Managing Knowledge Networks

The information context of the modern organization is rapidly evolving in the face of intense global competition. Information technologies, including databases, new telecommunications systems, and software for synthesizing information, make a vast array of information available to an ever expanding number of organizational members. Management's exclusive control over knowledge is steadily declining, in part because of the downsizing of organizations and the decline of the number of layers in an organizational hierarchy. These trends, as well as issues surrounding the Web 2.0 and social networking, mean that it is increasingly important that we understand how informal knowledge networks impact the generation, capturing, storing, dissemination, and application of knowledge. This innovative book provides a thorough analysis of knowledge networks, focusing on how relationships contribute to the creation of knowledge, its distribution within organizations, how it is diffused and transferred, and how people find it and share it collaboratively.

J. DAVID JOHNSON has been Dean of the College of Communications and Information Studies at the University of Kentucky since 1998. He has also held academic positions at the University of Wisconsin-Milwaukee, Arizona State University, the State University of New York at Buffalo, and Michigan State University, and was a media research analyst for the US Information Agency. He has been recognized as among the one hundred most prolific publishers of refereed journal articles in the history of the communication discipline.

Advance praise

"This book is about making the jump from IT to KM; from engineering potential information flow, to managing effective information flow. No one can know all the information relevant to our work and interests. We rely on friends, colleagues, and productive accidents for cutting-edge information and for blinders to information it is socially acceptable to ignore. Our points of access are connected in a network around us, and *Managing Knowledge Networks* provides frameworks for surviving and thriving in that network. Johnson draws on his years of research on human communication to speak simply with clarity, coverage, and examples. Addressed to academic and practical audiences, this book would be equally useful for an upper-division college course, a graduate seminar, or a manager responsible for information access and flow in the organization."

    RONALD BURT, Hobart W. Williams Professor of Sociology and Strategy, University of Chicago Booth School of Business

"What makes this a great book is its comprehensive treatment of an interdisciplinary topic – knowledge management – through a laser-like focus on one fascinating issue – knowledge networks. Nurturing them, monitoring them, diversifying them, and using them will be the knowledge professional's toolkit in the coming decades. More and more innovation is not the answer to our organizational challenges. Value-added processes must come into play. David Johnson provides a terrific perspective for business leaders and organizational researchers – knowledge networks – and clarifies how they work in relation to innovation, organizational learning, and work performance."

    JAMES W. DEARING, Ph.D., Senior Scientist at the Institute for Health Research, Kaiser Permanente, Director of the Cancer Communication Research Center, and Co-Director of the Center for Health Dissemination and Implementation Research

"By marrying knowledge management to networks, Johnson derives important insights about the social and relational nature of knowledge. His dynamic view of knowledge and its management in knowledge networks is both innovative and insightful. This book will hold great interest for scholars and practitioners alike."

    MARSHALL SCOTT POOLE, David and Margaret Romano Professorial Scholar, Professor in the Department of Communication, and Senior Research Scientist at the National Center for Supercomputing Applications, University of Illinois at Urbana-Champaign

"David Johnson's book presents a comprehensive examination of how information and communication networks have evolved over time in personal, work, and broader environmental settings. What is unique about this book is that it taps into and synthesizes years of important research in communication network analysis and applies it to current day thinking and problems. This book is a must-read for anyone interested in studying networks."

    ALEX M. SUSSKIND, Associate Professor of Food and Beverage Management and Academic Area Director for Hospitality, Facilities, and Operations, School of Hotel Administration, Cornell University

Managing Knowledge Networks

J. David Johnson

CAMBRIDGE
UNIVERSITY PRESS

CAMBRIDGE UNIVERSITY PRESS

Cambridge, New York, Melbourne, Madrid, Cape Town, Singapore, São Paulo, Delhi

Cambridge University Press
The Edinburgh Building, Cambridge CB2 8RU, UK

Published in the United States of America by Cambridge University Press, New York

www.cambridge.org
Information on this title: www.cambridge.org/9780521735520

First published 2009

Printed in the United Kingdom at the University Press, Cambridge

A catalogue record for this publication is available from the British Library

Library of Congress Cataloguing in Publication data
Johnson, J. David.
Managing knowledge networks / J. David Johnson.
    p.   cm.
Includes bibliographical references and index.
ISBN 978-0-521-51454-5 (hardback)
1. Online information services.   2. Expert systems (Computer science)   I. Title.
QA76.55.J64   2009
006.3′3 – dc22   2009030743

ISBN 978-0-521-51454-5 Hardback
ISBN 978-0-521-73552-0 Paperback

To my mother, Edna Horn Johnson.

Contents

Figures

Tables

Boxes

Cases

Information technology

Key researchers

Methods

Preface

Managing knowledge networks (KN) within organizations has taken on enhanced importance in recent years because of the decline of middle management and other changes in formal organizational structures, the growth of information technologies, and our increasingly competitive global economy. KN can be manifested in a variety of forms: project teams, research groups, advice networks, professional communities, communities of practice, support groups, and so on. Individuals increasingly find that they must determine for themselves what choices they will make, distilling the information they have gathered in their personal networks to knowledge that results in strategies they can pursue as they act in an ever more complex world. The awareness of the operation of KN is, quite literally, an important survival tool for individuals. In turn, resulting individual learning and actions determine how organizations adapt to rapidly changing environments and innovate to meet new challenges.

I have been conducting network analysis, innovation, and information research for over three decades now (Susskind *et al.* 2005). This book represents a culmination of this work: a bringing together of what have been complementary, although separate, strands of research. As such it draws on my books and research articles in these diverse areas, hopefully resulting in a useful synthesis of ideas applied to the increasingly critical problem of understanding the role of KN in contemporary organizations. My first book, *Organizational Communication Structure*, placed network analysis within broader intellectual traditions relating it directly to formal, spatial, and cultural approaches to structure. *Information Seeking: An Organizational Dilemma* applied many of these structural approaches to the problems individuals confront when they seek information in organizations. It also explored the darker sides of individual action that I will discuss later in this work. My most recent work, *Innovation and Knowledge Management: The Cancer Information Service Research Consortium*, draws on my work on innovations, and my more recent interest in knowledge management, to analyze an elaborate case study of how these themes unfolded in a major provider of health information to the general public.

As Dean for the last decade of the College of Communications and Information Studies at the University of Kentucky I have had a unique opportunity to be exposed to the range of disciplines necessary for a holistic understanding of these issues. Our college is currently developing an undergraduate program in information studies that will address this critical manpower need in our modern economy. In the tradition of land grant universities we have also tried to address these issues in more pragmatic ways. For example, as part of the Commonwealth's New Economy proposals we partnered with Decision Sciences to propose a Knowledge Innovation Management Center. We have also focused on Kentucky's Senate Bill 2 which would be instrumental in developing regional health information exchanges of electronic medical records, forming consortiums of vendors, providers, and insurance companies to try to control medical costs and improve quality. In addition to my research work with the Cancer Information Service, I have also been involved in Australia's Cooperative Research Centre for Freshwater Ecology in the development of their unique knowledge brokering partnerships with practitioners.

Typically the operation of the tools related to network analysis have been closely guarded. Fundamental (and often elementary) ideas related to structural research are masked with jargon and mathematics that make them inaccessible to all but those few individuals who have a mathematical/statistical background and/or who were trained in a limited number of graduate programs which focus on network analysis. While much of what is said in this book could be (and has been) expressed in mathematical terms (often in my own writings), I purposively have avoided them in this book. My desire is to acquaint a range of readers with the underlying substantive and pragmatic issues related to managing KN. I seek here to broaden the appeal of structural research along a number of dimensions and as such the book is intended to reach a wide audience. Accordingly, I have written the book in such a way that it will be appropriate to diverse audiences. I use summaries, charts, tables, and figures to make the book more accessible, especially to advanced undergraduates. The book also relies on boxes (equivalent to "sidebars") in the tradition of Ev Rogers' *Diffusion of Innovations* work (Backer *et al.* 2005) to illustrate substantive points with case studies, more elaborate descriptions of key researchers, emerging information technologies, and methodological approaches. The interested reader can consult the Further Readings noted at the end of each chapter for many excellent introductions in very concrete terms to such pragmatic issues as how to conduct a network analysis. This book focuses on general issues, providing readers with analytic frameworks that should be useful in specific situations as well as being applicable to the future in a way that discussions of particular, fleeting technologies is not. In writing this book I came to a deeper understanding of the many dilemmas and paradoxes posed by KN and the importance of managerial judgment in resolving them.

I would like to thank Paula Parish, Commissioning Editor for Business and Management at Cambridge University Press, for believing in this project. I would also like to thank Nathaniel E Johnson and Sally Johnson for their technical assistance.

Acknowledgments

The author and publisher are grateful for permission to reproduce portions of the following copyrighted materials.

Table 4.1. Reprinted from J. D. Johnson, on contexts of information seeking, *Information Processing and Management*, 39: 735–760. Copyright ©2003, with permission from Elsevier.

Table 2.1 and Figure 6.1. From J. David Johnson, *Information Seeking: An Organizational Dilemma*. Copyright ©1993 by J. David Johnson. Reproduced by permissions of Greenwood Publishing Group, Inc., Westport, CT.

Figures 7.1 and 7.2. From J. David Johnson, *Organizational Communication Structure*. Copyright ©1993 by Ablex Publishing Corporation. Reproduced by permissions of Greenwood Publishing Group, Inc., Westport, CT.

1   Introduction and overview

> In an information economy, organizations compete on the basis of their ability to acquire, manipulate, interpret and use information effectively.
>
> (McGee and Prusak 1993, p. 1)

> While we will consider various knowledge transfer issues and strategies . . . many of them come down to finding effective ways to let people talk and listen to one another.
>
> (Davenport and Prusak 1998, p. 88)

> Building competitive advantage involves creating and acquiring new knowledge, disseminating it to appropriate parts of the firm, interpreting and integrating it with the existing knowledge and ultimately using it to achieve superior performance . . .
>
> (Turner and Makhija 2006, p. 197)

> The grand challenge is knowing what to deliver to whom using what mode when and how quickly.
>
> (Satyadas, Harigopal, and Cassaigne 2001, p. 436)

The information context of the modern organization is rapidly evolving. Information technologies, including data bases, new telecommunications systems, and software for synthesizing information, make a vast array of information available to an ever expanding number of organizational members. Management's exclusive control over knowledge is steadily declining, in part because of the downsizing of organizations and the decline of the number of layers in organizational hierarchies. These trends make our understanding of informal communication networks, particularly those focusing on interpersonal relationships, the human side of knowledge management (KM), increasingly critical for understanding organizations. Knowledge is inherently social, with knowledge networks (KN) linked to innovation, learning, and performance (Swan 2003).

These trends have resulted in quicker response times and reduced coordination and relay costs because of the linkages that have been removed from the hierarchy. They are made possible by advances in information technology (IT). They put increasing responsibility on individuals to become active seekers, rather than passive recipients, of information, especially for decision support and problem solving. For technical and managerial positions, those most adept at identifying sources of information, who can then acquire and synthesize it, will be the most successful in these new organizational environments. KN have become a critical survival tool for individuals, facilitating uncertainty management, social support, and, ultimately, advancement in careers. Those who have the appropriate synthetic abilities and information-seeking skills are likely to be more satisfied and productive, the targets of active recruitment and retention efforts.

Not too long ago, knowledge in organizations was the exclusive preserve of management. Still today, in many organizations, it is kept from people. In part, organizations are designed to encourage ignorance through specialization and rigid segmentation of effort (Kanter 1983). So there is a constant dilemma for organizations: the imperative, in part stemming from efficiency needs, to limit the availability of information, and the recognition that structural designs are flawed and circumstances change, requiring individuals to seek information normally unavailable to them. How these conflicting imperatives are resolved is a critical question for the contemporary organization and, perhaps, the central challenge for its management. Unfortunately, while volumes have been written on formal organizational design, comparatively little is known about the forces that shape the development of knowledge within organizations. The comfortable world where one's supervisor provided authoritative directives concerning organizational activities is changing to one where organizational members must make quick, informed decisions about how goals should be accomplished.

While "Man's very survival depends on paying attention to aspects of the environment that change" (Darnell 1972, p. 61), individuals have free access to an often bewildering wealth of information. They have to choose between a variety of information sources. There are literally millions of articles published every year in the organizational and technical literature, making it nearly impossible for even the most dedicated individual to keep abreast of recent advances. For example, it has been calculated that physicians need to read an average of nineteen original articles each day to keep abreast of their fields (Choi 2005). This overload of information forces decentralization of effort, with increasing responsibility passing to individuals, and organizational effectiveness being determined by their ability to gather and then act intelligently on information.

In effect, lower-level employees must often do the traditional work of management, who cannot possibly keep up with the in-depth information related to specific technical issues. Baldridge award winning companies recognize this in their total quality efforts, believing that empowering workers to solve problems is critical to their success (Hanson, Porterfield, and Ames 1995). In fact, managers are increasingly irrelevant to the information-seeking concerns of technical employees whom they supervise, because they lack the requisite technical knowledge. Recognition of the limits of management and other sources also requires individuals to confirm and corroborate information by using multiple sources, thereby creating complex KN.

Actors operate in information fields where they recurrently process resources and information. These fields operate much like markets where individuals make choices (often based on only incomplete information, often irrationally) that determine how they will act. This contrasts directly with formal approaches to organizations that tend to view the world as rational, known, and that

Table 1.1. *Formal and informal approaches and knowledge
network concepts*

Knowledge network concept	Approach	
	Formal	Informal
Knowledge	Uniform	Contextual
Knowledge flow	Top-down	Multidirectional
Knowledge type	Explicit	Tacit
Design	Road map	Incomplete
Technology	Paper system	Digital
Dominant relational factor	Authority	Trust
Individual roles	Manager	Brokers
Who benefits?	System	Individual

concentrate on controlling individuals to seek values of efficiency and effectiveness, particularly regarding the timeliness of decision making (see Table 1.1).

In spite of (or maybe because of) the abundance of available information, organizational members' lack of knowledge about important issues is a significant problem confronting organizations. There is a growing recognition that information channels used by management can be easily avoided by certain groups, since they are not as captive an audience as they once were. As we shall see, the forces preserving ignorance may be far more compelling than those resulting in knowledge acquisition.

Most treatments of KN focus on their many benefits; yet, it can be viewed as having many negative consequences. Most threatening to management is their loss of control, since knowledge may be inherently destabilizing. Enhanced information seeking for one group in the organization also increases the possibility of collusion between members of informal coalitions, to the detriment of other organizational members, much as occurs with classic insider trading in financial markets.

The more control that managers have, the less effective their organizations may ultimately be, especially in terms of obtaining the critical answers that they need for pressing questions. Kanter (1983) has argued that a major barrier to innovation in American organizations comes from a narrow focus on departmental/unit/division concerns. Imbalances in the distribution of information in organizations are a key consequence of this differentiation which often benefits the interests of individuals in privileged or specialist positions (Moore and Tumin 1949). Organizational power structures, particularly management, reap benefits from hoarding information, since it is widely thought that information is power.

Segmented concern, as opposed to a concern for the good of the entire organization, is a direct result of the differentiation of the organization into specialized groupings that focus on particular tasks. In the classic formal organization, substantial barriers arise to the integration of organizational effort. This effect is often related to the development of silos or chimneys around different organizational functions. These barriers include informal rules that discourage individuals from developing cross-unit relationships. But these relationships are the most critical ones for innovation since they are the vehicles for sharing information and perspectives. Diverse perspectives result in the development of synthetic ideas and approaches that are holistic and concerned with the overall organization and new directions for it.

On the other hand, with their increasing responsibility, there is also an increasing burden on individuals. It may be unfair to make employees responsible for every aspect of their performance, especially in these highly uncertain times. In this new era, individuals must confront the world very much as a scientist, constructing practical theories upon which they must act. This may be establishing a set of expectations that only the best educated can achieve. Will people make the right choices; do they know enough to weigh and decide between the often conflicting pieces of information they will receive? Human beings are far from optimal information seekers, and, while information is a multiplying resource, attention, by implication, is a zero-sum resource.

All of this also raises the question of whose information is it anyway? Knowledge that to an employee is necessary for the accomplishment of his/her job, may be seen by management as an intrusion into its prerogatives. In addition, the same piece of information may be irrelevant to one organizational member who has it, but critical to another who does not.

Knowledge

Increasingly, generating and manipulating knowledge is seen as a core function of our economy, the "only sustainable way for organizations to create value and profitability in the longer term" (MacMorrow 2001, p. 381). Managers who possess the judgment to act quickly to solve the various dilemmas associated with KN and develop approaches that best facilitate knowledge creation and transfer, resulting in continuous innovation, will have substantial competitive advantages over their fellows (Real, Leal, and Roldan 2006). Of course, in commercial settings this is not done for altruistic purposes, but to insure competitive advantage for the firm (Stewart 2001). In government and non-profit organizations the motives may be slightly different: enhanced prestige and better services for clients, as well as reacting to demands of stakeholders (Eisenberg, Murphy, and Andrews 1998). So we are often forced to ask the more functional question of KM to what end: be it fostering creativity, enabling innovation, or increasing competencies (MacMorrow 2001). As we shall see, the answer to this question is often quite complex, with multiple purposes, often representing different groups, simultaneously at play.

In Chapter 2 I will explore knowledge as a concept and its various manifestations in great detail. I will also trace its relationship to various other concepts including data, information, and wisdom. I will contrast it to ignorance, which as we have seen is often encouraged in organizations for very sound reasons. Most of the recent excitement surrounding knowledge in organizations is associated with its management. KM has been loosely applied to a collection of organizational practices related to generating, capturing, storing, disseminating, and applying knowledge. KM can be viewed as a system for processing information. It is strongly related to IT, organizational learning, intellectual capital, adaptive change, identification of information needs, development of information products, and decision support, so intimately that it is often difficult to say where one approach stops and another begins.

In many ways KM can be viewed as an innovation that is rapidly diffusing among organizations. It also falls in a class of meta-innovations that enable other innovations to occur in an organization. Indeed, the pursuit of KM often is based on the premise that it will lead to better decision making and a flourishing of creative approaches to organizational problems. So, the ultimate outcome of effective KM is the rapid adoption or creation of appropriate innovations that can be successfully implemented within a particular organization's context. Greater knowledge intensity leads to greater profitability for commercial firms and higher levels of innovation. Ultimately, knowledge has become the source of wealth creation and economic growth (Florida and Cohen 1999; Leonard 1995; Stewart 2001).

Network analysis

Knowledge is also inherently a social phenomenon that develops from complex communicative interactions in social structures. Communication structure research, which encompasses hierarchies, markets, and networks, has been traditionally viewed as a central area of organizational communication theory. There are many different approaches to communication structure. The two used most frequently to analyze organizational communication systems are the formal approach, the primary focus of most traditional KM, and the informal approaches, especially network analysis, that I will focus on here. An organization's communication structure consists of both formal and informal elements, as well as other ingredients, and is not reducible to either (March and Simon 1958). However, to most organizational researchers this fundamental distinction captures two different worlds within the organization, worlds that have different premises and outlooks and, most importantly, different fundamental assumptions about the nature of interaction. These differences are highlighted in Table 1.1 and will be elucidated in more detail throughout this work.

Informal approaches recognize that a variety of needs, including social and individual ones, underlie communication in organizations and that, as a result, the actual communication relationships in an organization may be less formally rational than designed systems (Johnson 1993). Informal structures function to facilitate communication, maintain cohesiveness in the organization as a whole, and maintain a sense of personal integrity or autonomy. KN are increasingly the means by which knowledge is diffused, disseminated, and created. They reveal how people actually go about seeking information, how it is distributed, and how people collaborate to create new knowledge.

In contrast to the paper system and rules technology of classic formal approaches, Nohria and Eccles (1992) suggested that several factors related to new technologies make entirely new organizational forms, such as networked organizations, possible. First, IT increases the possibilities for control and decreases the need for vertical processing (e.g., condensation) of information. Second, new technologies facilitate communications across time and space. Third, they increase external communication, thus blurring traditional lines of authority within the firm. Fourth, IT enhances flexibility within the firm by decreasing the reliance on particular individuals for specialized information. Electronic markets, which we will describe in more detail in Chapter 4, are increasingly the means by which industries collaborate to translate knowledge into action.

Network analysis represents a systematic means of examining the overall configuration of relationships, both formal and informal, within an organization. The most common form of graphic portrayal of networks contains nodes, which represent social units (e.g., individuals, groups), and relationships, often measured by the communication channel used to express them, of various sorts between them. Because of its generality, network analysis is used by almost every social science to study specific problems. It has become the preferred mode for representing informal, emergent communication and associated information flows.

Recent years have seen a resurgence of interest in network analysis in the social sciences and even in the natural sciences (Newman, Barabasi, and Watts 2006), in part because of the development of such heuristic concepts as social capital and structural holes. Social networking, Web 2.0, and other collaborative technologies are viewed as a key feature of modern business approaches to how knowledge spreads within a company (Cross, Parker, and Sasson 2003; Mead 2001; Waters 2004). Some theorists (Contractor and Monge 2002) have begun to talk about the essential characteristics of KN and these networks are seen as a critical element of KM. They provide the foundation of social capital that enables the sharing and exchange of intellectual capital (Nahapiet and Ghosal 1998). Ultimately, an understanding of KN is a fundamental step for truly moving beyond IT and hardware to understanding the deeper, more social side of knowledge.

Plan of the book

The first part of this book focuses on the fundamentals, establishing a foundation for our understanding of the remainder of this work. In Chapter 2 I will define knowledge, distinguishing it from such common terms as information and wisdom. This chapter will also talk about the various forms that knowledge can take within organizations, critical distinctions that can be used in defining network linkages. Chapter 3 focuses on the burgeoning field of network analysis. It will describe how such basic concepts as entities, linkage, and boundaries can be used to build ever more sophisticated analyses of cliques, centralization, and integration, which are critical to understanding the transfer and diffusion of knowledge within organizations.

The next part focuses on the contexts within which knowledge is embedded. As Chapter 4 details, contexts shape and define knowledge, determining its distribution and the ways that people can be linked in organizations. Chapter 5 focuses on the the basic framework of an organization, its formal structure, and design issues that promote or inhibit the flow of knowledge. Much of the current excitement related to KN flows from new information and telecommunications technology which I will detail in Chapter 6. Chapter 7 dwells on spatial distributions that constrain the spread of knowledge. Organizational boundaries are becoming increasingly blurred, so in Chapter 8 we will focus on how firms bring the world outside into the organization through boundary spanning and the development of consortia.

The final part focuses on using knowledge and the pragmatic outcomes and policy issues associated with it. Chapter 9 develops a perspective on the role of KN in the critical organizational processes of creativity and innovation. Chapter 10 details the role of KN in productivity, efficiency, and effectiveness. We then turn to the related topics of the human and the dark side of KN. How people find knowledge and then use it for decision making are the subjects of Chapters 12 and 13 respectively. Finally, I sum up this work in Chapter 14 by focusing on policy issues, the importance of managerial judgment in dealing with KN dilemmas and paradoxes, and the future of KN in organizations.

Further reading

Choo, C. W. 2006. *The Knowing Organization: How Organizations Use Information to Construct Meaning, Create Knowledge, and Make Decisions*, 2nd edn. Oxford University Press.

Textbook description of knowledge in organizations. However, it touches only tangentially and very indirectly on KN.

Davenport, T. H., and Prusak, L. 1998. *Working Knowledge: How Organizations Manage What They Know.* Harvard Business School Press.

One of the first popular book-length treatments of the management of knowledge in organizations. Useful general introduction for managers, although it does not focus on the role of social networks.

Lesser, E., and Prusak, L. (eds.) 2004. *Creating Value with Knowledge: Insights from the IBM Institute for Business Value.* Oxford University Press.

Based heavily on the editors' work with the IBM Institute for Business Value and the associated Knowledge and Organizational Performance Forum, the readings in this work touch on several of the themes in this book. Especially

important is the section on social networks that contains several of Rob Cross's early studies.

McGee, J. V., and Prusak, L. 1993. *Managing Information Strategically*. Wiley.

Drawn from the author's work with the Ernst & Young Center for Information Technology and Strategy, with roots in the management information systems perspective, this book focuses on the strategic advantages for organizations of managing knowledge. Useful examinations of individual roles and information politics in organizations.

Fundamentals

2 Forms of knowledge

In this and the following chapter on network analysis I will concentrate on building a foundation for what is to follow. I start this work by defining the key concepts associated with knowledge, drawing careful distinctions between them. Needless to say these terms are at times used interchangeably and at times are taken to be quite different things in the burgeoning literature in this area. I then move on to a discussion of various classifications of types of knowledge, starting with the foundational one between tacit and explicit knowledge. These types could serve as the starting point for the definition of relationships in network analysis, the most critical move in any project relating to it. Finally, in part to serve as counterpoint but also to focus on critical dilemmas and questions of balance in organizations, to which managerial judgment must be applied, I discuss ignorance and the positive role it plays in organizations.

What is knowledge?

Knowledge runs the gamut from data, to information, to wisdom, with a variety of distinctions being made between these terms in the literature. While there is a generally recognized ordering among these terms (see Figure 2.1), with wisdom having the least coverage of any of the sets in the figure, they are often used interchangeably and in conflicting ways in the literature, resulting in some confusion (Boahene and Ditsa 2003). The increasingly limited set, or domain coverage, associated with higher-order terms also can be associated with greater personal interpretation (and resulting idiosyncratic meanings) (Boahene and Ditsa 2003) as one moves from data, a special type of information, to wisdom. This parallels the distinction between tacit and explicit knowledge and represents a progression of states (Holsapple 2003). It has also been suggested that value and meaning increase as one limits the domain coverage, and not surprisingly so does the difficulty in developing KM systems that capture the higher-order terms (Burton-Jones 1999).

Information

One of the most frequently made distinctions in the literature is that between knowledge and information. The word information is ubiquitous; it has even

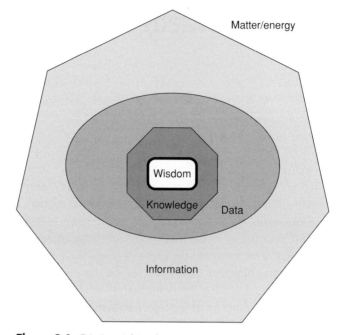

Figure 2.1. *Distinguishing key terms*

been used to define our society as a whole. As with any such central concept, several senses of the word are found in the literature (Case 2007). Unfortunately, some of these are also mutually contradictory.

Perhaps the most referenced to source for a definition of information is Shannon and Weaver's (1949) seminal work on telecommunication systems. Their central concern was how to send messages efficiently, with minimal distortion, over mediated communication channels. Yet, this work has always been troublesome because of its mechanistic, engineering transmission focus, which slights the meaning of messages, which is something fundamental to definitions of knowledge.

Shannon and Weaver (1949) developed an abstract definition of information based on the concept of entropy. Total entropy would represent complete randomness and lack of organization in messages. With greater entropy you also have higher levels of uncertainty, so that the more familiar a situation is, the less information it generates. In this sense something is information only if it represents something new; thus a measure of information is the "surprise value" of a message (Krippendorf 1986). However, it is quite possible that only an experienced person can recognize the unfamiliar in the most seemingly familiar of messages (Cole 1994; Rowley and Turner 1978). This also leads to the expert's paradox: the greater one's expertise the more likely one is to be successful in finding information, but the less likely is that information to be informative in this sense of information (Buckland 1991). Since most people associate information with certainty, or knowledge, this definition can be somewhat counterintuitive (Case 2007).

Much more globally, information is sometimes equated with any stimuli we register or recognize in the environment around us (Miller 1969). In this view, information involves the recognition of patterns in the basic matter/energy flows around us, i.e. everything else in Figure 2.1 (Bates 2006; Case 2007; Hjorland 2007; Farace, Monge, and Russell 1977). The other side of this view focuses on the nature of an individual's perceptual processes, arguing that they shape what we consider to be information, what we will perceive, and how we will perceive it (G. R. Miller 1969). But there is also a sense, a very important one for KN, that information is what you use to develop a higher level of comfort, perhaps even more of a feeling of familiarity with a situation. The more confident and sure you are about something the less uncertain it is (Farace, Monge, and Russell 1977). Thus, information can also be viewed as the number (and perhaps kind) of messages needed to overcome uncertainty (Krippendorf 1986). In this view, information is of value if it aids in overcoming uncertainty; the extent to which information does this also defines its relevance (Rouse and Rouse 1984).

Associated with the concept of information load, a critical problem that most organizations must confront, is yet a fourth sense of the concept of information, and one that encompasses in some ways the previous two definitions. In this fourth sense, information load is a function of the amount and complexity of information. Amount refers to the number of pieces (or bits) of information, somewhat akin to the accumulation of data. Complexity relates to the number of choices or alternatives represented by a stimulus. In a situation where all choices are equally probable, entropy is at its maximum. This fourth sense of information reflects the close association of information with decision-making processes, something we will return to in Chapter 13.

The senses and properties (e.g., timeliness, depth, breadth, specificity, quality, accuracy, quantitative/qualitative, hard/soft, etc. (Dervin 1989)) of information are many. In this work I will use information in its most general sense – the discernment of patterns in the world around us. Data, in this framework, are a special case of information. Data takes on the characteristic of facts – more isolated, atomistic elements. Data are often associated with information technologies because of the certainty of 0, 1 binary bits of information suitable for processing in a computer that can be recognized as either one thing or another.

The patterns that reveal information may often themselves represent the material world, but some of the most interesting implications of an information society come in how it differs from the societies that preceded it. Cleveland (1985) has offered several interesting distinctions in this regard. First, information is expandable, that is new knowledge often interacts with old knowledge to produce an exponentially increasing wealth of new information while leaving the old intact. The limits to expansion are primarily in the users of information systems, not in the systems themselves. Second, information is typically not resource hungry; it does not deplete a finite store of material resources, like mineral extraction industries. Third, information is substitutable, it can replace itself and it can be readily exchanged. Fourth, information is transportable by mediated means (e.g., telecommunications systems) that can overcome the limits of time and space of the material world. Fifth, information diffuses. It is hard to hoard information, to prevent its spread to others who have an interest in it – a fundamental focus of prior work in KN. Increasingly, we are living in a world where there are no secrets, at least not for long. Sixth, information is sharable, especially so because different parties may have considerably different uses for the same piece of information. Cleveland (1985) goes on to suggest that these characteristics of information are inevitably going to lead to the decline of hierarchies in organizations, just as they have led to the decline of authoritarian states, something that is increasingly recognized as popular wisdom.

Information also differs from other material goods in markets in that you cannot give the finished good to a partner to try out; once it is given, it's gone and cannot be returned since the customer retains its value (J. Roberts 2004). Information's value is dependent on its future use, something that its producer may not share in, which leads to the possibility of it being underutilized (M. J. Bates 1990) and problems with "free-riding" (Ba, Stallaert, and Whinston 2001). I will discuss these aspects in Chapter 12.

Defining knowledge

> Know-how embraces the ability to put know-what into practice.   (J. S. Brown and Duguid 1998, p. 95)

> Knowledge (or, more appropriately, *knowing*) is analyzed as an active process that is *mediated, situated, provisional, pragmatic* and *contested*. (Blackler 1995, p. 1021, italics in original)

> we define knowledge as *information that is relevant, actionable, and based at least partially on experience*.   (Leonard and Sensiper 1998, p. 113, italics in original)

Knowledge implies a deeper level of understanding than that represented by data or information (see Figure 2.1), although, similarly to information, it has often been defined in a variety of ways that are at times elusive (Birkinshaw, Nobel, and Ridderstrale 2002; K. G. Smith, Collins, and Clark 2005). *Merriam-Webster's Collegiate Dictionary* (4th edn., 1995) lists two elements that are critical to our understanding of the concept: (1) to have a clear perception or understanding of; . . . and (5) to have understanding or skill as a result of experience. Naively, then, knowledge sometimes approaches the meaning of truth (Boulding 1966) and becomes the basis for action (Satyadas, Harigopal, and Cassaigne 2001). Thus, not all ideas are considered intellectual capital, only those that can be applied in some form of production process (A. Dean and Kretschmer 2007). This is critical for organizations, since knowledge becomes something you can do something with. As a result it often leads to strategic advantages since organizations that have the best understanding of their environment and then act on it accrue competitive advantages, something we will discuss in much more detail in Chapter 11.

Knowledge is often the residue of thinking, or of reflecting upon experience (McDermott 1999). Wisdom represents the special case of actionable knowledge that "implies superior judgment and understanding based on broad knowledge" as defined in Webster's: (1) . . . the power of judging rightly and following the soundest course of action, based on knowledge . . . ; (5) a wise plan or course of action (*Merriam-Webster's Collegiate Dictionary*, 4th edn., 1995).

Knowledge is also something that is inherently social (J. S. Brown and Duguid 1998; McDermott 1999; Orlikowski 2002), bound to particular contexts (McDermott 1999; Swan 2003; Tsoukas and Vladimirou 2001), and something that can be communicated to others, even if it takes considerable effort and requires the development of mutually agreed symbols. Reflecting the work of American pragmatist philosophers such as Dewey and James, there has been a move away from objective views of knowledge to one that is fundamentally indeterminate and anchored in an individual's day-to-day interactions (Hjorland 2007; Nag, Corley, and Gioia 2007). Networks can help us become aware, familiar and cognizant of, recognize, and have a degree of certainty that often derives from social consensus. In this sense, then, learning represents knowledge acquired by study (*Merriam-Webster Collegiate Dictionary*, 4th edn., 1995).

Types of knowledge

> Many of these knowledge classifications take as their starting point the distinction made by Polanyi (1967) between tacit and explicit knowing. This classic distinction is then typically used to elaborate additional knowledge dichotomies, for example, local vs. universal, codified vs. uncodified, canonical vs. noncanonical, procedural vs. declarative, and know-how vs. know-what.   (Orlikowski 2002, p. 250)

It is important to distinguish between types of knowledge, since they can have different impacts on processes like knowledge transfer (Reagans and McEvily 2003). There has been a plethora of approaches to classifying types of knowledge. For example, Eveland, Marton, and Seo (2004) suggest the following scheme: declarative knowledge – being aware of something, knowing it exists; procedural knowledge – knowledge in use or the application of declarative knowledge; and structural knowledge – knowledge of how concepts within a domain are interrelated. Various metrics concerning its quality, validity, and completeness can be applied to knowledge (Satyadas, Harigopal, and Cassaigne 2001). Just as the Inuit developed more and more words for snow as they adapted to their environment, researchers and theorists are constantly expanding our vocabulary for understanding knowledge in organizations.

Tacit vs. explicit

> All knowledge is therefore tacit or rooted in tacit knowing.   (Polanyi and Prosch 1975, p. 61).

> we know other minds by *dwelling in* their acts   (Polanyi and Prosch 1975, p. 48, italics in original)

> For just as, owing to the ultimately tacit character of all our knowledge, we remain ever unable to say all that we know, so also, in view of the tacit character of meaning, we can never quite know what is implied in what we say. (Polanyi 1974, p. 95)

Fundamentally two types of knowledge, tacit and explicit, may be spread in networks (Nonaka 1991). The distinction between these two types of knowledge is derived from the work of Polanyi (see Box 2.1) who was concerned with developing a general philosophical system for describing personal knowledge in both the arts and sciences, applying it to a broad range of societal problems. Although he worked largely before the advent of contemporary KM, his general distinctions have been widely adopted and applied by organizational scholars to knowledge problems.

Box 2.1. Polanyi

Probably the most cited distinction in the knowledge-in-organizations literature is that between tacit and explicit knowledge that has its root in the work of Polanyi (Polanyi 1974; Polanyi and Prosch 1975). One of the reasons for his current popularity may be his critique of detached observation and subjectivity in science, which he felt should be displaced by his conception of personal knowledge (Polanyi 1974). His work is wide-ranging, as one might expect from someone who was a professor of both physical chemistry and social studies while at the University of Manchester, thereby bridging the infamous two cultures.

He was also very concerned with intellectual freedom, in his mind an essential societal precondition for the achievement of meaning. Since he seldom explicitly discussed his work in the context of formal organizations, one wonders what he might have had to say about the imposition of bureaucratic forms on the development of personal meaning, although the latter chapters of Polanyi and Prosch (1975) provide implicit compelling rationales for the move to market and cultural forms of organizations. He does suggest that a free society is one that does not interfere with what its members find meaningful, whereas a totalitarian one clearly does and tries to control this process by various means (Polanyi and Prosch 1975).

However, expert knowledge does depend on the application of traditional knowledge to which the seeker is in many ways a servant (Polanyi and Prosch 1975). The freedom of members of these communities rests on certain obligations and systems of mutual authority that also entail personal judgments (e.g., scientists forming hypotheses, lawyers preparing briefs). This process is accorded respect by society and certain things are left to communities of specialists to pursue; the mutual adjustment of these specialists then determines the ultimate directions of the societies of which they are a part (Polanyi and Prosch 1975). Mutual adjustment depends in turn on consultation or, in the case of business, competitive forces (Polanyi and Prosch 1975), and is clearly evocative of the operation of KN in organizations. However, this system of spontaneous order has several limits: first, the public good can be surrendered to these personal judgments; second, society is ruled by a privileged oligarchy; and, third, it can drift in directions determined by no one (Polanyi and Prosch 1975).

One example he uses to illustrate his perspective is the use of geographic maps. Maps are meant to represent parts of the earth's surface, but they are not necessarily the territory, as Korzybyski famously observed. They can be used for multiple purposes (e.g., aesthetically – as in decorations in formal libraries). For the purpose of finding one's way (Polanyi and Prosch 1975) users must do three things: associate their current position with a point on the map; find the best path to their desired position; and locate landmarks that help guide them towards it along the way. There are explicit, codified features of maps (e.g., scale, the meaning of particular symbols and lines). However, anyone that has tried to navigate a boat through an archipelago of geographically similar islands knows this is not as easy as it sounds. Successful outcomes are determined at least in part by the experience and tacit knowledge of the user. While the quality of the map may have an impact, it is how the user interprets it – the map cannot read itself nor can an explicit work on "map reading for dummies" perfectly determine better outcomes. What ultimately determines whether one ends up on the rocks or swimming off a sandy beach in a beautiful cove is the tacit knowledge of the user.

Contemporary technology, analogous to organizational KM systems, can play an important role by tracing appropriate paths, as Mapquest® does for highways, or giving the user critical feedback in locating their position and feedback related to particularly disastrous potential deviations. However, the judgment of the aesthetics of the cove still rests with the user.

Explicit knowledge is easily transferred because it can be encoded in a widely recognized symbol system, and traditionally it was the backbone of formal structural approaches (see Table 1.1). In the network literature this has also been referred to as migratory knowledge since it refers to information in books, designs, blueprints, and so on that can be easily moved from one location to another (Monge and Contractor 2003). In economics similar notions underlie the concept of general knowledge which is relatively inexpensive to transfer (Jensen and Meckling 1995). At times, definitions of explicit knowledge overlap with those of data.

Knowledge codification represents the translation of explicit knowledge into some written or visual format (E. W. Ford *et al.* 2003). It can increase the quality and speed of knowledge creation and distribution (Kayworth and Leidner 2003). While much attention has been paid to content in network analysis, the degree to which network members share similar meanings has received somewhat less attention, although some of the work on semantic networks touches on this issue (Monge and Contractor 2003) and the distinction made between manifest and latent link properties discussed by Johnson (1993) also addresses it. Fundamentally, for explicit knowledge to be transferred, there must be a shared symbol system with common meanings for the symbols among network members. This codification can take many forms – blueprints, documents, diagrams, and so on (E. W. Ford *et al.* 2003).

Tacit knowledge presents special challenges and can only be transferred under exceptional conditions (see Box 2.2). Tacit knowledge derives its value from being inimitable; it is hard to leverage because it is difficult to codify. However, codifying it makes it imitable, producing a basic paradox that organizations must resolve (Coff, Coff, and Eastvold 2006). This has also been referred to as embedded knowledge that is associated with craftsmanship and unique talents and skills that are particularly difficult to transfer across organizational or group boundaries (Monge and Contractor 2003) or, in economics, specific knowledge (Jensen and Meckling 1995). This type of knowledge has been described as "sticky" because it is difficult to spread as a consequence of issues such as causal ambiguity, absorptive capacity, retentive capacity, and the arduousness (e.g., maintenance over a distance) of the relationship (Szulanski 1996).

The key to tacit knowing is the functional relationship between subsidiaries and a focal target, which highlights the importance of from–to relationships (Polanyi and Prosch 1975). Thus, in the map example in Box 2.1, comparing a map to one's physical position in a space establishes a from–to relationship in which experience, tacit knowledge, is critical. This, then, can lead to meanings attached to the from–to relationship – I am lost, I am found. Thus, the person is critical to integrating the from–to relationship and establishing its meaning and cannot be replaced by a mechanical procedure. By focusing on the to, as codification often does, or the objects in a sense, we lose the subtlety of tacit knowledge, which is a basic problem with many KM systems.

Nonaka (1991) also developed a more dynamic, interactive approach to these issues, focusing on the implications of the spiral of knowledge and its articulation (converting tacit to explicit) and internalization (using explicit knowledge to extend one's own tacit knowledge). Thus professionals may gather large amounts of information to develop insights into deeper problems (e.g., financial trends) then articulate them, as financial brokers do, to specific buy and sell recommendations for their clients. The complexity of these processes for KN is developed more fully in Chapter 3.

Box 2.2. The lost knowledge of Stradivari

Antonio Stradivari (c. 1644–1737) and his sons possessed tacit knowledge of Stradivarius violin making that has not since been duplicated. The latent assumption underlying Western approaches to progress is that knowledge is cumulative; we build upon earlier generations adding to an accumulating knowledge base. But, as any archeology buff is aware, much knowledge has been lost to humankind over the years. This is, in part, because knowledge is contextual, social, and often dependent on the larger cultural system in which it is embedded. Sometimes knowledge loss is purposive, as in the case of colonial destruction of native cultures or closely held proprietary knowledge. At other times, it is the unintended consequence of other events, such as corporate merging and/or downsizing, where the tacit knowledge of those who are let go proves to be more vital than people thought.

The case of Stradivari, whose violins (there are approximately 600 still in use) command enormous prices because their sound quality cannot be recreated by modern means (Gough 2000; Pickrell 2004), has important lessons then for the fragility of tacit knowledge and the ease with which even the most valuable knowledge can fail to pass from generation to generation. Many hypotheses, some of which do not relate to knowledge transfer, have been advanced, then refuted, over the years for the inability to replicate these violins: the age of the wood; a little ice age that changed the quality of medieval wood; a unique source of ancient wood; special varnish; chemical treatment; soaking and/or drying of the wood; methods of storage and selection; the love and playing that the violin has experienced; the special shape and length of the instrument; and so on (Gough 2000; Pickrell 2004).

The real explanation, however, may lie in long practice of a craft and repeated experimentation. The most valued Stradivarius instruments come from the period 1700–1720. At this point he had been working for over thirty years in his craft, experimenting with different configurations and woods, passing on some of his tacit knowledge to his sons and others in his shop, which was then lost.

Some, like Ron Burt (2005), argue that there is nothing new under the sun, that everything that is new is actually a repackaging of the old, something that clever academics have long known. This is especially problematic in an academic culture that quickly devalues theories and gives little value to those who work in the framework developed by others. There is not a similarly attuned academic audience who appreciate and value the subtlety of tone in our work, in the way that any musician can recognize the distinctive voice of violins (Gough 2000).

Leonard and Sensiper (1998) have further elaborated the concept of tacit knowledge by identifying three different types of it in the context of developing innovation in organizations. A *guiding concept* resides at a high level of abstraction and is often metaphorical. It also may have totemic, visual quality that is often found in the realm of product design that captures the "style" of a particular company, such as Apple. *Collective tacit knowledge* arises from interaction in the same group and resides in the head of each socialized group member. *Overlapping specific tacit knowledge* arises from groups working on common, interdependent tasks. Another special form of tacit knowledge, embedded knowledge, resides in systematic routines (Blackler 1995), such as the rites and ritual of corporate life. All of these distinctions emphasize the social nature of knowledge captured by KN which at its root implies sharing experience at an increasingly fundamental, yet particular, level.

Ignorance

> they [Americans] judge that the diffusion of knowledge must necessarily be advantageous and the consequences of ignorance fatal.   (de Tocqueville 1835/1966, p. 148)

> perfect knowledge is itself impossible, and an inherently impossible basis of social action and social relations. Put conversely, ignorance is both inescapable and an intrinsic element in social organization generally . . .   (Moore and Tumin 1949, p. 788)

Ignorance and knowledge are inextricably intertwined concepts (Stigler 1961). Ignorance, as used here, refers to a state were an individual is not aware of knowledge relating to organizational life, including procedures, policies, cultural factors, and events – the everything else in Figure 2.1. So, ignorance exists when knowledge resides somewhere in the social system of which an individual is a part, yet the focal individual just does not have it.

Kerwin (1993) has developed a very useful classification scheme for mapping ignorance in terms of various levels of personal and societal (also read organizational) awareness and/or knowledge (see Table 2.1). Fundamentally, we can make a distinction between the things that are accepted as knowledge, though they might be socially constructed and subject to future paradigm shifts (Berger and Luckman 1967; Kuhn 1970), and things that are unknown. Typically, the number of unknown things is much larger than that of known things, but we have a tendency to focus on objects rather than their grounds (Stocking and Holstein 1993), so we concentrate on what is known rather than what is unknown. As we have seen, it is possible for the individual to know tacitly things that his/her social system as a whole does not yet accept.

Usually individuals will know much less than any social system of which they are a part. This is especially true of formal organizations, as the two ignorance

Table 2.1. *Mapping ignorance*

Personal knowledge	Social system knowledge	
	Known things	*Unknown things*
Known	Awareness	Known unknowns
Unknown	Ignorance	Unknown unknowns
Error	Error	False truths
Proscribed knowledge	Denial	Taboos

Source: Derived from J. D. Johnson (1996b, p. 70).

case studies in Box 2.3 suggest. Some observers are concerned with the ignorance explosion, the growing gap between what an individual knows and what is knowable. Indeed, there is growing concern with literacy and the general distribution of knowledge in various domains, especially health and the sciences.

While we are steadily increasing our knowledge of specific subareas, we are also decreasing the possibility of any one person knowing enough about each of the parts to integrate the whole (Thayer 1988). Of the things an individual knows, some will be in conscious awareness and others unconscious; things we do not know we know. Much of what we do in our social worlds, how we react to each other's nonverbal expressions, for example, is beneath our level of conscious thought. Intuition often falls in this classification and it is often extremely important for how upper-level managers make decisions (Simon 1987).

Next there are things we know we don't know – the known unknowns. This form of ignorance has also been termed conscious ignorance or meta-ignorance (Smithson 1993). Interestingly, these things often are also socially constructed and the pursuit of answers to them is the subject of intense scientific competition. Claims of knowledge gaps are used to support research programs and proposals, so scientists have vested interests in arguing for compelling known unknowns (Stocking and Holstein 1993). Known unknowns, when considered to be irrelevant, are not perceived to need further inquiry or information seeking (Smithson 1993). But, when considered to be important, these things are often the object of intense information searches. The operation of markets often depends vitally on the pursuit of known unknowns (Geertz 1978). Many high-tech genetics firms are searching for the locations of genes that are known to exist; it's just a question of where they exist. So, the very reason for the existence of some organizations is to discover a known unknown.

Perhaps more problematic for organizations are the things we do not know we do not know, the unknown unknowns. These are the things that are most likely to result in surprises and environmental jolts. So, if we are in the airplane passenger business, and it turns out it is ridiculously easy to develop a means of instantaneously transporting individuals from place-to-place inexpensively and safely, this unknown unknown may just be lying in wait to demolish our

Box 2.3. Two ignorance studies

Certainly ignorance is pervasive in most organizations. Two classic research studies eloquently speak to this point. The first study was conducted at the Library of Congress by Eugene Walton (1975) then Assistant Director for Personnel and Quality Programs. This study sought to determine the effectiveness of downward communication concerning an affirmative action program. It was an early precursor to notions of stickiness and absorptive capacity, concepts we will cover in more detail in Chapter 9. Over a period of about a one year the Library of Congress used a variety of channels to increase the awareness of employees of this program: fifteen feature articles in its bulletin, three special issues of its newsletter, an exclusive bulletin board for information on the program, ten-minute tape-slide film presentations shown to a third of its workforce, supervisor–subordinate face-to-face communication, and group meetings. At the conclusion of this program almost one-half of the members of the organization responded to a ten-item quiz with four responses possible per item concerning its features. Employees responded correctly only 27 percent of the time in the aggregate, only slightly better than chance. Interestingly, employees who perceived a self-interest in the program (e.g., they might get promoted) showed no greater level of knowledge than those employees who said they lacked self-interest, although there was a benefit in knowledge gained associated with higher perceptions of source credibility.

The second study, conducted by the Opinion Research Corporation (reported in Smith, Richetto, and Zima 1972), also illustrates that the level of awareness among lower-level organizational members is no better when an item of organizational interest is at stake. A metals-producing company had a problem with declining profit margins, an issue of considerable importance to the long-term health of the corporation. However, research discovered that the level of awareness of this issue declined steeply at each level of the hierarchy: top officers, 91 percent aware; upper middle management, 48 percent; lower middle management, 21 percent; and first line supervision, 5 percent. This was especially critical since the lower levels of the organization were likely to be most aware of what problems existed in production and how they might be solved, and they were the ones who were going to implement actual solutions.

These two studies illustrate a general lack of awareness by organizational members of organizational procedure and policies (Walton 1975; Downs, Clampitt, and Pfeiffer 1988); indeed, "organizational members display an astonishing ignorance of organizational procedures and functioning" (Brown and McMillan 1988, p. 24).

comfortable world. Error, something we think we know, but do not, is most likely to be corrected through interactions with others, especially weak ties. This is an additional benefit of diverse KN; we are more likely to come into contact with others who can correct our mistaken assumptions. If we interact only with the same others about the same topics, we are most likely to share and reinforce our mistaken assumptions.

False truths are things that are unknown, but which we think we know. As Will Rogers has observed "the trouble isn't what people don't know; it's what they don't know that isn't so" (quoted in Boulding 1966, p. 1). False truths often form the conventional wisdom that is the basis for ongoing interactions; still, they are at times erroneous views of the world, which some fundamental questioning might overturn. But we do not question them, precisely because they are accepted as truths. Treating knowledge as provisional and constantly questioning conventional wisdom may be one key to resilient, adaptive organizations and is often recommended for effective decision making.

Denial – of things that are too painful to know – is a major barrier to knowledge transfer within organizations. As we shall see, individuals often have very powerful reasons for refusing to admit that something is true.

Perhaps even more troublesome for social systems are taboos, things that societies agree should not be known by their members because they threaten their underlying premises. Most traditional cultures throughout history have been truth preservers, rather than truth pursuers, with information seeking permitted in only very limited, often highly personal domains (Thayer 1988). Forbidden knowledge (e.g., religious domains, shamans) is an area for which there are still significant penalties for individuals who engage in inquiry. Organizational elites and cultures, for example, may have a vested interest in protecting the basic authority relationships that are the fundamental organizing assumptions of hierarchies.

Ignorance, narrowly defined, concerns the things that we know that we do not know. So, for example we may know we do not know enough about how to work with the spreadsheet we are using in our job. We develop a search plan to address this shortcoming. We benefit greatly, however, in knowing the general parameters we need to search for. As we shall see, there are very compelling reasons for organizations to promote ignorance, to narrow the range of conscious known knowns for individuals (Smithson 1989). This creates a fundamental paradox for structuring KN: often preserving ignorance is more useful than promoting the transfer of knowledge.

Summary

The fundamental distinctions discussed here are critical to placing the literature in context in describing the scope of any knowledge network. They define the potential network in very direct ways, since what is shared/transferred in relationships is the most fundamental issue in developing a picture of KN. For example, a focus on explicit, highly codified contents should result in a very dense network with many cross-cutting ties. On the other hand, a focus on highly personal, tacit knowledge will usually result in a very fragmented network, with few weak ties and many structural holes. Those organizations that develop capabilities to share tacit knowledge widely have a unique resource that gives them competitive advantage (Ba, Stallaert, and Whinston 2001; Tippins and Sohi 2003).

Further reading

Kerwin, A. 1993. None too solid: medical ignorance. *Knowledge: Creation, Diffusion, Utilization*, 15: 166–185.

Very useful discussion of different types of ignorance, with applications to medical settings; serves as an interesting counterpoint to classic distinctions between different types of knowledge.

Nonaka, I. 1991. The knowledge-creating company. *Harvard Business Review*, 69: 21–45.

The article that started it all. Classic application of tacit–explicit knowledge distinction to differing types of knowledge in business settings.

Polanyi, M. 1974. *Personal Knowledge: Towards a Post-critical Philosophy*. University of Chicago Press.

Philosophical treatment of knowledge, developed the tacit–explicit knowledge distinction. Reviewed more completely in Box 2.1.

Smithson, M. 1989. *Ignorance and Uncertainty: Emerging Paradigms*. Springer-Verlag.

Comprehensive, book-length treatment of ignorance and its relationship to uncertainty.

Swan, J. 2003. Knowledge management in action? In C. W. Holsapple (ed.), *Handbook of Knowledge Management, vol. I: Knowledge Matters*: 271–296. Springer-Verlag.

Contemporary updating of the classic issues surrounding knowledge, with applications to innovation and KM. In Clyde Holsapple's definitive *Handbook of Knowledge Management*.

3 Network analysis

Network analysis is a highly systematic means of examining the overall configuration of relationships within an organization. The most common form of graphic portrayal of networks contains nodes, shown by circles in Figure 3.1, which represent social units (e.g., people, groups), and relationships (reflected in the lines) of various sorts between them. These elements of graphic representations are essential to most network analysis definitions: "In general, the term 'network' is taken to mean a set of *units* (or *nodes*) of some kind and the *relations* of specific types that occur among them" (Alba 1982, p. 42, italics in original).

Because of its generality, network analysis has been used by almost every social science to study specific problems.[1] Network analysis has been the primary means of studying communication structure in organizations for over three decades (Farace, Monge, and Russell 1977) and has become increasingly popular in management and organizational sociology as well (Borgatti and Foster 2003). In fact, so much attention has been paid to network analysis that a comprehensive review, particularly related to data gathering methods (Box 3.1) and computer programs (Box 3.2), of all material linked to it is beyond the scope of this chapter.

Naturally our focus here is on issues fundamental to KN, which will be developed in much more detail in subsequent chapters. Social networking technology is viewed as a key feature of contemporary business approaches to how knowledge spreads within a company (Cross, Parker, and Sasson 2003; Waters 2004). Since networks provide organizations with access to knowledge, resources, and technologies, they are a key source of competitive advantage (Inkpen and Tsang 2005). Job performance in today's knowledge-intensive organization is closely tied to an individual's ability to make the connections necessary to obtain the right information in a timely fashion (Cross and Cummings 2004). It is clear that informal, fluid structures characterized by individual autonomy are the key to creating knowledge (Nonaka and Takeuchi 1995). Horizontal flows through informal channels facilitate dissemination of incremental knowledge to relevant parties and its adaptive exploitation (Schulz 2001). Accordingly, KN are likely to be more fluid in terms of both agents and linkages, with changes in patterns based on evolving tasks, knowledge distribution, and agents' cognitive knowledge (Monge and Contractor 2003). A focus on KN examines how relationships

---

[1] Unfortunately, this has also meant there has been an explosion of vocabulary, with various traditions having different terms for the same concepts.

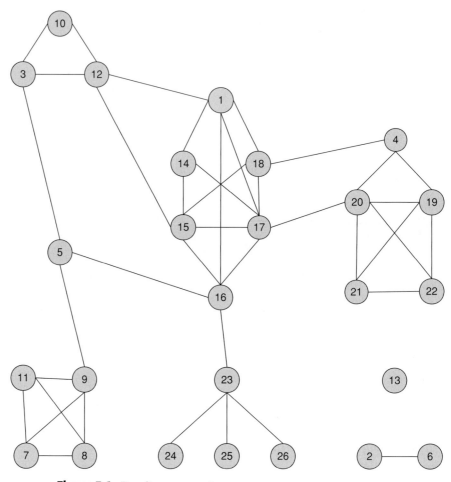

Figure 3.1. *Dazzling communigram*

contribute to the creation of knowledge, its distribution within the organization, how it is diffused and transferred, how people find information, and the collaborative relationships that link people in communities of practice (CoP).

Links as relationships

The analytical power and breadth of any network analysis is determined by how the relationships between nodes, referred to as "links," are defined. Links are the basic datum of network analysis (Rogers and Kincaid 1981; Wigand 1977); they are its fundamental property. Unfortunately, in most network analyses, linkages are defined very crudely, revealing relatively simplistic understandings of the communication process (Richards 1985) that often focus on explicit knowledge (see Box 3.1). For example, a typical network study might count the

Box 3.1. Network analysis methods

The major weaknesses of network analysis lie at the level of methods, particularly measurement. Methodologically, network analysis is perhaps the least robust of the commonly used social science techniques: "it should be observed that most network analysis procedures assume perfect measurement" (Farace and Mabee 1980, p. 384). A number of more specific problems are associated with this general difficulty.

First, there are several issues associated with the selection of the appropriate number of nodes to be included in a network analysis. A combination of data-gathering and computer analysis problems sharply limit the size of networks which can be examined. In practice there are also a variety of methodological difficulties associated with the collection of the data which, in effect, place ceilings on the use of particular methods for particular networks (e.g., observational techniques can only be used with very small *n*'s). These problems are exacerbated by the difficulties associated with sampling from populations to obtain network data (Alba 1982; Knoke and Kuklinski 1982; Marsden 1990; Monge and Contractor 1987). So, in practice, network analysis has been conducted on a census of the members of relatively small social systems.

The demand for a census of network members in traditional network analysis is impracticable in most organizational contexts. Recently, human subjects review committees have begun to raise fundamental objections to conducting censuses of respondents who are asked to report on their behavior involving others who may not have given their consent. However, owing to the nature of network analysis research, respondents must be identified. It is a basic requirement that researchers know with whom respondents are interacting. Thus, complete anonymity and confidentiality are not possible in network analysis research. These issues often raise ethical problems with the sorts of analytical outcome promised by many consultants: It is vital that the information contained in any study should not be used in a judgmental or punitive fashion, since respondents would be unlikely to furnish honest answers in subsequent ones.

Second, network analysis is very sensitive to methodological difficulties in data collection. For example, issues with missing data and reciprocity interact to create grave problems in determining which relationships should be analyzed. There is also considerable divergence of views as to which is the most important, subjective or objective measurement of networks, which is related to the problem of whether people can accurately self-report their communication linkages (Jablin 1980; Richards 1985; Monge and Contractor 1987). Indeed, some argue that it may be impossible to gather accurate network analysis data from individuals' self-reports of their communication activities (Bernard and Killworth 1977; Bernard, Killworth, and Sailer 1980; Bernard, Killworth, and Sailer 1982; Killworth and Bernard 1976; Killworth and Bernard 1979). While these conclusions have been questioned on a number of grounds (Burt and Bittner 1981; Farace and Mabee 1980; Romney and Faust 1982; Richards 1985; Tutzauer 1989), this line of research still identifies measurement as one of the major problems which network analysis research must grapple with (Alba 1982; Knoke and Kuklinski 1982; Newman, Barabasi, and Watts 2006; Richards 1985; Zwijze-Koning and de Jong 2005).

Fortunately, especially in terms of the automated auditing of network data, there have been a number of systematic attempts to come to grips with measurement issues (Danowski 1988, 1993) that also address some large- n problems, with small-world investigations tackling the whole Internet (Buchanan 2002; Newman, Barabasi, and Watts 2006; Watts 2003). Another interesting opportunity is to examine the corpus of e-mail communications available from various legal actions associated with E-Discovery, such as the Enron e-mail data set (Diesner, Frantz, and Carley 2005). Corman and colleagues' (Corman *et al.* 2002) recent work on Centering Resonance Analysis also lays the foundation for much more systematic measurement of network content, at least at an explicit level.

Although procedures involving self-reports have been questioned because of their accuracy, many still assert their validity on a conceptual level. As Richards (1985) maintains, since self-report reveals the person's perceptions of social reality, it often provides richer types of information than mere reliance on observations. Some have also argued, from balance theory perspectives, that self-reports of behavior are *more* meaningful than actual behavior, since they more closely reflect perceptions and thus are more closely linked to attitudes toward and reactions to a particular social system (Kilduff and Krackhardt 1994). In addition, it has been demonstrated that, while self-reports are often inaccurate, because of memory problems, in detailing what occurs for specific events, they are very accurate in detailing the typical structural relationships in systems (Freeman, Romney, and Freeman 1987). Researchers who have reanalyzed the Bernard and Killworth data have come to the opposite conclusion (Kashy and Kenny 1990). Even Bernard and Killworth have seen the utility of self-report for some problems (see Killworth, Bernard, and McCarty 1984). Indeed, while the accuracy of self-report network data has been questioned on many grounds, for pragmatic reasons it has been the predominant method used in network analysis (Marsden 1990).

Surprisingly low rates of reciprocation are generally reported in network analysis studies. Richards (1985) reports that confirmation rates, where both parties agree about the nature of a linkage, rarely exceed 30 percent. In a more comprehensive review, Marsden (1990) reports rates from various studies from 13 to 97 percent, with higher rates associated with intimate relations in denser networks, such as family ties, and lower rates in work-related networks characterized by weak ties. Marsden (1990) concludes that generally reciprocation rates are high enough to indicate that self-reports reflected actual events, but they must be interpreted with some caution because of potential inaccuracies.

At the operational level, network analysis has struggled to develop truly rich descriptions of relationships between actors (Susskind *et al.* 2005). The content of relationships has generally presented a difficult problem in network analysis research, with a variety of strategies developed to deal with it (Burt and Schott 1985). "... naturally occurring relations to other people are bundles of specific interactions, some consisting of many elements, others containing very few" (Burt and Schott 1985, p. 288). Typically, a network analyst makes a tradeoff, accepting simplicity at the dyadic level in order to examine complexity at the social system level. "The sociometric questions finally selected for a study can be no more than a compromise between the practical impossibility of gathering data on all kinds of relations in which respondents might be involved and the other extreme of initial hunches as to the correct identification of some minimal number of the most significant kinds of relations in a study population" (Burt and Schott 1985, p. 289). Researchers must also confront the problem of differential meaning between members of the study population and themselves (Burt and Schott 1985), which can directly be linked to tacit knowledge.

Given these measurement issues, a number of purported network studies focus on radial networks. Essentially radial, or egocentric, network data describes a focal network composed of an individual's overall pattern of relationships with others. This type of network is amenable to analysis by more traditional surveys and associated statistical analysis procedures focusing on issues such as the size of someone's immediate network and its heterogeneity (Laumann and Schumm 1992; Marsden 1987). Because of its focus on relationships, network analysis does not mesh well with traditional statistical analytic frames, such as analysis of variance (Kenney, Kashy, and Cook 2006). This is especially problematic for the discipline of communication, which at its root assumes dependence of actors.

number of production-related messages between two organizational members.[2] The preceding and subsequent chapters suggest various approaches to enriching our view of relationships. However, fully capturing the richness of knowledge flows in organizations is a great challenge.

Links can be conceptualized in a variety of ways and could reflect the various distinctions made in Chapter 2. It is very important, however, that any

---

[2] However, interesting attempts have been made to define linkages from the perspective of the respondent (Bach and Bullis 1989), in terms of their cultural properties (Eisenberg, Contractor, and Monge 1988), and in terms of the development of meanings (Corman and Scott 1994).

Box 3.2. Network analysis software

The recent explosion of interest in network analysis has been associated with the development of a number of computer algorithms with differing and often unique capabilities. These programs can produce differing results because of differences in focus; however, when programs are oriented to the same process (e.g., group density), there are generally great similarities in results (e.g., Rogers and Kincaid 1981; Rice and Richards 1985). Newcomers often find it difficult to grasp the many arcane methods, computer programs, and software associated with networks (Scott 2000). There has not been adequate professional reward for the time investment necessary for individual social scientists to write new, more user-friendly programs (Susskind *et al.* 2005).

Despite the development of a comprehensive software package, UCINET, network analysts are not quite in the same position as statistical analysts in the social sciences generally, where researchers rely on the companies that sell SPSS and SAS to develop software, market it to users (paying attention to factors which enhance marketability such as ease of learning and use), correct "bugs," and diffuse new applications (Friedkin 2001). As a result, researchers often have to use multiple software packages to complete any one study (Friedkin 2001). Happily, recent software developments are moving the field to a more mature state with full-featured analysis packages (e.g., NetMiner) and more attention to the rich visual imagery of networks (de Nooy, Mrvar, and Batagelj 2005). There has also been rapid development of software applications for commercial applications (e.g., Krebs's Inflow) and national security applications, especially those associated with tracking messages in telecommunications systems.

There are a number of general problems with network computer algorithms. First, the existence or non-existence of a linkage is much more important than subtle gradations in the degree of relationship. By design, or in practice, most network computer algorithms permit only primitive scaling, usually binary; really complete, rich descriptions of linkages are difficult to accomplish. Thus the difference between 0 and 1 is much more important than subsequent differences in numerical scores, as revealed in the general similarities found in comparing binary networks to scaled multivariate ones. Thus, in effect, a wealth of potential information on the relative intensity of relationships is "wasted" (Johnson 1987). Second, there are difficulties in detecting groups or cliques with precision and consistency (Alba 1982), with many different approaches to this fundamental issue (Scott 2000). Third, there are substantial limits to the size of networks that can be analyzed by particular algorithms and no consensus on how to deal with such fundamental issues as missing data and sampling.

An excellent resource for keeping up with developments in network analysis can be found at the International Organization for Social Network

Analysis website, *www.insna.org*. The organization also sponsors the annual Sunbelt Social Network Conference that brings together network researchers from a variety of disciplines. This website contains links to over two score of network analysis programs, most of which were developed for very specialized purposes. We will briefly review only a few of the more popular, accessible programs here.

GRADAP

Developed for a DOS environment, GRADAP (Graph Definition and Analysis Package) can define, manipulate, and analyze graphs of various kinds. It provides facilities for simple graphs, digraphs, and valued graphs, including the detection of cliques and components; all major types of point and network centrality measure; spatial autocorrelation; and variance degree. New graphs can be generated from the original data, with the help of selection, aggregation, and induction. Facilities to group points and lines in sets allow the analysis of subgraphs and partial graphs. It can interface with a number of relational databases. It is available at http://assess.com/xcart/product.php?productid=229andcat=32andpage=1. It is not especially user-friendly (Scott 2000) and has not kept pace with the recent development of other software.

NetMiner

Sold by Cyram Inc. in Korea, it appears to have many of the same features as UCINET, although it does not have the historical roots of that program nor the strategic placement of its developers in the network analysis research community. It has a special emphasis on exploratory network analysis and modern visualization techniques: www.netminer.com/NetMiner/home_01.jsp.

NEGOPY

While NEGOPY has been used in disciplines from agricultural journalism to urban planning, and by scholars and consultants in over twenty countries outside the United States, it is of interest now primarily for historical reasons (Susskind *et al.* 2005). NEGOPY is one of the few available programs which can fully assess issues related to the strength of communication linkages (see Farace and Mabee 1980; Rice and Richards 1985). Its algorithm is based primarily on matrix manipulations (see Rice and Richards 1985). NEGOPY identifies a number of *a priori* communication roles that fall under the classifications of participants (e.g., liaisons) and peripherals (e.g., isolates). It heuristically identifies groups according to specific criteria that can be set by the user.

More recently, Richards and his colleagues (Richards and Seary 2000) developed FATCAT and MultiNet, software that addresses some of the weaknesses of NEGOPY and is easier to learn and use. Released in 1988, FATCAT is for categorical analysis of multivariate multiplex communication network data. It can be applied to egocentric data. MultiNet, released in 1994 with updates through June 2004, extends FATCAT's functions to include univariate descriptive statistics plus cross-tabulation, analysis of variance, regression and correlation, four types of eigen analysis, p^*, and other analyses. It also performs continuous and discrete transformations, and does linear, log, power, z, and several other types of transform. It can use census or sampled network data.

STRUCTURE

STRUCTURE is based on the work of the sociologist Ron Burt, and, as such, has explicit linkages to his theoretical work (Burt 1982; Johnson 1988b). It produces density tables that focus on issues concerning structure at the subgroup level and relations among subgroups. This feature is useful in detecting the similarity of patterns among group members. Dissimilarities could indicate that individuals occupy unique roles such as bridges or are dominant members. Structural autonomy relates to the extent to which an individual's relationships may constrain his/her opportunities for individual action within a network. Cluster analysis and proximity measures tend to identify people with similar linkage patterns, which means that isolates and peripheral network members are as likely to cluster together. Somewhat uniquely, it provides for social contagion analyses related to cohesion and structural equivalence. STRUCTURE is also primarily of interest now for historical reasons and many of its more interesting applications are in UCINET.

UCINET

UCINET 6 for Windows (Borgatti, Everett, and Freeman 2002) appears to be the standard for network analysis research today (Scott 2000) and is available at www.analytictech.com. This package comes close to the ideal of a suite like SPSS or SAS. It allows for the import and transformation of a number of different network analysis data formats. It also contains a number of graphic visualization packages. It has a number of different means of calculating key network indices like centrality. Similarly, it has a number of different ways of determining cliques and groupings in networks. Like all network programs it can be somewhat tricky to use and it has only limited user support.

conceptualization be systematic and that it fully capture the various relational properties of interest (Richards 1985). Relationships reflect the nature of the bonding between interactants. In addition, "A relation is not an intrinsic characteristic of either party taken in isolation, but is an emergent property of the connection or linkage between units of observation" (Knoke and Kuklinski 1982, p. 10), a particularly important issue for the development of knowledge.

There are two primary types of relationship. Contextually determined relationships are associated with situationally or culturally determined roles. For example, Katz and Kahn (1978) viewed organizations as "fish nets" of interrelated offices. Contextual properties are intimately associated with asymmetry. Essentially asymmetry means that a relationship is not the same for both parties. This is an important property of organizational networks since there are a multitude of differences between organizational members, especially in term of status and the direction of communication. Thus power/dependence relationships are an especially important class of asymmetric relationship (Lincoln and McBride 1985).

Actor-determined relationships reflect the idiosyncratic bondings that characterize relationships between particular interactants. For example, importance, a variable that has traditionally been examined in network studies (e.g., Richards 1985), provides a direct assessment of the tie between an informal communication relationship and work performance. It can be associated with the more abstract concept of work dependency which relates fundamentally to the degree of access individuals have to needed task-related information (Johnson and Smith 1985). Often individuals in networks come to rely on their peers for work-related advice (e.g., Blau 1954). These peers are not formally assigned by the organization; rather, these relationships develop informally, often as a result of friendships. Thompson (1967) asserts that these work-dependent relationships determine communication channels in an organization to a greater degree than such factors as affiliation, influence, and status.

Reciprocity refers to whether or not both parties to a relationship characterize it in the same way. Reciprocity has been considered primarily a measurement property of linkages (Richards 1985), but it can be directly related to substantive processes as well, such as selective perception and selective attention or the total volume of communication in an organization. For example, often a supervisor will not be as aware of relationships with workers as they are of the relationships with his/her bosses. So when asked with whom they communicate they will forget about a worker, but the worker will remember his/her relationship with the boss. This linkage is therefore unreciprocated; the worker believes it exists, but the manager does not. Unreciprocated linkages, linkages where one party does not agree that a relationship exists, are quite frequent in organizations. Monge, Edwards, and Kirste (1978), for example, report reciprocation ranging from 37 to 100 percent across a number of empirical studies.

Perhaps the most frequently made distinction between relational elements is that between interpretation and content (e.g., Bales 1950), a distinction somewhat akin to that between tacit and explicit knowledge. Interpretation represents the connotative meaning associated with expressed symbols. Cicourel (1972) and Pearce and Conklin (1979) have maintained there is a need to distinguish between the manifest acts represented by content and their underlying meanings for inter-actants. However, many network theorists confuse interpretation and content, treating both as synonymous with function and also with other forms of relationship.

"The content or function of the relation creates some of the messiest problems for network analysis" (Richards 1985, p. 112), especially so because most category schemes are incomplete and some behaviors can represent multiple functions. Content is the denotative meaning of symbols expressed during an interaction. This is the literal meaning of what is said: the meaning of the interaction to a third party who is unaware of the background of the actors and other factors that may influence the true meaning of symbols for interactants. Content is perhaps the most direct manifestation of the functions of a relationship; but some content can reveal multiple functions. For example, in sending a number of production-related messages to a worker, a supervisor accomplishes a production function, but s/he may also be accomplishing a social support one for the worker. While there are a wealth of potential schemes developed for describing the content of functional networks, there is not an especially high degree of consonance between them. For example, Berlo (1969) identifies three organizational communication functions – production, innovation, and maintenance – which only partially overlap with Redding's (1972) task, maintenance, and human functions. Indeed, Farace, Monge, and Russell (1977) suggest that different functional schemes may be necessary for different organizations and that functions may even differ at different levels of the same organization.

The means, physical method/channel, by which symbols are transmitted between parties in an interaction has also been frequently used as a way of operationalizing relationships. These channels might include the written word, face-to-face communication, telephone calls, or telecommunication networks. Properties of channels will be discussed in much greater detail in Chapter 7.

An important general property of a link is its strength. Typically the frequency of communication is used to indicate the strength of a link (Richards 1985); however, there are many possible indicants of the strength, each of which has different implications for KN studies. For example, wide-ranging contacts of short duration may indicate individuals are searching for potential sources, while a few focused contacts of long duration may indicate the development of tacit meanings.

Another way of characterizing relationships, one that allows complex simulations of the spread of information and the development of social systems, is in terms of a few simple interaction rules that govern their development into self-organizing systems. So the susceptibility of a node to infection (usually a disease, but sometimes a new idea) spread through direct contact with others can determine the extent of information cascades represented by threshold rules, and the connectedness of the system also has impacts (strong cliques inoculate against the spread of new ideas) (Watts 2003).

Combining link properties

The manner in which these various properties of links are combined can determine the analytical power and depth of any one network analysis, since a network is defined by the nature of the linkages it examines. For example, it might be very interesting to look at multivariate network properties. These are networks where strength is determined by more than one factor; by weight, frequency, and duration of a link, for example (see Johnson 1987, 1993). Operationally, if we wanted to look at a network that paralleled the organizational chart, an approach developed in more detail in Chapter 5, we would specify that only linkages involving production content, which are in writing, asymmetrical, and unreciprocated should be included. Alternatively, an informal network could be defined by production and maintenance contents, face-to-face channels, symmetricality, and reciprocated linkages. By examining two types of content, formal and informal, we can see how they overlap. This exploration of multiplex networks can give us a more in-depth view of any one individual's overall participation in an organization (Minor 1983). For example, the president of a corporation might be at the center of the production network, but relatively isolated from a social one. This would paint a picture of a relatively cold and aloof management style.

Multiplex networks

Multiplexity refers to the nature of overlap, or correspondence, between differing networks (e.g., friendship as opposed to work). The nature of these overlaps is of great pragmatic concern, since it can suggest the inherent capabilities of individual actors within systems, and it also has rich implications for the understanding of social systems generally. Organizations are actually composed of a variety of overlapping and interrelated networks of differing functions (Jablin 1980); however, functional dimensions are but one of the many dimensions along which network linkages can be multiplexed (see Eisenberg *et al.* 1985; Minor 1983). At its heart, multiplexity refers to the extent to which different types of network relationship overlap: "The relation of one person to another is multiplex to the extent that there is more than one type of relation between the first person and the second" (Burt 1983, p. 37).

The degree of multiplexity has been related to such issues as the intimacy of relationships, temporal stability of relationships, reduction of uncertainty, status, the degree of control of a clique over its members, performance, redundancy of channels, and the diffusion of information (Minor 1983). Multiplexity is also crucial to processes of social contagion, since it can be expected that individuals with a high degree of participation across different types of network might be more affected by contagion processes, such as the dissemination of knowledge, than those individuals involved in only one type of network (Hartman and Johnson 1989).

Perhaps the key, and often overlooked, issue in multiplexity studies is the association between different types of network and the conceptual phenomenon of interest. Accordingly, if someone is primarily interested in innovation studies, innovation networks are of primary importance. However, other networks may have great importance as well, particularly social ones (Albrecht and Ropp 1984). In addition, too high a level of aggregation of network contents (e.g., all work-related content) can create problems in interpreting data. For example, Krackhardt and Porter (1985) speculated that workers were more likely to talk about job duties than general organizational goals. Therefore, they argued it was less likely that cohesion-related social contagion would impact on commitment. Unfortunately, because of the operationalization of network function, this "post hoc" explanation could not be tested; however, when separate content networks were examined by Hartman and Johnson (1989) this assertion was called into question. So the first issue that confronts a researcher interested in multiplexity is what different types of network will be examined? As we have seen, this is a question whose answer may provide the researcher with at one and the same time too much and too little information, given the large array of functional category schemes which have been proposed.

On the other hand, there is neither much theoretical guidance nor specific empirical work that describes the linkage between particular functional networks and non-network theoretical variables. Hartman and Johnson (1989) examined the relationship between multiplexity and role ambiguity and commitment. They found direct associations between functional networks and these concepts. Role ambiguity was most directly linked to conflicting information or perceptions of roles, thus it is most closely linked to the uniplex network relating to job duties. On the other hand, commitment was most directly tied to organizational goals. In addition, the other functional networks of satisfaction and non-work impacted on commitment. As a result, the multiplex combination of these network properties had more of an impact on commitment than they had for role ambiguity. The results bear out the importance of specifying appropriate functional/content networks in the framework of multiplexity. The overall pattern of their results stresses the importance of carefully considering the nature of multiplex networks. In a KN framework, tacit relations are likely to be more multiplex and explicit relations are more likely to reflect weak ties.

Weak ties

The strength of weak ties is perhaps the best-known concept related to network analysis. It refers to our less developed relationships that are more limited in space, place, time, and depth of emotional bonds. This concept has been intimately tied to the flow of information within organizations and by definition is removed from stronger social bonds, such as influence and multiplex relations.

Notions about weak ties are derived from research on how people acquire information related to potential jobs (Granovetter 1973). It turns out that the most useful information comes from individuals in a person's extended networks – casual acquaintances and friends of friends. This information is the most useful precisely because it comes from infrequent or weak contacts. Strong contacts are likely to be people with whom there is a constant sharing of the same information. As a result individuals within these groupings have come to have the same information base. However, information from outside this base gives unique perspectives and, in some instances, strategic advantages over competitors in a person's immediate network.

Granovetter (1973) provided the key explanation of the importance of weak ties in binding large collectivities together, since the removal of strong ties which are often redundant has little impact on overall system connectiveness (Buchanan 2002). These weak ties are most often bridges that link different social worlds. So, weak ties are also crucial to integrating larger social systems, especially in terms of the nature of communication linkages between disparate groups (Friedkin 1980, 1982; Weimann 1983). Granovetter (1982) now maintains that this bridging function between different groups is a limiting condition necessary for the effects of weak ties to be evidenced. However, weak ties may be discouraged in organizations because of concerns over loyalty to one's immediate work unit and questions of control of organizational members. Strong ties may also be preferred because they are more likely to be stable and because, as a result of the depth of their relationship, individuals may be willing to delay immediate gratifications associated with equity demands (Albrecht and Adelman 1987b). Individuals to whom an individual is strongly tied may also be more readily accessible and more willing to be of assistance (Granovetter 1982). Strong ties are also essential for the sharing of tacit knowledge.

Weak ties provide critical informational support because they transcend the limitations of our strong ties, and because, as often happens in organizations, our strong ties can be disrupted or unavailable. Thus weak ties may be useful for: discussing things one does not want to reveal to one's close work associates; providing a place for an individual to experiment; extending access to information; promoting social comparison; and fostering a sense of community (Adelman, Parks, and Albrecht 1987).

Network configurations

Inherent in the concept of networks is a recognition of the complexity of social structure; however, network analysis is also concerned with the identification of particular configurations which reduce to a small number of specific network patterns. As a result, another great strength of network analysis lies in the variety of means available for examining configurations of relationships. In this section the focus will be on three primary means of depicting network configurations: communigrams, individual patterns of relationships, and network indices.

Perhaps the best-known, and at times most difficult, issue associated with the configuration of networks is where to draw the boundaries around them. This is especially problematic since boundaries imply some discontinuity in relationships; that relationships across boundaries are in some sense qualitatively different than those within the network's boundary. In one of the more extended discussions of this issue, Lauman, Marsden, and Prensky (1983) distinguish between realist and nominalist views of this problem. In the realist approach, the researcher adopts the vantage point of the actors in defining boundaries, while the nominalist imposes a conceptual framework which serves his/her own analytical purposes. This also fundamentally relates to how nodes are defined. Boundaries are a particularly difficult issue for KN given the leakage of knowledge across them and the advent of the Internet.

There are difficulties with each of these approaches. For example, an individual faculty member's realist network may be composed of graduate students and professionals at other institutions. These individuals may be more important for the faculty member than his/her department colleagues, who would most likely be the entities contained within the boundaries of a nominalist study. On the other hand, trying to define the boundaries of one set of nodes that encompasses all of a department's individual faculty members' relevant contacts would be a nearly impossible task, with grave methodological problems, especially those associated with sampling procedures.

Communigrams

Network analysis can be a very systematic and complete means of looking at the overall flow of knowledge within an organization. Given the increasing interest in visualization generally, and the more specific interest in small-world depictions of linkages within the Internet, there has been a rapid advance in graphic representations of networks. As a result, there has been near explosive development of software for generating communigrams with Mage 3D Visualization, NetDraw, and Pajek all available in UCINET, and NetMiner having a special emphasis on graphic visualization for exploratory analysis (see Box 3.2). Maps, reflecting how people are brought together, are also a critical component of the cartographic approach to KM (Earl 2001).

Figure 3.1 contains a communigram, a special type of sociogram, reflecting the network of communication relationships found in a sample organization, Dazzling (see Figure 3.2 for its organizational chart). The circles in the figure represent nodes, in this case individuals, and the lines indicate linkages. This form of graphic portrayal is very flexible, since the nodes can be any type of entity and the linkages represented by the lines can be of any kind (Farace and Mabee 1980). Nodes and the lines between them can be arranged in circles, randomly,

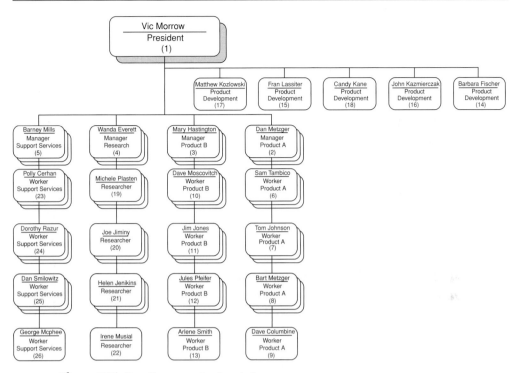

Figure 3.2. *Dazzling organizational chart*

on the basis of their attributes (e.g., demographic, hierarchical), or by algorithms (e.g., social proximity) (Katz *et al.* 2004).

Given the discussion in Chapter 2, we realize that there are many types of knowledge and it is unlikely we share the same level of knowledge with the broad range of people with whom we might interact. Figure 3.3 tries to capture this complexity. The essential backbone of relationships in this communigram, represented by the solid lines, are relationships in which information is shared relating to commonly understood explicit knowledge (e.g., management information systems, formal personal systems, formal production targets). Some relationships also involve the sharing of deeper levels of tacit knowledge associated with production processes and organizational specialties that are often lodged in formal organizational groupings. The dashed lines with letters represent idiosyncratic tacit knowledge (as well as more limited explicit knowledge) shared in groups, and some bridging roles. The most limited sharing of knowledge involves members 2 and 6 who only share information related to the plush walnut interiors of the current luxury automobile Dazzling manufactures. There is also the tight clique formed by members 3, 10, and 12 in Product B that coordinate the construction of a drive train (D linkages) of the current custom automobile produced by Dazzling. They also have tacit linkages with the President, who uses their knowledge to help shape the development of a new prototype (P linkages). Node 5, the Manager of Support Services, appears to be operating in a synthesizing

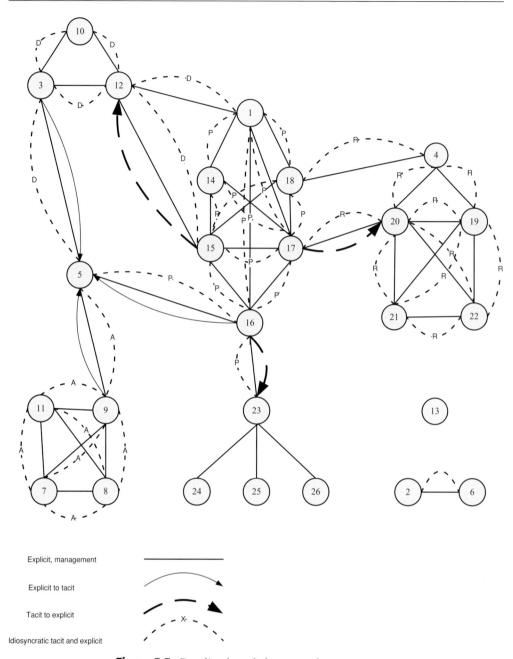

Figure 3.3. *Dazzling knowledge network*

role, having linkages representing several different types of tacit knowledge and converting explicit knowledge to tacit knowledge concerning the organization's overall operations. This manager also is in a key entrepreneurial position: since s/he knows how to frame ideas to differing groups based on their unique perspectives, s/he is more likely to have system-wide influence (Burt 2007). It should be noted that there is not a one-to-one correspondence between formal groups

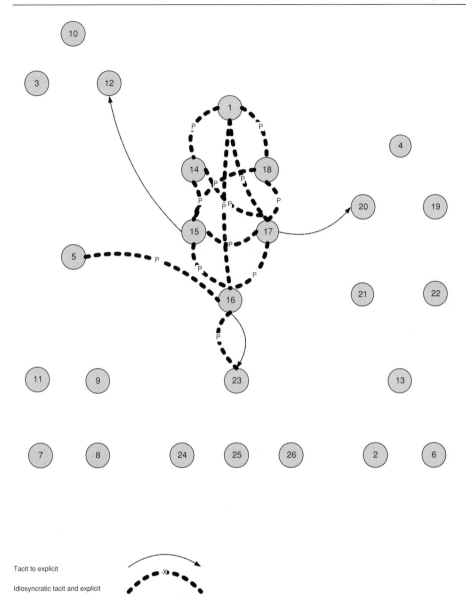

Figure 3.4. *Dazzling prototype knowledge network*

and the development of tacit knowledge. The group formed by 7, 8, 9, and 11 represents a cross-formal grouping of tacit knowledge related to the assembly of the final car components.

Figure 3.4 reveals another essential problem in representing knowledge in organizational networks. The presence of knowledge relationships for highly specialized tacit knowledge may be very fragmented within the organization and the possibilities of second-hand brokerage, or indirect effects, very limited (Burt 2007). As an example we present in this figure only the tacit knowledge related to prototype development, the most commonly shared type. We also represent in this figure attempts to translate this tacit knowledge for others in the organization to act on. So 15 may be developing blueprints of a prototype for 12, 17 may be developing specifications for a research project to test safety parameters for 20, and 16 may be drawing up job requirements for recruiting new workers to prototype the product for 23.

In sum, this figure shows how complex even a small organizational network might become if we tried to capture in a rich way the differing types of knowledge flow within it. Thus, it will not be surprising that there have been relatively few empirical studies of KN, in part because of the complexity of the undertaking (Turner and Makhija 2006). It also points to limitations in most, if not all, current computer software (see Box 3.2). These programs cannot capture this sort of rich description of linkages (Susskind *et al.* 2005), although most can cope with cruder descriptions of multiplexity. Many of Dazzling's members have external ties, particularly associated with their professions. They thus may be linked to much broader tacit networks that have the sort of scale that makes for some very interesting analyses focusing on the World Wide Web (e.g., Newman, Barabasi, and Watts 2006). However, the relatively small size of idiosyncratic tacit networks within organizations may make them more amenable to the limitations inherent in many network analysis computer programs and data-gathering techniques.

Individual patterns of relationships

> In the swirling mix of preferences characteristic of social networks, value is created by entrepreneurs strategically moving accurate, ambiguous or distorted information between people on opposite sides of structural holes in the routine flow of information.   (Burt 2002, p. 338)

> Boundary spanners are a rare breed, however, and few networks have many of them. That's primarily because most people don't have the breadth of intellectual expertise, the wealth of social contacts, and the personality traits necessary to be accepted by vastly different groups.   (Cross and Prusak 2003, p. 255)

Partly because of the emphasis on individual roles in sociology, social psychology, and organizational theory (e.g., Katz and Kahn 1978), early work in network analysis focused on typologies of network roles. More recent work has focused on individuals who position themselves within social structures to take advantage of opportunities. Before we turn to these issues, the contrast between cohesion and structural equivalence views of social contagion is an important theoretical frame for a discussion of the importance of individual positioning in social networks.

Social contagion

Over the last several years a major debate has developed within the social network literature about whether direct communication or forces related to competition are the major motive forces within social systems. Burt (1980) has argued that one motive force is the presence of competitors who occupy structurally similar positions. In contrast, a cohesion perspective, perhaps best represented in the work of Rogers and his colleagues (Rogers 1983; Rogers and Kincaid 1981), would suggest that direct communication results in changes in individuals.

Cohesion and structural equivalence serve as competing theoretical explanations of the impact of social context (the structural configuration of communication relationships) on social contagion processes. Cohesion perspectives essentially argue that communication contacts determine the development of norms. Thus, cohesion focuses on the socializing effect of discussions. The central assumption of the cohesion perspective is that the more frequent and empathetic the communication between individuals, the more likely their opinions and behaviors will resemble each other's (Burt 1987). Structural equivalence focuses on competition. In this view, supervisors could be expected to hold views similar to other supervisors because of their potential competitive roles in the network. This position requires that they maintain certain attitudes and behaviors. Thus, individuals may be the focus of similar information, requests, and demands from members of their role set, creating an information field which, when internalized, creates even more powerful pressures to conform than direct discussions with others. Employees in different functional roles rely on structurally equivalent referents for job-related information and on cohesive referents for general organizational information (Shah 1998).

Social contagion suggests an individual reaches evaluations about ambiguous objects through a social process in which the evaluations of all the proximate others in the system are weighed. As a result, people who are proximate with each other (in terms of their communication linkages) in the social structure tend to develop "consensual standards" (Burt 1982, p. 110) toward ambiguous objects. These consensual standards will trigger a homogeneous attitude that can be a reflection of tacit knowledge. When different individuals come to the same conclusions independently as a result of these processes this may be a key explanation of receptivity to tipping points. What one person says or does is contagious for other people within the same group. Thus, this theory suggests that ambiguous objects stimulate the contagion process which in turn leads to a social norm regarding a particular practice. However, the contagion process, the social mechanism, can operate in two conceptually related yet distinctive ways: cohesion and structural equivalence.

The first proximate mechanism that brings homogeneity is cohesion (Burt and Doreian 1982; Burt 1987; Burt and Uchiyama 1989; Friedkin 1984). The cohesion model has a long history of being used as a predictor of attitudes and beliefs in the social sciences.[3] The model posits that homophily between the ego (the focal individual, the object of influence) and the alter (others in a network who may influence the ego) can be predicted by the strength of their intense and mutual

---

[3] See a brief review by Burt (1987 pp. 1289–1290).

relations with one another. "By communicating their uncertainties to one another regarding some empirically ambiguous object, people socialize one another so as to arrive at a consensual evaluation of the object" (Burt and Doreian 1982, p. 112). Thus, the more frequent and empathetic the bond is between ego and alter, the more likely they come to share attitudinal and behavioral tendencies. As summarized in Hartman and Johnson (1989), "The ego is able to come to a normative understanding of the costs and benefits of specific actions and opinions in terms of the people with whom the discussions are held and thus reduce the ego's level of uncertainty" (p. 524). Where cohesion concerns influential relations among individuals within a primary group, structural equivalence concerns relational patterns among individuals who occupy particular positions (Burt 1982, 1987).

In the structural equivalence model, the driving force for similarity in perceptions is competition between ego and alter. The more the alter is able to substitute for the ego in the ego's role relations, the more pressure the ego feels to conform to the alter's attitudes or behaviors. "The ego comes to a normative understanding of the costs and benefits of the alter filling his or her role and a social understanding that is shared by others in similar roles" (Hartman and Johnson 1989, p. 525). From a structural equivalence perspective, direct communication contacts between individuals are not necessary for the development of a shared frame of reference (Burt 1982, 1987). Hartman and Johnson (1989) further explain that structurally equivalent individuals may experience more pressure toward uniformity because they "may be the focus of similar information, requests, and demands from members of their role set, creating an information field in which they are embedded, which, when internalized, creates even more powerful pressures to conform than discussions with similar alters" (p. 525). In sum, both cohesion and structural equivalence approaches to social contagion have been linked to the transfer of knowledge, with the former the traditional approach and the latter offering important new insights.

Network roles

An individual's communication role is determined by the overall pattern of his/her communication linkages with others. Some individuals, labeled "nonparticipants" (e.g., isolates), have relatively few communication contacts with others (e.g., 2, 6, and 13 in Figure 3.1). "Participants," on the other hand, form intense patterns which represent communication groups and linkages between these groups (e.g., 4, 19, 20, 21, and 22). Several research studies have found key differences between these two kinds of individual, with participants being more outgoing, influential, and satisfied (Goldhaber *et al.* 1978), and having more coherent cognitive structures (Albrecht 1979), and nonparticipants deliberately withholding information, having lower satisfaction with communication (Roberts and O'Reilly 1979), reporting less identification, variety, feedback, and required interaction (Moch 1980).

The most important communication role is that of a liaison (5 in Figure 3.1). The liaison links two or more groups, while not being a member of any one. This strategic positioning of liaisons has earned them the label of "linking pins", who, through their promotion of more positive climates and successful coordination of organizational functions, serve to hold an organization together (Likert 1967). More recently, the vulnerability of large scale networks like the World Wide Web to attacks on a few central positions has also been noted (Albert, Jeong, and Barabasi 2000).

The role of the liaison in the coordination and control of organizational activities is closely tied to the concepts of integration and differentiation discussed in Chapter 5. That is, as the organization divides into more and more groups, greater efforts have to be made at pulling these groups together through integrating mechanisms. These integrating mechanisms are crucial to organizational survival, since without them the organization would be a collection of groups each going off in its own direction. Typically, liaisons are the most efficient personal integrating mechanism because of their strategic positioning. Due to their centrality, and their direct linkages with others, liaisons reduce the probability of message distortion, reduce information load, and increase the timeliness of communication.

Unfortunately, liaisons are relatively rare occurrences, which is reflected in the generally low level of communication between diverse groups in organizations (Farace and Johnson 1974). More recent work on bridges, who are tied to each other but do not share ties with third parties, further emphasizes this point. Burt (2002) found that while bridges accrued significant social capital, had higher peer reputations, and higher compensation, these relationships decayed very rapidly in the environment of a large investment bank, with less than 5 percent surviving for four years. While bridge relationships have higher rewards, they are costly to maintain, since they are often not homophilous and third parties do not share in their costs. While they decay more rapidly than non-bridge relationships in the first two years, they decline more slowly in the third and fourth years. People who were more experienced bridges had their relationships decline more slowly.

Given their central role in organizational operations, it is important to understand the factors that make it more likely that an individual will come to assume the liaison role. Liaison emergence also is central to increasing the level of information which flows between diverse groups in organizations; and, as a result, to increasing coordination and control.

The first set of factors which causes liaison emergence is relational factors. Since network analysis is essentially a means of representing patterns of linkages, the quality of these relationships become important determinants of the patterns of linkages for individuals. So the overall satisfaction of an individual with his/her linkages with others can affect their frequency and duration. For a liaison, one such relational factor that is of critical importance is openness, which is generally conceived of as a willingness to impart or accept information. If information is to flow freely in an organization, then it is critical that network participants maintain the open communication characteristic of trusting relationships.

Another set of factors relating to a liaison's emergence is his/her cognitive abilities. Because the liaison stands at the center of organizational groups, this role has unique information processing demands. Liaisons must process information from diverse sources whose messages are often couched in different technical languages. In organizational contexts the liaison's information processing abilities have been associated with cognitive complexity. The highly cognitively complex individual is able to recognize important differences among bits of information (differentiation); perceive the relative significance of these bits (discrimination); and, finally, assimilate a great variety of information into coherent and/or novel perspectives (integration) (Schroder, Driver, and Streufert 1967). Indeed, several empirical studies have found a relationship between cognitive complexity and positions in communication networks (Albrecht 1979; Schreiman and Johnson 1975; Zajonc and Wolfe 1966). More recently, it has been argued that network range, or the diversity of one's contacts, affects a persons ability "to convey complex ideas across distinct bodies of knowledge" (Reagans and McEvily 2003, p. 247).

While relational and cognitive factors are essential to a liaison's role performance and are necessary for liaison emergence, motivational factors determine whether or not an individual will aspire to such a role and perform effectively within it. The emergent nature of network linkages is in part a picture of the more voluntary and spontaneous choices that organizational members make in their communication relationships. Thus, they may describe, in part, the need fulfillment strategies of organizational members. Typically liaisons in production communication networks can be said to fit into the classification of upwardly mobile individuals in organizations (Presthus 1962). The needs of upwardly mobile individuals are fulfilled within the organization. They are active seekers of information, who constantly survey the organization for information useful to their own advancement.

Traditionally, control in organizations has been viewed as occurring within the formal structure. Roberts and O'Reilly (1979) have argued that effective control in an organization corresponds to the extent to which networks link critical task groups. Increasingly, management functions can be viewed as similar to those of a liaison, a factor reflected in the finding that liaisons tend to be managers. An effective manager must also be able to perceive coherent patterns from diverse information inputs and to form clear judgments which can serve as the basis for organizational action. However, only a minority of all managers occupy liaison positions in informal communication networks. Those who are liaisons appear to use persuasion to accomplish their objectives. In fact, many of the characteristics of a liaison, openness, trust, sensitivity to others, and getting a wide array of input, have also been used to specify the characteristics of democratic managers and, more generally, of open communication climates. Thus, the liaison role points to the convergence of network analysis and formal approaches. It also is a precursor of the growing interest in markets, which makes critical assumptions about the motivations for voluntary interactions and the basic relational qualities necessary for the functioning of social systems.

Brokering structural holes

More recently an alternate view of liaisons has developed. Ron Burt (1992, 2000, 2007) has articulated the concept of structural holes in such a way that he brings together many of the themes of this book, explaining in more detail such phenomena as weak ties. He argues that much of market-oriented competitive behavior can be understood in terms of the access of individuals to "holes" in network structures. Structural holes are gaps or separations in communication network relationships and are framed as "disconnections or nonequivalencies between players in an arena" (Burt 1992, pp. 1–2).

A structural hole separates two entities who have dissimilar network relationships, and who are not connected to each other, but could be. Structural holes normally exist in a functioning network since network members do not share equal access to information or resources (Burt 1992). They provide opportunities for brokerage since actors can pursue their autonomous interests free of the constraints imposed by cohesive groupings (Burt 1991).

Holes are discontinuities in a social structure which create opportunities for information access to certain actors. For example, if two formal divisions which need to interact (e.g., product development and engineering) do not have formal integration links, then the individuals in these units who establish informal bridge or liaison linkages have an advantage over their fellows. While these ties may be weak, adding to the arguments presented earlier, they are also positioned in such a way as to provide unique information. Individuals can turn such relationships into "social capital" which gives them strategic advantage in the competition for scarce resources in the organization, such as promotion. A special case of brokerage comes when a person brokers relationships between asymmetrical groups. So, one who controls access to authority in an organization, or to resources in more informal coalitions, has additional possibilities for influence.

The information benefits of structural positioning revolve around the classic questions of who knows about opportunities, who participates, and when do they participate. Indeed, there is a growing recognition that knowledge networks "require a human hub or switch, whose function is as much to know who knows what as to know what is known" (Earl 2001, p. 225). Individuals who are correctly positioned (e.g., 5 in the communigram) know about key pieces of information earlier than others because of their unique pattern of ties. They can gatekeep the distribution of this information to others (or at least slow its progress) and they may know when and how the information is likely to diffuse to others in the social system.

They can also refer the information to targeted others who serve as their allies. Thus, if there is a training program associated with a key new technology in the organization, an adept individual can alert their mentee, who will then be on the cutting edge of developments and can keep their mentor informed. Taking these active steps moves an actor beyond the acquisition of information to the active control and manipulation of organizational resources based on the information acquired. Thus players can be "pulled" into entrepreneurial action by the promise of success.

Perhaps the most interesting application to date of the structural holes arguments comes in its implication for promotion. Burt (1992) has found that managers with networks rich in structural holes get promoted faster and at a younger age than their competitors. This is partially because the higher you go in organizations the more promotion is based on what you can accomplish with other people. Not only do these managers have the benefits described earlier, but they also are more known to others in the organization and may develop champions in unlikely places that are critical to their career paths. In this connection, one of the least effective strategies is to build strong, redundant relationships with your immediate supervisor. When your supervisor does praise you s/he is often by implication praising him or herself. (Look what a brilliant employee I have developed.) The supervisor also has a vested interest in protecting their investment by not advertising this unique resource to their competitors.

More recently, Burt (2003) has also found an association between innovative ideas and the structural holes of managers. Others have extended Burt's work highlighting its importance as a "starting point for conceptualizing the strategic use of network building to advance a given set of interests" (Pollock, Porac, and Wade 2004, p. 50).

Network indices

> The goal of network analysis is to obtain from low-level or raw relational data higher level descriptions of the structure of a system.   (Rice and Richards 1985, p. 106)

This goal is achieved primarily through the use of various mathematical formulae or indices, reflecting particular patterns of relationships (Edwards and Monge 1977; Wasserman and Faust 1994; Wigand 1988). These indices can inherently be linked to an issue of growing importance in communication, management, and social science research – levels of analysis – and, in part, account for the popularity of network analysis, since they are very sophisticated means of attacking levels-of-analysis problems.

If researchers are to avoid pure reductionism, they must systematically account for the impact of higher-order processes in organizations. For example, supervisor–subordinate dyadic relationships cannot be understood without reference to higher-order organizational processes, such as authority systems (Dansereau and Markham 1987). Similarly the aggregate of all supervisor–subordinate relationships may have important implications for group processes, particularly those associated with decision making and team building. Thus network analysis can be used as a systematic means of linking micro and macro perspectives on organizations. This section will focus on the inherent flexibility of network analysis indices in portraying configurations of relationships centered on pathways of relationships, an individual's positioning, and the group and/or systems level of aggregation, a common breakdown of the levels of analysis in network research.

Pathways

> We do not know all the people our friends know, let alone the friends and acquaintances of those people. It stands to reason that the shortcuts of the social world lie mostly beyond our vision, and only come into our vision when we stumble over their startling consequences.   (Buchanan 2002, p. 55)

Indices associated with pathways primarily deal with how easily a message can flow from one node to another node in a network and are intimately related to matrix manipulation (see Knoke and Kuklinski 1982). Graph theory has been centrally concerned with issues focusing on relationships and this has taken on increasing importance in recent years with the focus on linkages within the Internet and an expansion of the classical small-world problem (Barabasi 2003; Buchanan 2002).

Several definitional distinctions have been made concerning how two nodes might be connected by particular combinations of lines and other nodes (Borgatti 2005). Any sequence of lines is called a *walk*, while a walk in which each node and each line is distinct is termed a *path* (Scott 2000). A *trail* is a walk whose lines are distinct, but whose nodes are not (Wasserman and Faust 1994). These distinctions are important for assessing the flow of information in networks since they can differentiate the redundancy of flows and thus the likelihood of "stickiness," distortion, and other critical outcomes.

Walks that begin and end at the same node are termed *closed* (Wasserman and Faust 1994). Closure is an important property since it allows some feedback concerning how information has been processed (Katz and Kahn 1978). A path's length is determined by the number of lines and geodesic distance is determined by the shortest path, as in package delivery. Reachability focuses on how many links a message must flow through to get from one node to another, usually expressed in terms of the shortest possible path, an issue which has profound implications for an individual's ultimate influence in a social system (Barnes 1972; Mitchell 1969), given the likely limits of indirect contacts noted by Burt (2007) and our limited view of our information horizons (Krebs 2008).

Another way of conceptualizing this problem is in terms of the small-world studies originated by Milgram. These studies focused on the paths people actually used in getting a message to a relative stranger in another geographic location, with the usual finding that relatively few linkages (7.3 to reach a stranger across the continental USA) were needed to reach someone (see Barabasi 2003; Buchanan 2002). Other work has focused on the implications of the small numbers of acquaintances, some estimate as few as twenty-four, that would be necessary for everyone to be connected to everyone else in the world in a social web (Buchanan 2002).

Studies in this area have a number of implications for the flow of knowledge in organizations, especially in terms of efficiency and effectiveness (see Box 10.1 for more detail). They also are somewhat clouded because they represent possibilities, not necessarily what people would do in particular circumstances, and how their conscious choices about who may be the best source of information might shape the linkages they would go through (Barabasi 2003). Stated in another way, there are key differences between a broadcast search, in which everyone you know tells everyone they know and so on, and a directed search that is focused on limited content and the sources most likely to have it (Watts 2003).

It is the linkage of Granovetter's and Milgram's work that led to Watts and Strogatz's (1998) article in *Nature* that created newly aroused interest in this area in the context of the Internet (Barabasi 2003). While the Internet is composed of ordered networks of densely clustered local ties, linked by a few weak ties, it also appears to rely on a few highly centralized hubs that constitute "aristocratic networks of spectacular disparity" (Buchanan 2002, p. 119), enabling the rich to become richer through processes of growth and preferential attachment (Barabasi 2003). The power laws associated with these hubs help us to understand the dynamics of networks and how a few people come to be their focus (Watts 2003), and lead us to a discussion of individual positioning indices.

Individual positioning

Individual positioning indices, such as anchorage (Barnes 1972) and integrativeness (Farace and Mabee 1980; Wigand 1977), try to capture mathematically an individual's location within the configuration of relationships in a network. Structural autonomy relates to the extent to which an individual's relationships may constrain his/her opportunities for individual action within a network. Prominent actors, such as liaisons, are those most visible to others (Wasserman and Faust 1994). They may be the individuals most sought after for information, who have expert power, and who are viewed as most credible. These actors are prestigious to the degree they have ties directed at them, such as those requesting information, with many more relationships coming in than going out (Wasserman and Faust 1994).

The most commonly examined of these indices tries to reveal how central an individual is in a network. Freeman's scheme is the most often used (Scott 2000). He distinguished three types of centrality. Degree or local centrality refers to the number of immediate contacts an individual has, while closeness or global centrality refers to the number of ties needed to reach all others in a network. Betweenness centrality refers to whether an actor stands between two locations and thus has a strategic location as the shortest distance between two points in the network, thereby serving as a relay point. So, brokers have betweenness centrality since they are the go-betweens for transmission of messages from one grouping in a network to another and therefore can facilitate, impede, or bias the transmission of messages from different groups (Freeman 1977).

As with most network indices there is a variety of ways of calculating indices for individual positioning, which can have important implications for relationships to non-network variables. For example, Brass (1981) reports a study in which three different individual positioning measures were used in a study of a newspaper to examine their impact on job characteristics and such organizational outcome variables as satisfaction. Centrality referred to the extent to which a worker could reach others in the network through a minimum number of links. Criticality revealed the degree to which an individual's position was crucial to the flow of materials in a workflow network. Transaction alternatives referred to whether or not redundancy was built into the system in terms of inputs to particular individuals and their outputs to others.

While centrality and criticality were strongly related to job characteristics, they had different patterns of association. Transaction alternatives did not relate strongly to job characteristics. On the other hand, transaction alternatives and criticality had significant relationships to satisfaction, while centrality had non-significant relationships. Brass's (1981) findings point to the importance of measures of individual positioning in explaining non-network variables and also to the importance of carefully considering the wide array of different possible indicators in this category and conceptualizing their relationships to other variables.

Recently it has been suggested that in many ways conventional approaches to network analysis, which focus on relatively enduring relational properties, resulting in a view of the underlying structure of the organization, are too static to capture the fluid world of the contemporary organization. As in diffusion findings, it may be the case that the idiosyncratic flow of knowledge may be somewhat unique for individual cases. Thus, Liberman and Wolf (1997) have focused on the flow of knowledge in scientific meetings, casting it in terms of the exchange of highly specialized information in near-market settings. Recently, Borgatti (2005) has more fully developed the implications of this intuition for centrality indicators. He argues that these measures implicitly assume that messages will flow along the most direct, shortest possible path. However, in any one particular case they may follow different trajectory patterns and methods of spread. Through simulation results he concludes that most commonly used measures (e.g., Freeman's which are based on geodesics) are not appropriate for the more interesting types of flows and that researchers should carefully examine the properties of flows and desired outcomes (e.g., speed and frequency of reception) before using any one particular centrality measure.

Borgatti (2005) also discusses the implications of three different methods of spread – broadcast, serial replication, and transfer. In a broadcast situation, messages, similar to mass media transmissions, may be simultaneously sent in the same form to multiple others. Serial replication may involve some changes in the message at each of several consecutive points, as in gossip situations. Transfer refs to the decision rules at each point in a network (e.g., "Do I send the same message to the most relevant other I know of in my immediate ego network or do I alter it in some way for the first person I come in contact with?").

Groups and connectiveness

Network analysis has been most concerned with the means of identifying highly connected or dense patterns of relationships at differing levels. This has led to a variety of indicators and methods that are closely associated with the classic sociological focus on groups and cliques, or motifs, reflecting network roles at higher levels of patterning, in more recent parlance (Milo *et al.* 2002). This problem has direct analogs with issues related to the differentiation of the organization into formal groups, which we will discuss in more detail in Chapter 5.

Connectiveness and density

Perhaps the greatest level of development in network indices comes in the area of the relative connectiveness of larger social aggregates, either groups/cliques or the larger social system.[4] Essentially, the issue of connectiveness refers to whether or not all of the possible linkages in an aggregate are being utilized. So, even a group of seven has many possible combinations of internal linkages; the more of them that are in actual use, the higher the connectiveness of the group. This has important implications for processes like attitude formation in groups (Danowski 1980) and a group's relative cohesiveness.

Most recent attention to this issue has focused on density, which is determined by dividing the number of actual lines in a particular network by the number possible (Scott 2000). While centralization describes the degree to which cohesion is organized around particular nodes, density describes more holistically the level of connectiveness within a network (Scott 2000).

Cliques and groups

Cliques, which form because of greater levels of affiliation on some relational property, have always been of central interest in organizational behavior, at least back to the Hawthorne studies (Kilduff and Tsai 2003; Scott 2000). In the 1950s and 1960s there was extensive research on the issue of how small-group structures impacted performance and member satisfaction (Shaw 1971). After a long fallow period, work on group networks has focused on the balance between internal and external information ties needed to achieve optimal work performance (Katz *et al.* 2004). This is, in part, because of the profound influence of social context on individuals and their relationships with others (Kilduff and Tsai 2003).

The overlap of clique memberships (Katz *et al.* 2004; Kilduff and Tsai 2003) and the relative continuity of relationships in fractured social systems, such as virtual organizations, often make a clear identification of groupings difficult in

---

[4] See Edwards and Monge (1977) for an early systematic review of the different properties of a wide variety of early connectiveness indicators.

empirical work, with considerable attention being given to this in the development of computer algorithms and indices (Wasserman and Faust 1994). How people categorize their social world into affiliative groups is critical to how they go about searching for information in a directed fashion, since the first step will often embed certain assumptions about the types of people likely to have certain kinds of knowledge (Watts 2003). Highly dense, relatively isolated cliques can be expected to have high levels of tacit knowledge, while overlapping is critical to the sharing of knowledge and the development of common perspectives throughout an entire organization.

Summary

Recent years have seen a resurgence of interest in network analysis as a way of portraying the complex patterns of relationships in social systems. As we have seen, it offers many compelling advantages in the investigation of the flow of knowledge in organizations. First, it is a very practicable method for examining the overall configurations of relationships in a large social system, and can also provide an elegant description of them. Network analysis offers the most complete picture of the overall configuration of linkages yet developed, and certainly a much more complete view than that offered by the more traditional formal approaches alone. It is well suited for describing and analyzing more complex, modern organizational arrangements (e.g., consortia, matrix organizations, and so forth). Second, it provides very specific and direct information on the pattern of an individual's linkages, since networks are based fundamentally on the notion of dyadic linkages. It moves us away from an exclusive focus on the individual to a more conceptually correct focus on the relationship as the unit of analysis; it shifts the focus from what individuals know to how knowledge is shared within a social system through such processes as weak ties and brokerage. Third, it permits the derivation of a host of other measures from the aggregation of these individual linkages, including clique identification, roles, and metrics (for example, connectedness), and this data can be aggregated at various levels of analysis including interpersonal, group, and whole organization. In this regard it can be used as a systematic means of linking micro and macro perspectives of an organization, and the more contemporary focus on levels of analysis, to develop ever more sophisticated approaches to context.

Understanding networks can have emancipatory potential since it can acquaint actors with constraints and opportunities of which they might otherwise be unaware (Kilduff and Tsai, 2003). Their network of relationships constitutes an individual's social capital. Most fundamentally, network analysis is an expression of the social nature of knowledge, with Grover and Davenport (2001) and others viewing all knowledge as situated within a context. Network analysis, then, can offer a precise picture of how personal knowledge is situated or embedded within a broader social context, the subject we turn to in the next part of the book.

Further reading

Borgatti, S. P., and Foster, P. C. 2003. The network paradigm in organizational research: a review and typology. *Journal of Management*, 29: 991–1013.

Comprehensive overview of research on network analysis in organizations, particularly focusing on the management and sociology literatures.

Burt, R. S. 1992. *Structural Holes: The Social Structure of Competition*. Harvard University Press.

The seminal work on structural holes which primarily focuses on career paths, less so on issues related to knowledge transfer directly, although there is an extended discussion of weak ties.

Burt, R. S. 2005. *Brokerage and Closure: An Introduction to Social Capital*. Oxford University Press.

Focuses more directly on innovation and the role of brokerage in diffusing ideas within organizations. One of the reasons for the popularity of Burt's ideas is that his books move beyond the general overviews, so characteristic of work in this area, to richly developed empirical and theoretical treatments of his concepts.

Cross, R., Parker, A., and Sasson, L. (eds.) 2003. *Networks in the Knowledge Economy*. Oxford University Press.

Collection of classic readings that focus on many of the topics developed in this book, although most of the selections, like network analysis generally, only tangentially confront KN.

Monge, P. R., and Contractor, N. S. 2003. *Theories of Communication Networks*. Oxford University Press.

Systematic discussion of theories related to communication networks with an organizing scheme based on multilevels. Outgrowth of the author's handbook articles with some expansion on more esoteric topics.

Newman, M., Barabasi, A., and Watts, D. J. (eds.) 2006. *The Structure and Dynamics of Networks*. Princeton University Press.

Collection of contemporary readings from a very diverse array of sources, anthropology to physics, that capture the extension of networks to the world of the Internet.

Richards, W. D. 1985. Data, models, and assumptions in network analysis. In R. D. McPhee and P. K. Tompkins (eds.), *Organizational Communication: Traditional Themes and New Directions*: 109–128. Sage.

In-depth analysis of problems associated with operationalizing and conceptualizing the fundamental unit of analysis in network research – the relationship.

Scott, J. 2000. *Social Network Analysis: A Handbook*, 2nd edn., Sage.

Classic popular general introduction to social network analysis.

Watts, D. J. 2003. *Six Degrees: The Science of the Connected Age*. W. W. Norton.

Best-selling treatment of contemporary topics in network analysis, especially as they relate to the World Wide Web, by one of the leading researchers in this area. Some chapters focus on issues of importance to organizations, especially in terms of searching for information and the diffusion of information.

Contexts

4 Context

> ...we don't know who discovered water, [but] it was almost certainly not a fish.
>
> (McLuhan, quoted in Lukasiewicz 1994, p. xx)

> Despite repeated appeals for contextual inquiry and sensitivity to context...no one is exactly sure what is being requested or how to produce it.
>
> (Weick 1983, p. 27)

> The more contexts two people share, the closer they are, and the more likely they are to be connected.
>
> (Watts 2003, p. 126)

> Information is united with context, that is, it only has utility within the context.
>
> (Grover and Davenport 2001, p. 6)

A fundamental necessity of social action is that it must occur within a context. While context is central to all explanations of social science, it has been examined most often in micro, discourse-related processes or situational semantics. Knowledge is inherently embedded in particular social situations (Birkinshaw, Nobel, and Ridderstrale 2002). The relationship between context and information seeking is a problem increasingly viewed as the central issue in information behavior research (Cool 2001; Dervin 1997, 2003; Johnson 2003; Pettigrew, Fidel, and Bruce 2001; Talja, Keso, and Pietilainen 1999; Taylor 1986).

Generally, the persistent theoretical problem of accounting for individual action in a social context is seldom explicitly addressed and we are unaware of the different senses of "context" in use (Dervin 1997). Especially lacking is the identification of "active" ingredients of the environment that trigger changes in KN (Johnson 2003). In general, in conceptualizing our world, we have a tendency to focus on objects rather than their grounds (Stocking and Holstein 1993), focusing on messages or individuals, for example, rather than the contexts within which they are embedded. We concentrate on the processes we are interested in rather than on the more diffuse social contexts that frame, embed, and surround them.

Traditionally three senses of context have been used in organizational research (see Table 4.1). First, context is seen as equivalent to the situation in which an individual is immersed, with situations viewed as more important in determining behaviors than individual traits or dispositions. Second, contingency approaches move toward identifying active ingredients that have specific, predictable effects

Table 4.1. *Comparing three senses of context*

Dimension	Senses		
	Situation	Contingency	Frameworks
Explanatory power	Primitive	Precise	Rich
Individual's role	Passive	Match	Contextualizing
Subjectivity	Objective	Contingent	Interpretive
Duality	Separate	Interactive	Inseparable
Theoretic orientation	Positivist	Post-positivist	Post-modern

Source: Johnson (2003, p. 739)

on various processes. Third, major frameworks for meaning systems or interpretation are increasingly seen as critical to the development of knowledge. In the end, it is essential to the development of any theory that we explain the conditions under which it applies; this is the fundamental problem that examining contexts addresses (Baker and Pettigrew 1999). In this chapter, then, I will examine each of these intraorganizational approaches to context before turning to how organizations contextualize their external worlds.

Context as equivalent to situation

The first, and most primitive, sense in which context has been used is as equivalent to an elaborated list of situational factors (Chang and Lee 2001; Dervin 1997). So, a situational definition of context is simply an elaborate specification of the environment within which KN are embedded. For example, at the macro level, climate, cultural, and structural approaches have all specified lists of factors that can impact networks. So, Monge and Eisenberg (1987) discuss national character, socioeconomic factors, and type of industry as among the environmental factors that can shape emerging communication networks.

In the case of organizational climate and culture these enumerated lists can be extensive. Some climate approaches have sought to describe all the enduring factors present in an organization's situation that could be used to distinguish it from other organizations and that could influence the behaviors of organizational members. For example, in their seminal review of the climate literature, James and Jones (1974) describe the multiple measurement–organizational attribute perspective as one of three major approaches to climate. This approach specifies five major components of situational variance: context, structure, process, physical environment, and system values and norms. In the multiple measurement–organizational attribute approach, each of these components in turn has many elaborated elements, with context, for example, including technology, resources, goals, ownership, age, function, and so on. In this approach, climate becomes equivalent to a very elaborate specification of an organization's situation; and climate in James and Jones's (1974) treatment often becomes nearly synonymous with more commonly used senses of the concept of context (Denison 1996).

Situational approaches to context seek exhaustive, objective descriptions, but do not typically move to explanations of what the linkage is, if any, between situational factors (e.g., societal trends, information technology, constraints, information fields, search procedures, and so on) and the process of interest. Moving beyond lists of situational factors is the specification of limiting conditions (e.g., technology, life cycle, environmental niche) for a middle-range theory that suggests the context in which sets of propositions are operative. Thus, a contextualist might argue that any hypothesis is plausible in certain limited situations (McGuire 1983). So, recognizing the importance of KN to the operations of markets, I might state that a market approach to organizational structure explains the development of networks in highly competitive technological firms where members can freely exchange information with each other (Johnson 1996a, b). Thus, limiting conditions may be an intermediate step, specifying factors that are presumed to moderate relationships, but for which the exact nature of relationships are not specified, as in contingency frameworks.

Context as contingency

Contingency approaches move beyond the enumeration of factors in a situation to specify active ingredients in a context and their relationship to processes. A contingent approach to context is concerned with specifying key situational factors which produce predictable states of KN. Underlying these approaches is the more general assumption that an entity's (e.g., individual, unit) effectiveness is determined by the match (or fit) between its features, particularly structural ones, and its surrounding environment (Allen and Kim 2000). These congruence ideas have often been criticized on logical and theoretical grounds (Dalton *et al.* 1980), particularly because they often appear tautological or are used to explain relationships after the fact (Drazin and Van de Ven 1985; Fry and Smith 1987).

Match, contingency, and congruency

While the general ideas of match, contingency, and congruency are powerful heuristic concepts that have been supported empirically in many contexts, they are not without problems. Fry and Smith (1987) have developed a systematic conceptual critique of this literature. Essentially they argue for consistent definition and careful distinction of these concepts within the framework of a general approach to theory building. They argue that congruence is a concept that is defined by the relationships of a theory's variables. On the other hand, contingency is defined by system states where the integrity of the system is maintained, but in markedly different conditions.

So Lawrence and Lorsch's (1967) work on the match between differentiation and integration and an organization's environment would most clearly fall at the level of contingency, while their discussion of the importance of certain styles of conflict resolution is more of an example of congruence. Congruence is a prior requirement for contingency and a necessary, but not sufficient, condition for it. Thus, an organization in Lawrence and Lorsch's (1967) theory must have appropriate conflict resolution strategies if the match between differentiation and integration and the environment is going to occur, but this is not sufficient; the appropriate levels of differentiation and integration must also be in place.

Several other problems exist in this literature. First, a contingency view is often taken to explain research findings after the fact, but a true perspective on congruence and contingency requires specification of relationships before research is undertaken. Second, and somewhat relatedly, contingency perspectives often suffer from tautological or circular reasoning. It works because it works. It does not work because the proper match did not occur. Third, the fundamental systems notion of equifinality immensely complicates this picture. That is, many congruent systems might be established to maintain the system within the same contingent state (Fry and Smith 1987). It is possible that both a centralized communication structure coupled with authoritarian management and a decentralized structure coupled with democratic management can maintain a productive organization within the same general environment.

In sum, contingency approaches are more rigorous theoretically than situational ones, in that they specify the active ingredients in a context and their impacts on the processes of interest. However, these approaches have traditionally been more functionalist in character, slighting interpretive approaches, to which we now turn.

Context as frameworks and governance structures

> Not understanding that a fundamental intermediate purpose of managing knowledge is to create shared context.   (Dervin 1998, p. 39, citing Fahey and Prusak's eleven deadly sins of KM)

> . . . a connection that I make each time when I work with someone with whom I find some ground, some shared way of thinking about things. If I don't have that connection, it's tough for me to get going working with them.   (Kahn 1990, p. 707, quoting an architect on work interactions).

This section examines the various frameworks for governance structures within which debates, discussions, and dialogs occur within organizations. In one or another governance structure, some have identified each as what a network is, rather than one particular instantiation of the concept of networks. The concept of framework has a long history in the social sciences, especially in relation to discourse processes. Frames have been viewed as inherently delimiting, providing individuals with a situated context for action and for interpretations of particular "strips of activity" (Goffman 1974).

The concept of frames is most commonly used to indicate a way both of viewing the world and of subjectively interpreting it, with frames acting as sense-making devices that establish the parameters of a problem (Gray 1996). In organizational contexts, Schon and Rein (1994) have developed an extensive analysis of how frames affect policy conflicts. Similarly, Bolman and Deal (1991) argue four classic academic frames (structural, human resources, political, and cultural) contribute to a practitioner's sense-making in organizations. A frame, or the act of framing, usually refers to putting a perspective into words when one encodes a message (*American Heritage Dictionary* 1979), providing, for example, a definition, meaning, or conceptualization of an issue in a conflict situation (Putnam and Holmer 1992).

Here we will focus on frameworks that provide a more encompassing context for interaction within organizations. A framework for interaction is the set of interrelated conditions that promote certain levels of shared understanding of meanings, orient interactants to the nature of the event, and establish the ultimate purpose of continuing interaction (Johnson 1997b, 1998). A framework, then, is like a ground that opens doors to social worlds of situated knowledge and governing rationalities. Frameworks provide the basic support structures for cooperative relationships within organizations through the development of an inextricable linkage between context and meaning, which is increasingly viewed as fundamental to knowledge transfer.

A fundamental property of communication is that interpretation depends on context. Frameworks are both windows on the world and lenses that bring the world into focus; at the same time they filter out some stimuli (Bolman and Deal 1991). More post-modern views of context suggest individuals often enact their contexts (Weick 1969), choosing their own interpretations of the ones they are in (Dervin 1997). Often understandings attributable to various frameworks assume a taken-for-granted reality among interactants. Indeed, frameworks perform a number of critical functions for interactants: they are shared conversational resources; they provide a common emotional tone; they insure quicker responses; and they also provide a basis for temporal stability by insuring more continuous responses (Benson 1975; Collins 1981).

Structure as governance

Structural research has been the primary focus of research on these issues and it has been centrally concerned with examining enduring governance frameworks. Structure has five elements: relationships, entities, configurations, context, and temporal stability (see Table 4.2), and may be defined in these terms: "Organizational communication structure refers to the relatively stable configuration of communication relationships between entities within an organizational context" (Johnson 1992, p. 100). As Table 4.2 details, each of the approaches we will

Table 4.2. *Relationships between structure elements and knowledge and different types of governance framework*

Structure elements	Formal	Informal	Markets	Professional
Relationships	Hierarchical	Sentiments	Exchanges	Normative
Entities	Positions	People	Traders	Professionals
Context	Rules system	Social/personal/ climate	Embeddedness	Practice standards
Configuration	Organizational chart	Sociogram	Bazaar	Guild/clan
Temporal stability	Equivalent to organization's	Limited	Dynamic	Generations, common law
Knowledge	Rules	Intuition	Explicit	Tacit

discuss – formal, informal, markets, and professional – has different manifestations of these key elements. They also provide the human framework within which knowledge can be created, shared, and transferred, with different types of knowledge valued in each.

Structure determines what is possible in large organizations since it enables action within a governance framework. "Networks make the achievement of output goals (such as production) possible" (Farace, Monge, and Russell 1977, p. 179). The existing structure of an organization limits what is possible, if only by inertia, and at times quite formally. Geertz's spider-web metaphor, which is often cited in studies of organizational culture (e.g., Pacanowsky and O'Donnell-Trujillo 1982), may also be quite appropriate here.[1] At one and the same time a spider-web constrains and enables action. A spider, like an individual in a network, can make new strands in a web to meet new needs – but until it does, there are some things it will not be able to do, since the web constitutes a real boundary to action.

Without a predictable pattern of recurring relationships, coordinated activity within the organization would be impossible. The more constraints that exist, the more things occur in predictable patterns, and the more people know about their organization. "Structure is a fundamental vehicle by which organizations achieve bounded rationality" (Thompson 1967, p. 54); structure provides organizational members with the limits within which efficiency may be a reasonable expectation. Thus, when you increase constraints you increase what is known and knowable about organizational operations. The sum total of these constraints determines the manifest communication structure of a system. In turn, these forms of control affect a firm's ability to leverage knowledge (Turner and Makhija 2006).

---

[1] Indeed, a network program, Pajek, is named for the Slovenian word for spider (de Nooy, Mrvar, and Batagelj 2005).

Indeed, structure is often viewed as an information-processing tool (Mackenzie 1984). One of the clearest implications of the dysfunctional aspects of a lack of structure comes in information overload. Structure permits an organization to process more information. Since a lot of distinct information is processed by means of specialization, this information is then filtered before it is processed by other units. Thus more information can be processed, since some responsibility is delegated to particular units and everyone does not have to handle the same information. As a result, structure reduces information overload in organizations and thereby increases the efficiency of their operations. Ironically, in reducing information overload, a valuable contribution to organizational efficiency, organizations reduce the availability of information, which can reduce organizational effectiveness, particularly in terms of decision making. This also has obvious implications for the distribution of tacit knowledge within an organization.

Comparing formal, informal, market, and professional structures

> As it is the power of exchanging that gives occasion to the division of labour, so the extent of this division must always be limited by the extent of that power, or, in other words, by the extent of the market.   (Smith 1776/1952, p. 8)

> In sum, formal and informal organization are inextricably linked. Hierarchical organizations are deeply connected to wider networks, while informal networks straddle and interpenetrate the boundaries of hierarchical structures. (Powell and Smith-Doerr 1994, p. 380)

> In part, communication structure is planned; in part, it grows up in response to the need for specific kinds of communication; in part, it develops in response to the social functions of communication. At any given stage in its development, its gradual change is much influenced by the pattern that has already become established. Hence, although the structure of the network will be considerably influenced by the structure of the organization's task, it will not be completely determined by the latter.   (March and Simon 1958, p. 168)

Formal approaches, which, as we saw in Chapter 2, rely heavily on explicit knowledge and well-understood code systems, were the first to systematically examine structure, but increasingly the power of informal forces came to be recognized in organizational thought. The entire structure of an organization is composed of elements of both, with other ingredients as well – with the tension between formal and informal a critical issue for the social life of information and innovation (Brown and Duguid 2002). Attempts to systematically compare formal and informal groupings and their impacts on the levels of role ambiguity essentially found more similarities than differences between the two types of grouping and suggested a complex set of contingencies in which one or the other would have the most impact on role ambiguity (Hartman and Johnson 1990). Somewhat similarly, other studies have found that these two approaches related to such key organizational factors as beliefs, stylistic characteristics, and channel usage (Johnson *et al.* 1994). Much work remains to be done to determine the nature of overlaps and differences between informal and formal views of structure, with some arguing that the views are so divergent it is impractical to consider both simultaneously (Blau 1974). In many ways they represent diametrically opposed positions on what structure is (Dow 1988), with both perspectives also appealing to different underlying metaphors, mechanistic and organismic respectively (Johnson 1993; Morgan 1986). More recently, the advent of IT and global competition has pushed the envelope of formal structures, with contemporary writers focusing on the virtual characteristics of structure, which have direct analogs to KN.

In much of the literature on the interrelationships between structural approaches the focus has been on markets, hierarchies, and networks. Hierarchies are fairly close to the meaning of formal approaches developed here; however, networks have had various meanings, with some focusing on a much more narrow meaning and coming to reflect primarily the more informal trusting relationships that develop in ongoing associations (Thompson 1991). Formal structure can also be encompassed within network conceptions (Monge and Eisenberg 1987), so both hierarchical and market approaches could be considered to be differing instantiations of networks (Frances *et al.* 1991).

A formal approach, discussed in detail in the next chapter, was the earliest systematic specification of the underlying basis for interaction within organizations and in many ways the other frameworks were established in opposition, or counterpoint, to it (Johnson 1993). In fact, informal communication studies, the precursors to the modern interest in communication networks, became a residual category including a wide array of potential frameworks (e.g., sentiments, informal influence, and so on) for interaction. Thus, exchange rests on individuals pursuing their rational self-interest, common to markets, while normative frameworks depend on operations of larger collectivities, most clearly represented in the professions. The introduction of tacit knowledge also suggests a need for the more explicit introduction of culturally related normative elements, captured most clearly in the professions (see Table 4.3). In Table 4.3 the four structural governance types are classified by level of tacit knowledge sharing and by their relative emphasis on cooperation or competition. So, markets, for example, are characterized by low levels of tacit knowledge sharing and high degrees of competition. Negotiated order, as we shall soon see, often develops from idiosyncratic mixes of the other frameworks (Johnson 1997b). Let us now turn to a more explicit discussion of the elements of structure and how they relate specifically to each of these four governing frameworks.

Formal

Administrative rationality in the Weberian sense has always been a central concern of the formal approach and with it has come the assumption that structures are designed to control behavior in such a way as to produce efficient/effective operations (Pfeffer 1978), controlling competitive instincts to produce cooperative behaviors. Thus, structures are conceived as fitting into a preconceived

Table 4.3. *Levels of tacit knowledge sharing, coopetition, and governance frameworks*

| | | Coopetition | |
		Competitive	**Cooperative**
Tacit knowledge sharing	**High**	Professional	Informal
	Low	Markets	Formal

rational plan, rather than viewed as representing rationality after the fact (Weick 1969).

Formal frameworks essentially represent the bureaucratic world of the organization, with its specification of patterns of super- and sub-ordination and other hierarchical relationships between parties in a relatively permanent framework (Weber 1947). An hierarchy provides a framework for action by specifying control patterns, routinizing production, and implementing plans (McPhee 1988). The kinds of behavior individuals can engage in are specified in company manuals and output targets are detailed in formal performance reports (Baliga and Jaeger 1984). Usually formal frameworks require only a limited form of understanding, based on system rules, training, and a legalistic understanding of relationships between positions. Actors are presupposed to be driven, or motivated, by the requirements of the positions they occupy in the formal structure of the organization.

The context of formal structure lies in the "official world" of the organization. Most often it can be conceived of as embedded in its formal authority structure, usually associated with bureaucracy. In this context, communication is conceived as flowing along the pathways delineated by the organizational chart and the content of communication is limited to those production-related matters that concern the organization. While this formal approach constitutes a limited view of the role of communication in organizations, this still may be, especially operationally, its most important role, and certainly one that management must at least try to control.

Informal

Often interaction, which is initially based on one of the preceding frameworks, results in collective sentiments. Friendship and other more emotional ties often provide the underlying basis for relationships. Traditionally, this has been cast as a primary basis for informal structures. The shared understandings characteristic of these relationships are often dependent on the depth of emotional involvement. Classically, sociograms were used to represent the overall configuration of these relationships (Moreno 1934). Sentiments recognize the often neglected place of emotions (Mumby and Putnam 1992) and the desire for affiliation in organizational life. They also represent a more intuitive, subjective view of knowledge.

The degree of affiliation felt between interactants determines the temporal stability of relationships, which can be fleeting, and the degree to which parties' sentiments may override other bases for relationships, such as exchange. Thus, exchange relationships may be essentially the same for friends as for strangers, except for the greater trust and likelihood of being involved in the first instance. However, exchange relationships between individuals with deep emotional ties may be more characterized by "bad trades," where equitable exchanges of material resources are not realized (Clark 1984).

Markets

More recently, yet another view of structure, a market approach, which shares much with both network and formal approaches, and rests on economic and exchange assumptions, has emerged. Markets focus on exchange relationships (see Table 4.2) and the paramount importance of trust in characterizing them. Exchange conceptions of relationships within organizations may be the most popular modern framework (see Cook 1982; Hall 2003), partially because of their linkage to underlying economic theory. As Bellah *et al.* (1991) point out, the underlying cultural value of Lockean individualism is also dominant in our larger cultural frame. In this view, individuals are seen as driven to maximize rewards through their interaction with each other. Basically an exchange represents: "The action, or an act of reciprocal giving and receiving" (*Oxford English Dictionary* 1989).

Obviously, an exchange relationship can rest on extremely rudimentary understandings of others, based on such fundamental issues as fair price and trust that the other party will follow through on bargains. Relationships are seen from a utilitarian perspective, with the primary bases for continued relationships resulting from a perception of mutual gain. For communication scholars, information exchanges are the critical focus (Eisenberg *et al.* 1985). However, exchange relationships, once started, develop assets in and of themselves, based on their start-up costs, which make it more likely they will continue and endure (McGuinness 1991). Thus, exchange is sometimes viewed as the most fundamental of the frameworks, at least in terms of providing the initial starting point from which others might develop.

The unique attributes of information discussed in Chapter 2 also require special consideration when discussing the specialized world of knowledge and electronic markets (see Box 4.1). First, some information is perishable (e.g., reacting to a coup in an oil-rich state for energy companies). This means it is not stored or inventoried in the same way as other commodities. Second, knowledge does not have the same value for all parties. The same piece of data may be totally irrelevant to some, and the missing piece of a billion dollar puzzle to others. Third, the parties have different costs – search costs for buyers and the value returned for

Box 4.1. Electronic markets

The market frame provides a major approach to organizational structure. In general, the efficiency of markets depends on information symmetry, product standardization, customer homogeneity, a large number of suppliers, and common currency, with Grover and Davenport (2001) suggesting that KM is essentially a problem of creating effective and efficient marketplaces. Markets are central to global economies, facilitating the exchange of commerce, information, and trust, and IT plays a major role in supporting electronic markets (EM) (Wigand, Picot, and Reichwald 1997). EM such as Inventory Locator Service (ILS) in the airline industry, SABRE, American Gem Market System, and TELCOT in the cotton industry are interorganizational information systems that link multiple buyers and sellers (Choudhury, Hartzel, and Konsynski 1998) facilitating business-to-business (B2B) exchanges (Ordanini 2005). They identify potential trading partners, help in selecting particular partners, partly by providing access to price information, and facilitate transactions (Choudhury, Hartzel, and Konsynski 1998). EM operate best in commodity-type markets where the good is not complex and costs are low (Choudhury, Hartzel, and Konsynski 1998). Content syndication networks (e.g., iSyndicate) provide a special case of EM that are rich in their KN implications.

Malone, Yates, and Benjamin (1987) and Bakos (1991) assert that organizations involved in EM will reduce their transaction costs associated with the search for competing suppliers. In EM, it is possible to change relationships with suppliers, competition is open, and information is more readily available than in hierarchies, which are characterized by organizations controlling a vertically integrated supply chain (Salazar 2007). But reducing costs and inventory may not be the main point; in certain markets like ILS, greater assurance of the quality of airline parts is the primary benefit (Choudhury, Hartzel, and Konsynski 1998).

Supply chains represent a middle ground between markets and hierarchies. Supply chains are networks of separate organizations that jointly transform raw materials into distributed products often with unique, idiosyncratic intranets which have knowledge-based advantages. Creating value involves a sequence of activities for which KN are critical: gathering, organizing, selecting, synthesizing, and distributing information (Christiaanse and Venkatraman 2002). The specific type of information in this chain determines the basis of expertise exploitation (Christiaanse and Venkatraman 2002).

Managing supply chain and other interorganizational systems, which are automated IT systems shared by two or more companies, has become a key source of differential performance among firms and thus has direct relationships with their competitive advantages (Saeed, Malhotra, and Grover 2005). The initiators of these systems (e.g., Wal-Mart, General

Motors) have particular leveraging advantages in these relationships (Saeed, Malhotra, and Grover 2005). Historically firms needed to buffer or have slack resources to deal with uncertainties associated with lack of information; enhanced coordination reduces these problems (Saeed, Malhotra, and Grover 2005). EM with suppliers focus on efficiencies of routinization and electronic integration, with lower selection, negotiation, and transaction execution costs derived from long-term relationships (Choudhury, Hartzel, and Konsynski 1998). These EM also result in substantially lower inventory costs (Choudhury, Hartzel, and Konsynski 1998).

EM underscore the need to account for network structures and environmental factors when utilizing transaction costs approaches. The ability to successfully integrate and implement technology in organizations has provided organizations with a competitive advantage by helping them reduce transaction costs. EM can obscure boundaries between organizations, suppliers, and others, while technology reduces the cost of preparing and monitoring agreements, thus introducing elements unforeseen by Coase (1937). EM between businesses, suppliers, and consumers have both direct and indirect (leakage) effects (e.g., market share, orders from other suppliers, inferences from actions of directly informed parties) on information sharing (Li 2002).

EM may challenge the role of conventional intermediaries, forcing them to higher-end value-added contributions based on their unique knowledge (e.g., summary judgments of the bottom-line, true value of a transaction), rather than just the mechanics of matching buyers and sellers (Choudhury, Hartzel, and Konsynski 1998). Brokers provide the human side of technology integration in social networks (Salazar 2007). B2B exchanges provide platforms for knowledge brokers filling structural holes (Ordanini 2005). Linking buyers and sellers in EM substantially reduces buyer search costs (Banker and Kauffman 2004; Choudhury, Hartzel, and Konsynski 1998) and facilitates partnership effects by leveraging the possibilities of sharing information, experience, and knowledge, while also reducing negotiation costs (Ordanini 2005).

sharing knowledge for sellers. This is a critical element of transaction costs, since some members of specialized units within organizations are valued to the extent they provide valuable information to others (e.g., corporate librarians). Among the most important costs, which leads to an emphasis on firms and hierarchy, is the transfer of tacit knowledge (Kogut and Zander 1996), with firms seen as "superior vehicles for the accumulation of specialized learning" (Kogut 2000, p. 409).

Markets, through the mechanism of exchanges, operate to diffuse information rapidly to interested parties (von Hayek 1991) in an overall configuration often described as traders in a bazaar (Geertz 1973). In focusing on exchanges this approach provides a theoretical focus for the development of relationships between interactants, who may otherwise lack compelling motives to interact. Indeed, we may seek exchanges with others because they are not like us and they have resources that we do not possess.

This view also suggests a broader conception of information as something that can be shaped and modified in exchanges, then interpreted in different ways in the collectivity as exchanges proceed. Thus, markets have an inherently dynamic view of information exchanges, with individuals being compelled to change their ideas as a result of the reactions of others. This contrasts directly with the view of information in a hierarchical approach as a relatively unchanging commodity that should be passed with minimal transformations from one part of the organization to others (Powell 1990).

While markets have been seen as occurring outside the context of formal organizations, they have been recognized as containing many authority properties found in organizations, and organizations with complex, multidivisional structures take on market characteristics (Eccles and White 1988). "The internal operations of real-world firms are controlled by a blend of authority and market-like mechanisms" (McGuinness 1991, p. 66).

The nature of the relationships is determined by notions inherent in exchange; achieving a fair price for a good or service. In pure market exchange relationships the only thing that may matter is the value of the goods exchanged. In network-based exchanges normative controls may also be operative in the relationship (Lorenz 1991; Powell 1990) and the consequences of untrustworthy behavior may cloud concurrent and future interactions (Kirman 2001). An emerging emphasis on markets and economic conceptions of organizations has focused attention on the embeddedness of economic relations (Granovetter 1985; Johnson 1996a) which has led to social capital perspectives on brokerage relations (Sawyer *et al.* 2003). In fact, for those organizational members who are unscrupulous in their relationships, the possibility of their behavior being sanctioned internally provides a positive incentive to interact outside of the firm (Eccles and White 1988).

Networks of information exchanges, which also contain market elements, are particularly useful structures for organizations composed of highly skilled workforces which possess knowledge not limited to particular tasks (Powell 1990). Indeed, more generally it has been argued that knowledge flows may be best accomplished by informal organizational structures because of problems in recognizing the significance of information and communicating it effectively and efficiently (Gupta and Govindarajan 1991). This form of decentralization often reduces the possibility of information overload, and attendant delays and imperfect planning orders, within these organizations. Thus, in organizations like universities, it may be better to minimize intrusive formal structures and promote wide-ranging interactions, while providing a framework in which trading relationships can occur.

The availability of information concerning costs and beneficial exchanges is critical to the operation of a pure market (Levacic 1991). Indeed, inadequate information is one source of market failure (Levacic 1991). Thus, markets place a premium on KN. Inadequate information can take many forms. One form concerns problems in price and trust that go to the heart of exchange relationships (Levacic 1991). Opportunistic sellers selectively reveal, distort, and withhold information, if they perceive they can do so without penalty (Lorenz 1991; McGuinness 1991). Another set of issues deals with uncertainties, especially concerning future (and often unknown) contingencies (Levacic 1991). Of course, acting in a market (and observation of the actions of others) produces essential feedback and critical information that can be used dynamically to refine future market behavior (Krizner 1973).

The market approach, especially as it relates to transaction costs, has been used to specify those conditions under which an organization will try to subsume certain relationships under its formal umbrella (Williamson 1994). Uncertain transactions that recur frequently and require substantial investments of money, time, or energy are more likely to occur within a hierarchy. For example, organizations in the United States are increasingly incorporating legal divisions into their formal structures. Enhanced familiarity with, and responsiveness to, an organization's idiosyncratic legal problems offset the "costs" of bureaucracy because they provide a means (e.g., formal structure) for adjudicating unforeseen problems in the relationship, and the naturally opportunistic impulses of actors (e.g., lawyers in outside firms) are controlled by authority relationships within the organization (Granovetter 1985; Powell 1990, discussing the work of Williamson). In this view, organizations are islands of planned coordination relationships, often revealed in intra-group communication, and perhaps represented by professions (to which we now turn), embedded in a sea of market relationships (Powell 1990).

Professional

In some ways organizations become umbrellas for various professional guilds, like the legal divisions to which we have just referred. "They must be little republics of their own" (Polanyi and Prosch 1975, p. 204). These professions come together to pursue loosely defined larger objectives (e.g., universities and the pursuit of knowledge). So, shared norms of performance, or a shared philosophy of management, have been seen as a basis for members of multinational organizations to communicate with each other (Baliga and Jaeger 1984). Relationships between and among professions are often governed by such normative expectations (Cheney and Ashcraft 2007) (see Table 4.2).

Over the last three decades, cultural factors, which norms encapsulate, have assumed a central place in our theories of organizations. Culture is seen as providing an interpretive framework within which communication is possible; a macromedium for interaction (Johnson 1993; Poole and McPhee 1983). One of the impetuses behind the focus on communities of practice is the recognition that knowledge is social, that it moves better within communities than between them (Brown and Duguid 1998). Perhaps nowhere in our society is socialization more intensive than in the preparation of a professional. So much so, societies also delegate enforcement of practice standards to professional organizations. Professionals also form exclusive KN and jealously guard their prerogatives, especially in relation to knowledge claims in specific areas (Cheney and Ashcraft 2007).

A key element of this socialization is the development of elaborate semantic systems of tacit understandings (von Hayek 1945). The more elaborate and refined the framework, the more effective the communication. An advantage of strong cultures is their enhancement of shared understanding between actors, with a norm of mutual adjustment through consultation within a system of mutual authority that governs competition (Polanyi and Prosch 1975). Clan controls result in high goal congruence and common interests, most appropriate when transformation processes are imperfect and measures of outcomes are low (Turner and Makhija 2006). Interaction is also provided with a normative base that expresses the underlying cultural values. This strong emphasis on socialization of succeeding generations reinforces the temporal stability of KN associated with professions.

They develop near-clan forms of identity associated with their unique tacit knowledge. Indeed, the overall configuration of a profession is perhaps best reflected in conceptions of guilds and clans. But in many ways strong professions transcend particular organizations and make the latter's boundaries more permeable. Membership in a profession provides access to a much larger, scalable tacit knowledge community outside the organization. This is a key weakness of the other approaches to context, which primarily focus on what happens within a network defined by the firm, with limited tacit knowledge communities.

Negotiated order

The growth of different organizational forms highlights the importance of governance structures, particularly interorganizational relationships (Eisenberg *et al.* 1985), federations (Provan 1983), and multinational corporations (Ghoshal and Bartlett 1990; Gupta and Govindarajan 1991). These new forms must discover underlying bases for interrelationships among their increasingly pluralistic sub-groupings. A central issue for many organizations, then, is how to create contexts that promote cooperative climates and the trusting relationships necessary to produce agreements on a course of action (Fiol 1994; Johnson 1997b, 1998), which some have argued is best accomplished by convergence on particular frames (Drake and Donohue 1996) or, alternatively, ambiguous central concepts (Eisenberg 1984). It is on its face somewhat paradoxical that a focus on specialization also gives rise, as Adam Smith noted long ago, to an emphasis on market relations and cooperation, with individuals longing in a Durkheimian sense to belong to a moral order and in a Weberian view with routinization and rationality (Kogut and Zander 1996)

One important element of organizational design is trying to focus the firm on just those activities that create the most value (Roberts 2004). This has led to the contemporary concern, especially in the era of outsourcing, with which elements should be internal to the organization and encompassed in its formal structure, and which should be outside it. Theoretical approaches to this problem have relied heavily on transaction cost perspectives (Coase 1937; Williamson 1994). The fundamental unit of analysis in this perspective is a transaction that involves a transfer of property rights. Transactions can be differentiated in many ways: specificity, frequency, duration, complexity, uncertainty, performance measurement, connectedness to other transactions, and information asymmetries (Sawyer *et al.* 2003). The question becomes which governance mechanism is the least costly way to carry out a transaction (Sawyer *et al.* 2003), which is one way of describing relationships, the central property of KN.

There are at least four different types of costs: contact costs associated with information searches, contracting costs, monitoring costs (e.g., quality, secrecy), and adaptation costs (Sawyer *et al.* 2003). For our purposes, perhaps the most important cost is that of transferring tacit knowledge (Postrel 2002). Hierarchies tend to lessen contact and contracting costs, but may not be very efficient at finding the optimal price. There is also a quite natural human tendency to exercise ever more control when performance problems are experienced, which may partially explain its prevalence, even though it "is the organizational form of last resort" (Williamson 1994, p. 91). In general, the more costly, important, and complex the transaction is, the more it will be brought under hierarchical governance. Thus, transaction costs become a way of identifying boundaries – what is a contextual factor and what lies within a particular system. These issues are also illustrated in Box 4.1 on electronic markets (EM).

Governance structures are provided for the individual within the larger organizational context. However, it is possible for an individual to act with others, with their unique mix of the foregoing frames, to choose among themselves what frame (or combination of frames) will govern their interactions. It is also possible for two interactants to decide mutually on an idiosyncratic basis for interaction (Nathan and Mitroff 1991). This possibility creates the underlying conditions for change (Strauss 1978). Indeed, the absence of a dominating frame, or the lack of rigid specification when one or another applies, creates the possibility of flexibility within an organization. It also may be a key factor in the evolution of knowledge-sharing communities, such as open source software ones (O'Mahony and Ferraro 2007).

Relationships formed on the basis of the unique characteristics of actors, in opposition to existing organizational forms, require substantial negotiation among interactants, especially about forms and desired outcomes. The growth of electronic markets (see Box 4.1), which allow buyers and sellers to interact directly, encouraging disintermediation, further complicates these issues for organizations by increasing the blurring of roles and boundaries (Sawyer *et al.* 2003). So two parties communicate with each other to arrange the nature of their future interaction by mutual agreement, much as a reporter decides with a source what is on and off the record. This negotiation is designed to establish a stable ordering of the relationship, governing interactions within it, and to move to a state where the underlying base for the interaction is taken for granted. At times this negotiation might be explicit, verging on the establishment of contractual terms; at other times it might grow out of ongoing interactions.

Within organizations, frameworks for interaction differentially impact KN. For example, strong organizational norms can severely restrict the content and interactants available to individuals, but, interestingly, because of the increased sophistication of shared understandings, they can enhance the effectiveness of knowledge transfer. They also can improve efficiency by clearly delineating roles and relationships. In contrast, exchange-based information seeking has few barriers, but limited breadth and only moderate levels of effectiveness and efficiency, in part because of the differential understanding levels of the two parties. Some relationships may further facilitate transfer of tacit knowledge by operating simultaneously within several frames, a key role for management in the modern organization (Postrel 2002). Thus, a chief counsel in an organization has professional knowledge as well as formal authority over other lawyers. So, frameworks within organizations shape KN in different ways; these different frames then can become the underlying basis for defining relationships in KN.

Contextualizing the world outside

While the primary focus of this book is KN within organizations, the information environment represented in the world outside the organization is naturally also important and we will discuss it in more detail in Chapter 8. It is often the primary source of highly technical, specialized information, especially for professionals like engineers. Cosmopolitan organizational members and professionals often consider organizational boundaries to be artificial and do not, often to the consternation of upper-level managers who view information as proprietary, carefully guard tacit knowledge.

Professionals in different organizations share information with each other informally (e.g., TGIFs, association meetings) and formally (e.g., trade journals). Scientists also form invisible colleges that share information and act as a resource for their members in information searches. The most productive scientists are often those who communicate most outside the boundary of the organization (Allen 1966). These invisible colleges then cut across the membership of more formal organizations localized in particular geographic areas. In many ways, KN in this context are a special case of intraorganizational information seeking since the invisible college has many characteristics of an organization, as the communities of practice literature discussed in Chapter 8 articulates. In this instance, the individual is really a member of multiple networks with different KN functions.

Environments also create imperatives for organizations to seek certain kinds of information (Wilensky 1968). It has often been noted that more complex organizational environments require more complex internal organizational relationships, especially communicative ones. These environments also provide a critical stimulus for information seeking among organizational members (Huber and Daft 1987). The environmental scanning that results is a special case of KN (Choo and Auster 1993; Thomas, Clark, and Gioia 1993).

Of course, not all organizations will feel the same imperatives to seek information. Emery and Trist (1965) have developed a very useful categorization for analyzing different organizational information environments. They argue that there are four different types: placid, randomized; placid, clustered; disturbed reactive; and turbulent field. Placid, randomized organizations have the simplest organizational environment, with no direct competitors or interest groups. Organizations in this category are becoming increasingly rare, and may be only represented by a very few governmental organizations which are no longer relevant to today's environment.

A placid, clustered organization has groups in its environment who are interested in its performance, but it does not have direct competitors. Electric utilities, which need to be responsive to customers, government, and environmental groups, would be examples of this type of organization. The internal structural arrangements of these organizations change to reflect their environment, with customer relations units, for example, charged with relating to customers. These relationships often cue information seeking within the organization, with customer service representatives serving as boundary spanners who need to broker queries from customers to the internal organizational environment. These boundary spanners become the mechanism that operationalizes environmental cues to the internal organizational structure (Spekman 1979), a process described in more detail in Chapter 8. These positions are critical to innovation and the diffusion of ideas between and within organizations (Czepiel 1975; Daft 1978). One problem they can create is imbalances in information within the organization, with some units of the organization reacting to customer concerns, for example, and others ignoring them (Marchand and Horton 1986).

The next two types of organization identified by Emery and Trist (1965) not only need to react to the environment in which they find themselves, but also need to become much more proactive in their strategies to uncover information outside their environment and discover means of assimilating it into internal organizational operations. Beyond the structures characteristic of placid, randomized organizations, disturbed reactive organizations have to deal with the presence of direct competitors. They must create strategic planning capabilities to optimize their efforts in relation to their environment and potential competitors. They also must create more active ways of discovering what their competitors are doing and what their customers want (e.g., marketing surveys). These organizations are in the exceedingly tricky business of seeking information about the future, so that their current plans and operations can be positioned to prosper, not only today but also in the near and far term. This concern with reacting and adapting, with an eye to future survival, naturally puts additional force behind an organization's KN.

If an organization is not successful in these efforts, then it may find itself in a turbulent field situation, where the organization's existence is directly threatened. Two types of situation are characteristic of turbulent fields. The first is when the environment of the organization has changed so that the organization's goals are no longer meaningful. For example, while the March of Dimes succeeded in its original goal of fighting polio, if it had not reformulated itself to focus on birth defects, its existence as an organization would have been threatened. In this context, an organization must search its environment for information that will help it while it is rediscovering what it is and searching the environment for niches in which it can prosper. Obviously, the intensity level of this search is high, since the very survival of the organization is at stake.

A competitive organization threatened with takeover or bankruptcy is the second case where elements of the environment are directly threatening the existence of the organization. In this situation, organizations, such as Chrysler in the late 1970s and early 1980s, find that the line separating them from their environment becomes increasingly blurred, with elements of their environment becoming increasingly intrusive in internal organizational operations. Chrysler placed a union official on its board of directors and government agencies and banks had effective veto power on decisions relating to the development of product lines. KN for organizational employees in this context become increasingly complex, with the familiar sources and pathways for information no longer the place to seek definitive answers to their questions. In fact, a form of meta-information seeking, involving answers to questions such as "Who is in charge here?" and "What constitutes an authoritative answer?", often precedes any searches for substantive answers to questions.

The proactive strategies necessary for the survival of organizations in disturbed reactive and turbulent field environments generally fall into one of two classes: placing sensory apparatus into the environment to collect information and deciding what categories of information it is vital for the organization to collect. Thus, organizations play a very active role in enacting their environment.

The first means by which they do this is in their placement of sensory apparatus, scanning and search mechanisms, used to apprehend the world outside (Miller, Fern, and Cardinal 2007). All of us have a noosphere, a layer of information that surrounds us, which can be apprehended by our senses (De Chardin 1961) and that we create in a very real way from our tacit knowledge (Polanyi 1974). Similarly, organizations place sensors in their environment that allow them to process information. So a competitive organization may: reach out to customers through marketing tools such as telephone or face-to-face mall intercept interviews; have lobbyists roaming the halls of the legislature; have lawyers talking to regulators; have observers outside another organization's research facility; have buyers on site purchasing commodities, and so on. These individuals act as the eyes and ears of the organization; they enable it to experience its environment, and when coupled with correct interpretation, permit an organization to respond adaptively.

The arrangement of an organization's noosphere rests on an its interpretation of what are the important elements of its environment. Based on this interpretation the organization decides on the placement of resources needed to experience these elements. How the environment is enacted by organizational members determines how information is brought into the organization, but even more importantly it determines what is brought in and how it is likely to be evaluated (Weick 1969). An organization's members are likely to only recognize information that they have identified *a priori* as important and to categorize the information based on their understanding of the world.

If we could reconstruct how the great railroad barons at the turn of the last century reacted to the advent of flight, it would provide a useful example of organizations' interactions with their environment. They probably read about it in the newspapers with some curiosity, but did not perceive it to be the start of a new transportation system that would eventually supplant their thriving passenger railway systems. In short, they failed to define adequately what was important in their environment, to conceive of alternative ways of doing their business, and to expand their noosphere to gather detailed information about this phenomenon. An adequate recognition of what was important would have led inevitably to much greater information seeking related to the future development of this new means of transportation. In sum, the world outside the organization has many implications for KN.

There is an increasing tendency to suggest that individuals and groups are not only shaped by context, the classic approach of contingency and situational perspectives, but can in turn shape contexts (Giddens 1991; Gresov and Stephens 1993), if only by how they activate and interpret them (Baker and Pettigrew 1999; Branham and Pearce 1985). Interestingly, notions underlying negotiated order are also revealed in Giddens's arguments concerning the production and reproduction of institutions (e.g., Contractor and Siebold 1993; Poole and McPhee 1983). In other words, by how we perform our roles, we can change the nature of our institutional contexts. Individuals can only shape contexts if they understand their active ingredients and how they act upon them. In a pragmatic sense, there may be no richer area of study for individuals who desire to shape the world around them (and to understand how they are shaped by it) (Dervin 1997).

Karl Weick (1969) makes this point forcefully for organizations in his classic concept of the enacted environment, suggesting that instead of organizations responding deterministically to outside stimuli, actors constitute by their actions the environment to which they think it is important for them to respond. These factors may drive individuals to create and dissolve ties which can then create operational linkage between environmental and KN change (Koka, Madhavan, and Prescott 2006). Once this environment is constituted then it becomes possible both to reduce uncertainty and to operate in a boundedly rational manner (Simon 1991).

Summary

In this chapter we have traced the development of work on context from specification of situational factors, to active ingredients that have contingent effects, to the multiplicity of governance frameworks in the modern organization. These governance structures, formal, informal, markets, and professions, establish the medium for relationships to develop and ultimately for KN to form. Finally, we described the active role that organizations play in contextualizing their world.

Perhaps the simplest, most powerful, reason for focusing on context, on the ground of KN, is that we will never understand KN unless we do (Dervin 1997; Georgoudi and Rosnow 1985). It is perhaps the major area for growth in social science research, since it has been so understudied. More careful delimiting of the contexts in which particular hypotheses and theories apply is a major undertaking, with inconsistent results challenging us to understand the impacts of context (McGuire 1983; Perry 1988). New insights may come from rubbing different contexts together. In this part of the book we will focus in greater detail on formal, technological, spatial, and interorganizational contexts that form the "givens" of KN. By broadening our horizons and studying processes across contexts, by moving beyond the self-imposed limits of our intradisciplinary boundaries, we may in the end develop a more mature understanding of KN.

Further reading

Emery, F., and Trist, E. 1965. The causal texture of organizational environment. *Human Relations*, 18: 21–32.

Classic typology of different environments of organizations as well as discussion of different types of interorganizational relationships needed to prosper in each.

Johnson, J. D. 2003. On contexts of information seeking. *Information Processing and Management*, 39: 735–760.

Systematically compares two different contexts of information seeking, cancer-related and organizational, and how different views of context inform our understanding of this basic process, which is often the driving force for the development of KN.

Kenney, D. A., Kashy, D. A., and Cook, W. L. 2006. *Dyadic Data Analysis*. Guilford Press.

Primarily a statistical treatment of a basic analytic problem – the parties to dyadic relationships are not independent of each other as most traditional statistical techniques assume. Details various implications of this basic issue for a variety of dyadic relationships, including those embedded in larger networks.

McGuire, W. J. 1983. A contextualist theory of knowledge: its implications for innovation and reform in psychological research. In L. Berkowitz (ed.), *Advances in Experimental Social Psychology*, vol. XVI: 1–47. Academic Press.

Foundational article for anyone interested in context. Advances the argument that we can only really understand theories by pushing the boundary conditions under which they may apply, which then leads to knowledge of the contingent conditions that should be applied to a theory.

Williamson, O. E. 1994. Transaction cost economics and organization theory. In N. J. Smelser and R. Swedberg (eds.), *Handbook of Economic Sociology*: 77–107. Russell Sage.

Systematically links economic views of transaction costs to traditional organizational theory, bridging these two separate views of organizational behavior, with special implications for network linkages.

5 Designing knowledge networks

> The challenge faced by managers is how to restrict great amounts of upward communication that may result in overload, and at the same time ensure that relevant and accurate information is transmitted up the hierarchy.
>
> (Glauser 1984, p. 615)

> If intelligence is lodged at the top, too few officials and experts with too little accurate and relevant information are too far out of touch and too overloaded to cope. On the other hand, if intelligence is scattered in many subordinate units, too many officials and experts with too much specialized information may engage in dysfunctional competition, may delay decisions while they warily consult each other, and may distort information as they pass it up...
>
> (Wilensky 1968, p. 325)

> "Structural secrecy" refers to the way division of labor, hierarchy and specialization segregate knowledge... Structural secrecy implies that (a) information and knowledge will always be partial and incomplete, (b) the potential for things to go wrong increases when tasks or information cross internal boundaries, and (c) segregated knowledge minimizes the ability to detect and stave off activities that deviate from normative standards and expectations.
>
> (Vaughan 1999, p. 277)

Formal structure is one of the fundamental tools for managing knowledge in organizations. Some have viewed formal structure as one instantiation of networks, with relationships defined by asymmetry and work-related content transmitted in written channels. But, as we will soon see, there is much more to the study of formal structure. Early approaches to studying formal communication structure in organizations concentrated on the organizational chart and the flow of messages vertically and horizontally within it. Later researchers concerned with formal structure tended to focus on more abstract variables, associated with both formal relationships and the organizational chart, such as configuration, complexity, formalization, and centralization (Jablin 1987). In general, reviews suggest that formal approaches focus on the configurations resulting from the following characteristics of structure: formal authority relationships represented in the organizational hierarchy; differentiation of labor into specialized tasks; and formal mechanisms for coordination of work among these tasks (Dow 1988; Jablin 1987). These characteristics, along with the notion of goal or purpose, have been seen by some to represent the very essence of what an organization is (Schein 1965). In this chapter the focus will primarily be on the communicative elements of formal structure, especially in terms of their implications for KN and how managers might rationally design their organizations.

Traditional views

Jablin (1987, p. 391), in discussing formal communication structure, defines configuration as the "shape of an organization resulting from the location and distribution of its formal roles and work units." Thus structure has certain properties which have almost a "physical" objective character, at least as pictured on the organizational chart, which have become represented in terms of indices which capture these differing properties. This has been reflected in the persistent appeal of the conduit metaphor for formal approaches, which tends to see structure as offering a series of "pipelines" for the flow of information in an organization (Axley 1984). This flow of explicit information, particularly in traditional perspectives, reflects the information processing view of formal structure.

Early research programs related to communication structure in organizations concentrated on the organizational chart (see Figure 3.2), which has also been referred to as the "organigram" (Rogers and Agarwala-Rogers 1976). The formal organizational chart is embedded in the assumptions of the classical approach to rational management. It specifies very clearly who reports to whom and, in effect, constitutes a map for the routing of communication messages, as well as the location of certain types of knowledge. Given the importance of the visualization of these relationships, a variety of software packages have been specifically designed as tools to manage them (see Box 5.1). It still, as it has been for generations, is the most popular method of describing organizational structures.

In general, information load is determined by such factors as size, transmission rules, and degree of interdependence (Downs 1967). Organizations which severely constrain their structures substantially reduce their level of information load. The more severely constrained the structure, the more the organization is divided into autonomous groups and the less the general distribution of knowledge. Some have gone so far as to suggest that the classic forms of bureaucracy "are invitations to intelligence and communication failures" (Lee 1970, p. 101), because of this rigid segmentation of information sources.

The central impetus underlying the development of formal structures, then, is the differentiation into entities, undertaking specialized subtasks, who depend on each other and therefore must communicate to coordinate their activities. Long ago Adam Smith (1776/1952) cogently argued that the wealth of nations depended on "the skill, dexterity and judgment with which its labour is generally applied" (p. 1) and that the primary way this was accomplished was through the division of labor. The increase in efficiency from differentiation was a result of the greater dexterity and focused attention of the worker, the savings in time resulting from focusing on a single task, and the invention of machines that

Box 5.1. Visio: a drawing tool

Structural design tools rely on graphics of complex configurations of relationships. Even the most basic computer software recognizes the need for this sort of tool for managers. Accordingly, both Microsoft Word and PowerPoint, as well as a variety of other word processing and presentational software, have tools embedded within them that permit more sophisticated, refined, professional drawings of such structural basics as organizational charts.

The structural professional should go beyond these basic tools and have some familiarity with more powerful tools that permit sophisticated images of a vast array of business processes, such as complicated web pages or telematic information systems. In this book I have used Visio® to draw most of the charts and figures I have used as examples. It is especially intended for those of us who cannot draw and have a limited aesthetic sense.

In Visio® a drawing page and associated stencil are used as the starting point for constructing sophisticated images. Working with a Wizard to guide one through a drawing process, or starting with just a stencil and a blank page, communigrams, organigrams, and flow charts of work processes can all be produced. One can also import data bases from other programs, like Excel, to generate organizational charts. This is an especially useful feature for updating and modifying charts based on changes in other files such as telephone directories.

Fundamentally the stencils represent a variety of entities and relationships. So on the organizational chart stencil, for example, you have various hierarchical positions (e.g., executives) and types of relationships (e.g., top-down reporting). Interestingly, these stencils embed a number of standards (as well as visual assumptions) for drawing common features of organizational charts. For example, top executives have bigger boxes of somewhat different shapes than holders of other formal roles in the organization. The issue of standard graphical representations is an important one because of the widely varying representations found in the literature. One can also supplement these standard stencils with vendor specifications for more technical drawings of a telecommunications network, for example. It can also be linked to Visio Maps and data bases to prepare reports on sales for particular geographical regions.

One source of the power of Visio® for the structural analyst is the variety of different stencils available (e.g., office layouts and building plans, organizational charts, and project schedules). Flowcharts has a variety of different features, including special stencils for Total Quality Management diagrams. The basic flow chart stencil contains the essential tools necessary for drawing network communigrams and figures associated with complex work diagrams, as well as depictions of complex work processes. Internet diagrams are suited for sorting out complex web pages. Finally, Network, which focuses not on organizational communication networks but rather on telecommunications and computer technology networks, is an additional advantage of this program for communications professionals. The analyst can also modify stencil pages by creating custom stencils for a particular purpose.

Visio® can be used in conjunction with a variety of other software; for example, buttons can be added to the toolbar in Microsoft Word® since the Visio organization is now a subsidiary of Microsoft. Its research feature links it to a variety of Internet-based features.

would help workers in performing their tasks. Today we would probably add the focused attention that also permits the development of ever more sophisticated levels of tacit knowledge; which is only made possible by concomitant ignorance of others' work in organizations (Becker and Murphy 1992). This focus on differentiation also implies a concomitant growth of commerce, since individuals will now have to exchange goods they previously produced themselves. In this sense then: "Every man thus lives by exchanging, or becomes in some measure a merchant" (Smith 1776/1952, p. 10).

Downward communication

Downward communication originates from upper levels of management and is targeted to lower-level personnel. This type of communication is meant to control the organization and the operations of its personnel. Typically, downward communication messages, since they are official, are very formal and usually written. Katz and Kahn (1978) describe five types of downward communication content. Job instructions account for the bulk of downward communication messages. These are usually very direct messages which instruct an employee to perform a specific operation at a particular place. Messages dealing with a job rationale attempt to put an employee's job in the context of others' work and tell an employee why it is important that they do particular things. Organizations typically do not answer the "Why am I doing this?" question of workers very well, leaving it up to the workers to decide what aspects of jobs are important and what they should concentrate on. With the growing professionalization of the workplace and the concomitant growth of tacit knowledge, this sort of delegation is often jealously protected. Somewhat related to job rationale is the indoctrination to the goals of the organization, which is intimately related to organizational socialization. These messages attempt to communicate to workers what the central values of the organization are and thereby what it is the organization is trying to accomplish.

Probably the two biggest failures in downward communication content lie in feedback about performance and in information about organizational procedures and practices. Often organizations fail to adopt systematic means of providing members with feedback (such as appraisal interviews) and when they do adopt them they tend to perform miserably, seldom providing appropriate feedback (Ashford, Blatt, and VandeWalle 2003). Employees want to know how well they are doing and what they need to do to improve, but many elite organizations operate under the informal norm that "no news is good news." That is, management operates under the assumption that they have hired excellent employees and, therefore, expect excellent performance. The very fact that someone is employed and is not being criticized is considered enough feedback. But employees also realize that many times supervisors are unwilling to confront them directly with bad news. So this silence could indicate either approval or disapproval. Employees are often uncertain and anxious about how well they are doing. Manipulative managers will exploit this uncertainty, feeling that the resulting stress and tension will produce higher performance, but as Peters and Waterman (1982) point out, excellent companies have the opposite philosophy. They believe that positive employee recognition is the best motivator. As we saw when discussing brokers in Chapter 3, more contemporary views of structure focus on self-governing entrepreneurs who can exploit their social structures.

Organizations often have powerful motivations to keep employees in the dark concerning procedures and practices as well. This area is one that raises many potential ethical questions concerning organizational behavior. For example, the cost of medical insurance is rising astronomically. In this situation, is it in the profit-making organization's best interest financially to send out complete and detailed information concerning health insurance? Or should its humane concern for workers offset any considerations of the cost involved? There are a host of other problems with downward communication as well. One of particular importance is the persistent problem of the distortion of downward communication messages. These messages often do not arrive in a timely fashion and they are not sufficiently targeted to insure that they are distributed to the proper mix of individuals. Shortcomings in downward communication often set the stage for active information seeking on the part of lower-level organizational members who want to rectify critical shortcomings in the information they receive, and can account for the development of informal networks.

Aside from direct monetary benefits (e.g., withholding information about fringe advantages), and the presumed benefits of keeping people on edge, organizational power structures reap a number of other benefits from hoarding information. It is widely recognized that knowledge is power. And it may be no accident that those higher in the hierarchy are typically better informed than those who are lower (Jablin 1987). The purposive exclusion of groups in the organization from information also deprives them of the information necessary to participate successfully in organizational decision making. So, for example, a common response of management to workers pressing ideas for change is that the workers do not have all the facts and if they did they would hold the same position as management. Thus information is purposively manipulated to maintain the relative power of various groups. Lower-level employees, especially skilled technicians, can also accumulate power by not sharing information with management (Eisenberg and Whetten 1987).

Upward communication

Formal structure reduces uncertainty, thus lending predictability to organizational activities (Pfeffer 1978). For organizations, this predictability is critical to the smooth functioning of day-to-day operations. Organizational members must feel confident that certain messages will flow to certain locations at certain times. It is often noted that management in particular abhors unpredictability; as a result, they often spend considerable time designing organizational structures (e.g., formal organizational charts) that contribute to a subjective feeling of certainty. One of the reasons that informal structures remained hidden in management thought for so long is that awareness of their existence inevitably diminishes management's feeling of control over organizational operations. Indeed, structures are often designed to minimize, or at least regulate, individual variation in organizations (Dalton *et al.* 1980).

The classic principle of management by exception states managers only deal with exceptions to established procedures and policies. It is natural and expected that management will not know everything that is occurring below them in the hierarchy. If management knew everything, they would quickly become over-loaded with information and be unable to do their jobs. For example, if the manager of even a small assembly plant knew everything that was going on beneath him or her, the manager would have to be able to do the work of 1,000 people. So it is critical that information be filtered and condensed before it is given to an upper-level manager. The central problem for upward communication is how this can be done while retaining the critical information that management needs to control current organizational activities and to direct future operations of the organization. So it has long been recognized that the flow of information needs to be restricted, even to managers, since they have limited time to attend to, interpret, and respond to feedback, and by implication managers will be unaware of some organizational activities. This problem is exacerbated since "many have noted that organizations and their leaders are generally intolerant of feedback, particularly dissent..." (Ashford, Blatt, and VandeWalle 2003, p. 789) which leads to real costs in detecting and correcting errors.

However, the transmission of regular, negative feedback to upper management is essential if subunits of an organization are to be integrated into the system and work to desired organizational goals (Glauser 1984). One generic problem that is difficult to overcome is the differences in perspective between supervisor and subordinates, with subordinates unable at times to judge what information might be deemed to be important to supervisors. Like all vertical communication, upward communication (communication from workers to bosses) tends to be formal, in writing, and flows along the formal chain of command represented by the organizational chart. Upward communication is more important for control than for coordination of organizational activities. Without adequate upward communication from workers, management cannot react to change quickly enough to prevent major problems from developing. For example, if a salesperson does not communicate to managers that customers are becoming dissatisfied with the organization's product line, then the organization will not have a new one in place when the customers' dissatisfaction becomes decisions not to buy. Without feedback (workers providing management with their reaction to messages) the impact of downward communication is unknown, although many managers wrongly assume that just because an order is given, workers will do what they are told. Upward communication is also critical if an organization is interested in reacting to the problems and concerns of its workers. If workers have input into decision making through upward communication, they are more likely to react positively when decisions are implemented.

Horizontal communication

Horizontal communication occurs at the same level, or sideways, across the organizational chart. This type of communication is usually informal, face to face, and personal, taking on the coloration of more contemporary views of networks. Since it is much faster and more attuned to the personal needs of communicators, horizontal communication also tends to be used more to coordinate activities and was a precursor to a more contemporary focus on KN.

Perhaps the best known body of research relating to horizontal communication is Keith Davis's (1973) work on the grapevine.[1] The grapevine represents the informal flow of communication along primarily horizontal channels. Davis argues that the grapevine is a key indicator of the health of the organization, since it reflects the involvement of workers in the organization and their interest in its activities. Thus the grapevine can serve management's interests by making sure that workers have alternative means of getting the information they need. The grapevine is particularly active in times of high uncertainty, especially when critical problems are facing the organization and people tend to spread information in which they have a personal stake. Surprisingly, despite the negative view people have of rumors, Davis (1973) has found that most information spread along the grapevine is accurate (estimates ranging from 75 to 95 percent).

Perhaps the primary reason why research related to formal views of structure has been neglected recently is that the world of organizations has become increasingly complex, which is reflected in the introduction of concepts like the grapevine, diagonal communication, and complex modes of integration. One of the first transitional attempts to deal with the complexity of communication in organizations was Katz and Kahn's (1966) notion of communication circuits,

---

[1] See Hellweg (1987) for a review.

which have direct relations to the KN concerns with pathways I discussed in Chapter 3. They argued that there are five major characteristics of communication circuits or networks in organizations. The first is the size of the loop, which reflects the organizational coverage of a particular message. Does it reach the entire organization or only one part? Another important characteristic is whether a message is repeated or modified as it passes through a circuit. Modification indicates that the message is altered in some way as it goes through the organization. The third characteristic is the feedback or closure (no response is received) character of the circuit. Feedback implies that a response is received to a message, whereas in a closed circuit there is no response. The final two characteristics, efficiency and fit with systemic functioning, will be addressed in detail in Chapter 10. Katz and Kahn's (1966) description of communication circuits is important because they recognized that more flexible approaches to communication structure were needed and that there were various relational elements of circuits which had crucial systemic impacts.

Summary

The context of formal structure lies in the "official world" of the organization. Most often it can be conceived of as embedded in the formal authority structure of the organization, usually associated with bureaucracy. In this context, communication is conceived as flowing along the prescribed pathways of the organizational chart and the content of communication is limited to those production-related matters that concern the organization. While this formal approach constitutes a limited view of the role of communication in organizations, this still may be, especially operationally, the most important one, and certainly one that management must at least try to control.

Perhaps most importantly, the traditional view of communication structure reinforces some dangerous assumptions that managers often hold; that messages flow along the conduits represented by the organizational chart without blockage or interruption, that management is in charge, and that messages actually reach their destinations (Axley 1984). It also suggests that information will be provided to individuals who need to know and that, therefore, individuals should play a more passive role and not engage in active information seeking. So there is a constant dilemma for organizations: the imperative, in part stemming from efficiency needs, to limit the availability of information, and the recognition that structural designs are often flawed and circumstances change, requiring individuals to seek information normally unavailable to them. However, the design of formal structure, and the rewards associated with it (e.g., promotion) often specifically discourage the sharing of information (Powell 1990). Indeed, some might argue that "to extract information from those who have it typically requires the bypassing of regular organizational structures" (Wilensky 1968, p. 324).

Indices

Research related to formal approaches has focused on various indices of the overall configurations of formal structural relationships at a macro level (Jablin 1987). An index provides researchers with a systematic way of describing an organizational property in terms of a precise combination of other attributes. Many of these indices derive from the differentiation of the organization both vertically (e.g., number of hierarchical levels) and horizontally (e.g., number of separate work groups). Such differentiation, as we have seen, is often a precursor to the development of tacit knowledge. These indices have direct analogs to those discussed in Chapter 3.

Complexity

Complexity (or horizontal differentiation) is related to the number of different formal organizational groups. There is fairly clear evidence that horizontal complexity relates positively to the frequency of communication (Jablin 1987), especially with the need for coordinating diverse occupational specialties (Hage, Aiken, and Marrett 1971). It also has implications for creativity, as we will see in Chapter 9.

Hierarchical level

Research in this area focuses on the vertical differentiation of the organization into various status levels. Studies have generally found that the time spent in communicating increases as one rises up the organizational ladder, but that the nature of the communication is heavily dependent on the nature of the organizational context (Jablin 1987). For example, Bacharach and Aiken (1977) found that department heads engaged in more formal communication of all sorts than subordinates. These diverse inputs result in unique tacit knowledge at the apex of the hierarchy.

Centralization

Centralization refers to the degree to which authority is concentrated at higher levels of management (Jablin 1987). As we have seen, centralization is also a concept that has been used to refer to a person's positioning in a network of communication relationships. There are limits to how much organizational operations can be centralized. These limits are primarily determined by task factors and the capabilities, primarily information processing ones, of decision makers (Pfeffer 1978). There is also an inevitable tendency for managers, because of their positioning in networks, to develop idiosyncratic perspectives that are difficult to communicate to others who have more fragmented views of the organization, often as a result of the locally dense structures within which they are embedded.

Span of control

Span of control is defined in terms of the number of subordinates a supervisor has (Porter and Lawler 1965). Greater vertical differentiation is usually associated with smaller spans of control, which concomitantly lead to greater supervision over individual workers. While it could be assumed that reduced spans would lead to greater control by management over organizational functions, it may paradoxically lead to less control, since it increases the number of levels of the hierarchy and thus can lead to increased problems in vertical communication (Pfeffer 1978). Span of control has other negative consequences. Not all workers require close, personal direction by a supervisor, especially more entrepreneurial knowledge workers. So, when professionals are the subordinates, there may be more consultation with subordinates by supervisors rather than close supervision (Brewer 1971). Low levels of span of control may result in unnecessarily increased administrative costs (Pfeffer 1978). High levels of span of control may also encourage more individual initiative and growth (Porter and Lawler 1965). In summarizing this literature Jablin (1987) concludes that while frequency of communication is affected by span of control, the mode and quality of communication is not necessarily affected.

Formalization

Formalization, as operationalized by the number of rules existing in an organization, has been another key index of formal structure. The notion of rule has always been central to theorizing about organizations (e.g., March 1994; Perrow 1972; Porter, Allen, and Angle 1981). The earliest thinking about bureaucracy noted the importance of rules for determining the actions of organizational members and every bureaucratic organization has an elaborated set of formal rules. Formal rules have also been seen as one primary means used by organizations to control the activities of their members and the extent of this formalization has traditionally been considered an important element of organizational structure. "Rules for gathering, storing, communicating, and using information are essential elements of organizational operating procedures" (Feldman and March 1981, p. 171). Rules can severely constrain the developments of particular types of knowledge in organizations. "The major advantage of rules is that they provide predictability. They specify who is to do what, when, where, and sometimes how" (Hage and Aiken 1970, p. 21). In a larger sense, this is the role of design approaches, to which we now turn.

Design

In this section we start a discussion which will be continued in later chapters that focus on productivity, decision making, and strategies for finding information. Here our focus will be on the conscious design of formal communication structures constructed to achieve certain purposes, one of which is promoting the flow of knowledge in organizations. In terms of KN, the effects of design have often been latent rather than manifest, that is design decisions would often achieve certain effects because of their underlying impacts (Gittell and Weiss 2004). So, strict principles of super/subordination found in bureaucracies imply that organizational intelligence is best lodged at the apex of organizations, where decisions are made based on the synthesis of a variety of sources of information. Little credence is given in this framework to the tacit knowledge of those close to the information; rather the focus is on the development of the tacit understanding of key administrators.

Since the formal approach almost exclusively conceives of the organization in terms of authority relationships between formally defined positions, it has been heavily influenced by Weber's work on bureaucracy. Even when non-authority relationships are considered they are defined in terms of their association with ones of authority, such as the traditional breakdown between formal and informal structures. This focus on formal relationships centers this approach on managerial concerns and also tilts the direction of this approach to more rational views.

This view of relationships substantially limits the breadth of coverage of formal approaches. But this limitation may be a strength to managers whose primary pragmatic concern is how they can consciously and rationally plan to improve the operations of organizations. As a result, organizational design efforts are essentially related to the formal approach and they are concerned with controlling behavior so as to produce a more efficient/effective organization (Pfeffer 1978).

Design is often viewed as a coequal element of organizational effectiveness along with strategy and environment, with all three elements needing to fit and/or correspond with each other, and structure seen as following strategy (Roberts 2004). It is probably the height of folly for an organization to develop a strategy of pursuing innovative products in a turbulent environment and to insist on having a rigidly bureaucratic, top-down structure (see Box 9.3), so the appropriate clustering of a number of dimensions is often critical to successful design (see Table 5.1).

The symptoms of poor design are legion. They include lack of coordination, excessive conflict, unclear roles, misused resources, poor work flow, reduced responsiveness, proliferation of *ad hoc* entities (e.g., task forces, committees) and virtual positions (Mackenzie 1986), "grey areas" in which the responsibilities of different entities are unclear, and so on (Nadler and Tushman 1997). Developing a winning strategy through design combines both art and science and may be the ultimate act of managerial creativity (Roberts 2004). So, designers can be considered master builders who lay the foundation for all that follows in the organization, with the architecture they develop the context for KN.

Deciding on what is central

The critical question that designers must face is what theme will be emphasized, what value will be stressed in their design, just as architects must balance function with aesthetics. Traditionally designs have faced tradeoffs relating to a variety of concerns, with strategy often implicit in the choices that are emphasized (Nadler and Tushman 1997). Box 5.2, on design elements, discusses traditional approaches to this problem that often emphasize achieving productivity goals; here we will emphasize the centrality of uncertainty reduction in controlling the flow of information, a traditional focus of organizational design (Duncan 1988).

It is has become commonplace to say we live in a highly uncertain world, one whose tempo is dramatically increasing, with too much productive capacity, too many emerging competitors, and too much variety (Galbraith 1995). In designing organizations, adaptability to ongoing change, with a built-in capacity for continual redesign, is increasingly a key driver in design decisions (Nadler and Tushman 1997). As Friedman (2005) has suggested, if our attention is diverted for even a moment, as it was in the United States after 9/11, whole new competitive forces may arise for the contemporary organization. In alignment with classic definitions of uncertainty we have too many alternatives, a plethora of products, and splintering market segments. Given all these secular trends, a key question for organizations is who should absorb uncertainty – customers, management, or knowledge workers.

A traditional, if often implicit, way of approaching this problem is planned ignorance, which is often essential to organizational efficiency. By definition a specialist assigned to a functional division focuses on a limited domain of knowledge. The broader the domain, the less sophisticated the specialist. Indeed, one way to increase the efficiency of communication is to minimize the need for it by such strategies as coordination by plan, where units concentrate on fulfilling formally assigned tasks that fit into the larger whole (March and Simon 1958). This design strategy purposively encourages ignorance of the operation of other subunits.

At relatively low levels of uncertainty an organization can rely on rules and programs, the hierarchy, and goal setting to accomplish integration. These strategies constitute the traditional formal managerial structure of an organization and they will be used in sequence as uncertainty increases within an organization. Rules and programs refer to procedures established in advance for relatively predictable organizational behaviors. Each unit contributes its part of the larger project without much need for communication between units. For example, a plan may be in place that specifies in great detail the contribution of each unit in a production process. However, even the most detailed plan often runs into difficulties in implementation. Exceptional circumstances may arise which require

Box 5.2. Design choices

our problem is not only that we do not know enough but, more
fundamentally, that we do not know what we need to know.   (Tsoukas
1996, p. 18)

Given the distributed character of organizational knowledge, the key to
achieving coordinated action does not so much depend on those "higher
up" collecting more and more knowledge, as on those "lower down" finding
more and more ways of getting connected and interrelating the knowledge
each one has.   (Tsoukas 1996, p. 22)

Every approach to formal design has specific strengths and weaknesses as
detailed in Table 5.1. Managers need to be aware of these and be prepared
to constantly monitor the potential weaknesses so that they can be
ameliorated through their actions. They also must realize that there is a basic
shift in their responsibilities as design becomes more complicated, since
formal design is the context within which organizational processes and
routines occur that constitute one form of tacit knowledge (Choo 2006;
Tsoukas 1996), and they are no longer the ones who are the ultimate focus
of these processes (e.g., decision making) (Galbraith 1995). It is important
that the ultimate goals of a particular design be kept in mind, especially
since they provide the markers against which success can be measured and
are a key element of an organization's strategy (Roberts 2004).

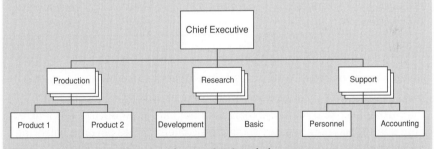

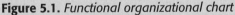

Figure 5.1. *Functional organizational chart*

Classically, designers have contrasted functional and product approaches
to design, as represented in Figures 5.1 and 5.2 respectively. Functional
approaches, or U-form, are probably what everyone thinks of first when
considering a formal organizational design, and their primary objective is to
maximize efficiency through specialization and formal authority. They are
best used when stable performance on routine tasks is required (Walker and
Lorsch 1968). The functional chart in Figure 5.1 represents a division into
three areas, production, research, and support, with further specializations
(e.g., personnel and accounting) under them. This type of specialization,

Table 5.1. *Design principle*

Dimension	Function	Domain	Customers	Knowledge
Content	Explicit	Domain-specific	Customer-specific	Tacit
Internal transfer	Segmented	Interdependence-based	Customer liaisons	Gap fulfillment
External transfer	Minimal	Domain focus	Boundary spanning	Gap fulfillment
Knowledge creation	Minimal	Domain-specific	Individual customers	Maximized
Innovation experimentation	Low	Moderate	High	Higher
Innovation implementation	Resistance	Domain-specific	Individual customers	Knowledge-driven
Problem solving	By exception	Domain-specific	Individual customers	Problem-specific
Recruitment/retention	Specialization	Dual considerations	Personal service	Knowledge workers
Certainty of personnel	Highest	Bifurcated	Relationship-dependent	Uncertainty maximizers
Formality/control	Highest	High	Lower	Lowest
Environmental adaptability	Low	Moderate	High	Highest
Timely response	Low	Moderate	Highest	High
Efficiency	Highest	High	Low	Lowest
Effectiveness	Lowest	Moderate	High	Highest

made famous by Adam Smith's (1776/1952) description of pin production, permits the growth of large-scale economies, as well as a concomitant interest in trade to achieve the maximum benefits of production efficiencies. For contemporary organizations, the classic dilemma has become balancing increasing specialization with ever greater imperatives to coordinate their efforts (Qian, Roland, and Xu 2003). The functional approach has many advantages:

• It is the starting point for most organizations
• Highly efficient
• Permits standardization
• Maximize investments (e.g., capital equipment)
• Beneficial for people with low tolerance of ambiguity; provides a stable and secure work setting (Dess *et al.* 1995)
• Works best in organizations of small size, with long product development and life cycles

It also has many disadvantages:

- Bottlenecks; decisions pile up at top
- Segmented concern
- Product variety is problematic since specialization assumes one size fits all
- Barriers to cross-functional, lateral relations (e.g., silos)
- Slow to respond to environment
- Lacks customer and stakeholder orientation

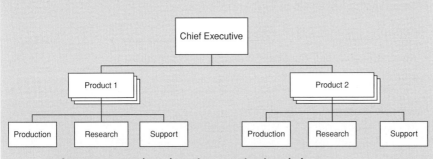

Figure 5.2. *Product domain organizational chart*

Functional designs have been increasingly supplanted by domain-based designs that focus on a particular type of tacit knowledge critical to the organization. There are many domain-based designs, with bases in geography (e.g., plant/facility, country), markets, and process/technology being popular. Interdependence-based internal transfer of information and external relations are dependent on the domain, i.e. on whether there is a regional, product, or process focus.

Product-driven, or M-form, design is probably the most popular of domain design types. Figure 5.2 contains an organizational chart organized by product groups with a functional specialization approach under the product groupings. The primary objective of this type of design is to emphasize different organizational products, recognizing that functional specialization needs might vary across them (e.g., different design teams are needed for sports cars vs. trucks, different human resource functions are necessary for knowledge workers vs. unionized industrial workers) (Walker and Lorsch 1968). Recruitment is complicated by some blending of functional specialization and domain (e.g., entertainment lawyer), but sometimes this can aid retention because a dual specialization may limit mobility. One difficulty with functional approaches is that innovation/experimentation tends to be uniform, on a system-wide basis, whereas in M-forms different divisions can try different things without impacting the whole (Qian, Roland, and Xu 2003). However, as we shall see in Chapter 9, the transfer of best practices across different divisions is inherently problematic (Szulanski

1996). This sort of approach is usually the next evolutionary stage in an organization's growth and it is adopted for its advantages:

- Focus on products
- Shortens development cycles
- More responsive to customers
- More responsive to environmental changes
- Enhances coordination, or lateral relations, across functional specializations within products
- Develops higher levels of tacit knowledge

However, it also has key disadvantages:

- Reinventing wheel; duplication across each product line
- Non-standard approaches to common problems
- Knowledge developed in specialties (e.g., personnel) within products difficult to spread; sticky
- Missed opportunities for knowledge sharing
- Lose economies of scale, common investments in capital
- Customers and other outsiders often do not know who to go to

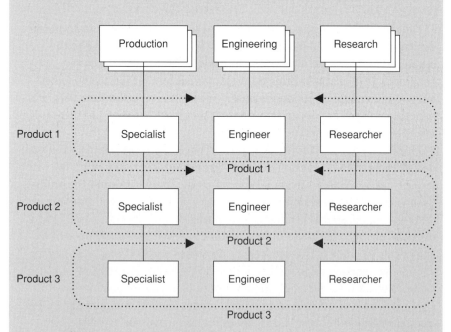

Figure 5.3. *Matrix organization*

An attempt to get at these issues, which by and large failed, was matrix approaches, that tried to merge both into a hybrid (Duncan 1988). In Figure 5.3 one such approach is represented, with production, engineering, and research functions arrayed across the top and three products represented vertically. The first researcher in this design is assigned to both a research division and a particular product line. This divided authority, with concomitant problems for the researcher, is one reason why successful matrix structures have been difficult to achieve in practice (Galbraith 1995). This form also has problems with determining priorities, and it is difficult for outsiders to negotiate. Public goods are hard to maintain. In general, the failures of traditional design approaches to deal with our rapidly changing world has led to a number of approaches to reducing both internal and external boundaries through modular, virtual, and barrier-free types of design (Dess *et al.* 1995).

As Table 5.1 details, customer-based approaches may serve as precursors to more explicitly knowledge-based approaches and considerably dampen the functional specialization legacy in the interest of making customer service supreme. Organizational members in essence serve as customer liaisons who do the navigation of the organization for customers, in effect serving as their broker. The unique tacit knowledge they develop is of the customer. Knowledge creation, innovation implementation, and problem solving are all oriented to their needs. Individuals recruited for these positions must be highly adaptable and responsive to customer needs, ready to serve them in an instant. Effectiveness becomes totally dependent on the relationship between the customer and their liaison. As a result the organization becomes considerably less efficient because of the lack of internal knowledge and generalized learning, and because of the need for slack resources to respond to specialized requests. Hospitals are experimenting with this sort of coordination of care networks to better serve patients (Gittell and Weiss 2004).

Figure 3.2 represents another approach to hybrids, emphasizing classically functional designs combined with a recognition of the importance of product development in a lateral, team-based approach that requires communication across functionally specialized groupings. These sorts of lateral relations are also a tool that managers can use to correct some of the weaknesses of particular designs (Galbraith 1995) and have become an increasingly important element, and often a perplexing one, of contemporary designs.

Knowledge-based designs focus on free-flowing communication, pushing information up because of minimal layers in a hierarchy; a mixture of generalists and specialists (Postrel 2002); the importance of brokers; decentralization that permits knowledge to be immediately applied to problems by those entrepreneurs who discover it; and with lots of free-flowing links outside the organization. All of this is similar to the market-based structures discussed in Chapter 4.

Knowledge-based designs must address common reasons for market failures (Matson, Patiath, and Shavers 2003): first, lack of codification mechanisms, which inhibits the spread of tacit knowledge; second, the lack of incentives to codify and share; third, a lack of external knowledge sources with whom one can freely share information, partly because of classic protectionist concerns (e.g., intellectual property); fourth, ineffective and uncoordinated delivery systems, which we shall discuss more in the next chapter; fifth, a lack of awareness of the value of information to others, both internal and external to the organization. (For example, whole new industries have grown up in unanticipated ways around weather and GPS information systems advances.); sixth, a lack of brokers and intermediaries to turn to for knowledge sharing, which we discuss in more detail in Box 9.2.

Knowledge-based designs need a different graphical approach that can capture the complexities we described in the tacit/explicit network. Since KN are so fluid, drawing simple boxes and lines gives an inappropriate permanence and an illusion of control that also fails to capture the layering of knowledge. Clearly network-based diagrams, somehow linked to pools of knowledge which can be tapped, may approximate what is needed, as we attempted in Chapters 2 and 3.

The fundamental goal of this sort of design is to analyze, create, or transfer knowledge to solve problems. The primary strengths of knowledge-based designs include:

- Adaptability
- Maximize innovation
- Maximize creative problem solving
- Heighten growth and organizational learning
- Retention of people who have a high preference for uncertainty, or need for cognition
- High adaptability to turbulent environments
- Focus on employee development (Keidel 1984)
- Entrepreneurial freedom
- Highest effectiveness in terms of fit to environment

On the other hand, the primary weaknesses of knowledge-based designs include:

- Uncertainty; frustrating to traditional employees (Keidel 1984)
- High possibility of disorder
- Very risky
- Hard to explain to others; institutionalism perspectives
- Who's in charge?
- Low security
- May not deal with equity issues well
- Low preservation of public goods

- Free-riders
- Lower efficiency in terms of standardization and capital equipment
- Inhibit common vision and integration of organizational efforts
- Intellectual property ownership issues
- High level of trust needed to facilitate relationships (Dess *et al.* 1995)
- How does an organization go about forgetting (Govindarajan and Trimble 2005)?

Several new types of structures – modular, hypertext, and so on – have been suggested to promote the types of collaborative relationships and knowledge generation associated with KN (Gold, Malhotra, and Segars 2001). One type of experiment is cellular organizations built on principles of entrepreneurship, self-organization, and member ownership (Miles *et al.* 1997). The cell metaphor implies both a functional orientation and internal structure, coupled with a need to interact with other cells to perform larger functions. Another approach involves viewing the firm as a distributed knowledge system where individuals manage the tensions between normative expectations, personal dispositions, and the local context when they can only know a portion of what is known throughout the organization (Tsoukas 1996). This combination of interdependence and independence allows teams to develop and share know-how that promotes overall adaptability and innovation. The efficiency of KN markets depends on such issues as information symmetry, product standardization, customer homogeneity, a critical mass of suppliers, and a common currency to facilitate trades (Grover and Davenport 2001).

Another type of early metaphoric approach is associated with holographic organizations derived from brain functioning (Morgan 1986). Holography captures how processes develop where the whole can be encoded on all of its parts. For example, memory is distributed throughout the brain and can be reconstituted from its parts. This is done in part by rich connectivity between parts that can be reorganized as the organism learns to adapt to new demands.

Essentially, most organizations are now in a one-to-many framework, a top-down approach. But more modern approaches are many-to-many, representing extreme solutions to coordination and collaboration problems, with an implicit questioning of the old saw that hierarchy is inevitable. Thus, we have new forms of collectives, cooperation that appears almost leaderless (e.g., smart mobs), an emphasis on the wisdom of crowds in social networking software, Wikipedia, open-source software, and so on. Many of these approaches do not consider networks as givens, but rather as design elements of the organization that can be shaped deliberately (Lorenzoni and Lipparini 1999).

coordination by management to insure that proper levels of relationships are maintained between units. This intervention by the hierarchy insures completion of the project. As uncertainty increases, management may decide that it is more efficient to coordinate units by establishing targets for them. Management lets the units themselves decide how the targets will be achieved. Coordination is achieved by each unit reaching goals set by management.

As uncertainty reaches high levels, however, the traditional hierarchical approach runs into difficulty and the organization is confronted with strategies that involve a departure from traditional perspectives of coordination. Essentially the major choice an organization faces is whether to reduce the need for information processing or increase its capacity to process information (Galbraith 1973; March and Simon 1958; Watts 2003). Thus organizations can be improved not by producing more information, but by reducing the amount any one subsystem must handle (Johnson and Rice 1987). Reduction in need depends primarily on the strategies of creation of slack resources and creation of self-contained tasks, which are both aimed at reducing the need for communication between units (Galbraith 1973), and by implication increasing their ignorance of other organizational operations.

Managing interdependence among units by coordinating and controlling their activities is critical to organizational design (Pfeffer 1978). The greater the interdependence among work units the greater their need for coordination (Cheng 1983). In turn, the higher the levels of coordination required, especially by more personal mechanisms, the greater the volume of communication (Hage, Aiken, and Marrett 1971). These processes are also crucial because of the many communication problems associated with hierarchies, such as blockage of information and slowing of message flows, as well as the natural tendency for rivalries to develop between functionally separated units (Lee 1970).

A variety of means (e.g., matrix, human relations, and formal integrating mechanisms) have been used to encourage interaction between entities of the formal organization, which the organizational chart in effect serves to isolate (O'Neill 1984). There is a relatively rich literature on various levels of coordination (Crowston 1997; Malone and Crowston 1994), which is also reflected in such notions as loose coupling and the strength of weak ties, which was covered in Chapter 3. Perhaps the most comprehensive, systematic discussion of this issue, especially in the context of formal structural approaches to design related to information processing, is found in the work of Galbraith (1973, 1974).

Galbraith's central assumption is that the greater the uncertainty faced by the organization the more it must concentrate its efforts on communication, particularly integrating mechanisms designed to increase the levels of coordination among work units (Galbraith 1973, 1974). These integrating mechanisms, especially the more personal ones (e.g., liaisons), also overcome some of the inherent communication problems (e.g., failures to report critical information) of the hierarchy (Lee 1970). The organization's capacity for handling communication related to coordination will determine how much interdependence, and relatedly differentiation, it can handle (March and Simon 1958) and may be the key limiting factor in knowledge-based designs. The creation of lateral resources involves much more personalized integrating mechanisms, such as liaisons, task forces, and teams, which should result in a greater awareness in organizational members of each other's activities. However, they are extremely costly in terms of communication (Cheng 1983; Hage, Aiken, and Marrett 1971) and in some contexts may be inefficient (Lawrence and Lorsch 1967). Recent approaches to this problem, such as communities of practice, implicitly take these sorts of relationship outside of the control of management, in effect creating leaderless (or at least manager-free) teams that define their own problems and membership and address problems of mutual concern.

In general, task characteristics have been argued to be the most influential factor in determining interpersonal and group communication patterns in organizations (Jablin 1987). For example, Simpson (1952) found that mechanization reduced the need for close supervision and vertical communication, since machines dictated the work pace for subordinates. Mechanization correspondingly increased the need for horizontal communication among first-line supervisors related to joint problem solving and coordination of the work. Workers' needs for information differ according to the requirements of the positions they occupy. Often jobs are reengineered to minimize the need for someone to seek information, an approach that has been labeled by its critics as deskilling. Thus, the institution of plans in bureaucratic organizations is designed to reduce the amount of information processed (Galbraith 1973).

There are many potential design dimensions, which then determine the scope of the firm, that need to be balanced in particular approaches (Roberts 2004) (see Box 5.2), each with different implications for the development of tacit knowledge and its dispersal throughout the organization. Traditionally, functions which highlight what overall business a firm is in and what specializations are needed to accomplish its strategy have driven formal structures. More recently, especially for conglomerates and very diverse organizations, product-driven designs, which may require different specialization mixes, have been used. Geography is particularly important for multinational corporations since it often reflects dramatic differences in contexts, especially in terms of government regulations and national cultures, that can be turned into sources of competitive advantage (Almeida and Phene 2004). Organization by customers, clients, stakeholders, or other external publics is also increasingly important. For example, professionally oriented universities (e.g., free-standing colleges of law), may be considerably different than liberal arts or research-oriented ones. These types of design are relationship-management driven; relationships are viewed as the firm's most fundamental asset (Gulati and Kletter 2005), much as the fundamental defining element of KN is the nature of the relationship.

Finally, as we cover in more detail in Chapter 6, workflow processes, especially technology-determined ones, can influence design approaches. For example, technological imperatives heavily influence the content of communication that flows within a role set, although the amount of this communication can also be mediated by spatial factors (Katz and Kahn 1978). Role-set communication is one of the most direct indications of interdependencies and coordination requirements existing within an organization. In fact, as Katz and Kahn (1978) note, occupants of the formally assigned offices to which roles are tied are usually associated with a few others who are adjacent to them in the workflow structure or the hierarchy of authority of an organization. Thus, "Generally, role behavior refers to the recurring actions of an individual, appropriately interrelated with the repetitive activities of others so as to yield a predictable outcome" (Katz and Kahn 1978, p. 189).

Katz and Kahn's (1978) role episode model provides a good framework, then, within which to examine the impacts of knowledge acquisition on task performance. A role is defined as the total requirements with which the organizational system faces the employee. A role set might be composed of the focal person's supervisor, subordinates, and those others with whom the member must work. In other words, the role set is a focal network of relationships emanating from the individual. Each member of the role set has expectations about the focal person's behavior; role sending occurs when these expectations are communicated to the focal person. Thus, members of a role set are likely to be the immediate, local source of knowledge.

Unfortunately, there is often not a clear overlap between formal organizational charts, which focus on hierarchical status and power relationships, and the actual flow of work represented by interdependence concerns and the interlocking roles that often determine the flow of knowledge in organizations. Specialization of function revealed in differentiation of the organization's formally assigned roles, further reinforced by professionalization, obviously also relates to the distribution of information, with jobs and associated skill sets overlapping substantially with tacit knowledge. Formal approaches excel at the development of pools of knowledge, but they minimize the circulation of knowledge among them. These issues also relate clearly to the dilemma of how we leave it to the "man on the spot" to translate his tacit knowledge to act in particular circumstances in a timely manner, while preserving the larger interests and goals of the organization (von Hayek 1945).

Dilemmas of design

The primary factor that makes design more of an art than a science is the resolution of many conflicting concerns, with Keidel (1984), for example, emphasizing the need to balance control, cooperation, and autonomy. Alternatively, March (1994) has emphasized the critical choice between exploration and exploitation of knowledge, or search and stability in Rivkin and Siggelkow's (2003) terminology, that we will discuss in much more detail in subsequent chapters. The central problem then is to try to maximize complementarities (Roberts 2004) to achieve synergies rather than energy-draining conflict and artificial supremacy of one concern. Change in one element of structure (e.g., recruitment in Table 5.1) is seldom effective since we are talking about complex systems of relationships; rather we should look at coherent clusters of changes (e.g., recruitment/retention, certainty, formality, and adaptability) that work together to achieve desired effects (Rivkin and Siggelkow 2003).

In the attempt to balance opposing organizational design imperatives, knowledge has, historically, not often been taken into account. Tangentially, however, there has been a recognition that one central design element is who will absorb uncertainty/complexity and by implication be forced to learn new things. Conventional bureaucracies tend to place this burden on their clients, while more modern approaches tend to suggest managers and/or workers should be the primary individuals who cope with uncertainty in the service of other primary objectives of the organization (e.g., having a true customer orientation). Customers generally could not care less about the internal organizational design and do not really want to be placed in the position of having to negotiate it to get the outcomes they desire (Keidel 1984).

Ultimately, rational decision choices require careful thinking about what is really valued in the organization. At times formal structures can offset other weaknesses such as geographic dispersion and the loss of closeness-desired relationships because of the growth of organizations. The fundamental issue is what competitive advantages does an organization really want to develop. Managers also must be prepared to accept that there are parts of structure that are legacies that really cannot be changed (at least at acceptable costs for the resulting benefits that may accrue) (e.g., disbanding traditional academic units in universities), but which have no real function. As Krackhardt (2007) has pointed out we will not be able to understand networks until we consciously try to change them.

Summary

In summary, there are a number of weaknesses inherent in the formal approach. First, it offers only an incomplete view of KN, since it captures only a limited subset of possible relationships (Brewer 1971; Rogers and Agarwala-Rogers 1976). Second, the formal approach ignores the active roles that individuals play in shaping their focal communication networks and in seeking information (Monge and Eisenberg 1987). Third, it also offers only a somewhat awkward and heuristically limited portrayal of the configuration of communication patterns, which is increasingly a problem in portraying knowledge-based designs. Fourth, the reification of formal structures in organizational design reduces the adaptability of the organization to change, since once structures become official they become more difficult to change, thereby increasing organizational inertia.

There are several key strengths to the formal approach. First, it deals directly with the issue of predictability as it relates to control, especially in vertical communication. The organizational chart was originally intended to map out patterns of control across the whole organization, thus making relationships between interactants clear, at least in terms of who was in charge. This chart can also be a map of where knowledge resides in organizations. Fundamentally, it should identify people who are expected to know certain things. This gives management a useful tool for designing organizational structures. It is somewhat of a paradox though that management's prime means of control is so ineffective. Second, the organizational chart is often a reflection of temporal stability; it reflects rationality after the fact (Weick 1969). This means that after people in the organization have been behaving in a particular way long enough, these relationships tend to be formalized on the organizational chart (Connolly 1977). Once relationships are specified in the chart they take on a permanence that they might not have otherwise had. Third, the organizational chart also reveals a guide to action, suggesting how things should occur in the organization. Members of the organization should realize, however, that this guide is only a practical starting point, a framework, which they may need to flesh out and deviate from to meet new problems and concerns. Finally, this approach's focus on authority relationships might be quite appropriate, since arguably these relationships form the core of most organizations.

Further reading

Downs, A. 1967. *Inside Bureaucracy*. Little, Brown.
    Classic description of the operations of bureaucracy from a political science perspective.
Galbraith, J. R. 1973. *Designing Complex Organizations*. Addison-Wesley.
Galbraith, J. R. 1974. Organizational design: an information processing view. *Interfaces*, 4: 28–36.
    Seminal descriptions of the interrelationships between communication, coordination, and uncertainty reduction in organizational design.
Galbraith, J. R. 1995. *Designing Organizations: An Executive Briefing on Strategy, Structure, and Process*. Jossey-Bass.
    Update of his classic works for managers with an emphasis on more complex modern design approaches.
Glauser, M. J. 1984. Upward information flow in organizations: review and conceptual analysis. *Human Relations*, 37: 613–643.
    Very useful synthesis of classic literature on formal communication structure in organizations.
Jablin, F. M. 1987. Formal organization structure. In F. M. Jablin, L. L. Putnam, K. H. Roberts, and L. W. Porter (eds.), *Handbook of Organizational Communication: An Interdisciplinary Perspective*: 389–419. Sage.
    Overview chapter with findings related to indices from the handbook series edited by Jablin, the leading expert, until his untimely death, on supervisor–subordinate communication issues.
Katz, D. and Kahn, R.L.1978. *The Social Psychology of Organizations*, 2nd edn. Wiley.
    The definitive, comprehensive system treatment of organizations as interlocking roles.

6   Technology

The social reality of technology implementation is highly complex. Different technologies are brought into different social settings for distinct reasons, often with opposite effects and thus complex theories recognizing the emergent and socially constructed nature of technology are needed.

(Liker, Haddad, and Karlin 1999, p. 576)

At a fundamental level, technology may be defined as organizational actions employed to transfer inputs into outputs. It can be viewed not just in the narrow sense of focusing on machines needed to produce physical goods, but in the broader sense of any systematic set of techniques which leads to organizational outputs. Naturally an understanding of technology is fundamental to our understanding of organizations, but little is known about the precise impact of technology, particularly IT given the unique attributes of information discussed in Chapter 2, on KN.

Technology has a number of potential impacts. Most importantly, it determines the human composition of organizations. The diversity of skills needed in the contemporary organization increases the heterophily of its members and generally heterophily can be associated with a variety of communication problems (Rogers 1983). Different occupations also have different knowledge needs (Case 2007). Engineers, for example, are much more likely than scientists to be interested in information that is directly and narrowly relevant to their jobs (Allen 1977). Second, technological factors also have a significant impact on the spatial environment of organizations, something we shall discuss in detail in the next chapter. Third, technology has a direct impact on the structural design of organizations.

In spite of often rosy predictions, the impact of information processing technologies has been a matter of some controversy, as has its relationship to corporate productivity (Mahmood and Mann 2000), profitability (Hoffman 1994), quality (Deveraj and Kohli 2000), and competitive advantage, as we shall discuss in detail in Chapter 10. This has been widely described as the productivity paradox – the perceived lack of increased output resulting from increased investment in IT (e.g., Sircar, Turnbow, and Bordoloi 2000; Zhu and Kraemer 2005). There appears to be a complex set of mediators that determine the ultimate success of the technology use–outcomes relationship (Timmerman and Scott 2006). There is a consensus that eventually, often with a considerable lag, new information technologies have an impact on organizational structures (Huber and McDaniel 1988) and other payoffs (Deveraj and Kohli 2000; Mahmood and Mann 2000), often by providing new ways of organizing, with some arguing that the United States has recently reaped an IT dividend in enhanced productivity.

While computerization of information should make it possible for organizations to deliver the right information, at the right time, to the right place, accomplishing this has proven to be much more difficult than it would appear on the surface (McGee and Prusak 1993). It also must be understood that information systems can only capture a small proportion (some have estimated as low as 10 percent) of the information available in organizations. The other 90 percent resides in people's heads, the social system, paper files, and so forth (McGee and Prusak 1993). While optimists wait for the next generation of computer software and hardware, realists are increasingly looking at the organization itself, especially its culture and structures, as the major impediment to improved information processing (McGee and Prusak 1993). Thus, technology, seemingly the most rational and objective of organizational factors, because of its linkage to values of efficiency, is heavily influenced by cultural factors and by existing formal power relationships within the organization (Sept 1989).

Some have argued that the primary reason information technologies fail is that their designers do not recognize the information politics of their organizations (McGee and Prusak 1993). Increasingly it is argued that the optimal political structure is akin to a federalist system with many checks and balances and explicit negotiations between sovereign states (e.g., professional groupings) within the organization (Hoffman 1994; McGee and Prusak 1993). Part of what is negotiated is who has access to what information.

While information technologies make a vast array of information available to an ever expanding number of organizational members, management's exclusive control over information resources is steadily declining, in part because of the downsizing of organizations and the decline of the number of layers in the organizational hierarchy, which were in part made possible by IT. These trends make our knowledge of communication channels, especially new media, increasingly critical for understanding how organizational members acquire knowledge. Here we will primarily focus on them and IT, given their central importance for both KM and KN, but first we turn to a broader discussion of the general relationships between technology and work. We will conclude this chapter by discussing the overall knowledge infrastructure of organizations.

Technology and structure

In general, in organizational settings, a link has been found between technology and formal organizational structure, but there is some controversy over the extent of this relationship (Ford and Slocum 1977; Mohr 1971; Porter, Lawler, and Hackman 1975). However, there is some agreement that the relationship is stronger at the unit level than at the macro-organizational level (Alexander and Randolph 1985; Van de Ven, Delbecq, and Koenig 1976; Withey, Daft, and Cooper 1983).

At the macro-organizational level a number of research programs have examined the linkage between formal organizational arrangements and technology. This research stream started with the classic work of Woodward (1965). The major conclusion of her extensive research program was that technical methods were the most important factor in determining organizational structure and the tone of human relationships inside organizations. Further she argued that no principle of management (e.g., span of control) was valid for all types of production system. Thus, this research program was instrumental in spurring the development of contingency approaches to organizational theory.

Woodward (1965) identified three major types of technology: unit, mass, and process. Unit or small-batch firms produce specialized products which require highly skilled labor (e.g., aircraft carriers) and, relatedly, in today's terms, tacit knowledge. Mass production generates products that have many standardized components, resting on explicit knowledge. A classic example is the assembly line operations of automobile manufacturers. Process production involves continuous flow technologies such as those found in chemical firms.

The findings of Woodward's (1965) study of a hundred firms in Britain indicated that several formal structural elements differed systematically across the three major types of technology. First, the number of authority levels increased with technological complexity. Second, span of control was highest for mass production. Third, administrative intensity was highest for process production. Fourth, written communication was greater in mass production organizations than in small-batch or process organizations. Fifth, unit production required day-to-day communication to coordinate activities, while mass and process production systems did not. In sum, Woodward's study found a relationship between formal structure and technology.

Other studies have also focused on formal organizational structure. For example, Simpson (1952) found that mechanization reduced the need for close supervision and vertical communication, since machines dictated the work pace for subordinates. Mechanization correspondingly increased the need for horizontal communication among first-line foremen in order to solve problems jointly and coordinate the work. Randolph and Finch (1977), more generally, found that technological certainty decreased the proportion of vertical communication and increased horizontal communication. Relatedly, task interdependence has been found to be the strongest determinant of information seeking (Cross, Rice, and Parker 2001). So, clear linkages have been made between technology and a variety of structural outcomes.

The special role of IT

> Other things being equal, then, information technology should permit the development of more elaborate and complex organizational structures.
> (Pfeffer 1978, p. 74)

New forms of electronic communication often open new possibilities for communication within organizational structures (Culnan and Markus 1987), with lower-level organizational members often having enhanced access to numerous others. As a result, decision processes move to lower levels of the organization and the organizational hierarchy is flattened (Fulk and Boyd 1991). Thus, a key factor in the introduction of new technologies is the removal of constraints from organizational members (Rice 1989). Many have argued that these new technologies create the possibilities for new organizational forms, like network organizations (Nohria 1992), or for the full operation of markets within organizations (Malone, Yates, and Benjamin 1987).

Indeed, developments in communication and IT have made the modern organization possible. Increasingly the convergence of IT, telecommunications, wireless, broadband, and so on is accompanied by more fluid intraorganizational structures and interorganizational networks (Salazar 2007). IT has a central and pervasive effect on organizational functioning since it often needs to be implemented on a system-wide basis, which makes it qualitatively different than other types of innovation (Sabherwal and Robey 1993). Information itself is distinct from physical commodities and IT requires organizational members to be trained to meet increasing levels of technological complexity.

IT has permitted the geographic dispersion of organizations across the world and the development of organizations of enormous size. But these developments in organizations over the last 150 years have also meant that the possibilities for face-to-face interactions have decreased, and that decision making, messages, and action are often separated from sources of information. As a result, the common core of meanings in organizations has been reduced, so that only simple, explicit messages (e.g., numbers in MIS reports) are commonly understood. In short, technology has had an enormous impact on communication in organizations historically and this impact is becoming more pronounced with the development of new media.

While it appears obvious that the impact of technologies would be dramatic, both structurally and spatially (Morgan 1986), especially in relation to the enhanced ability to control and coordinate organizational processes, this has not been the case in practice, with many promising technologies being used to do the old jobs in the old ways (Carter and Cullen 1983; Johnson and Rice 1987). For example, a word processor is treated as a fancier version of a typewriter and used for essentially the same functions. However, the promise of electronic media rests in the new capabilities they offer organizations, particularly in areas such as new ways of addressing communication (e.g., public bulletin boards); the storage and retrieval of communication (e.g., automatic storage of transcripts of electronic meetings); and control over access to and participation in communication, as we describe in more detail in Box 6.1.

Rice *et al.* (1988) detail the sorts of impacts that one information processing technology, electronic message systems, could possibly have on KN. First, it reduces the need for synchronous communication such as telephone calls.

Box 6.1. Social networking

Social networking services are primarily technology and software facilitators for people to form relationships with each other. So, "Facebook is a **social utility** that **connects** you with the people around you" (www.facebook.com/; bold in original). Their advent on the World Wide Web is one of the reasons for the current excitement related to network analysis. Typically, they define a universe of users, or entities, through directories. They also can define the types of relationship users would like to have with others. (Linkedin.com also identifies people by company to develop professional networks to power careers and get answers.) Users are often seen to be members of particular communities and, in some applications, social networking sites facilitate the development of communities of practice, such as Yahoo! groups, around particular interests and activities. Others, like Meetup, seek to build communites of practice that then facilitate face-to-face meetings in various cities, in part through the use of mapping utilities.

The content features of these web sites, especially in terms of facilitating the flow of complex information in various forms (e.g., graphic, visual, and so on), is one of the reasons for the excitement underlying their application to KN. One way this is accomplished is through social tagging of web sites by various users on del.icio.us, for example, which then becomes a way of sharing communally identified web sites. These features have been associated with the development of Web 2.0 which encourages the development of collective intelligence through the democratic participation of users (Boulos and Wheeler 2007).

Technologies associated with the sites enhance a number of differing possibilities for interacting: babble, chat, blasts, blogging, discussion boards, e-mail, loops, pokes, requests, reviews, shouts, tagging, Track Back Ping, and so on. Strategic advantage accrues to web sites that can provide innovative approaches to facilitating linkages of various sorts. In terms of reciprocity, access to more detailed information is often dependent on both parties agreeing they have a relationship of a particular sort (e.g., friendship). To achieve maximum benefits, as for other communication technologies, critical mass obviously makes a big difference.

The primary focus of most of these applications is on radial networks rather than more complex patterns, although some sites, such as the Friends of a Friend (FOAF) project, have tried to expand to larger network views. But Myspace's browse function lets you search through extended networks for people meeting particular demographic classifications and its search feature allows you to try to find people by affiliations. Social network sites can make visible more indirect contacts (e.g., friends of friends), thus facilitating the development of other ties.

In organizational applications these sites offer considerable possibilities for sharing and transferring information that may be used to enhance creativity and innovation. IBM's famous innovation jams and world jams relate directly to the research of its social computing groups. These jams attempt to provide a safe place where every employee can ask for and suggest practical solutions to problems they identify. An example for a professional community is Sermo, an increasingly popular online community for physicians to share information. It allows all participating doctors to rate postings that are often made in response to information queries. Postings are then archived for easy reference.

Social networking sites also provide a way of defining and growing elite communities whose access is by invitation only. For example, immobile.org is an executive community for leaders in the wireless industry. The proliferation of such sites as Diamond Lounge raises a number of questions related to their exclusionary practices, the classic concerns of conspiracy theorists (e.g., the Trilateral Commission), and the potential for monopolistic practices.

Second, it can increase the frequency of communication through a widening of professional and social connections. Third, it can increase efficiency by reducing media transformations (e.g., data files on disk to computer tape) and shadow functions (e.g., time wasted on unanswered telephone calls). Fourth, users may perceive they have greater control, improved communication, and greater access to information.

The significance of IT integration cannot be understated given its importance in terms of: level of financial investment; its role in strategy and developing competitive advantage; the possibility of disruptive innovations changing industries overnight; the relatively high failure rate; and its relation to a digital society. IT has been seen as critically important to firms in securing competitive advantage, but the findings in this area have been mixed, suggesting a critical role for mediating variables such as organizational learning (Tippins and Sohi 2003). More specifically, complementarity and cospecialization are particularly important, since they draw on idiosyncratic firm-based resources that cannot be easily mimicked by other organizations (Clemons and Row 1991; Tippins and Sohi 2003).

Cospecialization exists when one resource has little or no value without another. So, buying a computer system has little benefit if organizational members do not know how to leverage IT. First-movers have difficulty sustaining competitive advantage since imitators actually have several key advantages – newer technology, learning from competitors mistakes, and, as a result, lower costs, thus ameliorating any competitive advantages with IT adoption (Clemons and Row 1991).

Organizations use IT and KM in electronic markets (see Box 4.1) as a way of achieving efficiencies and cost savings. Malone, Yates, and Benjamin (1987) and Bakos (1991) assert that organizations involved in electronic markets (EM) will reduce their transaction costs associated with the search for competing suppliers and this will result in shifts from hierarchies toward market forms of organization.

In markets, it is possible to change relationships with suppliers, competition is open, and information is more readily available than in hierarchies, which are characterized by organizations controlling a vertically integrated supply chain.

IT allows organizations, through KM, to identify, record, connect, and utilize valuable organizational knowledge by preserving it in ways that make it easily available for use by different groups. This may include mundane knowledge such as customer data bases, problems that have occurred with products, and so on, but can also be used to preserve expertise from employees or knowledge about who experts are in an organization (Monge and Contractor 2003) or to link suppliers and organizations in EM.

Broadly, information systems perform several essential functions for organizations. First, they support the development of large-scale operations by increasing possibilities for control and decreasing the need for vertical processing of information, often by the development of explicit code systems. Second, they perform basic business transactions (e.g., from scanning purchases to payment of accounts). Third, KM decision support systems often result from the combination of basic business transaction information with software that develops trend information, as well as reporting the current status of organizational operations. Fourth, they monitor the performance of organizational members. Fifth, information systems retain corporate memory through records held in corporate data bases. Sixth, they maintain communication channels through which information is accessed and reported (Gurbaxani and Whang 1991). They can specifically enhance the performance of executives by creating new channels for sending and receiving information, filtering information, reducing dependence on others, leveraging time to concentrate on the most important tasks, and diminishing complexity (Boone 1991). Seventh, IT enhances flexibility within the firm by decreasing the reliance on particular individuals for specialized information (Nohria and Eccles 1992). Eighth, new technologies facilitate communication across time and space. Ninth, they increase external communication thus blurring traditional lines of authority (and associated transaction costs) within the firm (Nohria and Eccles 1992). A professional in an organization is as likely (if not more likely) to seek answers to questions from professionals outside the organization as from his/her supervisor within it. Somewhat relatedly, easier access to top management through e-mail increasingly makes middle management intermediaries superfluous (Contractor and Eisenberg 1990). Finally, computer-mediated communication, which we explore more fully in the next section, makes KN more egalitarian, potentially diminishing status differences and promoting access to a wide range of others.

Information carrier technologies

Information carriers are the primary repositories of information available to individuals within their information fields. The communication literature has traditionally focused on three primary classes of information carrier: channels,

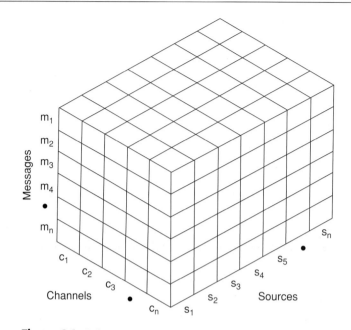

Figure 6.1. *Information carrier matrix* (Source: *Johnson 1996b, p. 48*)

sources, and messages (see Figure 6.1). There are multiple channels (e.g., trade publications, meetings) from which information can be acquired; within each of these channels there are a wide variety of sources, and each of these sources can contain a variety of messages. So, while the print versions of the *Financial Times* and *Tatler* share many channel similarities (e.g., lack of immediate feedback between source and receiver), each of us would recognize critical differences between them as sources (e.g., credibility). Similar differences in characteristics might occur for different messages emanating from the same source. So I might trust my supervisor to give me advice on work-related problems, but not what car to buy.

The relationship among these different carriers is somewhat akin to the relationship between compounds, molecules, and atoms in chemistry. Messages are the essential building blocks of which the other units are composed, the irreducible components of all carriers. Sources, somewhat akin to molecules, contain relatively stable combinations of messages. So, over time, we become very familiar with the repeated stories and themes of our close associates. Channels, like compounds, consist of more complex structures of sources that share similar attributes. So, there may be inherent similarities (e.g., preferences for new technologies, willingness to change) in individuals who use a channel like e-mail. By and large, communication researchers have focused their efforts within each of these classes of carrier, rather than assessing the things that are in common across them or processes like information-seeking that may underly them. While each information carrier has its own unique properties, there are also some dimensions (e.g., perceived utility) that transcend the differing types of carrier.

Channels have been variously defined as "an information transmission system" (Goldenson 1984, p. 137) or "the means by which the message gets from the source to the receiver" (Rogers and Shoemaker 1971, p. 24). Channels are also often seen as constraints, as in the conduit metaphor; thus a message has to stay within a channel (Axley 1984). As the preceding illustrates, and as Berlo (1960) has noted, channels have become one of the more ephemeral communication concepts.[1] Relying on the metaphor of a person on one shore trying to reach another on the opposite shore, Berlo distinguishes between three senses in which channels are used: "modes of encoding and decoding messages (boat docks), message-vehicles (boats), and vehicle-carriers (water)" (p. 64). Here we will stress mainly the sense of channels as message-vehicles, the contrivances by which messages are delivered. Thus "a channel is a medium, a carrier of messages" (Berlo 1960, p. 31).

Channels, as we saw in Chapter 3, have been one of the ways in which linkages have been defined. Since channels are the largest aggregate of the different types of information carrier, they are usually the first branch of an individual's decision tree on how they should pursue knowledge. So, my first decision when confronted with a work-related problem might be to consult co-workers, manuals, or trade publications.

General properties of channels can impact an individual's relative evaluations of them as disseminators of information. The print media, such as newspapers and magazines, are more appropriate for detailed, lengthy, and technical material, while brief, simple ideas are more effectively communicated via broadcast channels (Atkin 1981). Mass-mediated channels tend to provide information of a general nature with considerable efficiency in reaching large audiences quickly with a message (Schramm 1973). Interpersonal channels are more effective in reducing uncertainty because they provide social support, enhance confidence in suggested outcomes, and are tailored to individual needs and questions because of their immediacy of feedback and the situation specificity of their communication (Schramm 1973). For these reasons, interpersonal channels are seen as more useful in presenting complex, serious information and are generally preferred for the transfer of tacit knowledge.

Sources are particular nodes/locations of information and are akin to entities in traditional network approaches. "A *source* is an individual or an institution that originates a message" (Rogers and Shoemaker 1971, p. 251, italics in original) or "A person or place that supplies information" (*American Heritage Dictionary* 1979). While interpersonal sources, such as supervisors, may share many similar attributes, they also differ along dimensions, such as personal dynamism, trustworthiness, and credibility, that have been the classic concerns of persuasion

---

[1] This confusion is exacerbated by the frequent use of "media" as a term to refer to channels (e.g., Daft and Lengel 1986).

research. Some have found that the source of information is more important than the type of information a message contains (Hanser and Muchinsky 1978).

Messages consist of the words, symbols, or signals used to transmit a particular content emanating from a particular source within a particular channel. For example, Berlo (1960) distinguishes between a message's code, content, and treatment. Codes are groups of symbols that can be structured in meaningful ways. Treatment refers to the decisions sources make in arranging both content and codes. To Berlo (1960, p. 169): "Messages are the expressions of ideas (content), expressed in a particular way (treatment), through the use of a code."

As Figure 6.1 reveals, individuals can pursue knowledge within an information matrix formed by channels, sources, and messages. Thus, for example, I may start my search with a decision to consult a mediated communication channel, but I also may decide that I want this channel to contain authoritative information, as well as a personal touch. This unique hybrid of properties is represented by the customer support hotline of my computer software supplier. After placing a call I might decide that a particular operator is inexperienced, so I might then decide to call again or to link up the computer bulletin board focusing on this product. This new source I evaluate to be more credible, partially because of the nature of the messages it contains. While I can accept the other user's message concerning the need for a particular macro, I consider the linkage she is suggesting between printers and textual representations to be far-fetched and discount it. In other words, I move within this matrix, making decisions about how I will go about pursuing the information I want related to particular topics, which information I will accept and discard, and whether I need to continue my search within the matrix. Typically, research related to carrier selection has ignored the dynamic nature of this process (Froehlich 1994; Saunders and Jones 1990).

The route I follow in pursuing my search within this matrix reveals a number of characteristics of my search. For example, Lenz (1984) argues that search behavior can be characterized by its extent, or the number of activities carried out, which has two components: scope, the number of alternatives investigated, and depth, the number of dimensions of an alternative investigated. Lenz (1984) also identifies the method of the search, or channel, as another major dimension of the search. Applying this to the information-seeking matrix, an individual might choose the method of consulting the newspaper, decide to have a narrow scope by only consulting the local newspaper, but investigate every article about business within the paper, thus increasing the depth of the search.

In sum, communication channels are a fundamental way of defining relationships in KN and they are increasingly associated with technological capabilities in organizations. Electronic media have been found to diffuse leadership in groups, promote the formation of subgroups, and focus attention on the task (Culnan and Markus 1987), all factors that may promote KN. Communication technologies, such as bulletin boards, permit the sending of messages to a communication space that is characterized by potential similarities among messages and communicators, rather than to specific individuals. This enhances participation and access by saying that all individuals who share a similar interest can come to the same electronic space to communicate (Culnan and Markus 1987). Technologies such as bulletin boards, chat rooms, and e-mail also can reduce interpersonal coordination costs, as in the use of the dashboard visualization software described in Box 6.2.

Box 6.2. Dashboards

A car's dashboard contains a number of instruments that help the driver to use what is a complex system that interacts in many ways with its outside environment through an expanding array of sensors. Some of the visual displays signal that appropriate action needs to be taken quickly (e.g., a significant decline in oil pressure, or rise in water temperature), others give feedback on current performance (e.g., miles per hour), while still others provide longer-term information (e.g., maintenance is required, oil life is diminishing). More modern vehicle dashboards also have "drill-down capability" (e.g., projected range, miles per gallon) to provide more detail on particular areas of concern to drivers. As this sketch indicates, to be useful, a careful balance must be struck between providing too much information, which may distract the driver from the task at hand, and too little, with careful thought being given to which indicators are really critical to system performance. Increasingly the dashboard metaphor is applied to complex KM systems that combine the various elements of an organization's knowledge infrastructure into one simple, easily grasped knowledge display.

This area is very trendy and associated with a lot of buzz around Web 2.0 and visualization. Web 2.0 applies because dashboards often become the focus of collaboration efforts since their indicators can serve as cues for multiple users to take action. So, for example, a dashboard associated with an electronic medical records health information exchange may report an increase in the number of strange, deadly, viral diseases in a particular region. A visual cue on various health professionals' dashboards (e.g., on their personal web pages) that things had gone in to the red zone would signal the need to take a variety of public health measures. As a result, direct coordinating communication, and attendant delays and breakdowns, would be minimized, since a number of actors would attend to their element of the problem according to a pre-existing plan, implying a near structural equivalence, as opposed to a cohesion approach, for confronting this problem.

Increasingly, users of dashboards can customize their displays, drawing on a diverse array of information sources in creating "mash-ups." Essentially, mash-ups are software tools that allow users to easily customize the information they choose to attend to by creating unique information fields drawing on sources ranging from conventional corporate intranets, to public information from the World Wide Web, to unique proprietary data bases. These mash-ups can be shared with others and used in different formats for Blackberry-type devices, so they are not limited to desktop applications.

Visualization, which is inherent in the dashboard metaphor, is more broadly used to understand the vast amounts of digital data currently available and is increasingly important to the National Science Foundation, which has a special funding initiative related to Foundations of Data and Visual Analytics, as well as to a number of other governmental agencies and commercial firms. Especially critical in the output of these initiatives is the possibility of generating insights that can lead to meaningful action. These insights in the past have often rested on the tacit knowledge of users who could recognize patterns in very complex data. In a way, these systems are meant to make knowledge explicit that in the past was inaccessible or only known to a very limited group.

Historically, specialized information systems have always been developed for particular groups within organizations. For example, sophisticated executive information systems (EIS) were made available for top management (Matthews and Shoebridge 1993). In part, these systems recognized the conflicting pressures relating to centralization we have discussed elsewhere. Well developed EIS permit increasingly sophisticated monitoring of performance (McGee and Prusak 1993), while not obtrusively interfering with the operations of lower-level organizational employees. Unlike more well known MIS systems, which are primarily inflexible means of accumulating data, EIS focus on the analysis, presentation, and communication of data, the monitoring of exceptional performance, and keeping tracks of trends. They also permit "what-if analyses" that determine the impact of various changes on organizational performance.

This area is very trendy, with constantly emerging new approaches, but these surface manifestations suggest a number of compelling needs and continuing problems. The fundamental problems increasingly relate to the development of data bases and the quality of information that is put into them (Kalman *et al.* 2002). These are often enormous undertakings, as we will see in Box 8.3, with especially grave problems in combining information based on different formats and vocabularies. The benefits of these data bases are often opaque to the people whose goodwill is needed to insure good information is submitted (Kalman *et al.* 2002). As we shall reiterate in the concluding chapter, compelling needs relating to knowing what to attend to and how to translate data and information into actionable knowledge that is easily understood may be the fundamental problem confronting the future development of KN.

Interest in channel selection also stems from pragmatic issues of efficiency, particularly related to the claims of proponents of new technologies, and effectiveness. New media enhance efficiency by: transforming or translating one medium to another (e.g., voice to data); reducing shadow functions (e.g., busy signals on telephone calls); overcoming temporal unavailability through asynchronous communications (e.g., telephone tag); communicating more rapidly and efficiently to targeted groups; selectively controlling access to communication; increasing the speed of transmission of information; increasing user control; creating more specialized content; permitting multiple addressability, computer-searchable memory; reducing the number of links used by individuals in decision making; and enhancing individual perceptions of being informed (Culnan and Markus 1987; Huber 1990; Huff, Sproul, and Kiesler 1989; Markus 1994; Perse and Courtright 1993; Rice 1989). Although at times, what appears at first to be efficient merely adds complexity to the organization's information fields. So, for example, increased e-mail use often leads to a desire for more face-to-face communication (Contractor and Eisenberg 1990), as can work in virtual teams (Timmerman and Scott 2006).

Knowledge infrastructure

In this section, I will discuss several classes of technology that can be used to develop a firm's knowledge infrastructure, at times referring to specific software packages and technologies that are currently available. But, as even the most casually interested reader is aware, information technologies are rapidly changing. So, my task is to acquaint the reader with general concerns and issues; for specific discussions of current technology the interested reader probably would be best served by such magazines as *Scientific American*, *Business Week*, and *PC Magazine*, among a host of others, which track more recent developments.

In the following sections, I will look at the KN possibilities created by new technologies in several areas. In essence a corporation's information architecture has three primary components: data storage, data transport, and data transformation (Cash *et al.* 1994). While I will discuss these components separately, increasingly it is their blending and integration that is creating exciting new opportunities for KN.

Data storage

Traditionally, in bureaucracies, data storage has meant physical storage of information in filing systems. Needless to say, modern ideas of storage have broadened conceptions of this function considerably to include verification and quality control of information entering a storage system. Security systems for the stored information, which directly relate to KN, are also increasingly important. For example, many electronic means of communication allow an organization to store for future retrieval what would have previously been unrecorded interactions, such as those that occur in electronic mail and group decision support systems (see Box 13.2). Who should have access to this often more informal and personal information?

Security issues, however, also involve means to insure that no one can tamper or change information residing in a data base (Hoffman 1994). The viability of information also includes issues like shelf-life of data. The long-term ability of media like computer disks to store and to retrieve information physically is one aspect of this problem. Increasingly salient is the related issue of the meaningfulness of the keywords and software assumptions that categorized the original information. This also raises the issue of how old, irrelevant information is culled from any storage system. A not so apparent problem of public data bases, like the Internet, is the lack of quality control in the information available to users.

Data bases

Data bases are repositories of information that become key elements of a corporation's memory. Essentially they provide a means for storing, organizing, and retrieving information. Shared data bases are at the center of developing information systems, since they provide a common core of information to which all members of the organization have access (Malone, Yates, and Benjamin 1987). As we shall see in the next section, usually they must be combined with sophisticated electronic access, such as the Internet, to achieve their full potential for KN. When they are, then, they can form one element of an integrated network involving both humans and information terminals as entities.[2]

One of the earliest forms of data base, and one that was a critical technology in the early development of bureaucracies, was the vertical file system. Files provided physical access to permanent records that were typically alphabetized by some topical system. For example, all personnel records for a particular division kept in alphabetic order and perhaps color-coded by rank. As organizations grow, files become increasingly unwieldy and, as the sophistication of questions increases, they become unmanageable, in spite of cross-referencing. So, if I am a manager at UPS and I want to link performance records of my domestic managers with purchase orders from particular suppliers, I have probably exceeded the capabilities of physical storage systems.

As anyone who has created a simple data base (e.g., personal investments, recipes, bibliographic references) is aware, creating and maintaining a data base requires considerable investments of time and energy and associated opportunity costs. The creator of a data base hopes to achieve some advantage from this investment (e.g., complementarities in a resource-based view of strategies

---

[2] See Kane and Alavi (2008), for an interesting application of this integrated approach involving hospital information systems.

discussed in Chapter 10). Making data bases available to large numbers of others raises several interesting dilemmas for their creators, since users often have very little investment in them, but often may reap substantial returns from their use. While this use by others does not diminish their value to the original creator, the developers may be envious that they did not think of this new application of their work (Connolly and Thorn 1990). There is a human tendency to limit the free access of others to data bases or not to create them in the first place, hoping to get a "free ride" from others, a topic we will return to when we discuss the human side of KN in Chapter 11. Managers can offset the cost side of the equation to some extent by separately rewarding contributions to the development of a common corporate information infrastructure, such as data bases, beyond what an individual might expect for his/her own immediate application.

Electronic storage enhances the possibilities of linking various data bases to make increasingly sophisticated searches. Data bases, when coupled with powerful search engines and the linking capabilities of modern relational data bases, also encourage ever more complex questions. Historically, these systems have often been inaccessible. Modern data bases provide the possibility for every organizational employee to have easy access to enormous amounts of ever more complex information (e.g., storing expert profiles and organizational stories).

Data transport

The previously mundane world of data transport is increasingly the stuff of lead stories on the evening news, from providing easier access to information on the Internet through Googling, to providing new business opportunities through revised telecommunication laws, to the possibilities of broadband. Essentially data transport involves the acquisition and exchange of information.

Telecommunications

Telecommunication systems, such as fiber optic cables, wireless, and satellites, provide the hardware that links individuals, enhancing access to information. For KN, the critical issues here revolve around the carrying capacity of a particular system and the ease, range, and timeliness of access. Fiber optic systems are vastly superior to traditional metal wire systems because of their increased carrying capacity; they permit, for example, the transmission of moving visual images that eat up enormous volumes of information bits. Without this increase in carrying capacity, the movement toward merging entertainment companies with cable and telephone companies would be impracticable.

Similarly, satellite systems create new possibilities for instantaneous answers to even the most seemingly mundane questions. For example, the answer to the simple question of where I am, can be given with amazing specificity from global positioning satellite systems. From one new technology whole new industries have been spun off, with associated hardware and software. For example, one traditional problem that trucking and delivery companies have had is keeping track of where their distant employees are. Now, if I want to know where truck x is at a particular time, I can receive a nearly instantaneous answer that is accurate to within 50 feet. This creates a quantum leap in my ability to control my operations and to maximize the use of my resources. So, if I get an order from a customer, and I know I have a nearby, empty truck dead-heading back to the warehouse, I can call up the driver on my cellular telephone and much more quickly respond to my customer.

Data transformation

Combining data bases and telecommunications with software creates telematics, which allows increasingly sophisticated searches for information, and analysis/ interpretation of it once it is compiled. One reason for the excitement behind the Internet is its easy access (both in terms of cost and lack of other barriers) and the increasing user friendliness of search engines like Google® that permit access to web sites. In addition, data-mining programs, a form of artificial-intelligence expert system, can continually look for new statistical and visual representations of data, linked in ways that it would be very difficult for even the most diligent human researcher to have the patience to do.

Information centers

Developing "information centers" is one strategy for enhanced information seeking often employed by larger organizations (Daft and Huber 1987). These centers share many characteristics with traditional corporate libraries. Unfortunately corporate libraries seldom interacted with the real users of information and, as a result, became increasingly marginalized (Broadbent and Koenig 1988; McGee and Prusak 1993). Information and referral centers can take many forms, such as hotlines, switchboards, and units within organizations (e.g., micro-computer support groups) where an individual can go to get answers to pressing concerns. They serve three primary functions: educating and assisting people in making wise choices in sources and topics for searches; making information acquisition less costly; and accommodating a range of users (Doctor 1992).

In many ways the most useful thing referral services can do is put people within the organization who have the information in touch with those who seek to acquire it, hence the growth of corporate yellow pages (McGee and Prusak 1993). These yellow pages essentially expand on the traditional organizational chart by listing specific areas of technical expertise. So, for example, organizational members may not understand that their information technology office can also conduct communication network analysis as a diagnostic tool for determining user telecommunication needs. A detailed listing of functions, rather than organizational titles, can often facilitate the searches for organizational members. Relatedly, push technologies can take a more active role in insuring people get needed information. So, dynamic profiling at Intel updates employee profiles automatically based on their e-mail and web searches to provide them with a constantly changing mix of information, thus shaping their information fields.

Control, centralization, and technology

How we arrange our structures to accomplish our work obviously has a profound impact on the development of KN. Traditionally, organizational theory has focused on more macro-level impacts, but the special role of information technology has introduced a wide range of issues. IT allows organizations to identify, record, connect, and utilize valuable organizational knowledge, by preserving it in ways that make it easily available for use by different groups. This may include mundane knowledge such as customer data bases, problems that have occurred with products, and so on, but can also be used to preserve expertise from employees or knowledge about which people are experts in an organization (Monge and Contractor 2003). Communication researchers have also focused on the role of channels as one expression of relationships and often the most obvious manifestation of new information carrier technologies. A firm's information architecture, composed of data storage, data transport, and data transformation, increasingly is the source of exciting new opportunities for KN to provide unique strategic advantages for organizations. Technology facilitates our work, enhances human capabilities, and allows us to transcend human limits. It also increasingly may intermediate human functions on a macro scale, as well as the micro one we have been focusing on in the literature.

Centralization is one area where two competing positions concerning the impact of information-processing technologies have been fully articulated. Some have found support for the position that enhanced information-processing capabilities leads to greater centralization of decision making and control by management (Beninger 1986; Reif 1968; Whisler 1970), while others have found a negative relationship between more centralized information-processing technologies and decentralization (Carter and Culnan 1983) when size was controlled (Pfeffer and Leblebici 1977) or when computers were geographically dispersed (Blau and Schoenherr 1971). Fulk and Boyd (1991) argue that organizations choose technologies that promote centralization (e.g., mainframes) depending on their current situations. Huber (1990) has argued for a contrary effect, with computer-assisted communication increasing centralization in decentralized forms and vice versa. More recently Andersen and Segars (2001) found that IT enhancing communication supported a decentralized decision structure that was associated with higher financial performance. This issue is particularly critical since it relates directly to the information-processing capacity of management. Computers can serve to increase this capacity, if they present information in a comprehensible manner (Carter 1984; Carter and Culnan 1983), but there are real limits to the capacity of individual managers to process information, and computers also can serve to vastly increase overload problems for upper-level management, which has led to the current interest in dashboard-type systems.

Computers might serve to decentralize decision making in two ways: by providing an extensive array of control mechanisms (e.g., automatic warnings when activities monitored by the computers go outside certain boundaries – a key element of dashboards) and by routinizing work activities (Carter and Culnan 1983). Some computer technologies do enhance administrative intensity by increasing the efficiency with which managers can monitor the activities of workers (Carter and Culnan 1983). This raises the issue of what decentralization really is since management constrains activities in these instances (Pfeffer 1978).

It is possible that both views may be simultaneously correct. Centralization may have increased, not at the level of upper management, but at lower levels with an especially functional locus. So, lower-level decision makers in the MIS department or editors in a newspaper office, for example, may be at the nexus of organizational information flows (Carter and Culnan 1983).

While decentralization moves decisions closer to the organizational action, it may move it further away from strategic issues emerging outside the firm and from the perspective of top decision makers (McGee and Prusak 1993). So, some have called for a flattening of an organization's information environment so that key decision makers are not far from operations and vice versa. Traditionally the discrepancy between these organizational components was ameliorated by middle managers who could serve a critical bridging function, but as we have seen their numbers are steadily declining (Cash *et al.* 1994). So the tension between general strategic information and specific, tactical operational information often directly relates to issues surrounding centralization and decentralization.

The effects of new technologies on centralization also relate to the more general arguments concerning the impact of new media on the democratization of the workplace through changes in authority relationships. While it would appear that these technologies offer the potential to empower lower-level organizational employees in a variety of ways, in actual practice existing rules and norms tend to limit the use of new technologies for this purpose (Komsky 1989). Ironically, the same technologies that can serve to increase democratic participation in the work-force, also can heighten control and centralization, depending on how they are implemented (Cheney 1995).

Brokers also play a role in understanding the intersections of technology and human systems, given their central role in KN. They focus our attention on the often neglected role of human agents. Human agency in IT integration cannot be understated, as people need help in deciding on and adjusting to new technology. Paradoxically, technology often increases the importance of human agents and brokers. Information systems typically emphasize finality rather than the reflection, thinking, and learning (Solomon 2002) that only human agents can perform.

Summary

In this chapter we have reviewed the ways that technology can shape KN. Technology and structure are inextricably interwoven. The linkage between them has been sharpened by the growth of information technologies such as social networking and dashboards. Communication channels, representing information carriers, have also taken on increased importance with the growth of distant, electronic communication. We also examined the larger knowledge infrastructure of organizations, composed of data storage, data transport, and data transformation, and its importance for the development of KN. As a way of integrating the chapter we examined the issues of centralization and control and their impact on the development of KN.

Further Reading

Berlo, D. K. 1960. *The Process of Communication: An Introduction to Theory and Practice*. Holt, Rinehart and Winston.
Classic work on the fundamentals of communication with a thorough treatment of communication channels.

Cash, J. I., Jr., Eccles, R. G., Nohria, N., and Nolan, R. L. 1994. *Building the Information-Age Organization: Structure, Control, and Information Technologies*. Irwin.
Early comprehensive overview of the interaction between IT and organizational structure.

Form, W. H. 1972. Technology and social behavior of workers in four countries: a sociotechnical perspective. *American Sociological Review*, 37: 727–738.
General description of implications of workplace technology on the ability of workers to interact with each other; noise and mobility found to be key factors in the amount and quality of communication.

Woodward, J. 1965. *Industrial Organization: Theory and Practice*. Oxford University Press.
The findings of this study of a hundred firms in Britain indicated that several formal structural elements differed systematically across the three major types of technology. This research laid the empirical groundwork for contingency theories.

7   Spatial distributions of knowledge

> ... some bodies of knowledge emerge over time in a process of coevolution
> with the location in which they are embedded.
>
> (Birkinshaw, Nobel, and Ridderstrale 2002, p. 279)

Spatial dimensions of time–space relations are fundamental to most scientific inquiry. However, for a long time the social sciences have been spatially "blind," unattuned to the effects of distance and positioning on human interaction, but advances in geographic information systems have demonstrated the rich possibilities for visualization by approaching problems spatially. "... spatial structure is now seen not merely as an arena in which social life unfolds, but rather as a medium through which social relations are produced and reproduced" (Gregory and Urry 1985, p. 3). In fact, spatial factors also represent a larger movement in communication and management theory, since some view space as equivalent to context in providing the medium within which social interaction is embedded (Hatch 1987; Pfeffer 1982).

An irreducible fact of human existence is that individuals are located within a physical world. While individual locations in space may be attributable to a number of factors, they provide the basic context within which all communication occurs. Indeed, it has been argued more generally that fixed physical distances between nodes are one source of stability in network structures (Barnett and Rice 1985). As Pfeffer (1982) has pointed out, examination of communication structure and spatial factors serves as a very attractive alternative to traditional approaches to organizational theory. This is especially so in his view since physical characteristics are among the most enduring in an organization, and particular activities can come to be associated with particular locations. In other words they provide a context within which knowledge is embedded.

As Pfeffer (1982) has suggested, then, it appears that examination of spatial factors has rich potential for increasing our understanding of organizational behaviors. Examination of spatial factors also offers the promise of a fecund ground for future development of theory since it is one of the major, if not *the* major, sources of constraint on the activities of organizational members. However, this promise has been largely ignored in recent decades, in part because of the focus on the Internet and its ability to transcend physical distance. But, we are still located in a physical world that constrains the development of KN and also informs network members in ways that gives richer meaning to their relationships.

Physical location adds considerably to the capacity of interactants to interpret messages (Rapoport 1982). It is well known that the personal space characterizing an interaction reveals characteristics of relationships (e.g., status differences) (Aiello and Thompson 1980). Distance, in fact, can become a way of defining relationships.

Physical factors often have symbolic value for organizations and those who interact within them. Thus, organizations are increasingly using corporate architecture to define themselves to the public (and to their own members). The routinization provided by this architecture is often a crucial factor in the success of franchise operations like McDonald's, since they provide customers with a predictable, comfortable environment in which to pursue their projects (Rapoport 1982). In addition, members of a culture who share the same physical space are exposed to the same ambient stimuli, thus providing a common experiential base and opportunity to jointly interpret events (Hackman 1983). Thus culture, when combined with physical factors in an organization, provides a major source of temporal stability and provides a context within which communication structures are formed and tacit knowledge developed.

For our purposes the physical environment will be considered to be those elements of the built environment which surround and affect, by their spatial and functional elements, KN. The primary force which determines the impact of the physical environment is the effect it has on interactants' spatial relationships.

Steele (1973) has defined the physical environment of organizations by six main functions: (1) shelter and security; (2) social contact; (3) symbolic identification; (4) task instrumentality; (5) pleasure; and (6) growth. While Steele's framework was perhaps the first systematic attempt at specifying elements of the physical environment which relate to organizational functioning, it was not directly developed to deal with KN. On the other hand, Davis (1984) provided a framework for directly examining the linkage between the physical environment and organizational communication. He specified three primary dimensions of the physical environment which related to communication. The first dimension Davis identified, physical structure, related to architectural factors and semi-fixed features which act to regulate social interaction. Physical stimuli, the second dimension, refers to aspects of the physical setting (e.g., noise) that intrude into the awareness of individuals and thus influence their behavior. Finally, symbolic artifacts, such as furnishings and the amount of space assigned to individuals, are elements of the physical setting which guide the interpretation of the social setting.

According to Buttimer (1980) there are at least five distinct levels of analysis of social space. First, sociological space, at the social-psychological level, investigates a person's position within society. Second, interaction space focuses on the behavioral level, investigating activity and circulation patterns. Third, the symbolic level investigates images, cognitions, and mental maps (see Matei and

Ball-Rokeach 2005). Fourth, the affective level focuses on patterns of identification and territory. Finally, a morphological level factor-analyzes population characteristics to produce homogeneous "social areas." This chapter will concentrate on interaction space which focuses on behavior, investigating activity and circulation patterns and examining their implications for KN. To pursue that objective we first must explore the notion of fields.

Fields

An individual's information field provides the context and the starting point for individual knowledge acquisition. Individuals, of course, are not totally free of constraints governing their actions. They depend on others for information and for services and the general societal framework in which they are embedded restricts the range of questions and alternatives that can be pursued. For an upper-level manager an information field might be incredibly rich, including access to computerized information retrieval, specialists, other managers the individual knows personally, and subscriptions to a wide array of publications. On the other hand, a lower-level organizational employee, in a remote outpost of the organization, might be limited in the sources he/she can easily consult for information. How is individual agency limited and shaped by the larger information fields and carriers that compose an individual's information environment?

An individual's information field provides the starting point for information seeking (Rice, McCreadie, and Chang 2001). It represents the typical arrangement of information stimuli to which an individual is regularly exposed (Johnson 1996b, 1997a), the information resources they routinely use (Sonnenwald, Wildemuth, and Harmon 2001), and the stable states of efficiency of foraging for information (Pirolli and Card 1999). The concept of field has a long tradition in the social sciences, from the seminal work of Lewin (Scott 2000) to interesting recent variants, such as the information horizons approach suggested by Sonnenwald, Wildemuth, and Harmon (2001).

Individuals are embedded in a physical world that involves recurring contacts with an interpersonal network of managers and co-workers. They are also exposed to the same mediated communication channels (company news bulletins, local newspapers, television news, and so on) on a regular basis. Typically an individual's local information field consists of an interpersonal communication network and information terminals (e.g., fax machines), both of which are embedded within a physical context. This physical context serves to stabilize an individual's information fields and in large part determines the nature of the information to which an individual is exposed on a regular basis.

The constraints of an individual's information field limit the degree to which that individual can act on his/her predispositions to seek information. The information field in which an individual is located constrains the very possibility of selecting particular sources of information. Yet, individuals can, if they so desire, arrange elements of their information fields to maximize their surveillance of professionally related information. They can regularly scrutinize company memoranda and subscribe to trade magazines with high proportions of professionally related content. In other words, individuals who are more concerned with their jobs are likely to mold their information fields to include a richer mixture of organizationally related information sources.

How they shape this field over time determines not only their knowledge of general organizational issues, but also their incidental exposure to information that stimulates them to more purposive information seeking. Thus, in a sense, individuals are embedded in a field that acts on them; this is the more traditional view. Yet, individuals also make choices about the nature of their fields; the types of media to which they attend, the friendships they form, and their professional specializations, which are often based on their information needs (Pirolli and Card 1999).

Naturally an information field can change to reflect changes in an individual's life, which at times are also directly related to changing needs for knowledge. For example, when an individual is assigned to an *ad hoc* group focusing on a major new organizational product line, his/her interpersonal network changes to include other workers who are proximate during the project. S/he also may be exposed to a greater array of mediated communication (e.g., pamphlets, videotapes, etc.) concerning the nature of this project. Thus, as individuals become more focused in their information seeking, they change the nature of their information field to support the acquisition of information related to particular purposes. In this sense, individuals act strategically to achieve their ends and in doing so construct local, temporary communication structures and fields that mirror these interests (Pirolli and Card 1999).

In summary, people are embedded in information fields that determine their level of awareness and knowledge of particular issues. The nature of these fields also determines the likelihood that they will be exposed to information that may trigger a desire to seek more information or to change their behavior in some ways. The presence of weak ties, infrequent, unidimensional contacts with outgroup members, may expose them to information that suggests the possibility of change should at least be explored and this may trigger an expansion of the individual's information field. In some ways the total of someone's information fields has analogs to the notion of social capital in that it describes the resources an individual has to draw upon when confronting a problem. When individuals share the same information field they also share a context which provides the information grounds for further interaction (Fisher, Durrance, and Hinton 2004) and the development and sharing of tacit knowledge.

Relationships

Space, like communication, is somewhat an ephemeral concept, since it is not composed of substances, but rather helps define relationships between them (Sack 1980; Urry 1985). "The physical environment presents everyone with a set of initial conditions upon which behavior is largely contingent" (Archea 1977, p. 134). For example, spatial factors associated with location and mobility constrain our selections of interactants. This constraint places limits on the range of individuals with whom we can interact, ultimately determining our access to particular types of information.

In addition to determining with whom we form relationships, the nature of the space within which those relationships are embedded will often determine qualitative elements of those relationships as well. Qualitative effects include such things as the tension resulting from spatial violations and also feelings of privacy associated with well-being. For example, excessive noise makes polite, subtle instructions nearly impossible and it can lead to isolation among workers (Ashforth 1985; Canter 1983; Mohr 1971).

The primary force underlying physical structure is the effect it has on spatial relationships between interactants. Particularly important initially is the dispersion of locations of actors throughout an organization. While physical locations may be attributable to many factors (e.g., cultural), in organizations these locations are largely tied to technologies. Location can determine the information to which one is privy and thus one's inclusion or exclusion from other organizational processes (Davis 1984). It provides a static framework within which interaction is embedded.

Two variables reveal contrasting dimensions of spatial relationships and their impact on individuals: social density, or the number of interactants in a space, and proximity, which refers to the spatial distances between interactants. Together these two variables also shape the development of tacit knowledge in organizations and whether an individual engages in distant or local searches for knowledge (Miller, Zhao, and Calantone 2006).

Social density

Social density refers to the number of interactants within a particular space. It affects the opportunities for communication and it is directly related to different types of technology (Form 1972). Increases in social density have often been associated with stress and withdrawal-oriented coping mechanisms, such as avoidance of communication (Baum and Valens 1977; Brower 1980; McCarrey et al. 1974). On the more positive side, an optimal array of interactants within one's physical environment can promote intellectual growth and stimulation (Sundstrom, Burt, and Kamp 1980). Thus it has been argued that at least moderate levels of social density are essential for stimulation and the promotion of task accomplishment (Szilagyi and Holland 1980).

Proximity

Proximity is the dimension of physical structure which has traditionally been most clearly related to communication processes in organizations. The classic work of

Caplow (1947), Festinger, Schacter, and Back (1950), and Gullahorn (1952) identified a relationship between increasing physical proximity and increasing levels of communication in various social systems. Guetskow (1965) referred to this empirical generalization as one of the most common found in the organizational literature. Generally it has been argued that proximity relates to work accomplishment through such factors as increasing information exchange, increasing task facilitation, increasing coordination linkages, job feedback, the use of libraries in R & D laboratories, and decreasing role stress (Allen 1977; Allen and Gerstberger 1973; Korzenney 1978; Szilagyi and Holland 1980). It has also been found, when examining workflow diagrams, that positions scoring high on organizational centrality were located at the geographic center of an organization (Brass 1981). In addition, in cross-cultural research, it has been found that proximity contributes to the development of strong groupings in R & D laboratories (Keller 1989).

Access

Social density and proximity could be considered to be primitive terms in our explanations of the impact of the spatial environment on KN. They are also clearly revealed in gradients, with high social density revealed in clusters of actors and elaborate contours (see Box 7.1). While these factors determine the initial encounters of actors, other physical factors may be needed to understand the maintenance of relationships and what happens after initial intercession. Perhaps the variable which best captures the relationship between KN and the physical environment is access. Access may also be the single most important criterion in evaluation by users of an information system (Rice and Shook 1986), the development of foraging fields (Pirolli and Card 1999), and information seeking more generally (Case 2007). Access can be enhanced by various mediated technologies that, in effect, create electronic propinquity, in Korzenney's (1978) term. Thus, differing technologies (e.g., telephones, faxes) profoundly affect the spatial dispersion of communication activities across physical spaces, which has been described by communication gradients (see Box 7.1).

Physical factors associated with location and mobility constrain to whom we can easily access for information. Physical space also influences the meanings given to interactions within it. The physical environment is rich in symbolic artifacts (Davis 1984) that can be the object of information seeking. So, while office arrangements with closed doors promote the sharing of confidential information, they also promote the perception that there are secrets within the organization for only the privileged few. Indeed, the relationship of formal design approaches to spatial elements has not been adequately addressed in the communication or management literature (Miller and O'Leary 1989), although industrial engineers and architects have been very concerned with these issues. Thus there is an extensive pragmatic literature on open office landscaping and a variety of computer programs designed to facilitate physical layouts of plants and offices, often explicitly based on communication between units. Naturally these techniques are

Box 7.1. Gradients

Communication gradients portray communication intensity in a physically bounded plane through the use of rich visual imagery. In general, gradients detail the rate of increase or decrease of the magnitude variables through topological or graphical representations. For communication research, gradients represent communication levels of varying intensity within some physically bounded plane, such as the floor of an assembly plant, but they could also be used to capture levels of knowledge. Thus they provide a picture of where various activities are within an organization. They also provide information on the linkage of communication levels with other organizational factors. For example, a gradient might reveal that communication is highest at the intersection of two hallways, and lowest at their dead-ends. Gradients have long been used to describe phenomena in other disciplines, such as geology and meteorology (Monkhouse and Wilkinson 1971), and are directly linked to more modern geographic information systems representations. Gradients can make a significant contribution to our understanding of KN by detailing the communication configurations which result from spatial and technological contexts.

The sample computer graph found in Figure 7.1 provides us with representations of communication intensity within the bounded plane represented by the map of a warehouse/distribution center found in Figure 7.2. The warehouse is dominated by very tall bins, well above eye level (represented by the solid black lines in Figure 7.2), and a conveyor belt (which is represented by the enclosed white space which meanders through the middle right of the figure). The graph found in Figure 7.1, provides a dramatic three-dimensional picture of intense communication areas within the warehouse. The grid which forms the plane plots out the location within the warehouse of communication activities, with the horizontal coordinates for work stations arrayed along the bottom and the vertical coordinates arrayed along the right side of the figure. These coordinates, then, represent locations of individuals at work stations in the plane of the warehouse, with dimensions shown by a scale of thirty-two horizontal units and twenty-seven vertical units of eight feet. The elevated areas represent peak communication activities along the z axis (labeled by the variable NUMCONT for number of contacts). The higher the elevation, the greater the frequency of communication. For example, the highest peak is represented by the warehouse manager's cubicle at coordinates 10, 10.

Gradients can be used to portray deeper-level communication processes, such as those associated with creativity and the development of knowledge. In addition, multiplexity can be examined in a variety of interesting ways. For example, color coding could be used to portray the different locations of various functional communication contents. Another approach could involve overlaying the rest areas and work stations on the same map using different

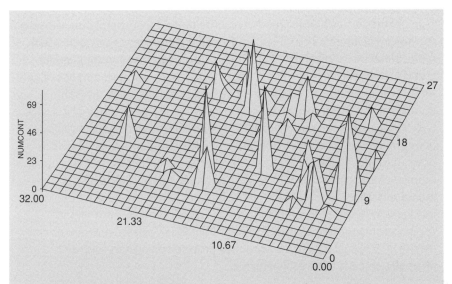

Figure 7.1. *Warehouse gradient* (Source: *Johnson 1993, p. 61*)

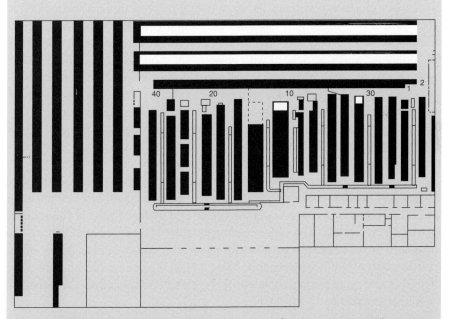

Figure 7.2. *Warehouse map* (Source: *Johnson 1993, p. 62*)

colors which highlight the functional linkage of particular communication behaviors to particular locations. Alternatively, in three dimensions, differing grids could be placed one on top of the other, with appropriate spacing between, to highlight the different intensity levels of particular locations associated with particular functions.

In general, it has been argued that some of the most useful discoveries in the history of science have been associated with visual imagery and visual representations (Klovdahl 1981). Today's advances in computer graphics and visualization offer us a host of opportunities for the development of new tools for examining KN. The gradient approach requires new ways of thinking about relationships. While, for network analysis, relationships typically are cast in terms of linkage, for gradients relationships might be better thought of in terms of relative intensities of communication which occur at particular locations. Location becomes an entity with its own unique properties and characteristics. While traditional approaches focus on individuals, roles, or groups as the entities, gradients broaden our thinking to include communication events primarily characterized by non-human organizational properties. Development of gradient-related techniques can lead to conceptual advances, since they provide researchers with an alternative means of investigating KN.

heavily rational and share many of the strengths and weaknesses of formal design approaches in general. Perhaps the most telling point in this connection is that when people first move into buildings they often complain about how formal things have become and how difficult it is to communicate (Canter 1983). Thus the formal networks associated with physical location need to be "fleshed out" by the actors to satisfy their individual needs. In this connection Canter (1983) has argued that, while having a minimal effect on formal networks, spatial factors can be expected to have a more pronounced effect on informal networks.

Increases in social density and in proximity also increase our physical access to others. Thus physical access provides the opportunity and occasion for interactions (Sykes 1983). In fact, one of the major problems for individuals in organizations comes in controlling the access of many proximate others to them. Archea (1977) has argued that privacy can best be understood in a framework in which each person is viewed as at the center of a dynamic field of information to which s/he adjusts. The individual's regulation of interpersonal behavior is influenced by his/her access to others for monitoring and the opportunities others have to monitor him/her (exposure). Indeed, open office environments are often viewed as a threat to privacy (Bennett 1977), with attendant negative associations for job satisfaction and performance.

Problems in social density which are associated with crowding reflect a loss of control by interactants of intrusions. They also impact on communication through the process of social withdrawal as a reaction to this overload of social information (McCarthy and Saegert 1978; Schmidt and Keating 1979). It has been suggested that managers can increase their control over their physical environment by (1) removing stimuli, (2) manipulating stimuli, and (3) arranging stimuli differentially in the work space (Davis 1984). People, in this context, can be viewed as stimuli, which can be arranged in space in such a manner as to promote or to retard KN. The quality, satisfaction, and amount of worker interaction is not only associated with these static, embedded elements of the workplace, but also with the more dynamic elements represented by mobility (Form 1972).

While both social density and proximity act to determine the access of individuals to each other, access is also affected by the relative mobility of individuals. Increasing mobility can be a direct result of technologies, but the necessity for this mobility can stem from utilitarian imperatives associated with problem solving as well. Information-seeking imperatives often demand that individuals transcend their local physical environment to seek out others on whom they depend for information. At this point, utilitarian concerns result in individuals seeking alternative pathways or channels for reaching distant others (Culnan 1983).

Mobility

Only when movement is introduced does the stasis represented by embedded elements transform itself into a dance which is characterized by relationships between interactants, with network analysis centrally concerned with revealing configurations of relationships. In fact, "the production and reproduction of social life depends upon knowledgeable human subjects tracing out routinised paths over space and through time, fulfilling particular projects whose realisations are bounded by structures of interlocking capability, coupling and steering constraints" (Gregory 1985, p. 297). Hägerstrand has developed rich visual imagery for representing the impacts of mobility (see Box 7.2).

The relatively limited assortment of others with whom there are frequently reciprocated contacts constitute a person's information field in Hägerstrand's (1953) more narrow sense of the term. This field sharply diminishes with distance from an interactant's position (Hägerstrand 1953). This assertion has an interesting corollary. The closer two interactants are, the more their information fields overlap, which could also have a bearing on the strength of weak tie notions (Granovetter 1973), which can be conceived of in terms of shared physical spaces as well as shared interactants. Akin to weak tie arguments, ties that span physical locations are related to job performance among engineers (Allen 1977).

Spatial factors can determine the pathways, physical or electronic, by which we access others. For example, job pressures when coupled with distance can lead to telephone use, and geographic dispersion can lead to the choice of channels such as electronic mail in organizational settings (Steinfield 1985; Steinfield and Fulk 1986). As a result, spatial factors can determine the method by which we reach other interactants. For example, Allen (1977) describes access in research and development laboratories as determined by gradually diminishing communication up to 50 feet away from an interactant, with communication beyond that characterized by a dramatic decline. Hägerstrand (1953) also describes this in terms of a cone with diminishing probabilities of communication with increasing distance. These factors led to Johnson's (1993) work on communication gradients (see Box 7.1) as a way of visualizing these structural impacts. This

Box 7.2. Hägerstrand

One of the most interesting bases for conceptualizing this dance of actors within the physical environment related to the emergence of human communication patterns is Hägerstrand's time-space paths (see Gregory 1985 for a discussion and critique). The central assumption of time geography lies in its recognition of the routinized character of daily life (Giddens 1985). "Hägerstrand's approach is based mainly upon identifying sources of constraint over human activity, given by the nature of the body and the physical context in which activity occurs. Such constraint provides the overall 'boundaries' limiting behavior across time-space" (Giddens 1985, p. 266).

The intersections of these time-space paths determines the opportunities for communicative encounters, since they reveal the availability or nonavailability of others (Hägerstrand 1982). The configurations of these time-space paths can then be represented as probability contours which indicate the likelihood that interaction will occur at any particular location (Gregory 1985). Hägerstrand's work can then be summarized in a tripartite theoretical grid:

(1) space and time are "resources" on which individuals have to draw in order to realise particular "projects," subject to:
(2) three "constraints":

   capability constraints which define space-time paths;

   coupling constraints which define space-time bundles;

   steering constraints which define space-time domains;

(3) these constraints are interactive rather than additive, and their prisms delineate a series of "possibility boundaries" in space and time which correspond to (or map out) an underlying and evolving "logic" or "structure."

dramatic decline may be the point at which an individual chooses to go to another plane, such as electronic channels, in his/her interaction with another. A gradient of individual information fields could reveal much about the probabilities of an individual receiving information from others in the organization and with whom they will choose to communicate. Therefore spatial factors affect channel selection in determinant ways, and channels, particularly electronic ones, can be viewed as the communicative surrogate of mobility.

Information terminals

The physical environment of the organization also can be seen as a space containing a set of locations or places each differing in their access to information (Canter and Kenney 1975), particularly information from outside an immediate physical location. To fully understand KN we should be concerned with the means by which the environment transduces, amplifies, contrasts or otherwise mediates the appearance of available information (Archea 1977). "An information *terminal* is a point within an informal social setting at which information is either entered into or retrieved from a formal communication network or information storage system" (Archea 1977, p. 126).

Information terminals are technological features that considerably increase communication levels at particular locations. They also can serve to expand someone's access to information. If a terminal is proximate, then the range of interactants individuals can contact is expanded and spatial limitations can be overcome to a certain degree. Enhanced information access through a rich information field also raises the probability that individuals will be stimulated to seek out information. Increasingly, open areas that promote access to information are being used in R & D settings. These areas provide an informal setting for face-to-face interaction and they also often provide teleconferencing facilities for interactions with others off-site. So, an individual whose office overlooks an open area, can easily keep track of the ongoing activities of others in their unit, and might be stimulated to ask questions concerning issues that relate to their projects.

Summary

The effect of spatial elements on KN comes primarily in determining the formation of relationships. The impact of physical factors on relationship development is quite pronounced and is associated with such factors as proximity, social density, and access. While much is known about the impact of these factors on dyadic relationships, very few studies have been conducted at the level of the entire network. In one of the few explicit treatments of this topic, Canter (1983) found that open office plans were associated with "loose" networks, while more traditional office arrangements were found to result in stronger, but more exclusive, networks. This study does suggest a direct relationship between the overall physical configuration of an office and that of its associated network.

Further readings

Allen, T. J. 1977. *Managing the Flow of Technology: Technology Transfer and the Dissemination of Technological Information within the R&D Organization.* MIT Press.
    Classic examination of networks in the context of R&D that specifically examines their linkage to physical factors in organizations. Contains the classic observation that engineers will only walk very short distances (50 feet) to

obtain information, a finding which led to the interest in open-office types of arrangements.

Hägerstrand, T. 1953. *Innovation Diffusion as a Spatial Process*. University of Chicago Press.

One of the first systematic treatments of innovation in general societal settings, this work places considerable emphasis on the spatial processes associated with diffusion, introducing key analytical concepts such as time-space paths and fields.

Johnson, J. D. 1988. On the use of communication gradients. In G. M. Goldhaber and G. Barnett (eds.) *Handbook of Organizational Communication*: 361–383. Ablex.

Systematic attempt to develop another set of analytic tools for communication structure research that directly links communication activities to physical locations.

Steele, F. 1973. *Physical Setting and Organizational Development*. Addison-Wesley.

Primer on the functions that physical settings serve for organizations.

8   Bringing in the world outside

In Chapter 4 we looked at the information fields in which organizations are embedded and discussed some broad conceptualizations of how organizations interact with their information environments. While this book has focused on knowledge within organizations, how knowledge is brought in from the world outside in collaborative relationships is becoming an issue of paramount importance (Gulati 2007). First, the world outside the organization is often the primary source of highly technical, specialized knowledge. Second, environments create imperatives for organizations to learn, to adapt to a changing world. Managers may even trust external information more, given that it is scarce, that it is less subject to scrutiny, and that there are not status or competitive implications for accepting it (Menon and Pfeffer 2003). Third, knowledge sharing is increasingly viewed as a vital mission for organizations that focus on service delivery (Wright and Taylor 2003). Finally, the development of tacit-knowledge communities in many cases is only scalable if individuals outside of the organization (e.g., other members of a profession, suppliers, or customers) can be included in KN.

Here I will first review the role of individual agents, boundary spanners, in bringing in information. Later I turn to more contemporary conceptions that emphasize the role of brokers, who sometimes serve as boundary spanners, but who also have broader roles, especially in the operation of consortia. Increasingly, knowledge and learning are the outcome of complex interrelationships between parties involved in consortia (Powell 1998). The operation of consortia has been increasingly central to theoretical work on organizations and, not so coincidentally, it is of increasing pragmatic concern to organizations, particularly related to the development and implementation of KM and innovations. Indeed, "the ability to interact and share knowledge with other companies is a distinctive organizational competence" (Lorenzoni and Lipparini 1999, p. 320). Particularly important, in this regard, is the relationship between researchers and practitioners that I will discuss in detail as a working example of these issues. Communities of practice, which contain people from within and outside the organization, have also captured increased interest. Finally, I will look at some common barriers to collaboration in knowledge generation and transfer and ways they can be overcome.

Boundary spanning

> Who proposes innovative ideas for adoption? Most new ideas probably
> originate with organizational members who span the boundary between
> organizations and technological environments.   (Daft 1978, p. 195)

Organizations, as open systems, need to sustain themselves by communicating
with diverse and dynamic environments. The external communication transferred across organizational boundaries interacts with the internal flow, affecting
structures, procedures, and control within organizations. The interaction with
the external environments, often cast as boundary-spanning activities, has been
demonstrated to be an indispensable element for modern organizations' ability
to survive and to succeed (Aldrich and Herker 1977). It also represents the first
systematic approach to how knowledge is brought into the organization from the
world outside.

Boundary spanners are individuals "who operate at the periphery or boundary of an organization, performing organizational relevant tasks, relating the
organization with elements outside it" (Leifer and Delbecq 1978, pp. 40–41).
In general, two levels of activity have been examined: first, boundary-spanning
activities occurring across working units within an organization – past research
has studied boundary spanners across different product teams, departments, and
project groups; second, boundary-spanning activities, in a more traditional sense,
between an organization and its environment. Adams (1976) has identified the following organizational roles as boundary spanners: marketing and sales personnel,
purchasing agents, dispatchers and traffic men, personnel recruiters, admission
and placement staffs, advertising and public relations workers, information and
intelligence gatherers and purveyors, legislative representatives, negotiators and
bargaining agents, and so on. Interestingly, there has recently been a growth in
the role of alliance relationship manager (Goerzen 2005).

Local search (within one's own work unit) has been contrasted with search
outside one's group, but inside the firm, and search totally outside the firm, but
within one's area of technological expertise. Radical search is both outside the
firm and outside one's technological competence. Rosenkopf and Nerkar (2001)
have found that the impacts of exploration on technological evolution are higher
when it spans the organization but does not go outside technological boundaries.
Staying within technological boundaries preserves common knowledge that is
essential for effective transfer (Carlile 2004). In this chapter I will focus on
boundary spanning outside the organization; local search and search outside the
group, but within the firm, is covered throughout this work.

Since organizations must adapt to their environments, a number of formal
structures and associated functional roles are created explicitly to deal with them.
So, for example, boundary spanners (such as department heads, customer service representatives) maintain external communication because of their formally
assigned roles. They are responsible for making communication contacts with

external information sources and supplying their colleagues with information concerning the outside environment, all the while maintaining an organization's autonomy (Aldrich and Herker 1977). As Johnson and Chang (2000) demonstrate in Box 8.1, the relationship between internal and external communication can be a complex one.

Box 8.1. The relationship between internal and external boundary spanning

Focusing on the Cancer Information Service (CIS), three models explaining how boundary-spanning communication develops over time were tested by Johnson and Chang (2000). First, in the functional specialization model, which stresses the formal side of the organization, individuals were posited to focus on either internal or external networks depending on their formal functional positions (e.g., customer service representative). Second, the communication stars explanation suggested that the two distinctive external and internal communication roles can both be played by one individual who is predisposed to high levels of communication (Aldrich and Herker 1977; Allen 1989; Friedman and Podolny 1992; Katz and Tushman 1981; Tushman and Scanlan 1981a, b). While it would seem obvious that there are finite limits to the amount of communication in which one can engage (Baker 1992), several empirical studies suggest that individuals who are high communicators in one setting are also high in others, and that heavy users of one information medium related to work are likely to be users of other media that also carry this same information (Carroll and Teo 1996; Paisley 1980; Weedman 1992), which is also a finding of more general media use studies (Berelson and Steiner 1964). This model underlines the informal side of an organization and individual predispositions. Stars acquire relevant information from their external contacts and filter and feed the information inwardly within the organization. Consequently they are perceived as influential by their peers, who seek them out for information (Paisley 1980; Reynolds and Johnson 1982).

A third model offers a cyclical explanation of individuals alternating their internal and external communication in a dynamic pattern because of the inevitable systemic, behavioural, and psychological consequences of boundary spanning. Individuals may shift on account of the systemic consequences of their boundary-spanning activities and dynamic organizational requirements. Strategically, boundary spanners might actively select one network (internal or external) on which to focus instead of attending to both networks, to avoid role conflict and to focus their work efforts. So, as suggested by the R & D literature, the importation of external ideas might result in considerable internal communication relating to the generation of internal innovations, which in turn are then exported to other organizations through external communication.

Johnson and Chang's (2000) results suggest a lagged effect, with high levels of internal communication in a preceding time period producing high levels of lagged external communication. In addition to their traditional representational and gatekeeping functions, boundary spanners in this organization also focused on developing community coalitions as a way of building political support from various stakeholders for their ongoing innovation efforts and also as a way of increasing the reach and impact of the organization, thus taking a more proactive role in resource dependence issues (Mizruchi and Galaskiewicz 1993). The CIS recognized a central tenet of organizations in competitive environments – they must seek cooperative relationships with other organizations.

Research has focused on boundary functions in terms of the information flowing in interorganizational relationships. Boundary spanners filter and facilitate information flow at an organization's boundary, and they cope with environmental constraints to maintain an organization's autonomy (Aldrich and Herker 1977). They "represent an organization to its environments, and the environment to the organization" (Eisenberg *et al.* 1985, p. 240). Thus they play two distinct structural roles: "a gatekeeper, who is a conduit for inflows to the group of which the boundary spanner is a member, and a representative, who is a transmitter of outflows from the group of which the boundary spanner is a member" (Friedman and Podolny 1992, p. 32). Tushman and his colleagues (Katz and Tushman 1981; Tushman and Scanlan 1981a, b) through their extensive research reinforce the distinction between gatekeeping and representational roles. Obviously, here we are most interested in gatekeeping functions.

Central to the definition of boundary spanning is the idea that these individuals process information from diverse sources and they represent the organization externally. Professionals in different organizations share information with each other informally (for example, at TGIFs and association meetings) and formally (for example, in trade journals). The most productive scientists are often those who communicate most outside the boundary of the organization (Allen 1966). These positions are critical to innovation and the diffusion of ideas between and within organizations. Boundary spanners become the mechanism that operationalizes environmental cues to the internal organizational structure and they accumulate power in organizations because of their ability to absorb uncertainty (Spekman 1979).

The integration and commitment of boundary-spanning personnel has always been problematic for organizations (Marrone, Tesluk, and Carson 2007). Boundary spanners are individuals who, while members of one social system, have links to another. Usually these linkages are discussed in terms of individuals who have communication ties to people outside their organization because of their formal organizational position. Informally, individuals are often more reluctant to cross boundaries, doing so only when the information is perceived as critical, there is a collective expectation that the information is relevant, and there is a perception that the boundary-spanners group is no longer functioning (Solomon 2005).

Consortia

> Collaboration has been called an "unnatural act between unconsenting adults."   (Wandersman, Goodman, and Butterfoss 1997, p. 274)

While in more stable times organizations could rely on individual boundary spanners, our increasingly complex and uncertain world has demanded that organizations be engaged in ever more complex types of relationship that I will broadly classify as consortia. Increasingly the sole purpose of these consortia is the creation and sharing of knowledge that provides partners with strategic advantages.

Consortial relationships are increasingly important because: (1) they can lead to the development, implementation, and evaluation of useful new ideas; (2) they can enhance the policy relevance of ideas that are tested, thereby facilitating translation; and (3) there is a greater likelihood of successful implementation if all parties have input early on.

A consortium can be defined simply as a collection of entities (e.g., companies, occupational specialties, community members) brought together by their interest in working collaboratively to accomplish something of mutual value that is beyond the resources of any one member (Cullen *et al.* 1999; Fleisher *et al.* 1998; *Merriam-Webster's Collegiate Dictionary*, 4th edn., 1995). Fundamentally, consortia are formed so that their members can accomplish more than they could do on their own but they are easily fractured if the needs of their members are not met.

Several developments reveal the increasing theoretical attention to consortia. First, there has been a reawakening of interest in this area with the emphasis on organizational cultures and the growing recognition that organizations are splintered into different functional groupings and "occupational communities" that form subcultures (Amabile *et al.* 2001; Gregory 1983; Johnson 1993; Keller 2001). This splintering provides a precondition for the development of structural holes that need to be bridged. Second, transaction cost perspectives, covered in more detail in Chapter 4, on economic behavior (Coase 1937), that contrast hierarchical and market approaches to the formation of organizations, have been a central theory for structural approaches to organizing because of their blending in unique network approaches to organizations. Third, and relatedly, the growth of different organizational forms highlights the importance of this problem, particularly interorganizational relationships, federations, alliance networks, clusters, and multinational corporations. These new forms must discover underlying bases for interrelationships among their increasingly pluralistic subgroupings (Keller 2001), that lead to the creation of multiple structural holes. Fourth, organizations often find that they are either strapped for resources or are pursuing projects of such magnitude that they must pool their resources. Developing cooperative relationships with other entities promotes the possibility of resource sharing and greater efficiencies. As Box 8.2 details, while there are many potential benefits to the parties in consortia, there are often as many, if not more, potential costs.

Box 8.2. Brokering researchers and practitioners

> The knowledge that researchers, teachers, consultants, and practitioners learn by themselves is different and partial. If it could be co-produced and combined in some novel ways the results could produce a dazzling synthesis that could profoundly advance theory, teaching, and practice. (Van de Ven 2000, p. 5)

> The transfer of knowledge from researchers to potential users is impeded, however, by the social separation of researchers from users. The two belong to different communities with few shared activities or sentiments and little social interaction ...   (Beyer and Trice 1994, p. 675)

Here we will focus on the naturally occurring structural hole between researchers and practitioners as a way of illustrating the many difficulties in framing consortia. The possibility of bridging this structural hole has been a recurring theme of leaders of academic disciplines (Applegate 2001, 2002; Cullen *et al.* 2001; Van de Ven 2000, 2002). It has also been noted, even for applied subfields, such as health, that the greatest shortcoming of academic research is its lack of relevance to practitioners, its inability to be translated (Babrow and Mattson 2003; Dorsey 2003; Thompson 2003).

In general for researchers there are considerable benefits that can ensue from interaction with practitioners; in fact they may have more to gain from researcher–practitioner relationships (RPR) than do practitioners. While both parties have things to gain from RPRs, they often have even more to lose, and this is seldom explicitly discussed. Both parties have substantial potential common benefits from a successful RPR, including securing both physical and material resources and intellectual stimulation (Cullen *et al.* 1999; March 2000). It is also obvious that policy makers see substantial benefits to be had from interaction between the various parties in the research enterprise, with increasing calls from the National Cancer Institute (2003) and the Fund for the Improvement of Post-Secondary Education (2003), among others, for holistic examinations of research problems through the development of synergistic relationships among often fractured disciplines (Wandersman, Goodman, and Butterfoss 1997). Many have suggested that a richer intellectual synergy can develop from combining theory and practice, resulting in greater understanding and a more comprehensive view of phenomena of interest. Such consortia can also make implementation of solutions more likely and increase the policy significance of research, resulting in greater society-level benefits. With such compelling advantages, one is left to ask: "Why don't these consortia develop?" The answers to this question lie in a closer examination of structural hole brokers (SHB).

RPR can easily be cast as a structural hole problem given the separate communities represented by these two groups (Cullen *et al.* 2001), with little communication occurring naturally (Amabile *et al.* 2001), but with considerable potential system benefits that could accrue from brokered linkages between them. Brokers who translate, coordinate, and align perspectives are needed, but these SHB also need to be able to address often conflicting interests (Kuhn 2002). The marketable commodity in this research environment is not individual scientific expertise, but the scientific capital one can bring to the table through the network of relationships one has with others. The substantial differences in the motives and perceptual frameworks stemming from the different cultures in which they are embedded (Rynes, Bartunek, and Daft 2001) highlight the importance of SHB in the emergence, maintenance, and dissolution of RPR. Do differences between researchers and practitioners really make a difference? If the overall system is to function successfully, there should be tension in these relationships. In a dialogic view, it is important to maintain and if anything sharpen these differences, while downplaying threats, if the overall system is to work. Ultimately achieving balance in all things is the central issue faced by an SHB. As Burt (2000) has established, sometimes SHBs are needed in situations where two parties are aware of each other, and may even have modest communication activity, but are so focused on their own projects that they cannot establish a meaningful relationship. The SHB acting as a *tertius*, or the third who benefits, strategically moves accurate, ambiguous, or distorted information to achieve control benefits (Burt 2000).

There is a cost in sharing ideas through less commonly used ties, since these ideas and relationships may actually weaken those that bind us to a particular profession. Some have suggested that the lack of utilization of social science findings by practitioners and policy makers is essentially attributable to their different frames – they have conflicting values, different reward systems, and different languages (Kuhn 2002). These obstacles are always difficult to overcome, especially where they relate to continuing unfilled manifest needs (e.g., publications or improved practice) of the parties. Failure to meet the earlier promise of relationships will result in a move to institutionalize trust through formalizing relationships (e.g., written contracts with performance obligations). In the end, the parties need each other's specialized contributions (e.g., access to a research site, research expertise, or improved practice) to gain the benefits of an overarching system (e.g., a granting agency) to which they must attend (Amabile *et al.* 2001; Cullen *et al.* 1999; Mohrman, Gibson, and Mohrman 2001; Walton 1985).

There are many advantages that accrue from RPR consortia. The primary advantage is the improved practice that can be achieved by accessing intellectual resources to solve problems. Second, the parties can gain a buffer to ultimate accountability by using each other as stalking horses who float trial balloons for their problem solutions, gaining the considerable benefit of having someone else to blame for changes or failures and thus spreading their risks. Third, practitioners can enhance their professional status by appealing to professional standards (Cullen *et al.* 1999). Fourth, especially when students or more junior faculty members are involved, practitioners can feel good about making a pro-social contribution to someone's education or career development.

While both parties have things to gain from RPR, they often have even more to lose, which can lead to difficulties in maintaining relationships and even to their eventual dissolution (Johnson 2004). One of the paramount values of any science is the objectivity of the researcher and the preservation of their ability to maintain their independence and integrity. Often practitioners, by questioning some taken-for-granted assumptions threaten researchers' autonomy in ways that call into question these fundamental principles. Practitioners seldom have any great concern for the integrity of the research process, especially relating to traditional scientific verities associated with rigorous research and internal validity (Killman, Slevin, and Thomas 1983). They will change interventions if they sense they are not working to the benefit of their project, since this is, after all, what they do daily in their operations. "Because sponsors' needs come first, program improvement second, and evaluator's needs are only a third priority, in many evaluation studies you'll have little control over the evaluation itself and none, typically, over the object of evaluation" (Dearing 2000, p. 8). Practitioners also may not respect researchers' needs for confidentiality of privileged scientific information, thus interfering with patent, publication, and other intellectual property rights (Keen and Stocklmayer 1999). All of these elements point to the critical need for the mediation of an SHB for the continued development of RPR.

Relationships with practitioners can also be very threatening to researchers' self-concepts, something to which an SHB must attend. First, as Goodall (1989) has articulated, researchers are often manipulated by skilled practitioners so that these practitioners can achieve their own ends. Second, critique from practitioners often centers around two contrasting themes of common sense and naivety: either "you're not telling us anything we do not already know" or "your ideas are so 'pie in the sky', or abstract, that they could never work." Since these judgments are often based on professional experience and anecdote, they are not easily refutable. They also may be quite telling, since we often seek to describe the world as it is, we lag behind real-world events, and often merely describe the experience of a skilled practitioner. So, practitioners often feel researchers are out of touch with real-world practices (Ford *et al.* 2003; Rynes, Bartunek, and Daft 2001), a critical shortcoming in this fast-moving world. Similarly, in our quest for methodological rigor, we often ignore variables, especially political and legal ones, that any practitioner must consider before implementing a new practice. Paradoxically, the more sophisticated our methods and theories, the less useful they appear to practitioners (Rynes, Bartunek, and Daft 2001).

One interesting feature of RPRs is that it is quite possible for one party to achieve his or her goals while the overall system fails. So an innovation might be adopted that benefits practitioners, but the research is so commonplace, or flawed because of lack of rigor, that it is not diffused through the academic literature. A true partnership with practitioners is very time-consuming, and the resulting rewards are typically slight, since it is seldom valued institutionally (Keen and Stocklmayer 1999).

More disturbingly, often a failed project results in interesting research. Herein lies a clear challenge for researchers. Often we learn as much or more from failed efforts in which we are involved as from successful ones. So our own individual goals are likely to be achieved regardless of the outcomes of the overall project. A key finding of the classic differentiation and integration literature is that the costs of integration can be quite high and only really need to be borne in certain organizational environments (Lawrence and Lorsch 1967). The personal investments of SHBs are significant. It is little wonder that so few people emerge in such roles. A focus on maintenance and dissolution also suggests that the need to recoup these costs can result in dysfunctions at the overall system level (Johnson 2004). Central to these dysfunctions is the need of the SHB to insure ties with the parties are non-redundant, or structurally autonomous in Burt's (1992, 2000) language. And we can often take comfort in the fact that we preserved the canons of our profession. Unfortunately citation analyses also indicate that relationships in which researchers define the problems and pursue their own questions are most likely to be successful in academic terms (Rynes, Bartunek, and Daft 2001). So in some ways you have the paradox of success: the more successful one entity in a system is in attaining its more limited individual goals, the more unlikely it is that the overall system will attain its wider objective (Senge 1990). Similarly, it has been found that centrality in advice networks, a fundamental property of SHBs, is positively associated with individual performance but negatively related to group performance (Sparrowe *et al.* 2001). So, in the end, developing and maintaining consortia is a central challenge for social systems generally, one that is fraught with many difficulties.

While the need for new organizational forms and the pressures to create them are great, success is difficult to achieve, particularly in the health area, as Box 8.3, on health information exchanges, demonstrates. Barriers to coordination are legion and are much more robust than the factors that lead to successful coordination, a topic we will return to later in this chapter. This aspect

---

Box 8.3. Health information exchanges

The fundamental difficulty in modern medical care is execution. Providing reliable, efficient, individualized care requires a degree of mastery of data and coordination that will be achievable only with the increased use of information technology.   (Bates and Gawande 2003, p. 2533)

In its simplest expression, electronic medical records (EMR) are a health information technology (HIT) that captures information about a patient's treatment in a particular context. In small or solo group practices this can include transcription of treatment encounters, e-prescribing, medical literature access, tracking of billing for services, patient scheduling, and potential reminders of screening or of chronic treatment. In this environment it has been estimated that the initial implementation cost (e.g., training, installation, software, staffing, and so on) per provider averages $44,000 per year, with ongoing costs of $8,500 (Miller *et al.* 2005). It takes approximately 2.5 years to recover initial costs, with the potential for substantial profits (e.g., efficiency savings, reduced transcription costs, fewer support medical record staff, and so on) thereafter; but there have also been cases of dismal failures (Miller *et al.* 2005). In group practices it has been estimated that the implementation of such systems might decrease physician income by 10 percent (Gans *et al.* 2005).

Essentially health information exchanges (HIE) are designed to encourage the interoperability of EMR in regions within the United States providing access for a variety of doctors and/or institutions to patients' records. Most health care occurs within regions because of patient's reluctance to travel long distances for treatment. For KNs they represent one of the more complex arrays of potential actors, especially in their formative stages, but also in their actual implementation and operation, with over thirty federal agencies involved (Brailer 2005; Thompson and Brailer 2004) and a hundred regions currently in various stages of piloting HIEs.

Here I will view EMRs in the broadest possible sense, to include their linkage in interoperable networks. Interoperability has been a classic problem in information science with almost all knowledge organization systems. In its most basic form it requires two or more systems to exchange and to use information without special effort on anyone's part (Zeng and Chan 2004). So, here we are looking not only at their implementation in an individual physician's office, which may be problematic enough (Miller *et al.* 2005), but also at their implementation in regions, which implies standard setting to facilitate common exchanges, itself an immensely complicated innovation (Halamka *et al.* 2005; Hammond 2005). So, to get their maximum benefit, we are looking at the bundling of a number of interrelated innovations (Hillestad *et al.* 2005; Taylor *et al.* 2005).

This innovation is in the early stages of adoption, with a few key early adopters already in place. One of the most frequently cited of these is in Indianapolis (Brailer 2005; McDonald *et al.* 2005) and is associated with the Regenstrief Medical Record System, a regional system that allows sharing of records of prior care at eleven hospitals as well as community clinics. However, nationally only about 10–16 percent of physicians currently use EMR in their offices, with 49 percent of physicians in a Massachusetts survey indicating they had no intention to use them (Lewin Group 2005). Small and medium-size practices – where 80 percent of medicine is practiced (Harris 2005) are often the most resistant to EMRs. The USA is significantly lagging behind other industrialized countries in this regard (Harris 2005).

From a KM perspective the most important function of EMRs (although the distillation of knowledge of various practitioners should not be discounted) is the possibility of conducting research based on data mining of large number of pooled medical records. The Indianapolis system has a data base on the treatment of over 3 million patients with 300 million online coded results. This allows for large clinical studies focusing on improving the quality of care for common medical conditions. EMRs also offer a potential early warning system for the emergence of various diseases, promote public health and preparedness, and accelerate the diffusion of knowledge and best practices (Thompson and Brailer 2004), as well as offering the possibility of enhanced financial controls (unnecessary surgeries, tracking waste/fraud/abuse). While moving to HIE considerably enhances the benefits of EMRs, it vastly increases the complexity of the problem.

Brailer (2005) estimates 5 percent of health care costs could be saved by improved interoperability of systems. The key to interoperability is getting the right information to the right place at the right time (Brailer 2005). It is estimated that nearly 30 percent of health care spending annually – 30 billion dollars – is spent on unneeded or duplicative care (Harris 2005). On a policy level this issue has become important enough that President Bush signed an Executive Order in 2004 setting a goal that the majority of Americans would have interoperable EMRs within ten years.

EMRs offer a number of compelling advantages:

- A reduction in the number of medical errors in the current system, which lead to 50,000 to 100,000 deaths a year (Brailer 2005; Harris 2005) and to 777,000 people being injured in adverse drug events in hospitals (Thompson and Brailer 2004).

- Increased consumer involvement in the choice of medical care (Brailer 2005; Harris 2005; Thompson and Brailer 2004).
- Currently 16 percent of GDP is spent on health care; lower estimates suggest that EMRs would save 112 billion dollars a year – 7.5 percent of health care spending – with higher estimates ranging up to 30 percent (Lewin Group 2005; Thompson and Brailer 2004).
- Managing chronic illnesses such as diabetes, which are growing dramatically, through coaching and home monitoring (Harris 2005).
- Increasing accountability for the quality of care (Harris 2005; Thompson and Brailer 2004).
- Reducing regional variability in care (Thompson and Brailer 2004).
- Enhancing coordination of care by eliminating administrative inefficiencies (Thompson and Brailer 2004).
- Accelerating the diffusion of knowledge and best practices (Thompson and Brailer 2004).
- Making it more likely physicians will prescribe generic drugs with resulting cost savings (Harris 2005).
- Strengthening privacy and data protection (Thompson and Brailer 2004).
- Promoting public health and preparedness (Thompson and Brailer 2004).

Developing these systems in the USA represents one of the most complex challenges known to KNs. The following barriers/objections must be overcome:

1. Privacy, including federal HIPAA regulations and often differing state requirements (Brailer 2005; Gottlieb *et al.* 2005)
   a. Hackers and security issues
   b. Confidentiality concerns
2. Proprietary interests of vendors in existing IT (Hackbarth and Milgate 2005).
3. Government regulations (e.g., anti-kickback rules that impede the sharing of technology) (Thompson and Brailer 2004).
4. Physician resistance
   a. Time
   b. Interference with traditional workflow that can be very complex and is already time-pressured (Walker 2005); threats to relationships with patients (Shortliffe 2005; Thompson and Brailer 2004)
5. Coopetition between medical providers within regions (Frisee 2005).
6. Technical problems
   a. Standards
   b. Common medical languages – the Regenstrief Institute's LOINC@ system now has a standard nomenclature of 33,000 observation terms

c. Data base architectures
d. Availability of broadband, hardware, software (Harris 2005)

Perhaps most importantly, the benefits of HIE accrue at system level, while costs are at the local level (Lewin Group 2005). But various groups have decided that the benefits of these systems outweigh their risks/costs, although the real benefits may take 5–10 years of diligent application to realize (Lewin Group 2005). Who bears the cost of maintaining software and investments in legacy systems is a vital issue. Thus there is a mismatch of motivations, with an absence of compelling ones for those who must implement the system.

explains the very high failure rates of consortia (Parise and Henderson 2004), with estimates of failure rates of business alliances as high as 60–70 percent (Gulati 2007; Gulati and Kletter 2005). Many barriers have been identified: the specific missions of cooperating agencies are often different (for example, providing social support vs. treatment for cancer patients); relatedly, outcome and effectiveness measures differ between agencies; search costs for finding appropriate partners can be high and it is often difficult to absorb the knowledge from truly diverse ones (Goerzen 2005); and there are high coordination costs (e.g., developing common vocabularies) in truly integrating the efforts of diverse organizations. In addition, members of coalitions may have multiple goals, they may resent the loss of decision-making latitude, and the cost of managing their linkages increases. Since it is difficult to mandate these often voluntary relationships, interest has increasingly turned to how communities develop around common problems and share knowledge to solve them.

Communities of practice

> Within a CoP, people collaborate directly; teach each other; and share experiences and knowledge in ways that foster innovation.   (Smith and McKeen 2003, p. 395)

The operation of communities of practice (CoP) has been increasingly central to theoretical work on organizations and, not so coincidentally, it is of increasing pragmatic concern to organizations, particularly in relation to the development of KM practices and the implementation of innovations (Wenger, McDermott, and Snyder 2002). Four general types of CoP have been identified: helping, where knowledge is shared; best practices development; knowledge stewarding that preserves knowledge for sharing; and innovating creative communities (Leonard 2006). CoPs represent the people side of KM and how it is negotiated communicatively (Iverson and McPhee 2002); interest in them grew out of a recognition of the importance of context in situated learning (Davies 2005). They are a nearly perfect object of KN research because of their fluid, informal relationships. Accordingly this literature would benefit from a greater appreciation of the classic group and social influence literature and more explicit incorporation of network concepts (Borgatti and Foster 2003; Cross, Rice, and Parker 2001) and an appreciation of the classic downsides associated with in-group, out-group dynamics (Wenger, McDermott, and Snyder 2002).

CoPs often discourage hierarchical relationships within the community and the community generates its own goals (Lesser and Storck 2004). CoPs are formed by groups of people who share tacit knowledge and/or learn through experimentation focusing on central organizational processes or problems (Brown and Duguid 1991; Lesser and Prusak 2004; Tidd 2000). CoPs form around communities of people who have areas of common interest (e.g., practices) within a domain and exchange information that results in improvements in the whole (Fontaine 2004; Huysman and van Baalen 2002; Kuhn 2002; Lesser and Storck 2004; Wenger, McDermott, and Snyder 2002) as demonstrated by the CISRC case (Box 8.4).

Box 8.4. Cancer Information Service Research Consortium

The strength of user innovation communities lies in the free revealing of detailed information about the innovation among members of the community.   (Huysman and van Baalen 2002, p. 4)

The Cancer Information Service (CIS) is an award-winning national information and education network, which has been the voice of the National Cancer Institute (NCI) for over thirty years (Marcus, Morra, *et al.* 1998; Marcus, Woodworth, and Strickland 1993). While the CIS has extensive outreach programs dedicated to reaching the medically underserved (Thomsen and Maat 1998), it is probably best known for its telephone service that has a widely available 800 number (1-800-4-CANCER). In the health arena, pressures concerning health reforms, relating particularly to the growth of information technologies and associated economic pressures, have resulted in a number of different approaches to consortia. The CIS itself is unique in many ways. Perhaps the best label for the new organizational form represented by the CIS is that of a contractual network.

The unique characteristic of the CIS in the 1990s was its geographic dispersion in nineteen regional offices (RO) serving the entire United States (Marcus, Woodworth, and Strickland 1993). What brought all the ROs together was a classic fee-for-services contract, which in effect hired existing organizations for a specified time to provide services toward the accomplishment of a common goal. Although the ROs were technically temporary, many of the offices had been in service to the CIS for over twenty years and had successfully competed for contract renewals (Morra *et al.* 1993). These offices, however, still retained their membership in their local sponsor or parent organizations (for example, cancer centers) and identified with and addressed their regional concerns. Yet there was also a strong normative thread that ran through the activity of this network, a commitment to providing high-quality information, free to the public, concerning cancer (Marcus, Woodworth, and Strickland 1993).

The Cancer Information Service Research Consortium (CISRC) was a consortium of cancer control researchers and CIS practitioners who formed a coalition to implement trials related to three major cancer control projects. Innovation often occurs within such communities of practice (CoP) whose members share a common set of goals and a core of shared knowledge (Fouche 1999). The creation of a consortia of researchers and practitioners in the CISRC added yet another level of complexity to the CIS.

Organizations experimenting with CoPs understand the learning needed in the flexible structures of new organizational forms (Smith and McKeen 2003). The CIS had a rich tradition of work with CoPs, primarily in the form of task forces. These task forces, then, represented the major sites of organizational learning and the generative mechanisms for change within the CIS. They prepared the CIS for what would become its most complex CoP to date, the CISRC, which was designed to address a major strategic objective of the CIS, demonstrating that it could perform higher-end knowledge generation and translation functions (Johnson 2005).

Over time, the CIS had become a community-based laboratory for state-of-the-science communication research (Marcus, Woodworth, and Strickland 1993) and had conducted more research on cancer-related information seeking than any other site, while simultaneously meeting its service goals (Marcus 1998a). The CISRC followed in this tradition; it employed a series of program project grants funded by NCI (Marcus 1998b). The creation of this consortium was, in part, a response to the lack of slack resources within the CIS, but it also recognized the reality that creating a new semi-autonomous structure is often necessary when embarking on an innovative organizational activity (March and Simon 1958). Companies seek to acquire knowledge from the outside when there is a capability gap – that is, when strategically important technical expertise is unavailable or inadequate internally (Leonard 1995).

The CIS, through the development of the CISRC, constructed a knowledge network with key research partners outside of its formal structure (Nonaka and Takeuchi 1995). This provided a strong formal base for relationships, with many associated informal contacts, that could be used to build an even broader coalition, combining to form a CoP. The CISRC represented a strategic alliance between researchers from a variety of institutions and practitioners within the CIS to implement three new intervention strategies. The CISRC was charged with implementing and evaluating preventive health innovations designed to reach traditionally underserved sectors of the American public (Marcus, Woodworth, and Strickland 1993). In this endeavor, the CIS needed to be creative in its attempts to manage innovation in order to generate organizational members' acceptance of change that at times could be challenged by geographic, institutional, and other, less tangible barriers.

Thus, in 1993 the CIS formed a CoP with several senior investigators to determine if it could serve as a dynamic laboratory for cancer control research at the same time as it was providing regular service (Marcus 1998b). Membership was diverse, following established practice, and included representatives from various functional roles in ROs, NCI's office of Cancer Communications liaisons, and outside expert advisory members and/or other interested parties (e.g., outreach partners). To insure appropriate collaboration, several committees served as means for the various groups to interact with each other. These included the Executive Committee, the Steering Committee, the Publications Subcommittee, the Members Council, and advisory committees for each of the projects (Marcus, Morra, et al. 1998). A unique feature of program projects of this sort is that they have shared resources on which all of the projects can draw, including in this case administration, survey research, and biostatistics. Thus, there was considerable complexity in the CISRC CoP, that was further complicated by four of the six major components being spread across the country at different host institutions. The consortium was designed to become a basic structure within which a number of innovations could be developed, thereby turning the CIS into an "innovation factory" (Hargadon and Sutton 2000).

The three new intervention strategies the CISRC piloted were designed to facilitate the dissemination of cancer information to the public. The first and third innovations were connected to the CIS 1-800-4-CANCER telephone service, utilizing the toll-free number as a nexus from which to disseminate cancer information to targeted populations. The second and third projects were tailored to the health information needs of traditionally underserved sectors of the American public. Project 1 ("5-A-Day for Better Health") involved the use of proactive counseling in the CIS to offer information about fruit and vegetable consumption to callers who would not ordinarily receive this information as part of its usual service. Proactive counseling was delivered at the end of a regular call, no matter what the caller had initially contacted the CIS about, in order to encourage callers to increase their fruit and vegetable consumption (Marcus, Heimendinger et al. 1998).

Project 2 was concerned with encouraging women to receive regular mammograms. This new intervention strategy reached out to women by making cold calls from the CIS to low-income and minority women in targeted communities in Colorado. This intervention strategy was unique in that it focused on making outcalls from the CIS, an activity that was substantially different from the traditional role of a telephone service that responds to calls placed by people in the community to a toll-free number (Crane et al. 1998; Crane et al. 2000, for follow-on study).

Project 3 ("Quit Today!" Smoking Program for African Americans) was a tailored, multichannel media campaign designed to increase the CIS call volume of low-income African American smokers and recent quitters. This project involved two interrelated studies. Study 1 focused on a paid media advertising campaign designed to motivate adult African American smokers to quit smoking and to call the CIS for help in doing so. Study 2 tested the efficacy of newly developed self-help smoking cessation materials and targeted CIS counseling tailored to the quitting barriers and concerns of African American smokers in motivating quitting compared with standard non-tailored CIS smoking cessation materials and counseling. For telephone information specialists, Project 3 was usual service, providing accurate, up-to-date information in response to caller requests (Boyd *et al.* 1998).

The CISRC operated within the larger political context of an evaluation of a federal government health information program. One implicit understanding related to the research was that the results would be utilized to demonstrate that the CIS could be used as a research arm of NCI. Thus, the CISRC was designed to develop the research potential of the CIS, to foster collaboration among investigators and the CIS network, and to move the service toward high-quality, peer-reviewed research (Fleisher *et al.* 1998).

These communities are particularly important for geographically dispersed, virtual organizations (Scarbrough and Swan 2002). Increasingly, attention has turned to ever more complex forms of communities such as those involved in open source software. In examining the case of Linux, Lee and Cole (2003) noted the importance in these communities of critique for error identification, correction, and rejection, which was critical to the evolution of knowledge.

Brokering structural holes in consortia

Bringing groups together to establish cooperative relationships, thereby closing the structural holes between them, is one of the classic problems of the social sciences (Johnson 2004). In traditional systems approaches, the problems of coordination and cooperation are typically viewed in terms of their system-level benefits, the clear need for groups to work together to achieve collective goals. This perspective focuses on linking groups to achieve common purposes arising from their shared interests, offsetting the differentiation into heterophilous groups by increased attention to integration. More recent approaches to this problem have focused on individual-level benefits that accumulate when gaps in social structures are filled. These market-driven approaches assume that opportunities arise from integrating disparate groups and that the "invisible hand" of the market will result in the establishment of cooperative relationships between groups, since actors will be motivated by their self-interests (Johnson 2004).

These perspectives also assume different roles for brokers, who act as intermediaries in the formation of cooperative relationships, thus creating conflicts between system-level and individual-level benefits. System approaches assume altruistic actors who will act to establish recurring direct linkages because of their contribution to overarching goals, while market approaches assume trusted actors motivated by self-interest who will act as go-betweens who accrue capital from transactions they mediate between groups. More colloquially, the first set of relationships might be thought of in the cultural form of family representatives who bring together couples for the interest of the larger kinship group, while the latter might be thought of in terms of merchants who act as go-betweens between buyers and sellers. While merchants will lose their profit if buyers and sellers discover they can directly interact, parties to a marriage (hopefully) will continue in their relationship with minimal interaction with the initial broker.

Studying brokering relations is especially important when there is an historical pattern where, despite compelling interests, groups do not naturally align; these situations often point to the dilemmas of the various parties, described in detail in Box 8.2, who often need brokers to successfully form cooperative relationships. Consortia are particularly interesting settings in which to examine these issues because of the voluntary nature of relationships within them, which often create a situation that is a mix of system/altruism and market/self-interest. Given the interest in new organizational forms, heightened competition, fractured communities, acquiring knowledge, and declining resources available to any one group, this topic has captured the attention of researchers in a wide range of disciplines.

Elsewhere I have used four factors that have been identified as key elements of both the classic and market approaches to structural hole brokering to develop propositions concerning the emergence, maintenance, and dissolution stages of consortia (Johnson 2004). A systems model developed for examining communication factors related to closer ties between entities that has been empirically tested in intercultural research (Johnson and Oliveira 1992; Johnson, Oliveira, and Barnett 1989; Johnson and Tims 1985) may be usefully extended to the context of the operation of consortia (see Figure 8.1). The fundamental premises of the model are based on the notion that, in a classic systems framework, perceived value/attitudinal similarities lead to behavioral intentions, particularly those related to future communication behaviors and relational ties, linked to the social distance between two communicators. This model stresses the balance between shared interests and threats that emerge in relationships with other groups. It also links these factors to homophily, a key feature of modern organizational demographic theory, as well as a continuing foundational factor in communication theory. Central to both systems theory and structuralist explanations of the problems that develop in intergroup relationships is the balance between differentiation and integration. Finally, market-driven approaches stress that trust is the most important factor in knowledge brokering (e.g., Davenport and Prusak 1998).

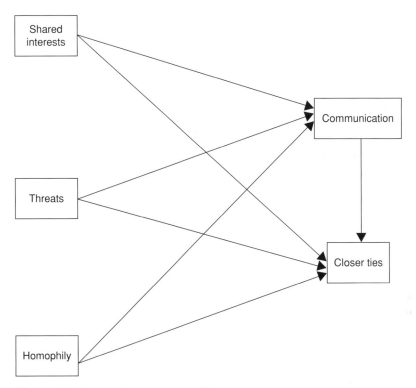

Figure 8.1. *Johnson's closer ties model*

Shared interests and threats

Social relations can be characterized in terms of a dualism of homogeneity and heterogeneity associated with shared interests and threats respectively; with the relative prevalence of one or the other determining the degree of enmity or amity in the relationships mediated by a structural hole broker (SHB) (Simmel 1955). Shared interests and threats should affect, in opposite ways, both communication and the desire for closer ties, and have classically been incorporated in systems frameworks.

Shared interests represent the direct, albeit sometimes idiosyncratic, benefits that accrue to the individual parties from continuing systemic relationships. Superordinate goals are also associated with shared interests because intrinsically they constitute cooperation, which can serve to reduce conflict. For example, individuals often desire improved economic prosperity within their own country through interaction with another one. Cooperation usually entails some sharing of benefits as a result of coordinated efforts. Interestingly, superordinate threats from third parties may also be a major inducement for cooperative relationships (Browning, Beyer, and Shetler 1995; Gibson and Rogers 1994). Indeed, Lawrence and Lorsch (1967) define integration in terms of the collaboration needed to respond to environmental demands. However, the goals/interests of different groups can reveal both shared interests and threats depending on whether they facilitate or impede each others' accomplishments. The closer ties model predicts that there will be a direct, positive relationship between greater perceptions of shared interests and the desire for closer relationships.

Perceived threats result from the perceptions of subsystems that their individual self-interest may be thwarted by the actions of the other party and that harm will result from a continuing relationship. Indeed, competition for scarce material resources can be viewed as a primary determinant of intergroup conflict. For subsystems to coact successfully, their perceptions of the benefits of common interests must outweigh the potential threats each perceives from the other. Perceived threats can lead to strain, conflict, and eventual discontinuance of relationships. For example, Park and Ungson (1997) found opportunistic threat and rivalry to be a strong indicator of the dissolution of joint ventures. As Sarbaugh (1979) has noted, the more the other is perceived as injuring the concerned party, the less effective communication will be, if it occurs at all. Thus, threats are posited to relate negatively to the brokerage of ties.

Homophily

As we shall see in Chapter 11, a large body of literature suggests that individuals have a tendency to interact with those similar to themselves; so, homophily has generally been considered a central communication variable. It has traditionally been defined as the degree to which parties "are similar in certain attributes, such as beliefs, education, socio-economic status and the like" (Rogers 2003, p. 19). Lawrence and Lorsch (1967), in discussing differentiation and the related specialization of function of different groups within systems, specified three primary areas where groups could be heterophilous: (1) they could have different orientations toward a particular goal; (2) they could have differences in time orientation; and (3) they could have differences in interpersonal orientation.

The degree of similarity between parties, which relates directly to perceived social distance, has been a central issue in both intercultural and organizational communication theory. It has been argued that effective communication, which results in fewer misunderstandings, is more likely to occur between homophilous communicators (McCrosky, Richmond, and Daly 1975; Rogers 2003). It is also more likely that homophilous communicators will have the appropriate absorptive capacity for knowledge to stick when transferred (Tsai 2001). However, heterophilous relations may input diverse views and truly creative approaches to problems (Klein, Palmer, and Conn 2000), as we shall explore more fully in Chapter 9.

Homophilous communicators are also more likely to be willing to accept information. Generally it has been found that increases in perceived similarity lead to closer relationships cross-culturally and that the communication in these relationships tends to be more effective. Or, stated in another way, "People's perception of other people determines to a major extent whether there is a communication attempt made" (McCrosky, Richmond, and Daly 1975, p. 323). In the closer ties model, homophily is posited to have direct, positive relationships on SHB.

Trust

As we have previously discussed, trust is an essential ingredient of long-term collaborative relationships in collectivities, and may be the most important attribute of network relations, at least in market terms. Since network analysis is essentially a means of representing patterns of linkages, the quality of these relationships becomes an important determinant of the patterns of linkages for individuals and the emergence of individuals in key network roles, such as liaisons.

Of course, trust may have many bases: process-based trust results from recurrent transactions; characteristic-based trust results from social similarity, and institutionally based trust is tied to formal social structures (Bradach and Eccles 1989). More recently, Levin *et al.* (2004) suggest that competence-based trust is critical in organizations, as well as a perception that others have benevolent motives. Thus, people would be more likely to trust individuals with whom they have had past successful relationships, who have knowledge in relevant areas, and who are homophilous, within an institutional framework that has strong norms of conduct and associated penalties.

Differentiation and integration

Relations among groups have also classically been cast in systemic frameworks, with groups viewed as systems components and the relationships between them heavily dependent on the nature of their communication, which relates directly to issues bearing on social distance. In any system there is a constant tension between the needs of component parts to differentiate, with concomitant growth of disparate values and attributes that can produce perceptions of threat, and the need to tie differentiated parts together so that they will orient themselves to the common, superordinate goals or shared interests of the larger system. Unfortunately, the differentiation of skills required by complex, modern organizations makes it increasingly unlikely that differing functional specialties will have similarities in outlooks. This too greatly impedes the transfer of knowledge between them.

Effective integration has become a considerable source of concern because of the increased organizational diversity that is a product of the greater technological and environmental challenges facing contemporary organizations. Among other effects, increased differentiation into more and more specialized subunits decreases system effectiveness, impedes coordination, hinders development of strong values and appropriate climates, and slows the diffusion of innovations within the firm, without a concomitant increase in integration (Johnson 1993).

Summary

The model of closer ties, emerging from classic system approaches, examines a closely intermeshed system of factors that can be expected to have strong, determinant effects on the desire for closer ties. Trust is the critical factor in modern market approaches, while differentiation and integration are the foundational forces in intergroup relations. Thus, these factors, while drawn from different theoretic traditions, recognize the blending of these forces in contemporary organizations and the need for more balanced, synthetic approaches to these problems. Each of these factors bears in direct ways on social distance between disparate entities and can be expected to play critical roles in the emergence, maintenance, and dissolution of ties mediated by an SHB and the need for more complex patterns of coordination in new organizational forms.

Brokers

> Most firms in biotech and pharmaceuticals have key individuals who function as network managers, "marriage counselors," and honest brokers. These individuals provide the glue that sustains relationships between parties who have ample opportunities to question one another's intentions or efforts. (Powell 1998, p. 237)

Interest in the emergence of individuals in key network positions is a long-standing one, given the voluntary nature of many relationships, especially those in consortia, that has emerged more recently in the context of B2B exchanges in value chains (Ordanini 2005). In fact, much more attention has been paid to these issues than the maintenance or dissolution of ties, a critical theoretical shortcoming in the eyes of Monge and Contractor (2001). Network analysis generally has been criticized for its static approach (Perry-Smith and Shalley 2003).

At the maintenance stage the focus of the SHB is on sustaining relationships developed in the emergence stage between the two parties. In doing this the SHB no longer dwells on shared interests and threats, unless driven to do so by events. In fact, one of the clear evidences of entry into this stage is a less visible, although still vigilant, role for the SHB. They now have the somewhat trickier task of balancing these factors, maintaining an appropriate level of distance between the parties. They do this in part because if the parties become too close, the SHB becomes redundant and will not recoup the considerable investment in forming these relationships. The parties start to see their similarities more clearly and develop an overarching identity as members of a functioning system, or team, something the SHB will encourage when the other factors start getting out of balance. This can be facilitated by shared outcomes. While process-based trust should start to develop between the parties, the personal assurance offered by the SHB is still the ultimate guarantee. Finally, comes the tricky matter of balancing differentiation/integration. While SHBs need to define a common workspace/focus, they also have to develop clear boundaries for each party's role (Amabile *et al.* 2001).

Burt (1992) has argued that weak ties are a special case of structural hole brokering. These weak ties can lead to the diffusion of innovation since they spread novel ideas through a system. However, widespread sharing can actually hamper innovation within a social system because of the development of common perspectives (Adler and Kwon 2002). So, preserving specialization is important for the continued development of a system and becomes increasingly paradoxical for KM and KN.

In spite of its prevalence and costs, much less attention has been focused on the dissolution of relations in consortia (Peng and Shenkar 2002). Relatedly, the interesting issue of what happens when we lose social capital, or are confronted with this possibility, has received scant attention (Adler and Kwon 2002). Here I will focus on what an SHB does to prevent the premature (before they have received their expected returns) ending of consortia. There are, of course, other possible roles an SHB can play in dissolution. One is that the SHB can grow satiated, having received enough of whatever reward s/he sought, and decide to move on to other challenges (or retirement). This may be particularly important for the perishable rewarding of curiosity. SHBs can act to nurture a replacement (with an appropriate fee) or they can easily (perhaps all too easily) move one of the four factors out of alignment and trigger the forces for dissolution, easily placing the blame for it elsewhere. They can also just accept the fact that events (e.g., a breaking of trust, the presence of a competing SHB) would require too much effort to overcome and resign themselves to dissolution. Some have argued that the growing presence of electronic commerce promotes disintermediation, or the potential that buyers and sellers will find each other directly without having to rely on human agents (Sawyer *et al.* 2003). In any case, the level of complexity and lack of tacit knowledge, typical of the parties negotiating the early stages of consortia, imply the necessity of the helping hand of a broker or the implementation of several tactics, to which we now turn, needed to promote the development of these relationships in KN.

Tactics for managing consortia

As our illustrative cases on HIE, the CISRC, and the Cooperative Research Centre (Boxes 8.3–8.5) suggest, developing consortia can be fraught with difficulties because of the many barriers that exist in these often very complex relationships. They are subject to many of the same basic problems that exist in any relationship between two parties (and remember relationships are the foundation of any network analysis) but they also are much more complex because they operate in many different cultural milieux and regulatory environments, and the stakes involved are often quite high. In this section I will sketch some tactics managers might use for overcoming specific problems in these relationships, given their importance to KN (see Table 8.1). The problems fall into three general classes: one-party, relational, and contextual. Managers need carefully to weigh the number of enablers that they apply to any one situation and evaluate the effort involved against the likelihood of success and the importance of the outcomes.

Box 8.5. Cooperative Research Centre for Freshwater Ecology

Australia has chosen a somewhat different path to formalizing RPRs than the US federal system of grant support. Their Cooperative Research Centre concept grew out of a concern that there be a more direct societal benefit from research programs and an earlier appreciation of the importance of translational research. This concept explicitly created a third-party funding mechanism that provided the initial risk capital to bring disparate parties together to address fundamental societal problems. In turn, there was an expectation that, as the centres matured, funding would emerge more directly from the work of the consortial parties.

The most interesting of these centres for our story is the Cooperative Research Centre for Freshwater Ecology, a critical pragmatic problem for Australia, whose founding director, Peter Cullen, although a natural scientist, adopted many knowledge management practices (Cullen *et al.* 2001). He recognized that the centre's fundamental problem was one of bridging structural holes between RPR where no prior relationship existed. However, while the director initially served as a liaison, filling the gaps between structural holes, he quickly recognized, partially because he was nearing his second retirement, that a more formal long-term solution was needed to maintain this consortium of researchers and practitioners. Serendipitously he cast this problem in the mid-1990s as a KM problem and started reading outside of his own science background for management solutions (Cullen *et al.* 2001).

In Johnson's (1996b) information-seeking broker concept (later cast as knowledge brokers, who bridged the gap between practitioners and researchers), the director found a synthesis of many of the traditional solutions suggested in the literature. This role could take on many of the characteristics of an ombudsman whose job was to monitor relationships to ensure that the parties were acting within the rules. These brokers had the classic ingredients of boundary spanners, with low affiliation needs and high tolerance for ambiguity. These special roles may be necessary, because it may be nearly impossible for someone to be simultaneously an actor, advocate, and researcher (Walton 1985). If a structural hole is worth bridging, then it is important to have redundancy and successors who can fill that role once the original liaison is gone.

The knowledge brokers in the Cooperative Research Centre for Freshwater Ecology were living embodiments of these characteristics. They were individuals who often started their careers as research scientists, but soon found that they enjoyed solving problems by applying research, a translational function. They served to broker relationships between practitioners (e.g., water companies) who gave a retainer to the centre and affiliated researchers who were conducting more basic research. They did not serve the entrepreneurial, impresario role of Dr. Cullen, but rather served to maintain relationships between necessarily specialized roles.

The initial act of creation of a consortium, the ultimate structural act of creativity found when bridging structural holes, is often performed by academic entrepreneurs like Dr. Cullen, but for continued benefits, the more mundane work of formalizing these relationships must also occur, something that the network literature seldom addresses. This knowledge-broker role is now formalized in the newly developed successor organization, the eWater Cooperative Research Centre. How these sorts of transitions are made is the critical issue for long-term system benefits accruing from RPRs. These larger system benefits are indeed compelling: greater likelihood of implementation of innovative ideas; greater understanding and more comprehensive view of the system of interest, resulting from a richer intellectual synergy that can develop from research informed by practice; and ultimately, a lower failure rate for consortia. They often require a willingness to create new organizational designs that formalize structural hole brokering.

One-party

One-party issues in consortial relationships essentially focus on the entities involved separately. An essential condition of economic relations, especially market ones, is motivation (Roberts 2004), and these issues often go to the core of a party's motivation.

Inertia

Inertia may be one of the most powerful, yet relatively benign, factors in the failure to develop consortial relationships. Habits are difficult to overcome and the new is coupled with uncertainty. Although inertia would seem to be relatively easy to deal with, establishing the momentum to change can be difficult. The tactics involved (Table 8.1) essentially involve destabilizing existing relationships in some ways through such approaches as job transfers, reorganization, or downsizing. If the same basic relationships are in place, the maintenance of the existing state can be made ever more costly (e.g., negative performance evaluations, layoffs). Of course, one can offer carrots, enticing the parties towards a more attractive future.

Threats

As we saw when we discussed the model of closer ties, threats are a major impediment to the development of relationships in systems. Threats themselves can take many forms. In the HIE case (see Box 8.3) they included the confidentiality concerns of patients and the proprietary interests of providers. Tactics for dealing with these issues (see Table 8.1) generally include: changing perceptions

Table 8.1. *Key problems in consortial relationships and tactics for addressing them*

Problem	Tactics
One-party	
Inertia	Destablize existing relationships
	Make maintaining existing state
	ever more costly
	Pull toward attractive future
Threats	Change perceptions
	Increase familiarity; build trust
	Third-party guarantees
	Exemptions from laws and regulations
	Offer compensating advantages
Resistance	Changes in organizational culture
	Work redesign
	Incentives
	Hierarchical mandates
Relational	
Lack of common ground	Stress or create homophily
	Create common vocabularies, standards,
	frameworks, and experiences
	Promote development of
	self-organizing systems
	Sponsor conferences
	Have brokers mediate
Shared interests	Working together necessary for goal
	accomplishment
	Stronger together than separately
Lack of vision	Demonstration projects to establish efficacy
	Benchmarking practices of other organizations
	Strategic planning process
	Providing job rationale
	What is the larger good, that I am unaware
	of, that this action can serve?
Contextual	
Internal bureaucracy	Ignore
	Find loopholes
	Use to your advantage
Regulations	Treat as an opportunity
	Coopt them
	Play different regulators off against
	each other
Third-party	Do not burn bridges; leave on good terms
	Legal actions
	Contextualizing human environment
	Provide them with some compensating
	benefit
	Source of seed money and expertise
	Facilitate information exchange
	Mobilizing stakeholders

that the threat exists, often by increasing familiarity, which may then build trust; removing the possibility of the threat being realized; mitigating its impacts (e.g., third-party guarantees); or offering compensating advantages.

Resistance

Resistance often occurs in asymmetrical relationships and can be countered by the classic influence strategies of persuasion, authority, and rewards (Fidler and Johnson 1984). Resistance to change has been a very popular topic in the management literature for decades, although recently it has been cast in terms of often legitimate objections to inherent problems in change itself (Dent and Goldberg 1999). The HIE case points to many sources of resistance among physicians – time, money, harm to patient relationships, and doctors becoming clerks/nurses because of the way orders are entered into the computer. Resistance to absorbing knowledge should be assumed and can take considerable time to overcome (Fink and Holden 2005).

Again, tactics for dealing with this may appear to be somewhat obvious, and some are shared with those used to address threats, but they are often difficult to accomplish in practice: changes in organizational culture, work redesign, offering compensating incentives, and hierarchical mandates. As Fidler and Johnson (1984) demonstrated in the case of innovation, using classic influence strategies can often be very costly (e.g., the communication costs involved in persuading someone to make a complex change).

Relational

Relational issues of coordination focus on the linkage itself, how the relationship itself might be characterized, which, as I argued in Chapter 3, is the critical issue in any network analysis. Sometimes tactics here involve changes in both parties, changes made with the overall relationship in mind.

Common ground

Homophily, as we have seen, is often an essential ingredient of relationships. Sometimes it can be created, as in a developing history brokered by an SHB (Johnson 2004). At other times, parties can help to create a basis for relationships through the development of common vocabularies (e.g., education and training programs), standards for technologies, and media (e.g., money) or frameworks (e.g., cultural norms) for exchange relationships. While at times this may verge on a third-party solution, usually these issues are in some ways mutually solved by consensual agreement among the parties. For our purpose the fundamental and most interesting common ground is shared understanding that rests on the medium of common knowledge (Miles and Snow 1994). Managers can encourage the development of markets, self-organizing systems governed by a few simple rules, or technologies such as Siemens' ShareNet that promote the widespread sharing of information directly from peer to peer (Voelpel, Dous, and Davenport 2005).

These systems can rely on key signals (e.g., visual dashboard indicators, discussed in Box 6.2) that result in individual actions to self-correct, in a cybernetic way, parts of the system.

Shared interests

In systems frameworks some sort of coorienting frame for a relationship is often a necessary condition for its continuance. However, while benefits accrue at a system level, costs are usually at a local level, so there is often a mismatch of motivations, with a lack of compelling ones for those who must implement the system. Shared interests can rest on many grounds (e.g. common goals) and are fundamental to the development of consortia, since only by working together can some goals be accomplished. Parties must feel that they have a deficit that only the other can satisfy. This need not be the same commodity. A mentor may need gratitude, while a mentee needs knowledge. Importantly, gaining recognition and reputation among a group of peers is often a key motivator for individuals to share knowledge (Voelpel, Dous, and Davenport 2005).

Vision

Change often depends on creating a vision of an attractive future pattern (Roberts 2004). Here demonstration projects that show that success is possible can often be important for establishing the efficacy of a new direction.

Contextual

Relationships and the actions of the differing parties are inseparable from the context in which they are embedded. Since many consortial relationships are embedded in complex legal, industrial, and cultural relations this is an especially important factor. For networks, it has long been argued that individual dyadic relationships are often shaped by the social dynamics that surround them (Parks and Adelman 1983).

Use of formal authority and coercion

All too often top-down implementation demands collaboration with other organizations as a result of mandates. Sometimes this can also have a coercive element when, in effect, a firm's leaders surrender to a stronger one. During the long course of bureaucracy a wide range of strategies, from active to passive resistance, have been used to counter this approach. Sometimes organizational members can just ignore mandates, hoping that they too will pass. One thing that formal rules do is protect weaker organizational members, who can find loopholes in them or turn them on their head to their advantage.

Government regulations

While often well intentioned, government regulations, like HIPAA or Sarbanes–Oxley, can create enormous complications for organizations. They can also create opportunities for strategic advantage for those firms that most rapidly adapt to them and for coalitions that form to exploit them. Of course, more Machiavellian strategies can also be pursued, with regulators at different levels being played off against each other or through the adoption of other classic, anti-bureaucratic strategies. Regulators can also be coopted and what was originally intended to do one thing can be turned on its head to do another. Often consortia can be formed with diverse memberships (e.g., consumers, activists, or interest groups) to accomplish these ends. Clever organizations often insure that they write the regulations with the exploitation of loopholes firmly in mind. These tactics often represent forms of contextualizing where an organization consciously pursues changes in its environment to improve its fit.

Third-party interference

One clear implication of KN is the importance of the spider-web of relationships within which parties are embedded. So, one purpose of studying networks is to determine the effects of third parties on relationships with others. As Mac Parks (Parks and Adelman 1983) has discovered for romantic relationships, often these third parties have a clear impact on the development of relationships (as do brokers), their duration, and on the terms on which parting occurs. Third parties can also exhibit jealousy and have things to gain from the weakening of a tight bond between others. Some may be inherently malicious, like hackers.

There may be legal remedies from some actions of third parties (e.g., as in alienation of affection lawsuits), but an understanding of the possibilities and appropriate preventive measures may be the best tactics. So, in a network context, establishing a new pattern of relationships, contextualizing your human environment, may in the end be the best protection.

A special case of third-party interference, that can be especially damaging because of its detailed knowledge, is that from a spurned, former consortium member. Indeed, hell may have no fury like these former partners. If a firm has been very successful in achieving its objectives it may outgrow former partners, leaving old friends behind when it moves to its new status. It is always important to separate on good terms, especially in a tightly bound industry. Demonstrating to third parties that they have something to gain from this relationship (e.g., creative product, growth in knowledge) may in the end be the best counter-measure.

At times, third parties can be the key to a successful relationship. Managers and the government can provide instrumental support, making success more likely. They can also provide a safety net and thereby reduce the risk of adoption. They can provide means of sharing experience/information exchange when they sponsor conferences or support web pages. Third parties also may be experts in developing consortial relationships, having tacit knowledge of the tactics we have discussed in this section.

Summary

In this chapter we have discussed how knowledge is transferred from the world outside and translated into actions within an organization. Our views of these processes have moved from focusing on one individual who was charged with working with one element of an organization's environment in a formal boundary spanning role, to the operation of brokers who act as intermediaries between various parties, to the conscious development of consortia as part of well-articulated strategies for organizations to gain strategic advantage in the development and transfer of knowledge and to also reduce uncertainty by exerting some control over elements of their environment (Klein, Palmer, and Conn 2000). As the case of the Cooperative Research Centre for Freshwater Ecology demonstrates (Box 8.5), consortia can both generate and transfer knowledge to larger social ends. This often requires very thoughtful management that is willing to invest some of its scarce resources in the integrating and brokering relationships needed for the success of these highly complex KNs. This is often revealed in the work of industry associations that set standards and play an increasingly important role in spreading knowledge, especially about technologies (Yates 2005).

Further reading

Adams, J. S. 1976. The structure and dynamics of behavior in organizational boundary roles. In M. D. Dunnette (ed.), *Handbook of Industrial and Organizational Psychology*: 1175–1199. Rand McNally.
   Early conceptual overview of boundary-spanning roles.
Aldrich, H., and Herker, D. 1977. Boundary spanning roles and organizational structure. *Academy of Management Review*, 2: 217–230.
   Classic early conceptual overview of boundary spanning with a special focus on its implications for structure.
Dyer, J. H., and Nobeoka, K. 2000. Creating and managing a high-performance knowledge-sharing network: the Toyota case. *Strategic Management Journal*, 21: 345–367.
   Provocative description of the interorganizational network of suppliers that has resulted in a unique resource that provides competitive advantage to Toyota by quickly creating and recombining knowledge from diverse perspectives.
Gulati, R. 2007. *Managing Network Resources: Alliances, Affiliations, and Other Relational Assets*. Oxford University Press.
   Systematic review of a decade of programmatic research on interorganizational networks conducted by the author and his colleagues. Focuses on the concept of network resources which reflects in many ways the social capital accruing from a firm's external relationships.

Johnson, J. D. 2004. The emergence, maintenance, and dissolution of structural hole brokerage within consortia. *Communication Theory*, 14: 212–236.

One of the few dynamic treatments of a network role, structural hole brokerage, tracing its evolution from initial emergence to factors that lead to its dissolution.

Wenger, E., McDermott, R., and Snyder, W. M. 2002. *Cultivating Communities of Practice: A Guide to Managing Knowledge.* Harvard Business School Press.

Pragmatic application of the ideas surrounding CoPs to organizational settings by some of the originators of the concept.

Pragmatics

9 Creativity and innovation

> While we will consider various knowledge transfer issues and strategies . . . many of them come down to finding effective ways to let people talk and listen to one another.
>
> (Davenport and Prusak 1998, p. 88)

> Innovations are not only adopted, implemented, and confirmed through social relations among people; they are also created, understood, and defined socially.
>
> (Dearing, Meyer, and Kazmierczak 1994, p. 17)

> . . . managers whose networks span structural holes have an advantage in identifying and in developing the more rewarding opportunities.
>
> (Burt 2005, p. 235)

> At times knowledge can be seen as the source of organizational innovation and change – at other times, however, it can be the very constraint on that change.
>
> (Hargadon and Fanelli 2002, p. 290)

> Glorification of exploration obscures the fact that most new ideas are bad ones, most changes are detrimental, and most original inventions are not worth the effort devoted to producing them.
>
> (March 1994, p. 238)

Creativity and innovation processes often determine how rapidly private and governmental organizations change to survive in an increasingly competitive world. As Schumpeter (1943) classically observed, creative destruction, replacing the old with the new, is a fundamental component of capitalist economic systems. A stagnant organization that cannot react to evolving environmental conditions will eventually find itself no longer competitive in an increasingly complex and technologically sophisticated economy. Economic prosperity increasingly depends on the development of new products and services. Innovation may be the ultimate service provided by KM organizations. Indeed knowledge is often seen as the primary driver of innovation (e.g., Amidon and Mahdjoubi 2003; Anand, Gardner, and Morris 2007; Nonaka and Takeuchi 1995; Swan 2003). The development of knowledge lays the groundwork for new action that may allow organizations to compete and adapt more effectively (Hargadon and Fanelli 2002).

However, in practice, creativity and innovation pose numerous challenges for organizations and in the end prove to be very difficult tasks indeed. It has been estimated that 90 percent of new ideas stop at the idea generator, only 3 percent develop the internal backing to become significant projects, and only 0.3 percent achieve commercial success (Howell 2005). Similarly, non-profit organizations have found that it is very difficult to disseminate and implement proven practices, much to the consternation of policy makers, as Box 9.1, on clinical and translational science, demonstrates.

It has become widely recognized in the literature that most approaches have a pro-innovation bias (Rogers 1995), partly because of underlying cultural beliefs in progress through technology. All of us, especially in our personal technological purchases (for example, Betamax VCRs), increasingly realize that early adoption can be risky and, at the very least, it is sometimes cheaper (for example, personal computers) to wait to adopt innovations. There are also real organizational costs to innovations: wasting resources on inappropriate technology, constant uncertainty resulting from perpetual change, lowered morale from unsuccessful adoption efforts, to name but a few. Implicit in most KM approaches is a return to a more optimistic view of the impacts of innovations on organizations and societies (MacMorrow 2001).

Distinguishing creativity and innovation

Creativity refers to the capacity to produce new ideas, with the additional implication in organizations that they must be of value in some way (Agrell and Gustafson 1996). We can also distinguish between creative processes and creative results, with innovations usually reflecting the latter. A focus on process also results in an emphasis on social, sense-making factors implicit in modern approaches to creativity (Drazin, Glynn, and Kazanjian 1999). The social side of creativity has been of increasing interest, especially in terms of arranging for diverse inputs in KN (Perry-Smith and Shalley 2003), that are often seen as an essential precondition for creativity (Joshi 2006). Invention implies a creative process that suggests bringing something new into being, although some question whether this is really possible, i.e., whether there is really anything new under the sun (Burt 2004, 2005). For management, creativity may be less of a critical issue than insuring that good ideas, regardless of their novelty, are successfully implemented. Innovation, on the other hand, implies bringing something perceived as new into use in a different context (Rogers 1995). More recent research also suggests that innovation is more fluid and interactive than earlier linear stage models suggested (Ferlie et al. 2005). It can be related to: (1) a product or service; (2) a production process; (3) organizational structure; (4) people; and (5) policy (Zaltman, Duncan, and Holbek 1973).

One of the central issues in the organizational innovation literature is the different types of structure necessary for different outcomes, something we discussed in greater detail in Chapter 5. For example, at different phases of the innovation process, different structures may be emphasized. Zaltman, Duncan, and Holbek (1973) have argued that organizations need one type of structure to

Box 9.1. Clinical and translational science

One of the most exciting recent developments in creativity and innovation research is the growing focus of the National Institutes of Health (2006), in part responding to Congressional pressure, on translational and dissemination research, which essentially encompasses the classic creation, transfer, and implementation framework we discuss in this chapter. The central issue for policy makers is that, while there has been an explosion of knowledge in the laboratory, very little gets translated into clinical practice and even less is widely and faithfully implemented (Bradley *et al.* 2004). So, what we know is not changing what we do, so producing troubling returns on investment for research. This is part of a more widespread problem that is generic to most organizations, with effective practices developed in one division seldom being spread to another (Dearing 2006; Szulanski 2003).

The evidence for widespread dissemination of effective practices is discouraging in health (Green and Seifert 2005; Klesges *et al.* 2005; Orleans 2005) and more general managerial settings (Szulanski 2003). It has been suggested that it takes an average of seventeen years for even a fraction of efficacious treatments to move into practice (Glasgow, Marcus *et al.* 2004). This is especially worrying because of the deterioration of clinicians' knowledge after they graduate (West *et al.* 1999). Much research has been done over the years, and very expensive interventions developed, that have little chance of actually being implemented in practice (Glasgow, Klesges *et al.* 2004; Johnson 2005; Klesges *et al.* 2005).

An interesting exemplar of an approach to these issues for health behavior interventions is the RE-AIM Framework developed by Glasgow and his colleagues (Glasgow, Klesges *et al.* 2004; Glasgow, Lichtenstein, and Marcus 2003; Glasgow, Marcus *et al.* 2004; Glasgow, Vogt, and Boles 1999; Green and Glasgow 2006; Klesges *et al.* 2005) (www.re-aim.org). Essentially this approach proposes that translation and public health impact is best evaluated along the following five dimensions: reach into target population, efficacy or effectiveness, adoption, implementation, and maintenance. This constitutes a relatively long-linked chain, with probabilities of success at each stage relatively slight, suggesting that the ultimate end-result is unlikely to be successful (Glasgow, Vogt, and Bowles 1999).

There seems to be an implicit assumption in most settings that if you build it they will come, and that if you make a better mousetrap it will be widely adopted. Thus, little attention (and fewer resources) is given to subsequent diffusion of ideas (Glasgow, Marcus *et al.* 2004). No one, especially the original researchers, has a clear responsibility for dissemination (Glasgow, Marcus *et al.* 2004; Johnson 2005) and little formal research, at least in health care settings, has focused on implementation (Oldenburg *et al.* 1999), the costs of which may outweigh the benefits of the intervention (Grimshaw *et al.* 2004). As we have seen there is often considerable inertia in social settings; resistance to new ideas; concern over diminishment of one's autonomy, personal judgment, and creativity associated with professions; and an unwillingness to adopt good ideas developed by others since that often reduces one's own status (think of researchers in academe). Especially important in medical settings, particularly private practice, is push-back from patients (Freeman and Sweeney 2001).

The NIH initiatives fit in with a growing, more general interest in translation science which focuses on "how evidence-based practices, programs, and policies can best be communicated for adaptation by practitioners in a societal sector for the benefit of their constituents" (Dearing 2006, p. 3). This is more specialized than the classic diffusion study since it focuses on evidence-based practices, is predictive and interventionist, targets practitioners, and draws on a wide array of disciplines to encourage spread (Dearing 2006).

Because of the focus on evidence-based practices, an important element of efforts in this area is a focus on fidelity (Glasgow, Klesges *et al.* 2004), since seldom are interventions adopted or implemented exactly as they were originally tested (Green and Glasgow 2006), which plays havoc with evidence-based approaches. Effect fidelity relates to the ability of an intervention to achieve the same effects across multiple contexts. This directly relates to the external validity of tests of a program. Implementation fidelity relates to the exact replication of a program across multiple settings (Dearing 2006). This aspect of fidelity directly conflicts with reinvention and the exercise of creativity and professional judgment by the adopting unit; it also fails to recognize that highly motivated, even dogmatic, recipients are likely to change the nature of interventions in their search for efficacious practices (Szulanski 2003). Some modifications may be absolutely essential for translating a practice to a new context; the question is one of balance and whether or not the core of what worked in the intervention is preserved (Green and Glasgow 2006). Of course, all this is further complicated by best practices often being a moving target (Szulanski 2003). Some have suggested that working on basic contextual factors (e.g., assuring appropriate levels of training and resources), while preserving the intervention, may be the best approach (Elliot and Mihalic 2004).

generate ideas (low formalization, decentralization, and high complexity), which reflects the market-driven forces necessary for informally generated ideas, while the opposite arrangement is needed for their effective implementation. So, implementation requires high formalization, centralization, and low complexity, the sorts of structural characteristic of classic bureaucracies. These very conditions also reflect the general historical trend of research studies related to innovation. In the 1960s and 1970s researchers focused on formal approaches and the implementation of innovation sanctioned by top management (Rogers 1983).

Table 9.1. *KN and creation, transfer, and implementation*

Network concept	Stage		
	Creation	*Transfer*	*Implementation*
Content	Tacit	Mix	Explicit
Key relational issue	Novelty	Contagion	Influence
Homophily	Low	Brokered	High
Multiplexity	Low	Low	High
Differentiation	High	Moderate	Low
Integration	Low	Weak ties	High

More recently, research has focused on more informal approaches and coalition building and teams, the social side of creativity.

In this chapter we will focus on three closely interrelated issues: first, the development of seemingly new ideas, especially in terms of the role of KN in creativity; second, the diffusion, dissemination, and/or transfer of these ideas across and within organizations, perhaps the critical function of KN, leading to their eventual adoption; and, finally, implementation of these ideas, which has typically been the focus of innovation research in organizations. We will use Table 9.1 as a touchstone for our discussion throughout the chapter. It relates each of these stages to key network concepts. As this table indicates, the chapter focuses on network concepts such as redundancy, social contagion and influence, homophily, multiplixity, differentiation, and integration, which we have discussed in greater detail elsewhere.

Somewhat similarly and more concretely, Table 9.2 reveals the often paradoxical and conflicting imperatives related to linkage patterns at each of the stages, which again will be amplified in the sections that follow. For example, while strong direct ties have compelling advantages for influence, the transfer of tacit knowledge, and potential spillover effects for resource sharing, they are costly to maintain and redundant, especially so with regard to the opportunity costs of reducing the number of weak ties we might have. On the other hand, indirect ties allow us to experiment and scan our environment widely for information, but they lead to difficulty transferring that knowledge – the classic search transfer problem identified by Hansen (1999). There also may be interaction, and potential substitution effects, between these types of tie, with interesting questions concerning whether, for example, the transfer of explicit codified knowledge entails that many indirect ties (which are easier to maintain) may be more beneficial than a few intensive direct ties (Ahuja 2000). Similarly, uniplexity, or a narrow focus, facilitates information sharing by making it more likely a common perspective will develop (Mohrman, Tenkasi, and Mohrman 2003). Social contexts of relatively dense ties with redundant others can inhibit creativity, but they also build trust and cooperation while aiding tacit transfer of knowledge, and influence

Table 9.2. *Linkage patterns for creation, transfer, and implementation*

	Stage		
Linkage pattern	*Creation*	*Transfer*	*Implementation*
Strong/direct ties	High conformity costs	Critical for tacit	Necessary for influence
Weak/indirect ties	Needed for new ideas	Aid diffusion	May increase resistance
Density	Inhibits	Aids tacit	Facilitates influence attempts
Brokerage	Facilitating	Critical role	Hand-off

attempts related to innovation implementation. They also establish the need for particular types of brokerage between locally dense groupings.

Creativity

> ... the development of knowledge may depend on maintaining an influx of the naive and ignorant, and ... competitive victory does not reliably go to the properly educated.   (March 1991, p. 86)

> The organizations producing more innovations have more complex structures that link people in multiple ways and encourage them to "do what needs to be done" within strategically guided limits ...   (Kanter 1988, p. 95)

While most early work on creativity has focused on unique individual attributes, here we will focus on structural features that promote (e.g., climate – especially related to risk-taking – existing knowledge/know-how, size, tenure, diversity, complex/challenging jobs, and supportive/noncontrolling supervision) and inhibit (e.g., bureaucracy, centralization, and formalization) creativity at the group and organizational level (Agrell and Gustafson 1996; Drazin, Glynn, and Kazanjian 1999; Kratzer, Leenders, and van Engelen 2004; Oldham and Cummings 1996; Smith, Collins, and Clark 2005). The initiation of innovations in organizations is more likely to occur in an internal environment where: people have easy access to information; there are permeable boundaries between organizational units; there are rewards for sharing, seeking, and utilizing new information; there are rewards for risk taking, accepting, and adapting to change, and the organization encourages its members to be mobile and to develop interpersonal contacts (Goldhar, Bragaw, and Schwartz 1976).

Most importantly for our story, particular network structures have been seen to facilitate creative action (Ford 1996), with communication explaining a substantial amount of the variance in the creative performance of innovation teams (Kratzer, Leenders, and van Engelen 2004). Highly redundant linkages impair creativity, in part because clique members have the same knowledge base, which results in similar world-views. Non-redundant linkages have often been associated with weak ties and the spread of novel information in social systems. In highly differentiated networks, weak ties are critical for the diffusion of innovations (Valente 1995). There is also a continuum of learning effects from the most rudimentary to the most complex that entail different network capabilities: information sharing, knowledge sharing, knowledge combination, and, finally, self-design, where newly combined knowledge yields a new practice that is embodied in a shared schema (Mohrman, Tenkasi, and Mohrman 2003).

Generally it has been argued that diversity in perspective is a necessary precondition for creativity (Albrecht and Hall 1989; Leonard 2006) or novel output (Taylor and Greve 2006). Diversity is a multifaceted construct, including professional training (Drazin, Glynn, and Kazanjian 1999), tenure, demographics, and function, which have all been related to creativity (Agrell and Gustafson 1996). Thus, group size has been positively related to creativity, in part because it increases the potential diversity of stimuli to which an individual is exposed (Agrell and Gustafson 1996). Individuals with many weak ties are exposed to information from a variety of sources. They are likely to perceive that they work in an innovative environment and be exposed to innovation-related knowledge. Information from diverse sources gives unique perspectives and is thus often a source of creative ideas (see Table 9.1). The most common source of new product ideas is users and clients (Leonard 2006), a form of weak tie not subject to formal influence.

At its heart, creativity often means combining old ideas into new patterns; the mechanism by which this is accomplished, the generative motor, lies in KN. Creativity, almost by definition, represents a new perspective on things; clearly, being in touch with different cohesive groups, perhaps through non-redundant and/or weak ties (Perry-Smith 2006; Perry-Smith and Shalley 2003), exposes one to different frameworks, leading to the perception of new approaches in a group that has not been so exposed. This results in a central focus on diversity as an essential ingredient for creativity. Creative abrasion, when different perspectives are directly confronted in discourse, can inevitably produce conflicts that managers must anticipate (Leonard 2006), since the very factors that can lead to creative outcomes in groups can also produce personal conflict, ineffective communication, and negative emotional reactions (Levine and Moreland 2004).

Disconcertingly the very factors that promote creativity initially may lead to diminished performance as time goes on. So, a number of factors inherent in diverse groups also serve as barriers to their developing creative products. For example, the lack of a common language/ vocabulary often impedes creative performance (Kratzer, Leenders, and van Engelen 2004). Lack of perceived similarity, in turn, is a major stumbling block for the exchange of information between diverse parties essential to creativity (Kanter 1988). In addition, group size is inevitably associated with the development of coalitions. However, the breaking up of a group into subgroups/coalitions has been found to diminish its creativity, in part because it limits the sharing of diverse perspectives (Kratzer, Leenders, and van Engelen 2004). Increased communication, in part because it results in the development of common perspectives, and tenure, which, in addition to resulting in common perspectives, increases the likelihood of centralization and subgroup formation, have been found to decrease creativity in teams (Kratzer, Leenders, and van Engelen 2004). This may be a rather natural process in large organizations, with the first increments of constraint more deleterious to creativity than any subsequent ones (Burt 2005).

Socially connected members of heterogeneous groups may also be more likely to self-censor their contributions than socially isolated members, with surprisingly low proportions of good ideas being followed through by managers who have them (Burt 2004, 2005). Maintaining dialog in the presence of disagreement, especially strongly held partisan beliefs, is a key element of political processes and has thus received systematic treatment in political science, with many elements being common with those we discuss here (Huckfeldt, Johnson, and Sprague 2004). Processes of self-censorship, especially when one does not hold strong views, are often coupled with false consensus effects, the projection on to others of similar perspectives to one's own, that further impede convergence to commonly held underlying attitudes (Huckfeldt, Johnson, and Sprague 2004). Because of the pressures to uniformity resulting from these processes, peripheral members of organizational networks often have the most creative (or, at the very least, different) perspectives (Perry-Smith and Shalley 2003), especially when this is coupled with ties outside of a social system (Perry-Smith 2006).

There is also some evidence to suggest that individuals can be more effective in combining diverse knowledge than teams, in part because of the social processes involved (Taylor and Greve, 2006). People who bridge structural holes have a "vision advantage" since they are exposed to a wider variety of new ideas earlier than others (Burt 2004, 2005). Somewhat akin to the communication stars explanation we discussed in Chapter 8, it has been found, that a combination of high internal centrality, which may constrain freedom of action, and a large number of external ties, which may be related to larger institutional conformity pressures, may not be the most conducive arrangement for creativity (Perry-Smith and Shalley 2003). Increasingly it is being recognized that there may be an underlying non-linear, inverted U-shaped element to these processes, with some contact (often through small-world processes) being necessary for stimulation, but with too much contact resulting in conformity pressures (Uzzi and Spiro 2005), although work still needs to be done on the contingencies involved for varying industries (Rowley, Behrens, and Krackhardt 2000). Or, stated in a different way, local search and reuse of existing knowledge results in rigidity, while expanding the scope of the search introduces the new, but also may introduce unreliability in organizational outputs (Katila and Ahuja 2002).

Knowledge transfer

> Innovation theory suggests that the close communication linkages among cooperative group members and between scientific communities will allow new ideas to flow easily and rapidly, resulting in a fast rate of innovation adoption . . . In addition, member "homophily" created by shared beliefs and backgrounds should lead to more effective communication of information on cancer control research and a stronger diffusion effect.   (McKinney, Barnsley, and Kaluzny 1992, p. 277)

> Research has shown that social integration is associated with the early adoption of normative innovations.   (Burt 1980, p. 329)

> The three benefits of bridging structural holes can be expected: Access to alternative opinions and practice, early access to new opinion and practice, and an ability to move ideas between groups when there is an advantage to doing so.   (Burt 2005, p. 23)

Network analysis and the literature on the diffusion of innovation have been intimately intertwined for decades. Now, social networking technology is viewed as a key feature of modern business approaches to how knowledge spreads within a company (Cross, Borgatti, and Parker 2003; Waters 2004). Knowledge transfer (also termed diffusion, dissemination, sharing, and adoption) has been a compelling issue in a variety of areas including technology transfer between developed and developing nations, between organizations, and within organizations. Here I will primarily focus on internal organizational transfer, given our focus on intraorganizational KN. Since knowledge transfer among organizational units can provide opportunities for learning, cooperation, and creativity, it has been directly related to organizational innovation (Tsai 2001), as well as to a number of other organizational processes (Reagans and McEvily 2003). To be effective, transfer implies a level of understanding that enables action (Jensen and Meckling 1995). In most of the literature, transfer seems to imply adoption, but as we shall see in the implementation section, bringing an innovation fully into use should never be taken for granted (see also Box 9.1).

Innovation diffusion is ultimately a social process of information seeking and transfer of ideas perceived as new that is a result of the creative processes described in the previous section. Rogers concluded that "in all cases it seems that social systems whose members are more closely linked by communication networks have a stronger diffusion effect and a faster rate of adoption of innovations" (1983, p. 235). Further, someone's positioning within the social structure is particularly important, with Becker (1970), for example, finding for public health officers that their centrality in communication networks was positively related to the adoption of innovations.

A variety of network factors are associated with the diffusion of innovations. The typical scenario for facilitating the adoption of innovations painted in the literature is: (1) identify the opinion leaders of a system; (2) expose them to sources of information they value; (3) increase the prestige value of the innovation;

and (4) reduce the risks associated with adoption (Becker 1970). Later empirical studies have found similar processes at work. First, the more multiplex someone's relationship, the more likely an individual is to be an early adopter (Bach 1989). Second, the more central they are the more likely they are to adopt (Czepiel 1975; Ebadi and Utterback 1984). If early adopters are central, then the diffusion of innovations is more rapid throughout the system (Valente 1995). Third, the more frequent and important their communication the more likely they are to adopt (Ebadi and Utterback 1984). Fourth, the more diverse their communication, the more positive the effects on technical innovation (Ebadi and Utterback 1984). Theoretically, the best description of the processes involved may be contained in the classic attitude change literature associated with influence in social systems.

Development of attitudes

Network analysis has traditionally had great difficulty moving beyond surface content to deeper levels of meaning associated with knowledge (Johnson 1993; Susskind *et al.* 2005). While, as we saw in Chapter 3, much attention has been paid to content in network analysis, the degree to which network members share similar meanings has received somewhat less attention historically, although some of the work on semantic networks touches on this issue (Monge and Contractor 2003) and the distinction made between manifest and latent link properties discussed by Johnson (1993) also addresses it.

Knowledge is the ultimate social construction and some would argue it cannot exist unless it can be shared in ways that eventually result in actions in social systems. In KM, codification and other manifestations of explicit knowledge are the ultimate end states in social networks of what can be a very long process relating to the development of code systems and construction of agreement as to what they refer to. Change is often assumed to be an ideational process implicating awareness, attitudes, and beliefs. As a result, social influence is critical to understanding the underlying dynamics and mechanisms of change (McGrath and Krackhardt 2003).

As we have seen in Chapter 3, over the last several years a major debate has developed about whether direct communication or forces related to competition are the major motive forces for innovation adoption (see Table 9.1). If competitors adopt an innovation and it is successful, this would put another individual at a competitive disadvantage. Thus the other has a structural interest in adopting innovations. This entails that an individual will adopt an innovation when a structurally similar *alter* does, even if they are not in direct communication contact. From this theoretical framework, members of systems may adopt and implement innovations because they perceive there is a competitive advantage *vis-à-vis* others in doing so. An interesting twist to these arguments is that a prominent person may be even more compelled to adopt normative innovations because they want to remain prominent (Burt 1980).

In contrast, a cohesion perspective, perhaps best represented in the work of Rogers and his colleagues (Rogers 1983; Rogers and Kincaid 1981), would suggest that direct communication brings about changes in the individual that result in the adoption of innovations. Thus enthusiastic supporters of an innovation, such as those in communities of practice, may directly communicate with members who were not involved in its development. This enthusiasm is contagious and the members decide to adopt the innovation because of the credibility and persuasiveness of their colleagues.

In sum, both cohesion and structural equivalence approaches to social contagion have been linked to innovation adoption, with the former the traditional approach and the latter offering important new insights (see Table 9.1). More recently it has been argued that they can have complementary effects on knowledge transfer, with cohesion easing it by reducing competitive impediments and tie strength impacting the transfer of tacit knowledge (Reagans and McEvily 2003). Subsequent analysis of the classic Coleman, Katz, and Menzel (1957) tetracycline study, a primary early source of support for cohesion perspectives, suggests that marketing efforts by drug companies were the primary sources of influence, and cohesion actually had very little impact (Van Den Bulte and Lillien 2001), thus reinforcing the importance of mass media as well as interpersonal influence (Valente 2006). This suggests that someone's information fields and (in a more encompassing sense) their structurally equivalent positions within KN may be the primary determinants of diffusion.

The formation of attitudes, and related cohesion processes, in human communication networks has long been a crucial concern in a number of the social sciences and this concern was perhaps the earliest attempt to approach the problem of knowledge development, albeit in a more limited way. Indeed, there have been a number of mathematical models which in essence argue, from a cohesion perspective, that greater amounts of communication result in more attitude similarities within networks. Recently, this intuition has been applied to non-controversial change efforts in exchange networks with trust associated with friendships and shared organizational identities, preventing the often natural withdrawal of organizational members into the self-interest of their cohesive groups (McGrath and Krackhardt 2003).

Traditional discrepancy models of attitude change have received empirical support in a number of contexts (e.g., Danes, Hunter, and Woelfel 1978; Goldberg 1954; Zimbardo 1960), and essentially hypothesize that attitude change is a function of the distance between initial attitudes and the rate of contact between any two communicators, a more formal expression of cohesion arguments. Similarly, especially for non-controversial change, the key structural issue is how to strategically promote the widespread, rapid communication of the underlying notions using structural leverage (McGrath and Krackhardt 2003). Interestingly, these authors also argue that for controversial changes, to reduce the probability of backlash and resulting counterinfluence attempts, it is better to let change unfold, demonstrating its effectiveness, by piloting it at the periphery, before attempting widespread change (McGrath and Krackhardt 2003).

Discrepancy approaches support the notion that if an individual communicates intensively within a group, then, over time, s/he will converge on the group's consensus. However, if the individual has ties outside of the group then her/his attitude will be some linear combination of the proportion of time s/he spends communicating with others and the nature of their disparate attitude positions. Danowski (1980) found some support for these notions in studies of groups within a large eastern US financial institution, although the relationships between group connectivity and member attitude uniformity were somewhat counterintuitive and more complex than expected. One major limiting condition to these processes is the amount of information that an individual already possesses relating to a particular attitude. Woelfel *et al.* (1980) argue that the greater the amount of information which has been previously communicated to an individual, the less the likelihood that future messages can induce attitude change. Huckfeldt, Johnson, and Sprague (2004), while recognizing the inertial, autoregressive force of an individual's existing information base, also suggest that an individual's positioning in low-density networks with ties to others who share their opinions will slow social change and the convergence on similar attitudes.

In organizations, partially because of their differentiation into functional group-ings, individuals within disparate groups will come to adopt unique perspectives often associated with their functions (Lawrence and Lorsch 1967) and their professions, as we saw in Chapter 4. It might be expected that if there were enough ties present between groups, then a whole organization network would eventually come to reflect a common position on a particular attitude (Abelson 1964; French 1956; Huckfeldt, Johnson, and Sprague 2004). The underlying assumptions of this particular perspective have been empirically supported in the work of Albrecht (1979), who found that key communicators were more likely to be cognitively and attitudinally integrated into their organizations. However, recognizing the openness of organizations to communication from other organi-zations, other institutions within the society (e.g., professional associations), and the mass media, it is unlikely that any organization will be isolated enough or long enough lived for the entities within them to come to convergence (Taylor 1968).

Similar arguments can also be advanced in the field of organizational culture. Erickson (1982), while developing arguments from a different conceptual base, especially those related to structural equivalence and related processes of social comparison, has suggested a somewhat similar notion can be found in the devel-opment of the belief systems of individuals in networks. A belief system is an organized diversity of attitudes that can be directly related to notions underlying organizational cultures. Erickson contends that too many ties between groups will result in a commonality of positions, but she offers an interesting twist to the previous arguments. She contends that a moderate amount of ties between divergent groups is likely to result in stronger opposing belief systems, since these groups can now define themselves more clearly in their opposition to other groups.

More recently, work in this general area has focused on semantic networks (Monge and Contractor 2003) and, most evocatively, in the work on Centering Resonance Analysis (CRA), drawing on theoretical developments in social cognitive theory (Corman *et al.* 2002; Kuhn and Corman 2003). This approach focuses on identifying discursively important words and then represents them as a network.

At its heart, CRA focuses on the issue of resonance represented by the common occurrence of words in structurally similar positions in text. Kuhn and Corman's (2003) work focusing on planned change rests on the assumption "that members' interpretations become *homogeneous* over time, due to the social influence carried by communication practices." (p. 200, italics in original). Bridging cognition and action makes social cognitive approaches appealing (Kuhn and Corman 2003). "Examining schemata can show how knowledge is dispersed among actors, as well as how collective knowledge works its way into the construction and reconstruction of their conceptual systems through participation in joint activity . . ." (Kuhn and Corman 2003, p. 199).

Other factors affecting transfer

Of course, other factors have been identified at one time or another as influential in the transfer process. Here I will review a number of them that are particularly influential for the operation of KN. I have crudely lumped them into either barriers or facilitators, but this is primarily because of the relative weight attached to them in discussions in the literature. At times they are one or another; at others they act paradoxically as both.

Barriers

Cultural factors

Strong cultures can severely restrict the content and interactants available to individuals in their KN, but interestingly, because of the increased sophistication of shared understandings, they can enhance its effectiveness. So, strong boundaries between professional groups slow the spread of knowledge and innovations (Ferlie *et al.* 2005). They also can improve efficiency by clearly delineating roles, relationships, and contexts within which individuals seek information.

Broadly speaking then, culture enriches our understanding of any information we gather while it restricts the range of answers we can seek, most obviously by specific rule structures governing the search process (March 1994). In the interpretive perspective of organizational learning, the organization is viewed as a system for giving meaning to data; these meanings are determined by participants in socially constructed processes, hence actions lead to under-standing (Daft and Huber 1987). An example of how culture limits organiza-tional choices is often found in innovation processes related to new technologies (Contractor and Eisenberg 1990). So, cultural factors, and how groups socially construct the use of new technologies, can often limit the effectiveness of group decision-making technologies in organizations (Fulk and Boyd 1991). Infor-mal rules also can significantly restrict the full usage of other technologies designed to enhance information sharing (Zuboff 1988). Organizations often adopt information technologies not for their technical capabilities but for their symbolic value, to demonstrate they are on the cutting edge (Nass and Mason 1990).

Perhaps the most direct assessment of the role that organizational culture plays is in issues related to the compatibility of the innovation with existing values, past experience, and the needs of adopters (Rogers 1983). The more compatible an innovation is along these dimensions the more likely it is to be adopted. So, innovations, such as word processing, are often "sold" to organizations as more efficient replacements for current practice or technology (Johnson and Rice 1987; Yates 2005). It is only later that an organization discovers their truly innovative features.

Integration

Integration, as Lawrence and Lorsch (1967) also argued, can lead to "an indis-criminate increase in connectedness [that] can be a drag on productivity, as people get bogged down in maintaining all their relationships" (Cross, Nohria, and Parker 2004, p. 51). Knowledge transfer can represent a considerable cost to the source, who must bring the recipient up to speed (Reagans and McEvily 2003). The difficulty in transferring complex information can lead to frustration on the part of the searching unit, who may in the end say it would have been easier to do this itself (Hansen 1999). Indeed, dense communication within organizations has been found to be related to low production, low morale, and an experience of chaos (Krackhardt 1994).

Kanter (1983) has offered compelling arguments that organizations that are segmented into different functional groups with strong barriers, especially infor-mal rule structures, between them are not going to be capable of generating or diffusing innovations. Thus, the extent to which knowledge is bound to a partic-ular context, its stickiness, also will influence diffusion (Hoetker and Agarwal 2007).

However, differentiation is necessary for the synergy essential to the creation of ideas, partly through the creation of requisite variety (Van de Ven 1986), but it also makes it difficult to insure the system-wide consensus necessary for their implementation. However, Hage (1999) has suggested that a complex division of labor is the key overlooked factor in promoting organizational innovation. Unfortunately the differentiation of skills required by complex modern organi-zations makes it increasingly unlikely that differing functional specialties will have similarities in outlooks (Lawrence and Lorsch 1967), which also means there are relatively simple, explicit code systems (for example, numbers) used to communicate across groups in contemporary organizations. Differentiation also entails that implementation is more likely to be successful within the confines of a particular specialized unit, which implies widely varying implementation stories for the same innovation in differing units.

Absorptive capacity

Generally organizations exhibit considerably different learning rates and, as a result, highly differential productivity gains (Argote and Epple 1990). Absorptive capacity reflects the ability to recognize the value of new information, assimilate it, and apply it (Gold, Malhotra, and Segars 2001). It is not enough merely to be exposed to knowledge; one must be able to internalize it, something that directly relates to tacit knowledge. So, both trialability and observability, classic attributes of innovations critical to their diffusion, often imply high levels of tacit knowledge (Leonard 2006). This issue has been raised in different ways in the literature: the presence of hooks, things in one's own experience to which one can attach new knowledge, in Leonard's (2006) term, or stickiness in Szulanski's (1996, 2003) term, evoking images of immobility, inertness, and inimitability.

Stickiness research seeks to address a common managerial frustration, the failure of best practices to spread in an organization (Szulanski 2003), which also directly relates to the case study on clinical and translational science (Box 9.1). One study found that only 13 percent of managers thought their firm was doing a good job of transferring knowledge internally, partly because of internal competitive forces (Hinds and Pfeffer 2003). Szulanski (1996) also discusses retentive capacity or the ability of a recipient to institutionalize and utilize new knowledge as an important factor. Absorptive capacity, as Lane, Koka, and Pathak (2006) demonstrate in their interesting review of the literature on this concept, is probably the one that has captured the most attention.

In their original research Cohen and Levinthal (1989, 1994) sought to explain, from an economic perspective, how R & D laboratories not only generate new knowledge but increase a firm's capacity to identify, assimilate, and exploit existing information. In other words, a firm must invest for the long term in resources that enable it to assimilate new information by expanding its knowledge base so that it can more readily absorb all sorts of information and translate it to actionable knowledge useful for commercial purposes. Several factors can increase the potential for units to have high absorptive capacity: cross-functional interfaces, participation in decision making, and job rotation, while others (e.g., elements of socialization processes) relate to a unit's realized capacity (Jansen, van den Bosch, and Volberda 2005). However, reverse engineering or mere observation of creative, innovative products may not fully capture the underlying tacit knowledge that goes into their production (Uzzi and Spiro 2005). This concept has been extended to represent all of a firm's dynamic capabilities for knowledge creation and utilization (Zahra and George 2002), something we will return to when we discuss strategy in Chapter 10.

Facilitators

A number of factors we have discussed (or will discuss) elsewhere act as facilitators for innovation. So, incentives, even such limited ones as getting credit, since people often do not remember sources of knowledge (Reagans and McEvily 2003), can encourage participation in KN associated with innovation. Proximity is also especially important to the diffusion of innovations (Hägerstrand 1953; Wejnert 2002). High levels of homophily are necessary for tacit knowledge transfer (see Table 9.1) which is why it often must be brokered. Homophilous communicators are also more likely to be willing to accept information (Berscheid 1966) and thus be subject to the greater influence necessary for eventual implementation. Multiplexity, which was discussed in greater detail in Chapter 3, obviously has direct connections to homophily. High levels of multiplexity promote deep relations of the sort necessary for tacit knowledge transfer (see Table 9.1), but it also increases density. Dense ties in social groups both limit the ties of members outside the group and the absorption of innovative external information (Oh, Labianca, and Chung 2006). In this section we will focus in more detail on trust, brokerage, and critical mass as critical facilitators to KN transfer.

Trust

Trust is especially important in spreading tacit knowledge because of its often private character (Reagans and McEvily 2003). Trust is a leap of faith, committing oneself to action before one fully knows the outcome. Network closure makes it safe to trust since there are consequences for misbehavior (Burt 2005). Trust emerges in reciprocal relationships, with reciprocity norms encouraging the symmetrical relations needed to clarify new knowledge (Schulz 2001). Relational and identity-based trust have been argued to be particularly important for communities of practice (Ford 2003) and may be a key ingredient of benevolence-based trust in Lesser and Prusak terms (cited in Levin *et al.* 2004). They also identify another key dimension of trust, based on another's competence.

Brokerage

Change agents and opinion leaders are the natural leverage points of change (McGrath and Krackhardt 2003), as are external brokers, as Box 9.2 details. Burt (2004) suggests there are four levels of brokerage associated with the dissemination of good ideas. First, and simplest, is just to make the differing sides of a structural hole aware of the interests and difficulties of the other group. Second, is to transfer best practices across the hole. Third, is to draw at first seemingly irrelevant analogies to the way differing groups behave, thus suggesting new ways of approaching old problems. Fourth, is to engage in true synthesis. In sum, "brokerage increases the risk of having a good idea" (Burt 2004, p. 359).

Box 9.2. External brokers

As we have seen there are numerous problems with transferring information within organizations, with internal linking roles such as SHB, liaisons, and bridges critical to these processes. These internal brokers are limited in various ways (e.g., distrust of motives of someone in another division) and often have multiple roles that mean they cannot focus on the transfer of information, which can often take heroic efforts, especially to effect change. To deal with this problem (and in recognition of an interesting opportunity) external organizations and agents have recognized that they can facilitate the transfer of information within an organization by operating as a liaison between two internal members while serving as a representative of a third party. The many manifestations (e.g., salespeople, consultants, directors of professional organizations, journalists, and so on) of this role provide an indication of how great the unmet need is in most organizations. It also points to the clear role of incentives in information transfer.

There are a number of these brokers in the medical arena, which sometimes has whole institutions and/or professional specialties focusing on this role. So, an initial impetus for the development of the Cancer Information Service was a recognition that up-to-date treatment information related to cancer was not diffusing rapidly. It was thought that by providing information to patients directly they could in effect educate members of the medical community about what treatment they needed (Johnson 2005). Because modern patient care is so fragmented and hand-offs of patients so problematic, patients and their families, are often thrust into these roles by default (Gittell and Weiss 2004; Groopman 2007).

As the classic tetracycline diffusion studies demonstrate, detail persons (drug salesmen) can play this role within a medical community (Burt 1987; Coleman, Katz, and Menzel 1957). These detail people often purposively manipulate the internal network of a hospital to achieve their end of facilitating diffusion of a new drug. Groopman (2007) describes an example where pressure was applied to a doctor to adopt a new drug by a physician who was identified as an opinion leader by the detail person. This physician attempted to use his informal influence (and often in these cases there is formal influence) to shape the other doctor's clinical judgment. But, this sort of influence may be critical to change, since there is well-known inertia and a limited array of drugs used in physicians' prescribing behavior (Groopman 2007).

On a larger scale, consulting, accounting, and design firms can serve this information transfer function for their clients. A prime example is IDEO, the award-winning product design firm, whose influence spans many industries (Hargadon and Sutton 1997). Because of their unique position, they can take ideas developed elsewhere and transfer them to entirely new settings. They create new products from the existing knowledge of disparate industries. Based on their work with this firm Hargadon and Sutton (1997) developed a four-step model of technology brokering: access to ideas, which IDEO's unique structural positioning highlights; acquisition of information by organizational routines; storage of this information into some form of organizational memory for future use; and, finally, retrieval. They point to the critical role of the transformation and combination of ideas through brokerage as having a determinative effect on innovation, and stress "the value not of invention but of inventive combination" (Hargadon and Sutton 1997, p. 748).

Organizations are increasingly realizing that their customers and clients can serve in this role and are engaging in more systematic efforts to incorporate their perspectives in the development of new products and/or applications for existing ones.

Threshold and critical mass

Valente (1995) in his systematic review of the literature on the diffusion of innovations adds threshold and critical mass as central generating mechanisms to diffusion processes. Threshold models of collective behavior suggest that individuals engage in behaviors when a sufficient proportion of others do, with individual thresholds varying. These thresholds also play a critical role in information cascades; they are, in effect, tipping points that cause widespread changes in social systems (Watts 2002). Critical mass represents the number of individuals needed before an innovation can spread to others. One problem for the diffusion of communication technologies is that a certain number of users is required to make them useful, a key factor in the diffusion of social networking sites. These two variables can interact with each other, since once an individual adopts an innovation it lowers other thresholds because of decreased risk. The more individuals who adopt, the lower the levels of risk, setting in motion a snowball effect (Watts 2002). In general, informal coalition building is critical to the development of innovation processes (Albrecht and Hall 1989; Kanter 1983), if for no other reason than some innovations, such as electronic messaging, need a substantial number of adopters for successful implementation (Rice *et al.* 1988), the topic to which we now turn.

Implementation

As specified in Table 9.2, implementation often requires a focus on strong, direct ties that lead to repetition and two-way communication. This promotes the possibilities of reinvention and interpretation, and extrapolation to local circumstances (Tenkasi and Chesmore 2003). However, traditionally research has focused on implementation by management of innovations through formal channels, rather than the informal communication processes that are linked to the initiation of innovations (Kanter 1983). Formally generated innovations are ones originating in upper management, using the traditional authority structure as the primary impetus underlying adoption. This is a unique feature of innovation within organizations; an entity of higher status and authority can decide to adopt an innovation that another segment of the organization must implement. In organizations the former unit has been termed the "adoption unit" and the process as a whole has been called "authority innovation decision" (Rogers and Shoemaker 1971). Formal networks can fail in organizational change efforts on two counts: they focus on information sharing within existing frameworks and they rely on proscriptive commands (Mohrman, Tenkasi, and Mohrman 2003).

Considerable research attention in the 1960s and 1970s was devoted to the relationship between formal structure and innovations, with a disheartening array of mixed findings. For example, the contradictory findings related to organizational size and innovation have been attributed to two offsetting processes. While size increases occupational diversity, it stifles innovation through the institution of more bureaucratic controls (Daft 1978; Kim 1980). There does appear to be support, with some cross-cultural verification in Korea, for the hypotheses that complexity and integration are positively related to innovation, and formalization and centralization are negatively related (Kim 1980). Thus adoption of technological innovations is more prevalent in organizations which are large, specialized, functionally differentiated, and decentralized (Kimberly and Evanisko 1981; Rogers 1983), factors which have also been found to relate to innovation adoption by lower-level decision makers in organizations (Moch and Morse 1977).

Successful implementation of an innovation can be conceived of as the routinization, incorporation, and stabilization of the innovation into the ongoing work activity of an organizational unit. For organizations, "the bottom line is implementation (including its institutionalization), and not just the adoption decision" (Rogers and Adhikayra 1979, p. 79). Advocating change necessarily results in increased uncertainty, which can lead to resistance to innovation by adoption units. Communication plays a key role in overcoming resistance, in part by reducing uncertainty. Complexity and risk are elements of uncertainty which are crucial to the ultimate implementation of innovations. Complexity in this context relates to the number of potential alternatives perceived in an innovation adoption. Risk is the perceived consequences to the adoption unit associated with the implementation of an innovation.

Reducing uncertainty is central to processes of innovation within organizations (Fidler and Johnson 1984) and can be a key outcome of KN. Uncertainty is a function of the number of alternatives (complexity), the risks associated with them, and the extent to which an individual can be sure of the alternatives (Johnson 1990). Overcoming perceptions of risk and complexity is crucial to inducing the level of involvement needed for successful innovation (Bennis 1965), since cooperative norms are often essential to the implementation of innovations (Reagans and McEvily 2003). Because new ideas are risky, workers initially share their ideas with members of their immediate network, which can provide the support an individual needs to reach individuals with whom they do not have strong ties (Ray 1987).

The reduction of uncertainty inherent in communication can decrease resistance to innovations, but usually decision units also must exert some degree of power and influence to facilitate implementation. In fact, the communication channels available to transmit the various types of power and information concerning innovations are the primary structural characteristics which affect innovation implementation. The commonly used types of power in organizational settings have different communication costs associated with them and they also result in different levels of involvement in adoption units. These communication costs are determined by the amount of resources expended in the transmission of a message (Farace, Taylor, and Stewart 1978). Some combinations of power, complexity, and risk can overload available channels, creating an upper limit to the capacity of an organization to implement certain innovations (Fidler and Johnson 1984). In more decentralized environments, messages from a wide range of sources may actually be more effective and less costly for an organization than exclusively relying on a top-down approach to innovation (Leonard-Barton and Deschamps 1988). The complexity and perceived risk inherent in innovations interact with types of power to determine the communication costs associated with their implementation.

The perception of risk often is a result of a lack of knowledge concerning the implications of an innovation (Strassman 1959), which necessitates additional information transfer to reduce uncertainty and is related to the point that knowledge transfer is inherently a learning process (Leonard 2006). The more risky the adoption of an innovation, the more likely it is that an adoption unit will be resistant, requiring more rewards or influence attempts on the part of the decision unit before the acquiescence of the adoption unit in its implementation (Zaltman and Duncan 1977). The various types of power used to overcome resistance to innovations are crucial in determining the success of innovative processes generally, since acceptance can be hindered through both passive and active resistance (Zaltman, Duncan, and Holbek 1973).

Complexity also affects the types of power that will be used to promote innovation implementation. For example, the more facets to an innovation, the more actions that have to be rewarded and, somewhat relatedly, the greater the volume of information related to persuasion. Thus the high communication costs of persuasion and sanction – and also, in this case, expert power – increase almost exponentially with greater complexity; however, the communication costs of other types of power increase more linearly because the invocation of these types of power is inherent in the messages concerning innovation (Fidler and Johnson 1984).

Fidler and Johnson (1984) described systematically the consequences of using various types of influence processes in innovation implementation, a key relational issue in Table 9.1. Using the classic framework of French and Raven (1959), they discussed the relatively high communication costs of using sanction and persuasion and the low costs of using legitimate and referent power. They also contrasted the higher levels of involvement induced by classic influence types of power, represented by persuasion, expert, and referent power, with the lower levels of involvement resulting from sanction and legitimate power. Expert power is obviously particularly important for KN and represents some special problems for the person exercising it. If every step leading to a judgment must be explained to the other party, especially in situations of high tacit knowledge, then very high communication costs may be involved. On the other hand, if just a summative answer is needed, its costs may be as low as those of legitimate power. Paradoxically the more an expert needs to explain, the less power they may ultimately have, since they are transferring their basis of influence to the other.

Johnson (1990) tested a model of the effects of persuasiveness, salience, and uncertainty on participation in innovations. This research focused on the role of informal communication channels in the transmission of influence attempts related to a new component of an existing program. It examined the initial stages of the development of innovations at lower levels in an organization. The communication channel typically used in this phase is primarily interpersonal, and these subformal channels reflect the informal authority structure of an organization (Downs 1967). Typically these more personal channels are more likely to be effective, since they meet the specific needs and questions of the receivers. This is a consequence of the immediacy of feedback and the situation specificity of the channel. As a result there is an inherent reduction of uncertainty involved in the use of these channels, since they lead to increased understanding of a proposed innovation, which may in part account for the somewhat more moderate impact of uncertainty in the model. Johnson's (1990) model was tested on data gathered from a large financial institution and the results suggested that the classic communicative variable of persuasion had a paramount impact on participation, reinforcing the notion that communication is central to innovative processes within organizations.

Generally, persuasive strategies have been found to be the most effective means of ensuring the successful implementation of innovations, especially highly risky and complex ones. Effective persuasion can best overcome resistance attributable both to lack of understanding and to fear; in addition, the use of persuasion results in a higher level of involvement. The moderately negative path between uncertainty and willingness to participate confirms the view that firms must build in an ethos of risk taking, a system of rewards for accepting and adapting to change, for innovation to prosper (Goldhar, Bragaw, and Schwartz 1976).

For informal channels, persuasion, or influence, is the primary means available to secure participation in an innovation. Persuasion rests on the capacity of an individual to cause changes in another's behavior by the use of more subtle, informal and often cognitively oriented means than those associated with sanction or authority (Fidler and Johnson 1984). In utilizing persuasion an individual communicates evidence, arguments, and a rationale advocating acceptance of an innovative idea and participation in an innovation. Since innovations within large organizations generally are initiated by an idea generator who must convince others to participate (Galbraith 1982), the willingness to participate in innovations is a critical outcome of communication. Since effective persuasion results in greater participation in the implementation of innovations it usually entails less resistance to the eventual implementation of innovations as well and is more likely to insure active involvement. There is a critical difference between effective communication, where each party understands the other, and persuasive communication, where one of them changes their opinion as a result of communication (Huckfeldt, Johnson, and Sprague 2004).

Organizational change

A classic problem in literature in this area relates to the degree and pervasiveness of organizational change embodied in any one effort. At one extreme, one might have a slight change in one organizational process, say different paper for time cards, that impacts very little else; at the other extreme might be an encompassing change in an organization's structure and climate, say moving from a hierarchical framework to a truly virtual, decentralized organization. The latter type of change is probably more aptly covered under the topic of organizational design on which we focused in Chapter 5. It is also a meta-KN type of change, since the flow of knowledge and fundamental network structures would also be implicated. Needless to say this type of change is very disruptive and very difficult to accomplish, in part because of the forces of inertia reinforced by the routines embodied in structure, but also because of the seemingly inevitable (and often rapid) development of centralized, differentiated structures that we discussed earlier in this chapter. It also evokes the classic knowledge transfer paradox, since fundamental change requires a certain level of tacit knowledge to implement, while at the same time introducing a significant learning problem (Tenkasi and Chesmore 2003).

In one of the rare systematic studies in this area, Mohrman, Tenkasi, and Mohrman (2003) used a grounded theory approach to examining such changes in eight organizations. Fundamentally these types of change represent sensemaking challenges that networks facilitate through both influence, which we discussed earlier, and organizational learning and resulting adaptation. They found that informal networks supplanting the traditional organizational hierarchy were critical to the successful implementation of fundamental organizational change efforts. These networks enabled organizational learning of new schemata in local units. In the successful organization, they represented a mix of system-wide and local learning: strong and weak ties that were both external and internal and across system levels were present. The networks facilitated implementation by sharing information, by providing capabilities to exchange and combine knowledge, and by enabling local self-design of new approaches representing new understandings and schemata.

All of this also points to the importance of paradoxes, the complex contingencies involved, with real difficulty in predicting end states. So, while diversity is directly related to creativity, it also is inversely related to the implementation of new ideas (Agrell and Gustafson 1996). Similarly, the breadth of someone's linkages might serve to provide an individual with a variety of information sources, as well as repetition of certain effects, which determine such contagion-related processes as attitude change. Thus there is the high relationship posited between multiplexity and implementation in Table 9.1 (Foray 2001). Conversely, low levels of multiplexity are associated with the creativity and the diffusion processes associated with adoption. Interestingly the balance needed between cohesion within groups, associated with high levels of work interdependence and associated cooperation, and the structural holes that need to be bridged by managers through weak ties, often determine the relative adaptability of organizations to change (Gargiulo and Benassi 2000). All this leads also to perhaps the ultimate paradox: the more people communicate, the more they converge on a common attitude, the less creative (different) the organization is. However, while cohesion limits creativity, it aids the spread and transfer of knowledge.

The key problem, then, for managers is to find a balance among these paradoxical forces in their design decisions (see Box 9.3). So connections should be neither too close nor too far, with a Miller, Fern, and Cardinal (2007) study suggesting that interdivisional knowledge is more likely to lead to an impact of an invention on a firm's subsequent technological developments than intradivisional or extrafirm searching and transferring. Interestingly, March (1991) demonstrates that in closed systems, as organizations become more knowledgeable and eliminate differences in understanding codes, they converge on equilibrium beliefs (that may or may not be accurate). Higher learning rates, somewhat disconcertingly, lead to achieving this equilibrium earlier. They also can produce "competency traps" where, because of initial success, teams quickly converge on limited courses of action and are unwilling to consider new approaches (Taylor and Greve 2006).

"Slow learning on the part of individuals maintains diversity longer, thereby providing the exploration that allows the knowledge found in organizational codes to improve" (March 1991, p. 76). This slow learning is facilitated by heterogeneity and greater specialization and the high communication costs associated with truly sharing diverse perspectives in groups (Taylor and Greve 2006). Similarly, in a turbulent environment, a moderate level of turnover, coupled with slow socialization (which permits an opportunity for the organization to learn from individuals) slows the development of an equilibrium that is not an adaptive one. All of this suggests the delicate, temporal challenges for organizations which wish to maintain diversity and the importance of processes that lead to uniformity of attitudes and behaviors and higher productivity (Balkundi and Harrison 2006).

Box 9.3. Designing for innovation

The big payoff of this approach is that by understanding how individuals search socially, we can hope to design more effective *procedures* by which robust organizations can be constructed without having to specify the precise details of the organizational architecture itself.   (Watts 2003, p. 289, italics in original)

Organizing to support the generation of new ideas is not hard. Research universities provide the model. Get bright, curious people together, give them time and resources and minimal direction, let them communicate with other smart people who will both share thoughts and subject ideas to rigorous examination, and make sure that the people whose ideas are judged best are rewarded in a way they value (not necessarily with lots of money!).   (Roberts 2004, pp. 253–254).

At different phases of the innovation process different types of structures are necessary for different outcomes. Formal structures can bar innovativeness within the organization if they are too rigid and confining. Hierarchical structures also interact with a sequential, linear view of innovation processes in organizations to further retard their development (Bush and Frohman 1991). Thus more formal organizations do not promote the level of flexibility necessary for individuals to initiate innovations and to allow for the collaborative relationships across hierarchical and functional relationships that insure successful completion of projects.

Kanter (1983) has offered compelling arguments that organizations which are segmented into different functional groups with strong barriers, especially with informal rule structures between them, are not going to be capable of generating or diffusing innovations. Differentiation is necessary for the synergy essential to the creation of ideas, but it also makes it difficult to insure the consensus necessary for their implementation. In this regard it is important that two distinctions be made when discussing innovation in organizations. First, innovation processes often need to be considered separately from the operating side of the organization (Galbraith 1982). Second, the rule structures governing the initiation of innovations may be considerably different from those governing their implementation (Rogers 1983; Rogers and Agarwala Rogers 1976).

Thus a balance must be reached between efficiency, which results from highly constrained systems, and effectiveness. While it is important to reduce information load, for example, it is also important to allow some leakage between units, so that new ideas and perspectives can be brought to problems. Total segmentation of an organization into isolated work groups may be just as harmful as no segmentation (Kanter 1983). Zaltman, Duncan, and Holbek (1973) have argued that organizations need a particular type of structure to generate ideas (low formalization, decentralization, and high complexity), which reflects the market-driven forces necessary for informally generated innovations. Market conceptions of networks may be especially useful for more qualitative information exchanges based on expert knowledge or ideas; they also create incentives for learning and the dissemination of information that promotes the quick translation of ideas into action (Powell 1990). This is also reflected in the work of Aiken and Hage (1971) that suggests that organic organizations, with decentralized decision making, many occupations, slack resources, and a history of innovation are more likely to be innovative. However, implementation requires high formalization, centralization, and low complexity.

Accomplishing both innovation and productivity poses a difficult problem for an organization since the two appear to require different structures (Kanter 1983). Some organizations choose to emphasize either innovation or productivity, recognizing the inherent difficulties in trying to accomplish both. For example, organizational efficiency can be improved not by producing more information, but by reducing the amount of information any one subsystem must handle (Johnson and Rice 1987). However, this strategy will be very deleterious to the development of innovations within the organization. In addition, Hage and Aiken (1970) have argued that the greater the emphasis on efficiency, the slower the rate of change. Some organizations try to "buy" their way out of this problem by acquiring innovative firms, but eventually they are faced with the same coordination–autonomy dilemma when these firms are grafted onto the existing structure (Puranam, Singh, and Zollo 2006).

Another strategy that many organizations adopt is to compartmentalize these processes, with very rigid structures in production processes and more flexible ones in R & D labs. The ignorance resulting from this sort of compartmentalization is often essential to the maintenance of system equilibrium. However, there have been very successful labs following this model, such as Xerox's Palo Alto Research Center, that produced wonderful ideas through exploration and that were exploited not by the host organization, but by other firms. At some level, at higher management's in this case, someone must multitask, combining both exploration and exploitation (Roberts 2004).

Combinations of structural dimensions can also be used to achieve synergies. For example, the old Bell Laboratories and other divisions of the Bell System used differing design elements to achieve appropriate levels of interdependence. So, application-related development was organizationally linked to more fundamental research, but spatially removed from it, while it was organizationally separated from engineering, but spatially proximate. This insured the proper mix of coordination between these units that a focus on one or the other would not have achieved (Morton 1971). Allen (1977) noted a similar phenomenon in R & D laboratories he investigated, finding that organizational members tended to communicate with those with whom they were formally grouped, but that this separation could be ameliorated by spatial designs.

However, although there is no research evidence to speak to this point, the most effective strategy in the long term may be to try to adopt a dynamic synergism between two differing structures, which sometimes overlap in messy and troublesome ways. In this regard, organizational incongruence may be related to overall organizational effectiveness, since it may establish the creative tension necessary to move to more productive organizational systems (Fry and Smith 1987).

More market-driven relationships may be a partial answer to this dilemma. This is an argument that is borne out by the research evidence that suggests individuals in liaison positions in informal networks are more productive (Downs, Clampitt, and Pfeiffer 1988) and also more innovative (Reynolds and Johnson 1982). Watts (2003) has suggested that when managers become overburdened in ambiguous environments it is best for them to delegate problem solving to their subordinates who then can conduct their own directed searches for information. After many such searches a new structure may emerge that instantiates these many repeated searches and embodies local wisdom resulting from trial and error. Somehow organizations must achieve a balance between stability and flexibility (Weick 1969); how to strike that balance, and resolve this dilemma, is still very much open to question.

Summary

In some ways what we have discussed in this chapter represents the conversion of tacit (intuitive) to explicit (manifestly known) knowledge that facilitates widespread action. So someone (or a group) that has a creative idea must develop a means of disseminating it to others that involves at least partial understanding of it, but implementation entails deeper knowledge and more explicit knowledge that can be easily operationalized. In the end, all organizational innovation processes must confront these factors, balancing the everyday press of operational issues against the needs of organizations to adjust to ever-changing environmental circumstances (Van de Ven 1986), with individual coping responses determined by balancing concerns for performance with culturally based normative responses and environmentally induced uncertainties (Lewis and Seibold 1996). Underlying these surface currents is the darker observation that creativity and innovation involve change and thus can trigger substantial countervailing social pressures, since people's lives are intertwined with ideas and there are numerous social interests attached to them.

Further reading

Burt, R. S. 1987. Social contagion and innovation: cohesion versus structural equivalence. *Applied Journal of Psychology*, 92: 1287–1335.

Reanalysis of the classic tetracycline diffusion study, contrasting cohesion and structural equivalence perspectives of social contagion.

Burt, R. S. 2004. Structural holes and good ideas. *American Journal of Sociology*, 110: 349–399.

Extends Burt's project on structural holes to the development and transfer of innovations in organizations.

Damanpour, F. 1991. Organizational innovation: a meta-analysis of effects of determinants and moderators. *Academy of Management Journal*, 34: 555–590.

In a way puts a period on the era of research on the impact of formal indices (e.g., formalization) on innovation.

Huckfeldt, R., Johnson, P. E., and Sprague, J. 2004. *Political Disagreement: The Survival of Diverse Opinions within Communication Networks.* Cambridge University Press.

A political science work focusing on opinion change in society, it describes the general processes of attitude change and their relations to social networks.

Perry-Smith, J. E. 2006. Social yet creative: the role of social relationships in facilitating individual creativity. *Academy of Management Journal*, 49: 85–101.

Perry-Smith, J. E., and Shalley, C. E. 2003. The social side of creativity: a static and dynamic social network perspective. *Academy of Management Review*, 28: 89–106.

These articles represent the most systematic research program coupling network analysis with creativity in organizational settings.

Rogers, E. M. 2003. *Diffusion of Innovations*, 5th edn. Free Press.

The last edition of Everett Rogers's classic work on the diffusion of innovations in a broad array of social settings. While this is one of the most frequently cited works in the social sciences, and it does specifically deal with authority innovation decisions, it has been supplanted in organizational settings by other works that focus on organizations and interorganizational consortia.

Zaltman, G., Duncan, R., and Holbek, J. 1973. *Innovations and Organizations*. Wiley.

Classic early work describing innovation in organizations.

10 Productivity: efficiency and effectiveness

> The major downfall of the network approach is that they are such sparse social structures that it is difficult to see how they can account for what we observe.
> (Fligstein and Mara-drita 1992, p. 20, quoted in Swedberg 1994, p. 270)

> . . . the exact contribution of communication processes towards outcomes is often hard to assess, and the connection is more intuitive than demonstrated or empirically proven.
> (Downs, Clampitt, and Pfeiffer 1988, p. 171)

> . . . the chain of conditions between amount of communication in the workplace and outcomes such as satisfaction, effectiveness, or other effects may be quite lengthy.
> (Zimmerman, Sypher, and Haas 1996, p. 200)

I will use productivity in its broadest sense here, focusing on the generation of wealth in organizations in a variety of forms entailing social as well as economic capital, which also suggests some degree of efficiency and of effectiveness. Since these terms are closely interrelated I will begin with some basic definitional issues. As the colon in the chapter title implies, productivity is a function of both effectiveness and efficiency, with the former term somewhat more difficult to define concretely.

Effectiveness details a desired outcome or result. It therefore implies some degree of rationality, intention, and purpose and could be closely associated in this sense with more functional approaches to organizations. It implies some martialing or matching of organizational outputs to particular goals that here I will discuss primarily in terms of contingency impacts and resource-based views of strategy.

Efficiency is fundamentally concerned with the level of input, particularly in terms of expending the least effort possible (for example, the amount of communication), which is needed to achieve certain outputs. We have at best a fuzzy idea of how much communication is needed to produce certain impacts in organizations (Johnson 2008). However, network analysis, through various linkage metrics, offers many precise and elegant ways (e.g., small world) of specifying the minimum number of linkages needed to contact others (see Box 10.1). Much attention has also been devoted to the efficiency of markets, which we have seen are directly linked to networks conceptually. Efficiency is obviously an important issue for organizations because it allows attention and

Box 10.1. Graphical representations of efficiency and effectiveness

As we saw in Chapter 3 there are a number of indices and graphical representations for various network configurations. In this box we will apply these to some basic issues of efficiency and effectiveness. To do this we will use a small network of seventeen nodes represented in a minimalist configuration in Figure 10.1. This is a highly efficient configuration since the minimum number of linkages is used to insure that everyone is connected, but it is also extremely hierarchical and suggestive of a very flat organizational chart with 1 at the center. As small network studies make clear (Shaw 1971), this might only be effective in a situation where there is a preexisting standardized plan, where everyone has a well-defined role and is engaged in a simple task. Otherwise, 1 would be quickly overloaded with the combination of coordination and problem-solving tasks.

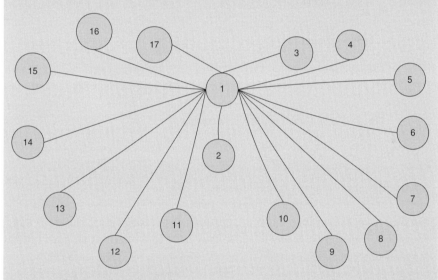

Figure 10.1. *Hierarchy*

In contrast, we could have a chart where everyone is connected to everyone else (Figure 10.2). This might be an effective chart, in the sense that a community could develop that has a high degree of tacit knowledge and the group is highly cohesive, but it is hardly an efficient one because of the highly redundant linkage patterns, which would result in considerable duplication of information.

Between these two extremes lie a number of different ways of approaching problems of efficiency and effectiveness. One, as we have reviewed in a number of ways, is the strategic positioning of individuals who can operate in key network positions revealing weak ties/bridges (10/11), centrality (1), and structural hole brokerage (1,2), all captured in Figure 10.3.

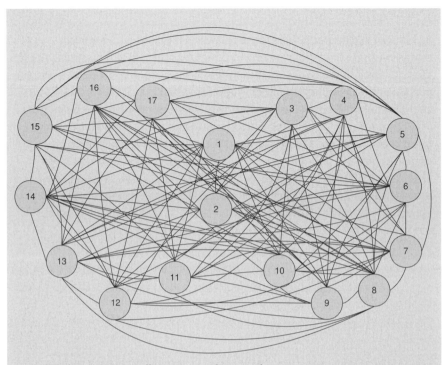

Figure 10.2. *Fully connected network*

As we reviewed in Chapter 3, there are a number of numerical indices that capture different nuances of positioning. As one can easily discern, 1 is the most central individual in this diagram, with direct ties to everyone in the network save 2. Members 2, 10, 11 provide some redundancy, but each has somewhat reduced centrality because they have to work through each other to reach other individuals in the network. Members 10 and 11 are classic bridges in the sense that they are clearly embedded in cohesive groups that do not overlap, but have a weak tie outside of that group that can facilitate knowledge transfer. Members 1 and 2 indicate differing types of brokerage: member 1 is clearly embedded in two apparently different social worlds, while 2 is more of the classic intermediary, who stands apart but acts to solidify the relationship between 10 and 11. While 1 may be more effective, 2's position is clearly more efficient. Another way of looking at these issues is what would happen if these individuals were removed from the system, since they are clearly the linking pins, in Likert's (1967) term, that hold it together, or the "cut points" whose removal fractures the system (Kilduff and Tsai 2003). A critical operational question then is how to repair broken linking pins, since it often takes a long time to develop such relations, and, because of their centrality, how much redundancy should be encouraged.

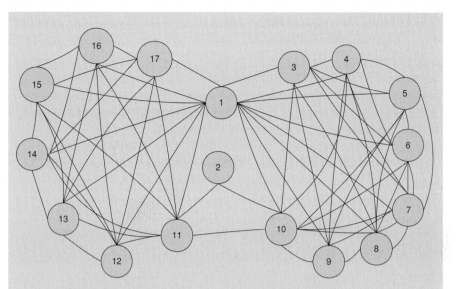

Figure 10.3. *Bridges, structural holes, and weak ties*

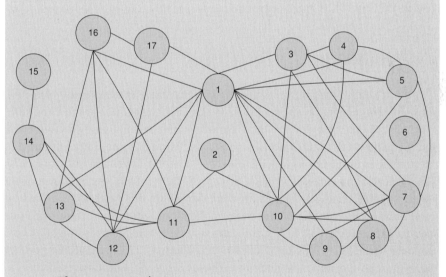

Figure 10.4. *Pathways*

Figure 10.4 captures yet another approach focusing on pathways and small worlds. We discussed pathways in Chapter 3 and they clearly focus on issues surrounding the inclusion of nodes, closure/feedback (such as a cycle or a path that returns to its own starting point), serial replication, speed, redundancy (a key indicator of effectiveness), and efficiency, in terms of the shortest distances between any two nodes. Member 6 in this figure is a pure isolate who receives none of the content in this particular network, a surprisingly common occurrence in empirical network research (Johnson 2005). Member 15 has the most tenuous linkages in this network, needing as few as four linkages to reach others by the most direct path, but as many as eleven by the most indirect. Generally, distance (or the geodesic) is determined by the length of the shortest path connecting two nodes (Scott 2000); however, information may not necessarily spread along the shortest path (Borgatti 2005; Newman 2005). One of the reasons that 1 is the most central is that he or she can reach the most people directly and requires fewer indirect linkages to reach everyone through these intermediaries.

In sum, as these graphs indicate, network depictions of productivity can be particularly rich in describing the operational conditions necessary to achieve certain levels of efficiency.

effort to be more profitably devoted elsewhere. It produces a desired effect for the minimum amount of effort, expense, or waste, or an attractive ratio of effective work outcomes to energy expended.

Productivity

While on the surface it may appear that there is a generally clear link between communication and productivity (Downs, Clampitt, and Pfeiffer 1988), somewhat disconcertingly very little is known about the relationship between KN and productivity (Provan and Milward 2001). This can be partially attributed to the general emphasis of the social sciences on psychological processes, such as attitude formation (Pfeffer 1978, 1982). As a result, much less is known about people's actual behavior than about what they think they will do. This lack of knowledge is also attributable to the complications which soon arise when one tries to explore what at first would appear to be a relatively straightforward outcome variable such as productivity. "Productivity is simultaneously one of the most important and most difficult variables for communication researchers to study" (Downs, Clampitt, and Pfeiffer 1988, p. 173).

However, for the organization and its ultimate survival there is probably no more important issue than productivity. While there is some evidence that communication relates to productivity (Lewis, Cummings, and Long 1982), it is often based on anecdotal data, on case studies, or on limited, one-shot research efforts (Downs and Hain 1982). However, improvements in worker effectiveness offer much potential for improving productivity, since a substantial amount of organizational costs are associated with labor, and thereby linked to communication (Downs and Hain 1982).

How much?

Most communication theories implicitly paint a picture of the prevalence and paramount importance of communication, with some arguing communication is the very essence of the organization, its constitutive element. Systems theories point to the importance of coordination and interdependence, interpretive theories focus on the sharing of perspectives in sense-making activities, discourse theories on the importance of dialog for collective action, and so on. There is also what has been described as a "communication metamyth" that more is better, with organizational members always desiring more communication, especially from formal channels, regardless of how much they were receiving (Zimmerman, Sypher, and Haas 1996).

At one end of the continuum, the communication needed to achieve certain impacts may be so overwhelming that it is foolhardy to even attempt such projects (Fidler and Johnson 1984). However, the empirical work that has been done on actual communication behavior suggests that, especially for innovation-related communication in organizations, people do not talk to each other very much (Johnson 2005, 2006, 2008). In spite of decades of research on organizational communication, we have at best only a fuzzy notion of what "dosage" is needed for particular effects (Johnson 2008). What volume of communication do we need to achieve particular purposes (Farace, Taylor, and Stewart 1978)?

On the receiver's side there has been a concern with impacts of communication overloads (Farace, Monge, and Russell 1977; Fidler and Johnson 1984), but there has not been concomitant interest in underloads and the, perhaps, related topic of ignorance (Johnson 1997a). Because of individual and system overloads, organizations must achieve efficiencies in their internal communication systems by message routing and message summarizing (Daft and Huber 1987; O'Reilly and Pondy 1979) or condensing (Downs 1967). Underload situations and organizational slack increase the opportunities of individuals for knowledge seeking, but it may not be clearly related to organizational objectives. Overload situations may increase the stimulation to seek information, with information junkies likely to seek more, especially for information related to enhanced performance. Some partial attempts have been made to grabble with dosage – contingency approaches to differentiation and integration, repetition, frequency, Zipf's (1949) law – but not an integrated approach. One of the more troubling issues in information seeking is the lack of persistence of information seekers and related issues of accessibility. In short, people do not typically put forward much effort and can easily be deterred by obstacles (Case 2005; Johnson 1996b, 1997a, Johnson *et al.* 2005).

My first research paper focused on the normative level of communication activities in a range of organizational networks (Farace and Johnson 1974). It demonstrated surprisingly low levels of communication generally in organizations. This is a finding that was again confirmed in my recent longitudinal research on innovation within the Cancer Information Service (CIS) (Johnson

2005). While communication has been viewed as central to innovation, surprisingly little communication occurred during the length of this project. It has been my experience that when the CISRC network analysis findings are shared with others that the first reaction is to question the quality of the data. It was partly this sort of response from CIS staff that led to our switch midway through the project to include facsimile and electronic mail communication in the communication logs in an attempt to uncover additional communication related to innovation. In the end, the weight of the evidence was compelling; it may be time to look more carefully at the match between desired outcomes and levels of communication.

Minimalist perspective

Simply put, it could be the case that not much communication is needed to achieve certain effects. In spite of the concerns of persuasion scholars for overcoming resistance, and such shibboleths of communication theory as repetition for getting a message across, in most organizations orders are orders. If my organization says that henceforward all of my communication related to invoices will be by e-mail, as long as the system is minimally intrusive, relatively easy to use, and not personally risky (or there are more risks for not going along), I do what is required of me. In most organizations this sort of compliance may not be difficult to achieve and the communication related to it may be minimal (Fidler and Johnson 1984), especially compared to the winning of hearts and minds assumed by most participation theories (Monge and Miller 1988).

Thus, a key question to be explored in future research is just what "dosage" is needed to achieve particular impacts (Johnson 2008). How many people and what amount of communication is needed to achieve threshold and/or critical mass effects (Watts 2003)? It may be the case that for a number of innovations, minimalist communication strategies, involving some mediated communication and intense interpersonal communication, leading to the development of tacit knowledge and involving only those immediately affected, may be the best approach. Dosage issues related to staging and the management of uncertainty determine how much information is necessary at different points, especially since acquiring more information can result in delays and increase costs (Gales, Porter, and Mansour-Cole 1992). Another twist on these questions is perhaps the most interesting unexplored question in structural analysis – why certain relationships do *not* occur (Johnson 1993).

Structural equivalence

Burt's (1987) introduction of structural equivalence notions to innovation research was perhaps the first systematic attempt to offer an alternative explanation to the classic taken-for-granted assumptions relating to direct interpersonal communication in diffusion theory (Valente 1995). This approach essentially argues that people's positions expose them to information that influences their actions regardless of their direct, cohesive communication with others. In addition, competitive motivations may impel individuals to act to maintain or to gain particular advantages. Through structural equivalence factors, organizational roles often bridge individual and organizational levels (Baldridge and Burnham 1975). From a structural equivalence perspective, it may be the case that *no* cohesive interpersonal communication is required to trigger the appropriate innovation implementation; that, indeed, experience is the best teacher, which directly relates to the development of tacit knowledge.

Tacit understandings

Another way of approaching this problem is through an individual's understanding of the underlying rules of a game. When I am passed the ball in soccer, I may be well drilled in formalized approaches, and see a pattern that activates a play that is implicitly understood by all of the other players. Thus, the high levels of formalization and socialization to professions may minimize the need for direct, interpersonal communication (Van de Ven 1976). Alternatively, I may go with the flow of events, reacting spontaneously, and experience the pleasurable sensation of jamming (Eisenberg 1990), where others react in concert with me and our combined actions achieve our ultimate purpose of scoring a goal. In both of these situations, direct overt communication is not needed; rather, tacit understandings of the rules of the game and what my actions entail within this established framework are what is required to play.

In these situations, the manager may act as a curious combination of coach and umpire, setting the overall rules framework and then making sure that they are followed. This approach also explains how people deal with so many competing task demands: in effect, some players let others carve out their own turf and delegate to them implicitly (or formally through task forces or more informally through communities of practice) the accomplishment of particular tasks. (As long as they have the ball, let them run with it, when they pass it off, then we will see what I do.) So, players do not become involved until they need to act.

Efficiency

Various approaches have been made to determining the efficiency of networks, with most detailing a relationship between the number of links necessary to perform a particular task (see Box 10.1). For example, short path links are better for obtaining knowledge than long ones; they are both more efficient because of fewer links and contain less possibility for distortion and error (Hansen 2002). Efficient networks minimize the number of direct contacts with decision makers; however, it also appears that supervisors will only delegate when overloaded with information (Bolton and Dewatripoint 1994). More formally, graph efficiency is the degree to which the number of links is the minimum necessary to prevent splintering the network into separate parts, the more efficient the more fragile the network (Kilduff and Tsai 2003) – some redundancy is needed for robustness and effectiveness. These latter two findings point to some broader concerns beyond a narrow focus on efficiency levels.

There also has been some attention devoted to the strength of particular links. So weak ties may facilitate search, but impede transfer. However, strong ties are costly to maintain (Hansen 2002); therefore they should be used most for tacit knowledge and other difficult transfer problems. In a study of an online graduate class's one-to-one postings (Russo and Koesten 2005) found that prestige and centrality were robust predictors of cognitive learning. A recent meta-analysis suggests that teams with densely configured interpersonal ties, which result in more information sharing and collaboration, attain their goals better and are more committed to staying together, in spite of the observation that large numbers of direct ties are costly to maintain (Balkundi and Harrison 2006).

Optimal match between structure and performance

The concepts of match, fit, congruence, and contingency have been used loosely in the literature to capture an essential idea related to structures – there is some optimal arrangement of structural elements that promotes the accomplishment of particular functions. For example, Tushman (1978) found in an R & D laboratory that effectiveness was a function of matching communication patterns to the nature of a project's work, particularly at the subunit level (Tushman 1979). Specifically, high-performing research projects needed more intraproject communication than high-performing technical service ones (Tushman 1978).

The idea of match permeates most of the literature related to organizational outcomes and has become a cornerstone of organizational theory, partly in reaction to the overly simplistic focus of classical management theory, which sought to discover *the* one best way of doing things in organizations (Lawrence and Lorsch 1967; Woodward 1965). This notion has been applied to many organizational outcomes: the relationships between differentiation and integration in different environmental circumstances (Lawrence and Lorsch 1967); the congruence between rules (both perceptual and actual) of the two parties in the supervisor–subordinate communication relationship and job satisfaction (Downs, Clampitt, and Pfeiffer 1988); the relationship between organizational strategy and structure (Egelhoff 1982; Fry and Smith 1987); media richness (Daft and Lengel 1986); the relationship between technology and structure (Fry and Smith 1987); and, finally, the match between communication structures and performance in small groups, to which we now turn.

Small-group communication networks

Perhaps more systematic research has been conducted on small-group communication networks than in any other area of research related to structures. The research results related to task performance and structure appear to fit quite well into a contingency theory framework (Lawrence and Lorsch 1967) and the idea of a match between structure and performance.

The experimental situation in small-group network studies (typically five individuals) constrained the written messages that could flow between group members (e.g., Leavitt 1951). The primary distinction was between centralized communication networks, where some individuals were clearly the hub in communication flows and could, in effect, act as gatekeepers for other individuals, and decentralized structures where there was more than one way of routing a message and no one individual dominated. Key men (*sic*) would be likely to be selected as leaders of centralized groups by other members (Leavitt 1951; Shaw 1971). In addition, there was also clear evidence that central members were more satisfied than peripheral ones and that the overall level of satisfaction was higher in decentralized groups (Shaw 1971).

Most of the research studies in this area focused on the performance of groups with different structures in simple and complex tasks. In reviewing this literature Shaw (1971) found clear evidence of a relationship between effectiveness in the performance of particular types of task and the relative degree of centralization of these groups. For simple problems, such as symbol identification, the centralized groups were more efficient in terms of time, sent fewer messages, and made fewer errors. For complex problems, such as sentence construction, decentralized groups took less time and made fewer errors, but they still sent more communication messages.

Shaw (1971) adopts the concept of saturation to explain these findings. For complex problems the most central person quickly becomes overloaded with both information and the burden of relaying information to other group members. When the group is faced with a simple task the volume of communication can be easily handled and there is a benefit to having a central repository of information. However, the independence possible in decentralized groups permits the sharing of the relaying burden of information among group members and it also results in a better "match" of individual capabilities to the problems confronting the group.

Guetskow and Simon (1955), in an interesting twist on these experiments, speculated that one of the reasons centralized groups were more efficient was that they had, in effect, been provided with a plan of action for making decisions. They discovered that if decentralized groups had an opportunity to discuss group organization after they had some experience in the task they became just as efficient as more centralized groups in performing simple tasks. Decentralized groups became more efficient by reducing the number of linkages that were used within the group. Other research studies have also suggested that there is a general trend over time for efficient groups to reduce the number of communication linkages used, to in effect become more structured or to match their structure to the task at hand (Katz and Kahn 1978). Indeed, some have argued that these processes can be generalized to a broad range of systems; that hierarchies are inevitable (Krackhardt 1989; Ahuja and Carley 1999).

Cost/benefit analyses

Work on information seeking has examined issues of effort and the avoidance of information (Case *et al.* 2005). The costs of information acquisition are many: psychological, temporal, and material. Most seekers appear to assume it is better to rely on easily obtained information – they have an answer after all, no matter how dubious – than to spend the effort necessary to get complete information. The "costs" in terms of extra time and effort for a complete information search, which also may result in delaying opportunities, complicating decision making, and increasing information overload, are real. There are also additional psychological costs, such as the loss of self-esteem and frustration, that result from an unsuccessful search (Hudson and Danish 1980). The classic law of "least effort" has been evoked to articulate why channels are chosen first that involve minimal exertion. The earliest expression of this was Zipf's (1949) law, a more general expression of a wide range of human behavior, which suggests that seekers will minimize their efforts, even when it means accepting lower quality content (Bates 2005; Case 2005). A corollary of this law is that people will tend to return to sources that they used in the past. Needless to say, in terms of KN, this suggests the sort of localized, relatively sparse communication structures actually observed in the empirical studies presented at the beginning of this chapter.

More recent work in this area has focused on information foraging (Pirolli and Card 1999), a form of cost/benefit analysis which assumes that humans maximize gains of valuable information per unit cost. Resource costs are the expenditures of time and energy involved in obtaining information. Opportunity costs represent what could have been gained by pursuing other activities. Accordingly, seekers minimize access costs by putting information resources close to themselves; they reduce costs of getting from one patch of information to another; they look for patches that are exceptionally rich in their yield; and they maximize nutritional return in their diet, avoiding "junk food" and paying attention to energy returned vs. handling time. A key issue for this approach is the notion of "picking up scents" that lead to valuable patches, something that may be a key driver in the development of particular patterns in KN, as we shall examine in greater detail in Chapter 12.

Effectiveness

KN effectiveness, or performance, is intimately related to issues of strategy and long-term adaptability to the environment in which a firm is embedded. While there has been little written directly on this topic, there are voluminous literatures on the related topics of the relationship between IT and organizational performance and the importance of interorganizational networks in the strategy literature. While we have focused on similar issues in Chapters 5 and 6 respectively, here we will more directly discuss their impacts on effectiveness.

Resource-based view

Most importantly for our story is the recent emergence of the resource-based view (RBV) school of strategy that has broad implications for KN. For a resource to confer a sustainable competitive advantage it must have value, rareness, inimitability, and non-substitutability (Melville, Kraemer, and Gurbaxani 2004; Pan, Pan, and Hsieh 2006). Resources include both capabilities (e.g., technical and managerial skills and processes such as system development or integration) and assets. Assets are tangible and intangible things used in processes, whereas capabilities are the patterns of use that transform inputs into outputs (Wade and Hulland 2004).

As we have seen in Chapter 8, consortial relationships are particularly difficult to form and sustain, and they are not easily substituted. Similarly, KN in general can have these properties, and if the integration of IT is also included, this triad can provide organizations that invest in them for the long haul with a considerable source of competitive advantage. Tacit knowledge transfer and effective KN may be the ultimate capability/complementarity, since they are not easily duplicated or imitated, they are less mobile (individual job transfers), and they do not lead to equifinal substitutability by other firms. Rarity of resources is the key source of sustained competitive advantage (Wade and Hulland 2004). Indeed, every firm can have resources that are difficult to replicate and that may not be mobile. These internal resources are the key to financial performance, and to the extent they cannot be duplicated, they have the potential to provide sustainable competitive advantage (Kearns and Lederer 2003). (An illustration of this point can be found in the tacit/explicit knowledge communigram of Dazzling discussed in Chapter 3.)

The significance of IT integration cannot be understated. Organizations undertake large investments in IT and these outlays come with considerable risks and benefits. Effective IT integration can be a source of competitive advantage by linking information technologies to organizational goals, enhancing performance and increasing efficiency. However, integration and implementation of IT are not uniform across organizations or even innovations, and the degree of organizational involvement in electronic markets, which can facilitate interorganizational relationships, can influence these processes as well. Interestingly, for interorganizational relationships, the benefits may not be located in specific firms, but in a whole supply chain of relationships (Lorenzoni and Lipparini 1999) and in its benefits ultimately to consumers (Melville, Kraemer, and Gurbuxani 2004).

As we have seen, while the focus of substantial investments, IT has had problematic relationships to profitability, specifically, and organizational performance, more generally (Melville, Kraemer, and Gurbuxani 2004), in part because ITs are imitable. In order to sustain first-mover advantages in IT, firms would need to become perpetual innovators, something that is very difficult to pull off in practice (Wade and Hulland 2004). However, the focus should not be on the technology *per se*, but rather on its impact on knowledge sharing and enhancements in management's knowledge base for decision making (Kearns and Lederer 2003). In an RBV the firm's internal resources are the key predictors of superior financial performance (Kearns and Lederer 2003; Wade and Hulland 2004). And, further, they contribute to its dynamic capabilities to reconfigure internal and external capabilities to adjust to changing environments (Kearns and Lederer 2003; Pan, Pan, and Hsieh 2006). However, information systems rarely contribute to sustained competitive advantage by themselves; they must be a part of a complex chain of assets and capabilities (Mahmood and Mann 2000; Wade and Hulland 2004). They are a necessary, but not sufficient, condition.

Configurational approaches

Configurational approaches to strategy provide a way of more directly assessing complementarities between KN and other organizational processes and their rarity. In general, it has been argued that there are three approaches to organizational phenomena (Ferratt *et al.* 2005; Lee, Miranda, and Kim 2004), which trace well the history of work on technology and productivity:

(1) universalistic: argues that there is a set of best practices across multiple contexts and situations;
(2) contingency: effects of processes on outcomes moderated by a variety of variables, especially those associated with contexts; the work of Lawrence and Lorsch (1967) on differentiation and integration discussed in Chapter 5 is perhaps the best early example of this sort of approach;
(3) configurational: focuses on bundles of attributes that exhibit synergistic, non-linear effects on outcomes.

This focus on commonly occurring clusters of attributes which can be linked to performance (Ketchen, Thomas, and Snow 1993; Lee, Miranda, and Kim 2004) is also linked to the classic system concept of equifinality (Gresov and Drazin 1997), with the adoption of one attribute limiting the adoption of others because of complementarity/fit/gestalt issues. Gestalts are feasible sets of internally consistent configurations, with research findings suggesting that configurational approaches are more predictive of outcomes than the other approaches (Lee, Miranda, and Kim 2004). For example, Andersen and Segars (2001) found that IT-enhancing communication supported a decentralized decision structure that was associated with higher financial performance. Indeed, it may be the case that only really gross differences in structures may make a difference in performance (Dalton *et al.* 1980), and, somewhat akin to catastrophe theory notions, there may be drastic change in organizational performance when certain thresholds are reached. This approach may also provide answers to resolving the many dilemmas and paradoxes posed by KN between differentiation and integration, tacit and explicit knowledge, and so on.

Summary

In recent years communication research has shown a curious tendency to ignore fundamental issues critical to practice. This is certainly the case with productivity, effectiveness, and efficiency issues. Even more troublingly, our comfortable shibboleths do not stand up to close empirical scrutiny. Most communication theories assume that more communication is better and imply that high volumes are beneficial for organizations, but the few studies that have been done suggest, at best, complex contingencies and cost/benefit equations. Some of these contingencies have been specified quite well for small-group research, which has a rich empirical tradition. The picture for efficiency is somewhat more tractable, at least in the sense that there are readily available graphic portrayals and associated indices that can describe it. KN effectiveness is becoming more and more a key element of any organization's strategy, especially in a RBV, with KN capabilities and complementarities a key factor in organizational performance.

Further reading

Downs, C. W., Clampitt, P. G., and Pfeiffer, A. L. 1988. Communication and organizational outcomes. In G. M. Goldhaber and G. A. Barnett (eds.), *Handbook of Organizational Communication*: 171–212. Ablex.
Classic review of organizational communication impacts on productivity.

Farace, R. V., Taylor, J. A., and Stewart, J. P. 1978. Criteria for evaluation of organizational communication effectiveness: review and synthesis. In D. Nimmo (ed.), *Communication Yearbook 2*: 271–292. Transaction Books.
One of the first systematic attempts to analyze communication effectiveness.

Johnson, J. D. 2008. Dosage: a bridging metaphor for theory and practice. *International Journal of Strategic Communication*, 2: 137–153.
Provocative essay relating the metaphor of dosage to effectiveness and efficiency issues.

Pirolli, P., and Card, S. 1999. Information foraging. *Psychological Review*, 106: 643–675.
Application of foraging metaphor and evolutionary thought to information seeking.

Shaw, M. E. 1971. *Group Dynamics: The Psychology of Small Group Behavior*. McGraw-Hill.
Systematic review of small-group communication network research.

Zimmerman, S., Sypher, B. D., and Haas, J. W. 1996. A communication metamyth in the workplace: the assumption that more is better. *Journal of Business Communication*, 33: 185–204.
Describes the "communication metamyth" that more is better, with organizational members always desiring more communication, especially from formal channels, regardless of how much they were receiving.

Zipf, G. K. 1949. *Human Behavior and the Principle of Least Effort: An Introduction to Human Ecology*. Addison-Wesley.
Developed Zipf's law of least effort which has since been applied to a wide range of social phenomena.

11 The human side

Connections are easy; relationships are hard.

(Lesser and Cothrel 2004, p. 29)

There are many elements of the larger organizational context, such as pay and promotion systems, which can impinge on human relationships in KN. However, the focus of this chapter will be on how the human composition of the organization affects the development of KN. Generally researchers have focused on the macro nature of the human environment either in terms of climate or cultural impacts, regarding these phenomena as the macro-media that flavor any interactions embedded within them and the resulting development of particular KN. For example, closed climates are likely to be associated with particularly constrained, fragmented networks that inhibit the free flow of information. Here I first discuss one aspect of macro-media, organizational demography, or the nature of the human composition of the workplace. How individuals come to understand their roles in organizations is a unique form of tacit knowledge which I discuss by focusing on role ambiguity. I then turn to the more classic micro issues related to motivations and individual ignorance, before returning to issues of status and face that blend these two perspectives.

Organizational demography

Organizational demography refers to the composition of the human membership of the organization in terms of such basic attributes as sex and age (Pfeffer 1982). It has been argued that the distribution of such attributes in an organization's population has important consequences for institutions and their members, especially so in the transfer of knowledge (McPherson, Smith-Lovin, and Cook 2001). So, as we discussed in Chapter 9, exposure to diverse membership in one's network has a positive impact on creativity and the adoption of innovations. However, there is also a natural tendency for people to communicate mostly with others like themselves, with whom it is often easier to share and transfer knowledge (Rogers 1983; Ruef, Aldrich, and Carter 2003; Tsui and O'Reilly 1989; Zenger and Lawrence 1989). In turn, cohesive groups may form negative perceptions of out-group members, further isolating them from potential knowledge transfers (Hansen, Mors, and Lovas 2005), particularly related to social categorization processes that impede information use (Dahlin, Weingart, and Hinds 2005). This, in turn, often means that women and minorities are excluded from informal networks, denying them access to restricted knowledge (Ibarra 1993).

Organizational demography can have pervasive impacts. First, demographic factors may affect recruitment practices and the degree to which an organization will defer to members once recruited. Second, they may affect modes of control (e.g., competitiveness stemming from a particularly large age cohort). For example, a large number of new members represented in a growing organization may insure bureaucratic rather than cultural forms of control since the new members have not had the time to be properly socialized. In any event, the higher the ratio of new members to old, the greater the proportion of communication which needs to be directed to the socialization of new members (McNeil and Thompson 1971). These issues may also impact the number of supervisors needed and their span of control (Pfeffer 1982).

A third issue related to demography is intercohort conflict. If a supervisor is a member of a different demographic grouping, as well as in a privileged position, this might further impede the development of relational qualities such as openness in his/her relationships with subordinates. There are also key differences in understanding of critical issues across generations, especially related to technologies and the impact of larger economic forces. The relative homogeneity of teams and their organizational context also has implications for their exposure to new ideas and level of conflict (Joshi 2006). Finally, these factors, in combination, can influence turnover within the organization. For example, the presence of a dominant cohort and substantial gaps among cohorts in university departments were found to be characterized by increased rates of voluntary retirements, resignations, and expired appointments (McCain, O'Reilly, and Pfeffer 1983).

One of the most researched issues traditionally related to organizational demography and networks focuses on proportional imbalances in organizational membership, particularly related to attributes such as gender. Kanter (1977) has argued that the integration of organizational members whose attributes are different from the work group majority is a function of their relative minority status. Thus tokens who represent a small minority, say 15 percent, of organizational members are subject to considerable pressures because of their visibility and uniqueness. However, as the balance becomes more even the impacts of different attributes becomes less pronounced. One of the most important impacts of tokenism is the isolation of token individuals from informal communication networks composed of majority members (Fairhurst 1986). Brass (1985) has found in a newspaper publishing company, with roughly equal numbers of men and women, that men and women were not well integrated into each other's communication networks and that women in particular were not well integrated into the dominant coalition. Naturally, these factors can impede the flow of knowledge.

A central question related to proportion concerns the impact of the distribution of relational states (see Kanter 1977; Pfeffer 1982, 1983). For example, can I be open when all others in my environment are closed? While this issue could be related to a variety of relational characteristics (e.g., trust and credibility) here the focus will be on openness, a variable which has received considerable attention in the literature historically (e.g., Jablin 1978) that cuts across multiple levels of analysis (Dansereau and Markham 1987), and that directly, almost by definition, impacts the willingness to share information. In spite of the fact that openness is crucial to the transfer of knowledge, there is considerable evidence that subordinates are unwilling to be open in their supervisor–subordinate communication relationships (SSCR) (Jablin 1978), with arguments that openness may not be beneficial in all circumstances, especially in terms of individual consequences (Eisenberg and Whetten 1987).

If individuals enter the organization with an essentially open approach to their relationships with others, what factors can cause this approach to change? One factor which might lead to change is the experience of asymmetry, that is some alters with whom the person has relations act in a closed manner. Now the key issue is at what point does the perception of closed relationships cause an individual to change his/her own behavior. Does just one particularly devastating experience cause change or is it likely that a substantial proportion of relationships with others need to be closed to lead to a negative reaction? Or is the person more discriminating? Does s/he reciprocate and behave towards others as these others behave towards them? Does the person have closed relationships with only those people with whom they are at risk (e.g., I want something from them or they can punish me in some way)? This guardedness might dissipate over time if a certain level of trust has been built up.

Issues of proportion, both of relationships and of prior experience, can have a substantial impact on the formation of informal networks. Naturally if a person has had consistently negative experiences, or consistently positive ones, s/he can be expected to respond with less or more openness, respectively, and contract or spread their contacts narrowly or widely. The really interesting issue is at what point in between these extremes does the individual tendency to react become more negative.

Jablin's (1978) study, which examined the content of messages within the SSCR, suggests that only a minimum amount of negative messages, especially those concerning the underlying relationship between the two parties, can act to close off a SSCR in some instances. Jablin (1978) argues that reciprocal acceptance by both parties is crucial to an open relationship. Thus the individual must perceive that both their messages and who they are as a person will be responded to positively before they will choose to be open. However, in an atmosphere of closed relationships the individual may not feel that this essential precondition is being fulfilled. Accordingly, subordinates are more likely to distort information when they perceive their supervisors are actively withholding information or are politically motivated (Jablin 1981). This of course has substantial implications for the flow of information.

The factors discussed in this section may also help explain why researchers often find much less informal communication than would otherwise be expected in actual communication networks (Johnson 2005). Indeed, it has been suggested that one of the reasons liaisons are sought out by others is that they are open with and trusted by other organizational members; however, liaisons are also very rare in actual communication networks (Johnson 2004). Indeed, the human environment within which communication relationships are embedded may discourage the widespread transfer and sharing of knowledge, except for certain unique individuals.[1]

Role ambiguity

Organizational members are also concerned about which behaviors are appropriate for their particular role in an organization (Pettigrew 1971), a unique form of tacit knowledge often associated with professions (Polanyi 1974). Role ambiguity refers to the predictability of the response of others in one's role set to one's behavior that results from clear behavioral requirements (Rizzo, House, and Lirtzman 1970). Role ambiguity is often experienced as a result of a member's uncertainty surrounding their job definition (Organ and Bateman 1986) and is a special case of tacit knowledge for organizational members dependent on communication in their role set, a special network that contains role-related content. This uncertainty is focused on the expectations which others hold for one's job performance and "the steps necessary to go about meeting those expectations, and the consequences of one's job behavior" (Organ and Bateman 1986, p. 389). Several antecedents of ambiguity have been hypothesized, including many structural variables such as formalization, participation in decision-making, span of subordination, size, and organizational position level (Greene 1978; Johnson *et al.* 1998; Kahn *et al.* 1964; Morris, Steers, and Koch 1979; Nicholson and Goh 1983; Organ and Greene 1981). Many negative psychological, emotional, and behavioral outcomes have been associated with ambiguity, including tension, burnout, anxiety, dissatisfaction, and absenteeism, as well as lack of commitment, low performance, low involvement, and reduced levels of autonomy (Brief and Aldag 1976; Fisher and Gitelson 1983; Jackson and Schuler 1985; Miller 1995; Van Sell, Brief, and Schuler 1981). When individuals experience a high level of role ambiguity they also experience anxiety, distort reality, and perform less effectively (Kahn *et al.* 1964). Thus, in general, the literature relates role

---

[1] Relatedly, very few studies have looked at the actual gain in knowledge as a result of mentoring (Swap *et al.* 2004), although it is often assumed.

ambiguity to negative employee perceptions of their work environments which may, in turn, affect their willingness to participate in KN.

Organizational relationships can be formally specified through role relationships in terms of work tasks (i.e., coordination and control of the workflow). Formal structure is designed to deal with role ambiguity through the prescription of specific behaviors required to perform one's task or one's formal role behavior. Kahn *et al.* (1964) found that when organizational size and complexity exceed an individual's span of comprehension, role ambiguity may result. Formal relations can result in continuity in roles through the communication of similar perceptions about a role. In general, it is believed that "organization-wide policies and procedures that serve to facilitate work flow activities reduce ambiguities . . . by defining role-related expectations" (Bedeian, Mossholder, and Armenakis 1983, p. 170).

Katz and Kahn's (1978) discussion of a role set is explicitly stated in structural equivalence terms, at least in terms of the specifications of relationships between a focal person (ego) and others. The role set is oriented toward the individual and is composed of all those individuals who send the individual role-related messages. Thus each individual can be expected to have their own set of individuals who target them for messages about role behavior. Cohesion can also be at play here in highly dense role sets. This information field can then be expected to influence their level of role ambiguity, depending on the clarity of its demands and the common focus of them.

However, this traditional view of the role set almost totally ignores three crucial possibilities. First, members of the role set communicate with each other in developing a mutual perception of the role expectations of a focal person. Second, a similar set of focal persons can communicate among each other and develop an alternative perception of their roles *vis-à-vis* common role sets. Third, focal individuals can also be members of a group and can also contribute to the development of shared perceptions of a role.

Indeed, groups can be formed based on shared perceptions acquired through similar patterning of communication relationships. In this instance the focus is on the impact of group-level networks on individual-level cognitive processes. As members of these groups come to a normative understanding about appropriate behaviors, a form of tacit knowledge, levels of role ambiguity should be reduced. Thus, varying levels of role ambiguity experienced by individuals can be explained through similar patterning of communication relationships.

Individuals of similar status, an important issue we will return to later in this chapter, tend to share information when facing uncertainty (Danowski 1980). Thus, as uncertainty about their jobs increases, organizational members will have a tendency to communicate with individuals with whom they share the same status (see Blau 1954). Therefore, once individuals are grouped based on similar communication patterning, they will have a tendency to share information about expected role behaviors and the consequences of alternative behaviors. In turn, the levels of role ambiguity within groups should be reduced as a result of this sharing of information.

Hartman and Johnson (1989, 1990) have examined these ideas in two articles dealing with the same organization, a non-profit lobbying organization in a large Eastern state. The first article (Hartman and Johnson 1989) found that for the whole network, role ambiguity had an higher association with structural equivalence than it did with cohesion and that it was associated with a more narrow band of network contents, particularly content related to job duties. However, recognizing that groups can be more influential than the organization as a whole in reducing uncertainty, Hartman and Johnson (1990) followed up this research with comparisons across formal and informal groupings. In general, the pattern of results provided moderate support for the hypothesis that groups had more of an impact than the entire network. The importance of utilizing both formal and informal structures to examine the relationship between structural processes and organizational outcomes is also apparent in the results. Although the relationships between formal and informal groupings did not evidence the superiority for informal groups that is implicit in many discussions of organizational communication, the results suggested that both formal and informal groups play key roles in the process of role ambiguity. It also appeared that role ambiguity was affected by group size and by the diversity of membership in groups, something we also saw in Chapter 9 was related to creativity.

I have also been involved in research which has related ritual importance and frequency to role ambiguity in a high-tech organization (Buster, Friedland, Eckert, and Johnson 1988). Rituals present an unique opportunity for members of an individual's role set to gather and present their expectations to a focal person. In general, this study found that the greater perceived importance of rituals and greater participation in them reduced the level of an individual's role ambiguity.

In new organizational forms, members, especially boundary spanners, are confronted with multiple, often conflicting messages about their role performance. New organizational forms often mean deskilling and offshoring except for a few highly talented knowledge workers. They "thrust a large number of its citizens into a condition of permanent survival oriented tension" (Child and McGrath 2001, p. 145). Indeed, a critical modern survival skill for individuals is to engage in sensemaking that results in unique individual survival strategies.

Increasingly some organizational members *expect* to experience role ambiguity while performing the duties associated with their role. This expectation may be particularly important in new organizational forms. Managing the tensions inherent in the paradoxes of stability and change is critical to the operation of alternative organizational forms (Harter and Krone 2001). Indeed managing the process of uncertainty reduction, not necessarily achieving it, may be the critical issue (Babrow 1992, 2001; Harter and Krone 2001). Thus individuals develop the skills necessary to function and even thrive regardless of their levels of role ambiguity. For example, it may be the case that one uses the ambiguity to find creative solutions in situations where ambiguity allows for more autonomy. In this way, role ambiguity empowers individuals to perform daily tasks without clearly contradicting their role prescriptions and therefore enables communication rather than hindering it. In fact, organizational members who resided at higher levels of the organizational hierarchy in a new organizational form reported significantly lower levels of role ambiguity than those members at the lower levels (Johnson *et al.* 1998). Like liaisons, high-status individuals seem to prefer some level of uncertainty in their lives.

Motivations

Structural perspectives typically focus on forces that act on individuals, rather than issues related to individual agency. So, there may also be a contagion effect which increases my willingness to share information with others in a growing, vibrant organization. In this situation a rising tide raises all boats and the success of my peers can contribute to my success as well. Organizations which are no longer growing become more characterized by zero-sum games, that is, I only succeed at the expense of others, which can have disastrous consequences on the flow of information in informal networks. However, Burt's structural hole arguments have reawakened interest in incentives and the related issues of individual motivations.

Obviously, individual learning orientations and curiosity, as well as the intellectual demands of their positions influence individuals' demand for knowledge (Gray and Meister 2004; O'Dell and Grayson 1998). The greater the need people have for certain types of information, the more likely they are to accept what they receive as credible (Wathen and Burkell 2002). On the other side of transfer relationships, a key factor in effective relationships is the level of engagement of the others – do they engage in problem solving rather than act as an "information dump" (Cross *et al.* 2004).

Commitment

Commitment is a concept that links individual motivations directly to organizational life and a number of studies have focused on its linkage to networks. Although the construct of commitment has been defined in many ways, the most common and extensive investigations of commitment have employed Mowday, Steers, and Porter's (1979) definition. Consequently, commitment is defined for our purposes as: (1) a strong belief in and acceptance of the organization's goals and values; (2) a willingness to exert considerable effort on behalf of the organization; and (3) a strong desire to maintain organizational membership (Mowday, Steers, and Porter 1979).

It has been generally argued that structural characteristics of an organization are antecedents of commitment (Steers 1977). Social integration, a concept intimately related to KN, has been found to be an antecedent to organizational commitment, especially in relation to a strong desire to maintain membership in the organization

(Buchanan 1974; Lodahl 1964). Thus positive relationships have been found between commitment and membership in informal cliques (Becker 1960), overall patterns of participation (Antonovsky and Antonovsky 1974), and group attitudes toward the organization (Buchanan 1974; Patchen 1970). On the other hand, a lack of integration seems to be associated with the development of negative attitudes toward the organization (McLaughlin and Cheatam 1977).

Studies have indicated that a positive relationship exists between network involvement and organizational commitment (Buchanan 1974; Eisenberg, Monge, and Miller 1983; Lodahl 1964; Salancik 1977; Salancik and Pfeffer 1977). Network involvement has been defined as the extent to which people establish and maintain direct and/or indirect communication contacts with others in their organization (Eisenberg, Monge, and Miller 1983). Research on this aspect of commitment has primarily focused on the role of cohesion, or direct communication contact, in developing within networks "a strong belief in and acceptance of the organization's goals and values," thus directly relating to the first element of the definition of commitment given above.

Following up on these ideas, Hartman and Johnson (1989) also focused on the relationship between commitment and Burt's (1982, 1987) theory of social contagion. Hartman and Johnson's (1989) study hypothesized that cohesion perspectives of social contagion would provide a better explanation of the relationship between communication networks and commitment than would structural equivalence ones. The results, which generally supported the hypotheses, suggested that commitment was a broader-based concept in network terms than role ambiguity, which significantly related to cohesion explanations of social contagion.

Moch (1980) found that people who were isolated in work networks looked to their jobs as alternative sources of meaning and of identity. Thus job duties and commitment (defined as network involvement) may serve as distinct sources of individual gratification relating to separable organizational processes. Eisenberg, Monge, and Miller (1983) found that for employees who were not involved in their jobs, involvement in job-related communication networks tended to lead to commitment. However, they also suggested that commitment could be increased by involvement in other networks. This contention was supported by the findings of the Hartman and Johnson (1989) study, particularly in the biplex network of job duties and goals, which when multiplexed was closer to Eisenberg, Monge, and Miller's (1983) operationalization.

More recently, Collins and Smith (2006) completed a study of how human resource practices affected the performance of 136 high-technology companies. They found that commitment-related practices, that demonstrated a long-term investment in employees, were positively related to organizational climates characterized by trust and cooperation. These commitment-based practices might include a focus on promoting internal candidates, assessing employees' broad fit to the organization rather than to a specific job, operating compensation practices that focus on group and organizational outcomes, and employing training and performance appraisal systems that emphasize long-term growth, team building, and firm-specific knowledge. Interestingly, these combination of attributes also reflect the historical interest in Theory Z (Ouchi 1981) and the search for excellence (Peters and Waterman 1982), and are linked more broadly to the macro culture and climate of the organization. They also reflect a long-term commitment to organizational learning that is critical to organizational innovation (Leonard 2006). These practices also contributed to shared codes and language that facilitated knowledge transfer, especially related to tacit knowledge. Most interestingly, these measures of social climate affected a firm's capability to exchange and to combine knowledge, a key source of competitive advantage in an RBV, which impacted revenues from new products and services and resulting growth in sales. Collins and Smith (2006) found support for these propositions as well as a relationship between them and employee turnover and tenure. In sum, commitment appears to be related to an individual's integration, and by implication learning, in KN. These processes also relate to the status dynamics I will discuss later in this chapter.

Free-riders and public goods

Commitment is important because it implies positive actions on behalf of the organization by individuals; on the other hand, free-riding suggests an exclusively individual focus. Knowledge can be construed as a public good that can be used in multiple ways. Like any public good, there is a constant tension between individual and organizational benefits. For example, getting individuals to contribute to a collective repository, such as a data base, can be a daunting challenge (Fulk *et al.* 2004; Yuan *et al.* 2005). Incentives not to share data are many, especially for data bases: effort needed to document, learning metadata standards, intellectual property concerns, competition, human subject protection/confidentiality concerns, and so on (Borgman 2006). Many intranets fail because individuals are not motivated to contribute to them. This happens in part because non-contributors cannot be excluded from benefiting. If everyone chooses to free-ride, then there is no common public good. This is further complicated by the value of knowledge being in the eye of the beholder, something we discussed in Chapter 2. Hoarding of information and dragging one's feet in sharing is also associated with competitive threats from the other (Hansen, Mors, and Lovas 2005). In some ways, specialization, and the entailed ignorance of the other's area of expertise, can also result in perceptions of free-riding.

Ignorance

> What one needs to know also depends in part on what others expect one to know.   (Wilson 1983, p. 150)

> . . . everybody is ignorant, only on different subjects.   (Will Rogers, quoted in Smithson 1989, p. 92)

All cultures develop rules which limit the sharing of information. Natural language is well suited for ambiguity and deception and often concerns for politeness lead us to equivocate, dissemble, and to tell others "white lies." We also may be limited in polite discourse in the extent to which we can self-disclose personal information. Conversely, others may be limited in the questions they feel they can ask us and the strategies they can pursue in seeking information. The line between natural curiosity and intrusiveness may be narrow. In fact, the Latin root of "nice" means ignorant, which also may explain why at a societal level good news tends to be more frequently, quickly, fully, and spontaneously communicated (Smithson 1989).

It has been assumed for too long that overcoming organizational ignorance is simply a matter of improving communication systems and processes. It is not that organizations do not gather information or learn things, but often they gather the wrong information for the wrong reasons from the wrong sources. So, many organizations will discount external information sources because of the not-invented-here syndrome, which can result in substantial declines in performance in R & D groups when membership is stable for an extended period (Katz and Allen 1982). Organizations also gather more information than they need to make decisions because of social norms (Feldman and March 1981). "People seem to seek not certainty of knowledge but social validity" (March 1994, p. 40).

Ignorance is different from ignoring, which often happens in an organization when an individual consciously knows that a problem exists, but chooses not to confront it. Ignorance can occur in several major areas and is very pervasive in organizations. First, individuals may be inadequately trained for the performance of their specific job duties. While this condition is interesting, it is beyond the scope of this book. Second, as we have seen in Chapter 2, individuals may be unaware of knowledge, readily available elsewhere in the organization, which has a direct bearing on their job duties. Third, ignorance of employee benefits, which has a direct bearing on the employee's personal life, is also widespread (Mitchell 1988), often in spite of government-mandated procedures for informing employees (see Box 12.1). Fourth, individuals can be unaware of the larger organization, especially its culture. Indeed, a rather common complaint in organizations is, "Why doesn't anybody know anything?" (Downs, Clampitt, and Pfeiffer 1988; Johnson 1993).

Given the pragmatic importance of this issue, it is somewhat surprising that it has received so little research attention (Guetskow 1965; Jablin 1987; Smithson 1989). Management often assumes that, if information is properly communicated, this problem will either go away or be improved (Axley 1984). The traditional literature has tended to focus on the many dysfunctional consequences of ignorance. First, ignorance is likely to result in considerable inefficiencies in organizational operations through such impacts as misunderstandings, the duplication of effort, working at cross-purposes, time delays, and so on (Inman, Olivas, and Golen 1986). Second, ignorance can lead to disastrous outcomes for organizations (Paisley 1980), such as the Challenger tragedy (Brody 1986; Lewis 1988) or the

Pinto's exploding gas tanks (Strobel 1980), where at least some organizational members knew that these outcomes were likely. Third, these inefficiencies and more dramatic outcomes are likely to have impacts on workers' feelings of stress, tension, burnout, and frustration that, in turn, can produce low morale, increased absenteeism, and worker turnover (Morrison 1993a, b). Fourth, ignorance can result in a lack of integration of the individual into the organization's cultures, contributing to a feeling of individual anomie. Fifth, ignorance may be associated with low levels of participation (Marshall and Stohl 1993) and commitment to organizational change efforts (Miller, Johnson, and Grau 1994). Sixth, ignorance of what is happening elsewhere in an organization is a major barrier to knowledge transfer (O'Dell and Grayson 1998).

The results of ignorance are well documented and organizations have engaged in various efforts to ameliorate it, but ignorance persists. Conventional approaches to this problem have focused on a variety of factors that lead to ignorance. For example, some have stressed the random nature of ignorance (e.g., the presence of noise or disturbances in a communication system) as a contributing factor. Others have emphasized the role of human cognitive processes (e.g., selective perception) (Kurke, Weick, and Ravlin 1989) and psychological processes such as denial (Smithson 1989). Still others have emphasized failures in communication as the cause for this situation. For example, surprisingly few, approximately 10 percent, pass on information they receive on the grapevine to others in the organization (Sutton and Porter 1968).

Segmentation inevitably leads to ignorance; structure enables and even encourages ignorance. It also leads to power imbalances, with units paradoxically becoming more powerful by avoiding dependence on others in loosely coupled organizations (Astley and Zajac 1991); yet, in organizations of any size "no manager will ever be knowledgeable enough to be independent of others' expertise" (O'Reilly and Pondy 1979, p. 133).

Ignorance is bliss

> ... there is something about the uninformed which makes them harder to reach, no matter what the level or the nature of information.   (Hyman and Sheatsley 1947, p. 414)

> ... brains have difficulty processing all the relevant information – there is too much, it may not fit with expectations and previous patterns, and some of it may simply be too threatening to accept.   (Mintzberg 1975a, p. 17)

> The art of being wise is the art of knowing what to overlook.   (William James)

In public communication campaigns Hyman and Sheatsley (1947) found some members of the public to be Chronic Know Nothings who appeared to have something in their psychological makeup that made them impossible to reach. Similarly, in organizational settings there appear to be several psychological factors which make it very difficult to reach certain groups of individuals. These psychological processes are directly related to the often irrational search processes in which organizational members engage (Huber and Daft 1987). It is in these areas especially that ignoring is not necessarily the same thing as ignorance.

Smithson (1989) has identified three normative roles underlying psychological perspectives on ignorance. First, is the "Certainty Maximizer" who tries to attain as much control and predictability as possible by learning and responding appropriately to the environment. Second, is the "statistician" approach, popular among managers, of treating uncertainty probabilistically when confronted with the unknown, ignoring ignorance where it cannot be overcome or absorbed, and selecting alternatives that maximize utility in the long run. Finally, is the "Knowledge Seeker" thesis that argues that individuals strive to gain full information and understanding, ignoring nothing that is relevant. When we discuss information and ignorance the image that is often fixed in our minds is that of the scientist valiantly struggling with some known unknown or a fictional detective trying to solve a particularly perplexing puzzle. However, beyond obsessions, curiosity, and creativity, lie a host of motivations not to seek information.

First, it is not uncommon for managers to avoid information that would force them to make a decision to overcome some problem. They can always claim that a decision was flawed because they were ignorant of a crucial factor in the initial decision-making process (Smithson 1993). If they refuse to confront it, at least they will not be involved (MacCrimmon and Taylor 1976) and they can avoid culpability and accountability (O'Reilly and Pondy 1979; Smithson 1989).

Second, ignorance can be used as a justification for inaction (Smithson 1989), as represented by the classic rationalization, 'I cannot do anything until I know more about the problem.' Risk-averse people may try to acquire more information as a way of avoiding errors (Gray and Meister 2004). Ignorance is often used as a justification for maintaining the status quo (Smithson 1993). Somewhat relatedly, individuals' perceptions of the extent to which they can shape or control events also will have an impact on their level of awareness. For many individuals it does not make much sense to learn more about things over which they have no control, so the powerless tend not to seek information (Katz 1968).

Third, the specialist might argue that you should be ignorant of my actions, otherwise you are suggesting that you do not trust me (Smithson 1989), a key factor in professional autonomy. Somewhat relatedly, trust is a major mediator of the open exchange of information (D'Aprix 1988) and of cooperative relationships in organizations (Smith, Carroll, and Ashford 1995). Especially in politically charged atmospheres, it is more rewarding to be closed (Eisenberg and Whetten 1987). In these contexts, seeking information in proscribed, taboo areas could result in sanctions that make ignorance a preferable alternative.

Fourth, often ignorance is a way of avoiding conflict. I can tacitly assume that someone agrees with me, when real knowledge of their position would lead to disputes (Smithson 1989). This is directly related to the strategic use of ambiguity in organizations, the purposive clouding of one's true meaning (Eisenberg 1984; Smithson 1993).

Fifth, ignorance can often be reassuring of a comfortable inertial state, whereas knowledge might lead to arousal to take action (Smithson 1989) or to fear. Adult learners have become highly skilled at protecting themselves from the pain and threat posed by learning situations (Senge 1990) and often information seekers who are conducting an unfamiliar search process, even one as simple as going to the library, experience considerable anxiety and frustration because of the unfamiliarity of the situation (Kuhlthau 1991; Taylor 1968).

Information carriers may be avoided because they increase uncertainty and thereby stimulate fear (Donohew *et al.* 1987; Swinehart 1968). Fear can play a major role in impeding information seeking (Atkin 1979). Fear may be so debilitating that it renders a person incapable of thinking rationally about a problem (Rosenstock 1974). Still, in some situations, a continued state of anxiety may be preferable to the possibility of having the validity of fears confirmed (McIntosh 1974). Acquiring more information and enhancing awareness can increase a person's uncertainty and relatedly their stress levels. As a result, individuals and organizations often choose to reduce this uncomfortable state through processes associated with denial and apathy.

Organizations, and the individuals within them, often deny the presence of disturbing information rather than confronting it, choosing instead to smooth over differences between units (Lawrence and Lorsch 1967). They do not want to know certain things or they hope problems will just go away. More generally, it has been argued that information seeking may not resolve ambiguity; rather, it may create more, as it forces us to confront an often mysterious and unknowable universe (Babrow 1992).

Sixth, while sometimes admissions of ignorance can enhance one's credibility (Smithson 1993) and might even justify action, at least in terms of delving into the known unknown, the very act of seeking information involves admitting one's ignorance (Conrad 1985). However, if it is an area in which one is supposed to be competent, then it may have untold consequences. Often claims of ignorance against others can be used to one's competitive advantage (Smithson 1993). Admissions of ignorance come at substantial cost to one's own ego. Some individuals just do not have the interpersonal skills necessary to form the informal network relationships necessary to acquire information (Wilson and Malik 1995). Others have such low self-esteem that they are afraid that any information they get will confirm their already low self-concept. As a result, individuals will only admit ignorance in certain limited situations, as demonstrated in the Blau research discussed in Box 11.1.

Finally, and fundamentally, as I have detailed, there are cognitive limits on the amount of information individuals can process, especially in short-term memory. Miller's classic observation that we can only viably keep seven things in mind at any one time establishes an absolute barrier to information processing. Beyond this absolute limit, the presence of additional information, especially in overload conditions, lowers even this limited capacity (Mintzberg 1975a). While it has become a truism that knowing how to search for information should be a major focus of our educational systems, rather than imparting perishable knowledge, the limits on short-term memory suggest having a sound and deep knowledge base is critical to management decision making (Lord and Maher 1990; Mintzberg 1975a).

There is evidence that individual information processing can be substantially enhanced by holding positions that demand higher levels of processing (Zajonc and Wolfe 1966) and by long experience in managerial roles. So, somewhat akin to chess masters who can instantly react to complex patterns based on experience, upper-level managers develop an intuitive feel for how to react to complex information patterns in organizations (Simon 1987).

Beyond the limits of memory, people have a limited ability to process and interpret information, an issue which is discussed in more detail in Chapter 13. They tend to exaggerate information they do register (Wales, Rarick, and Davis 1963). They consistently tend to a confirmation bias, ignoring or discounting disconfirming evidence. They often ignore their existing base of information (the base-rate fallacy) and will focus on compelling new information. So, for example, a prodigal employee, who has been a consistently low performer, may still be viewed favorably if there has been one recent positive experience. They also engage in the sample-size fallacy, generalizing from very limited experience. So, if one recent product has met with success in a new market, they may assume other products will meet with similar success. At best, humans are limited in their capacity to seek, to process, and to interpret information correctly (Smithson 1989).

In sum, ignorance is only one of many problems an organizational member has to confront. At times it is better to rely on easily obtained information than to spend the effort necessary to seek complete information. In short, the costs of overcoming ignorance at times outweigh the gains. (And what is amazing is how low the costs are that establish absolute barriers to information seeking.) It is even possible, at least for particular topics, to be sated, to have acquired enough information. In the end, there may be as many, if not more, reasons for not developing linkages in KN as for expanding one's network.

Social barriers to KN

Potential costs (e.g., interpersonal risk of admitting ignorance) of seeking information from others is critical to the development of KN (Nebus 2006), although other pressures (e.g., accessibility, time, risk of not knowing, the nature of the task) can ameliorate this (Borgatti and Cross 2003; Hirsch and Dinkelacker 2004; Xu, Tan, and Yang 2006), as well as personality traits like self-esteem (Madzar 2001). Indeed, the cost of seeking information within the organization may be so significant that people prefer to seek information outside of the organization itself, rather than to ask overt questions (Miller and Jablin 1991). A sense of being "safe" to ask dumb questions is important in seeking information (Cross and Sproull 2004).

Status

A critical factor that clearly impedes this feeling of safety involves the loss of face and status. In effect, low-status people are trying to "borrow" social capital of more central high-status others (Balkundi and Kilduff 2005).[2] So, status is an important predictor of KN outcomes (Argote, McEvily, and Reagans 2003).

Allen (1977) found that a significant barrier to face-to-face interaction in which advice is sought is the ego cost to the initiator of the interaction. Engineers would prefer not to lose esteem in the eyes of a colleague by seeking information from them. They would seek advice, however, in situations where they knew the other engineer socially, presumably because these more multiplex relationships have richer exchange arrangements. So, I may exchange my professional expertise with a colleague in trade for a lesson on how to play shortstop in the company softball team.

Similarly, in his classic study of a government bureaucracy, Blau (1954) found that advice seeking was related to perceived status within organizational groups (see Box 11.1). A member's status would be lowered by the constant seeking of information from higher-status members, especially when the other member did not, in turn, ask them for information. Members preferred exchange relationships where ties were more multiplex or there was a two-way flow of advice. Sometimes members preferred to share ignorance, even when this was explicitly proscribed behavior, rather than seeking out more authoritative information from a higher-status organizational member.

This is in some ways a variation of what Bianconi and Barabasi (2001) and others have found in relation to power laws and communication on the World Wide Web – the rich get richer, or the more ties someone has the more likely it is that others will be drawn to them. Similarly in group settings, because of power and dependence dynamics, members are more committed and more likely to help those seen as experts, a dynamic that frustrates group performance and learning (Van der Vegt, Bunderson, and Oosterhof 2006). Fundamentally, individuals' attempts to establish relations with others for the purposes of sharing information must be accepted by the others, and utilitarian concerns for both the value of information and the social standing of individuals determine acceptance. This may be why advice networks are so characterized by sporadic, asymmetric, and/or nonreciprocating relationships (Nebus 2006). The presence of ties between two actors also serves as a prism, an underlying informational cue that others can use to determine the quality of one or both actors in a market, and that indicates

---

[2] Relatedly, for many innovations the primary motivation is gaining status (e.g., think of the adoption of new products by trendsetters) (Bandura 2006).

Box 11.1. Advice seeking in a bureaucracy

In his classic study of a government bureaucracy, Blau (1954, 1955) found that advice seeking was related to perceived status within organizational groups. Interestingly, Blau's career was characterized by a mixture of methods used to study formal organizations, starting with qualitative approaches, then, somewhat uniquely, proceeding to more rigorous quantitative methods. In this study, Blau focused on a peer group of sixteen agents in a federal law enforcement agency that investigated business establishments. He made direct observations of their interactions, keeping track of the total number of contacts, contacts originated, contacts received, and, finally, an index of initiative in social interaction.

Competence was measured by supervisor performance evaluations and competent agents were found to have a disproportionate number of contacts as a result of ties initiated by others. This finding echoes the findings of the liaison literature that suggests individuals in central positions are often sought out by others because of their expertise. Inversely, the less competent agents, partly out of need, were more likely to take the initiative in seeking out others and cultivating relationships. However, competence needed to be tied with a perception that the individual was cooperative and willing to help others for them to be actively sought out.

Interestingly, contacts were also initiated with these individuals so that a person could raise their own esteem and standing in the peer group as a result of their association with a high-status other. However, members' status would be lowered by the constant seeking of information from higher-status members, especially when the other member did not in turn ask them for information. These dynamics also made even the most competent agents unwilling to ask for information for fear this would result in diminished status. In group settings, such as lunches, members could expose themselves to ridicule if they revealed their ignorance in informal discussions, which discouraged participation and integration of the less competent. Members preferred exchange relationships where ties were more multiplex or where there was a two-way flow of advice that was done seemingly indirectly in social settings.

As a result of these dynamics, sometimes members preferred to share ignorance rather than seeking out more authoritative information from a higher-status organizational member. Agents were supposed to work on cases individually under direct guidance of a supervisor. The cases they were assigned could result in difficult legal decisions and, given the issues around setting policy precedents, they were expected to consult with supervisors. However, as often happens, because of the performance rating and incentive systems, they were afraid of doing this since it might reflect on their competence. Instead, even though this was explicitly proscribed behavior, they relied on their peers to answer questions they might have. They often preferred to seek answers from those with whom they were friendly, regardless of their competence level, thus acting to pool ignorance rather than knowledge. But, as we have seen, this had other consequences, with these two dynamics providing powerful barriers to individuals in seeking answers to questions that might develop in their work.

their relative status and standing (Podolny 2001). So the infamous incident of a nineteenth-century financier walking across the trading floor with someone who wanted a loan from him, with the financier saying, "I will not loan you money, but others who see us together will."

A common theme related to demographic research, which bears directly on KN, is the relative isolation of certain groups (Fairhurst and Snavely 1983; Kanter 1977) and the oft-observed phenomenon of members of lower status desiring to communicate with higher-status others rather than each other (Ruef, Aldrich, and Carter 2003). For example, Allen (1977) has found in research and development laboratories, that non-PhDs were relatively isolated from PhDs. This isolation was due primarily to status differences: while non-PhDs could enhance their status by communicating with PhDs, PhDs would suffer a decrease in their status. Similarly non-PhDs communicating with each other reinforced their low-status positions. As a result non-PhDs did not communicate widely in these organizations. Indeed, an implied quid pro quo can inhibit the development of relationships more generally (Nebus 2006) with reciprocation-wary individuals fearing exploitation in exchange relationships and thereby becoming leery of accessing others' knowledge (Gray and Meister 2004).

However, isolated members may be more willing to share unique information as an instrumental means of enhancing their standing in a group (Thomas-Hunt, Ogden, and Neale 2003). Interestingly, since they have a lower standing in the group, they were also more likely to share divergent information, in part because they do not face the same social pressures as relatively connected members (Argote, McEvily, and Reagans 2003). Thus status differentials may actually facilitate organizational change by instituting a primary motivation for bringing in outside perspectives that undercut the points of view of existing organizational elites.

Group processes

Even more disconcertingly, correct information often has little impact on critical decision making because of group processes (Cross, Rice, and Parker 2001). How others view our relationships often determines how we view them as well. Thus the human environment in which structure is embedded affects the nature of our dyadic relationships and through them the structure of KN. Thus, as Box 11.2, on echo and bandwidth, suggests, the type of information that is shared often depends on perceptions of the overarching sentiments within a group that acts to silence organizational members, an issue we will continue to explore in Chapter 13. More generally, too much socializing may be a bad thing, in part because of the social costs of maintaining many, often redundant relationships (Cross, Nohria, and Parker 2004; Ibarra 1993) and, relatedly, because of the opportunity costs of relationships that are not developed (Cross, Borgatti, and Parker 2003).

Box 11.2. Echo in Project 2

> ...my summary conclusion is that network closure does not facilitate trust so much as it amplifies predispositions, creating a structural arthritis in which people cannot learn what they do not already know.   (Burt 2001, p. 63)

The research reported here was part of the Cancer Information Service Research Consortium (CISRC) project described in Chapter 8 that focused on implementing three public health interventions. In many ways Project 2 was the most interesting, novel, and fundamentally different of these interventions. It was concerned with encouraging women to receive regular mammograms. This new intervention strategy reached out to women by making "cold calls" from the Cancer Information Service (CIS) to low-income and minority women in targeted communities in Colorado. This intervention strategy was unique in that it focused on making outcalls from the CIS, an activity that was substantially different from the traditional role of a telephone service that responds to calls placed by people in the community to a toll-free number. The procedure of making outcalls was foreign to information specialists, who were trained to give information in response to callers' inquiries. Because of its unique approach this project was only piloted in one regional office (see Crane *et al.* 1998, and Crane *et al.* 2000 for the follow-on study).

Marcy Meyer (1996a), in her award-winning dissertation work examining the implementation of Project 2 over time, focused on weak ties, perceived organizational innovativeness, and perceptions of innovation characteristics over four points in time to examine the underlying theoretic dynamics. Longitudinally, this research explored the degree to which organizational members form general perceptions about organizational innovativeness based on their experience with a specific innovation.

Range and prominence measures are indicators of informal communication network structure (Burt 1991), specifically weak ties, which, as we saw in Chapter 9, have important implications for innovation. Individuals who are exposed to information about innovation from a variety of sources are more likely to perceive that they work in an innovative environment, and use that information to make evaluations about the pros and cons of innovation. Meyer's (1996a) study measured weak ties with the range measures of contacts and non-redundant contacts and the prominence measure of choice status (Burt 1991). Since these indices are characteristics of an organizational member's contact diversity, they are comparable to that individual's weak ties within the network (Granovetter 1973). In the interest of parsimony and as a result of detailed psychometric work (Meyer 1996b) the innovation attributes of relative advantage, observability, adaptability, and acceptance tapped one manifest trait, pros, while complexity and risk constituted cons.

Based on our previous discussions, it seems likely that weak ties, perceived organizational innovativeness, and the pros and cons of innovation are intimately connected constructs. Informal communication structure at one point in time should impact perceived organizational innovativeness and perceptions about the pros and cons of innovation at later points in time. An innovative climate should be a predictor of the degree to which organizational members will be supportive of a particular innovation. Likewise, organizational members should form general perceptions about the extent to which they work in an innovative climate through their experience with a specific innovation in the organizational context. In a detailed examination of various theoretical alternatives, Meyer and Johnson (1997) developed an optimal model of the interaction of these various factors. This research demonstrated that, over time, weak ties affected perceptions of innovation characteristics and perceived organizational innovativeness impacted perceptions of the pros. These findings suggest that climate is a predictor of the degree to which organizational members will be supportive of particular innovations.

Although weak ties affected perceptions of innovation characteristics, predicted links were surprisingly weak; the most notable effects were unexpected lag effects. This finding indicated that it takes time for organizational members to process novel ideas. Similarly, it has been observed that knowledge transfers are not instantaneous; it takes time for people to absorb information (Jensen and Meckling 1995). Although individuals with high levels of weak ties may be exposed to information about innovation from a variety of sources, this type of communication does not have an immediate impact on the degree to which they perceive that they work in an innovative environment, nor does it noticeably impact the degree to which they are supportive of particular innovations in the short term. In the long run, however, informal innovation-related communication can have more pronounced consequences for organizational members' evaluations of the pros and cons of innovation.

The "amplification effect" (Renn 1991) suggests that weak ties should impact future perceptions of innovations by amplifying existing attitudes toward their pros and cons. If people communicate with their weak ties about the favorable aspects of an innovation, then this could have a positive effect on attitudes toward innovation over time. If, on the other hand, organizational members communicate with their weak ties about the unfavorable aspects of the innovation, then this could have a negative effect on attitudes toward innovation over time. In contrast to the amplification effect, the "spiral of silence" phenomenon (Noelle-Neumann 1974) suggests that attitudes toward innovation may not necessarily get converted to talk among weak ties. Organizational members may hold dissimilar views about innovation, but the person with relatively less knowledge about the topic may fail to express his or her opinions because he or she perceives that he or she lacks expertise or is unwilling to go against prevailing opinions. In this case, vocal views about innovation would eventually become paramount in the network.

Congruent with the "amplification effect" (Renn 1991), the data suggested that weak ties do indeed impact future perceptions of innovation, by amplifying existing attitudes about both pros and cons. At least in this case, weak ties at Time 1 and Time 2 had relatively strong, negative impacts on perceptions of the pros of innovation at Time 4. The time lag between weak ties at Time 1 and Time 2 and perceptions of the pros of innovation at Time 4 may be due in part to the sparseness of innovation-related communication in this organization. This finding suggested that perceptions of innovation were influenced by the social amplification effect in highly segmented networks, but to a lesser extent, and at a much slower rate, than would be expected in dense networks. It also suggests the importance of studying the strength of strong ties (Krackhardt 1992) in securing support for innovation.

In addition, the lag effects mirror Weenig and Midden's (1991) unexpected finding that negative advice was obtained more frequently from weak ties than strong ties. It might be that organizational members were more likely to make negative evaluations of an innovation if they did not have a vested interest in it. Since perceived organizational innovativeness at Time 1 had a strong negative impact on pros at Time 4, organizational members may have been unsupportive of this particular innovation because they did not perceive it to be a good match with the current innovative climate of their organization.

Additionally, the unexpected finding that cons at Time 2 had a strong negative effect on weak ties at Time 3 points to a structurational account of innovation and communication (Lewis and Seibold 1993). Apparently, perceptions of negative outcomes associated with innovation can put a damper on future levels of innovation-related communication among organizational members. This finding puts a new twist on the old saying, "If you don't have anything nice to say, don't say anything at all." Unfortunately, this spiral of silence can have negative consequences for the course of particular innovations in organizations.

More recently, Burt (2001, 2005) has introduced the concepts of bandwidth and echo to explain these processes, associating them with structural holes, brokerage, and trust. The bandwidth hypothesis suggests that network closure enhances information flow, while the echo hypothesis suggests they do not because of an "echo" in the social system that reinforces predispositions, arising from redundant ties and social etiquette, not to reveal information that is supposed to be discordant with that held by the other. These processes inevitably lead to an inability to learn and adapt in cohesive groups; thus, "ambiguity plus network closure produces ignorant certainty" (Burt 2005, p. 222). More insidiously, gossip becomes a force of social cohesion, since we often define ourselves by what we are not.

Weak ties are more likely to share negative information, in part because they are not as aware of prevailing opinions in cohesive groupings. Favorable opinion is amplified by trust, while doubt becomes translated into distrust of those who spread negative views.

Summary

In this chapter we have looked at the human side of KN. We started at the macro level, examining the overall human composition of the organization, as represented in demographic approaches. We then turned to more classical individually focused approaches related to role ambiguity and motivations. Then we took a walk on the dark side, examining the role of ignorance and status in limiting the flow of knowledge in organizations.

Further reading

Allen, T. J. 1977. *Managing the Flow of Technology: Technology Transfer and the Dissemination of Technological Information within the R&D Organization.* MIT Press.

Systematic exposition of the information seeking of engineers in R & D settings, with extensive treatments of networks and the effect of physical settings.

Blau, P. M. 1954. Patterns of interaction among a group of officials in a government agency. *Human Relations*, 7: 337–348.

Blau, P. M. 1955. *The Dynamics of Bureaucracy: A Study of Interpersonal Relations in Two Government Agencies.* University of Chicago Press.

Classic description of the effects of status on information sharing, described in more detail in Box 11.1.

Hartman, R. L., and Johnson, J. D. 1989. Social contagion and multiplexity: communication networks as predictors of commitment and role ambiguity. *Human Communication Research*, 15: 523–548.

Systematic application of key network concepts to commitment and role ambiguity. The results suggested that commitment was a broader-based concept in network terms than role ambiguity.

Kanter, R. M. 1977. *Men and Women of the Corporation*. Basic Books.

Comprehensive analysis of the importance of gender proportions in organizations for career progression and status.

Pfeffer, J. 1982. *Organizations and Organization Theory*. Pitman.

Pfeffer, J. 1983. Organizational demography. *Research in Organizational Behavior*, 5: 299–357.

Early systematic descriptions of the impacts of demography on organizational structure.

12 Finding knowledge

> Yet it seems that information-seeking must be one of our most fundamental
> methods for coping with our environment. The strategies we learn to use in
> gathering information may turn out to be far more important in the long run
> than specific pieces of knowledge we may pick up in our formal education and
> then soon forget as we go about wrestling with our day-to-day problems.
>
> (Donohew, Tipton, and Haney 1978, p. 389)

The career and life winners of the future will be those people who know
where to go to find information, can then process large volumes of it, and,
ultimately, make sense of it by converting it into useful knowledge. As we have
seen, finding knowledge in organizations is a complex phenomenon and there
are many barriers that seekers must overcome. The previous chapters have been
devoted to understanding KN. In this chapter I turn first to individual strategies
that help people identify where knowledge might reside in a KN, what feedback
seeking they use to determine others reaction to them, and how they might
best forage for information. Management's role in KN becomes largely one of
setting an agenda that specifies what critical questions need to be explored, and
then facilitating and enhancing knowledge acquisition related to these issues by
creating rich information fields.

Individual strategies

In general, the focus of the literature has been on how information can
be provided to organizational members, rather than what motivates them to seek
answers to questions they pose for themselves; the latter process has also been
labeled knowledge sourcing (Gray and Meister 2004). We do not know much
about what motivates an individual to seek information, especially in terms of
the more prosocial seeking associated with personal growth, creativity, curiosity,
or sharing information with coworkers (Burke and Bolf 1986). One consistent
argument found in the literature is that people with high growth needs are more
likely to consult a wide range of information sources (Varlejs 1986). Organizations should nurture these individuals by providing them with the autonomy to
pursue their searches. In short, organizations must provide an environment that
values and encourages learning (McGee and Prusak 1993).

A state that organizations may wish to encourage is one where individuals feel that they are in the "groove," that they are jamming with the information environment around them (Eisenberg 1990). People want to maximize their cognitive load, as well as their enjoyment (Marchionini 1992); they do not like tasks or information systems that add to their frustration or interrupt their task performance. They prefer systems that are intrinsically gratifying, that have an intuitive game-like feel (Paisley 1993).

So, for example, people do not like "two-step" information systems that cite sources of information to which they must later refer. The concept of flow, which captures playfulness and exploratory experience, has been said to encourage people to use new and unfamiliar information technologies. Flow theory, most associated with the work of Csikszentmihalyi, suggests that involvement in a flow state is self-motivating because it is pleasurable and encourages repetition (Naumer 2005; Trevino and Webster 1992). A flow state exists when individuals feel in control of the technology (e.g., receiving feedback, or selecting from options), their attention is focused, their curiosity is aroused, and the activity in which they are engaged is intrinsically interesting. Increasingly the best computer software, especially that with multimedia capability, captures the conditions of a flow state.

As we have seen there is a major discrepancy between idealized behavior and the typical pattern of knowledge acquisition one finds in organizations. One way that organizations can address this problem is by being very careful in their recruitment and hiring practices to insure that they are selecting self-sufficient seekers. It must be recognized that information acquisition is an important life-skill that should be central to our educational efforts to produce lifelong learning, as well as in the training for particular professions. Most of our major life problems are associated with lack of knowledge, skills, or ability to assess risks. Information and the skills to acquire it are critical to surmounting these problems.

Another strategy is to increase the salience of these issues through better training programs that address optimal search behaviors (e.g., appropriate keyword selection) and acquaint individuals with unfamiliar sources of information. In general, organizations do not give their workers sufficient guidance on what are the optimal sources of information (Burke and Bolf 1986). Acquainting individuals with sources that are relevant (Saracevic 1975) and useful in their immediate work is the critical first step to developing better knowledge acquisition habits. Part of learning the tacit knowledge of a profession is learning how to acquire information and learning the relative value of different types of knowledge (Polanyi 1974).

In looking at the individual we must recognize that communication events in organizations are characterized by a complex of goals, with multiple motives. Strategies that individuals pursue can be complex; an information-seeking attempt may be masked as a persuasive message on another matter (Contractor and Eisenberg 1990). So I may go into my boss with a suggestion for improving work in the office, but the answer I am really seeking is whether s/he still values me enough to give me material support. In this section we will look at three issues: how people know where to go in networks; the feedback-seeking strategies related to individual work performance, and the more abstract perspective of information foraging drawn from evolutionary psychology.

How do people know where to go?

> While much research has focused on the issue of knowledge transfer, far less has considered the issues of individuals seeking out existing knowledge. The ability to do this may be constrained by the simple fact that those seeking knowledge may not be aware of those who have it . . .   (Kayworth and Leidner 2003, p. 245).

One of the things that characterizes effective KN relations is knowing what the other knows and when to turn to them (Cross, Rice, and Parker 2001). Partly growing from the classic debates relating to the validity of self-reports of network linkages, some have suggested that individuals have strong, albeit often crude, categorical intuitions of surrounding social structures, such that they know who is linked to whom in a stable network (Corman and Scott 1994; Freeman 1992; Freeman, Romney, and Freeman 1987; Romney and Faust 1982),[1] and by implication have some awareness of where information resides. Burt (2005) has suggested that people can be trained to see structural holes.

However, here we are not exploring how people get routine information from their strong ties, which may indeed have been formed to create an information field. Rather, we are interested in how people actively search for answers to questions that may exceed the capability of their existing network. This question is given some additional impetus by the classic findings of the information-seeking literature that people will seek information from interpersonal sources (Cross, Rice, and Parker 2001) who can summarize information for them in meaningful terms and are accessible; and that people are not very persistent nor sophisticated in their search behaviors (Johnson 1997a). It also addresses the organizational quandary of how to make connections between new knowledge and those who should have it (Schulz 2001).

Addressing this problem has traditionally been one compelling advantage of a formal organizational chart, which we discussed in greater detail in Chapter 5. The chart in effect provides a road map for confronting the problem (see Table 12.1). It clearly identifies who should have the expertise in particular areas, who is the authoritative source, and who has the training and experience. The formal organization, indeed, has been identified as a primitive computer (Beninger 1990) with a directory (job titles), programming language (formal rules), information storage systems (written records), and random access memory (managers' memories). All of this, of course, is rationalized, often explicitly, with relationships formalized (e.g., I have to respond to certain information requests

---

[1] Although they may have a more optimistic picture of their own positioning in this social structure (Kumbasser, Romney, and Batchelder 1994).

Table 12.1. *Searching for information*

Search concept	Structural approach	
	Formal	*Informal*
Information-seeking actions	Specified	Individual preferences, norms
Sources consulted	Formal roles	Personal attributes
Individual knowledge	Position-related Training Experience Recruited for	Need-driven Cognitive limits
Knowledge distribution	Planned	Random, historical, cultural
Comprehensiveness/reach	Organizational-wide reach	Localized, small-world
Directory	Job titles	Reputation
Programming	Formal rules	Informal rules, scripts, routines, cognitive limits
Storage	File systems, data bases	"Grey" literature, personal memory
Needs	Position requirements	Promotion, curiosity, status

because of job requirements). In the world of formal structure a search, then, often becomes a matter of formulating a question in the proper way and directing it to the correct formal role incumbent. However, it does little good to free up the possibilities of a search within new organizational forms, if everyone still goes to their supervisor because of ignorance of other potential sources (Krackhardt 1994), which we saw in the last chapter has various ego costs (Blau 1954, 1955). We return, then, to how individuals negotiate the more shadowy informal world for answers to their questions. This is something that Box 12.1, on work – life programs, suggests can be especially tricky for confidential information, where people might prefer more anonymous, web-based information (Case *et al.* 2004).

The literature has hinted at a number of factors that may shape searches for new information: relationships with weak ties, opinion leadership, the more general role of brokers, accessibility, and the status structures in which searchers are embedded. Prior experience with a source and that person's trustworthiness are particularly important. Cross, Rice, and Parker (2001) have described this in more contemporary terms as the degree of safety in a relationship that promotes both learning and creativity. (See also Box 12.1.)

Opinion leaders

Both the traditional opinion leadership (Katz and Lazarsfeld 1955) and network role (Reynolds and Johnson 1982) literatures suggest that people seek out knowledgeable others in their informal networks for answers to their questions (Burt 1999). Classically, opinion leadership suggests ideas flow from the media to

Box 12.1. Applying the Comprehensive Model of Information Seeking to work–life

The issue of work–life balance has received increasing attention across a range of disciplines, in part because of the wide range of problems confronting the contemporary work-force. Obviously, work and family are two of the most important realms of an individual's life, but these two realms can be detrimental to one another, leading to uncertainty and a need for information regulation.

Organizations typically use formal employee assistance programs (EAP) to address these issues, so they will be our pragmatic focus here. In the United States, the scope of the national problems in areas traditionally encompassed by EAP services is troubling. It is estimated that 10 percent of employees are impaired sufficiently to need behavioral health intervention (Poverny and Dodd 2000). Historically, EAP programs primarily focused on substance and alcohol abuse. Recently, there has been a move toward more broad-based programs that offer a wide range of benefits and approaches to address these complex problems. More comprehensive EAP services for employees might include programs addressing depression, stress, relationships, marital problems, compulsive gambling, career issues, financial and legal concerns, child and elder care, health and wellness, violence, and so on. Typically users of these programs are the most vulnerable organizational members; the programs are less likely to be used by high-status members and men (Poverny and Dodd 2000).

Finding help related to EAP in organizations is a complex task and there are many barriers that seekers must overcome. Ignorance of employee benefits, which has a direct bearing on the employee's personal life, is widespread (Picherit-Duthler and Freitag 2004), often in spite of government-mandated procedures for informing employees. Lack of trust and concerns over confidentiality may result in workers seeking informal or external sources of information for dealing with their problems, since they want to avoid being labeled or categorized in a way that is hard to remove (Geist-Martin, Horsley, and Farrell 2003). As a result, some employees may simply withdraw, often perceiving that their organization's culture demands that they suffer in silence.

In general, the focus of human resources departments has been on how information can be provided to organizational members, rather than on what motivates them to seek answers to questions they pose for themselves, and how individuals need to decide their own strategies for negotiating these dilemmas. One approach for examining these issues is found in the Comprehensive Model of Information Seeking (CMIS) and its application to communication networks in the workplace.

The CMIS has been empirically tested in a variety of cancer-related information-seeking (Johnson 1993; Johnson and Meischke 1993) and organizational contexts (Johnson *et al.* 1995a). Johnson (2003) has systematically compared these two contexts and their implications for the CMIS. The CMIS focuses on the antecedents that explain why people become information seekers, the information-carrier characteristics that shape how people go about looking for information, and the information-seeking actions that reflect the nature of the search itself.

The antecedents of the CMIS include demographics, personal experience, salience, and beliefs. A common theme in demographic research, which bears directly on communication networks, is the relative isolation of certain groups. This could then be extended to the stigma associated with substance abuse serving to isolate individuals from the main stream in most organizations (Dietz, Cook, and Hersch 2005). Information seeking can also be triggered by an individual's degree of direct, personal experience with the problem at hand, which for some EAP problems can be extensive and idiosyncratic.

In the CMIS framework, two personal relevance factors, salience and beliefs, are seen as the primary determinants in translating a perceived gap into an active search for information. Salience refers to the personal significance of information to the individual. An individual might wonder, "Is it important that I do something?" Potential costs (e.g., interpersonal risk of admitting ignorance) of seeking information from others are critical to the development of networks. As we have seen, a critical factor that clearly impedes this feeling of safety involves the loss of face and status.

Acquiring more information and enhancing awareness can increase a person's uncertainty and relatedly their stress levels. As a result individuals and organizations often choose to reduce this uncomfortable state through processes associated with denial, inertia, and apathy. Organizations, and the individuals within them, often deny the presence of disturbing information rather than confronting it. They do not want to know certain things or they hope problems will just go away. However, in this context where life problems can interfere with work, salience may be further enhanced by formal managerial interventions such as referral to drug treatment programs.

EAP information seeking is also affected by various cultural factors, since all cultures develop rules which limit the sharing of information. Natural language is well suited for ambiguity and deception and often concerns for politeness lead us to equivocate, dissemble, and to tell others "white lies." We may be limited in polite discourse in the extent to which we can self-disclose personal information. Conversely, others may be limited in the questions they feel they can ask us and the strategies they can pursue in seeking information. Fundamentally, an individual's attempts to establish relations with others for the purposes of sharing information must be accepted by the other, and utilitarian concerns for both the value of information and the social standing of individuals determine acceptance

(Nebus 2006). This may be why advice networks are so characterized by sporadic, asymmetric, and/or nonreciprocating relationships (Nebus 2006), and this may be especially true for EAP-driven interactions.

An individual's perception of the extent to which they can shape or control events also will have an impact on their level of awareness. For many individuals it does not make much sense to learn more about things over which they have no control, so the powerless tend not to seek information. Case *et al.* (2005) have articulated systematically why the avoidance of information may be very rational in particular situations where people have low self-efficacy or face threatening information about job performance (Ashford, Blatt, and VandeWalle 2003). It may be perfectly rational then to avoid information when there is nothing one can do with the answers one may obtain. If the threat is extreme, or if any potential responses are not expected to be effective, then an attractive alternative is to ignore the threat entirely – which in turn promotes cognitive consistency (Case *et al.* 2005). People who are officially referred to programs often have limited abilities to cope with their problems. They do not have a sense of self-efficacy that they will be able to correctly interpret and react to any new information with which they are presented. Use of the Web and formal onsite and offsite sources often require some sense of self-efficacy. An individual's belief in the efficacy of various programs also plays a role.

The information carrier factors contained in the CMIS are drawn from a model of media exposure and appraisal (MEA) that has been tested on a variety of information carriers, including both sources and channels, and in a variety of cultural settings (Johnson 1983; Johnson 1984a, b; Johnson 1987; Johnson and Oliveira 1988). Following the MEA, the CMIS focuses on editorial tone, communication potential, and utility. In the CMIS, characteristics are composed of editorial tone, which reflects an audience member's perception of credibility, or in more network organizational terms, the critical issue of trust, while communication potential relates to issues of style and comprehensiveness.

Utility, in both the CMIS and MEA, relates the characteristics of a medium directly to the needs of an individual, and shares much with the uses and gratifications perspectives (Palmgreen 1984). For example, is the information contained in the medium relevant, topical, and important for the individual's purposes?

Research on CMIS suggests it provides the "bare bones" of a causal structure, although the nature of the specific relationships contained in the model appear to be context-dependent. Tests of CMIS in health situations suggest the model works best with authoritative channels, such as doctors, that are the object of intense, goal-directed searches (Johnson 1993; Johnson and Meischke 1993), and for rational, programmed tasks that are more proximate to the individual (Johnson *et al.* 1995a). These characteristics certainly relate to the formal role of EAPs in organizations.

EAP information seeking is often emotional and irrational, governed by the dark side of informal networks. Because of the focus on the individual, EAP programs have seldom focused on social health, social capital issues surrounding one's social network of relationships including camaraderie with peers, communicating with superiors, and reconnecting with family (Farrell and Geist-Martin 2005). So, for example, not only do opinion leaders serve to disseminate ideas, but they also, because of the interpersonal nature of their ties, provide additional pressure to conform as well, a key factor in the success of drug and alcohol rehabilitation programs. They not only serve a relay function, they also provide social support information to individuals and reinforce messages by their social influence. In the classic small-world problem the task is for an individual to contact a distant target other (e.g., someone who knows how to cope with substance abuse), previously unknown to them, through intermediaries. However, EAP situations almost demand a directed search, rather than a broadcast one, because people will only ask people they can trust with sensitive, confidential information.

opinion leaders to those less active segments of the population (Katz 1957). Opinion leaders not only serve a relaying function, they also provide social support information to individuals and reinforce messages by their social influence. Social support is seen as being "inextricably woven into communication behavior" (Albrecht and Adelman 1987c, p. 14). Generally two crucial dimensions of support are distinguished, informational and emotional, with informational support being associated with a feeling of mastery and control over one's environment (Freimuth 1987) and emotional support being crucial to feelings of personal coping, enhanced self-esteem, and needs for affiliation (Albrecht and Adelman 1987b). Support has been associated with such critical organizational outcome variables as stress, absenteeism, burnout, turnover, productivity, and morale (Ray 1987). Support has also been directly tied to network analysis approaches.

Not only do opinion leaders serve to disseminate ideas, but they also, because of the interpersonal nature of their ties, provide additional pressure to conform (Katz 1957). How one person influences another is often determined by their structural positioning within a group (Katz and Lazarsfeld 1955). One classic finding of research into the relationship between interpersonal and mass media channels is that individuals tend "to select media materials which will in some way be immediately useful for group living" (Riley and Riley 1951, p. 456). Some have gone so far as to suggest that group membership can be predicted based on an individual's information-seeking preferences (Kasperson 1978), with suggestions that opinion leaders are information brokers at the edges of groups (Burt 1999). They are brokers twice over since through cohesive ties they pass information to weakly structurally equivalent individuals, thus triggering contagion across the social boundaries of groups (Burt 1999). However, the literature is less clear as to how people come to know who these others are. Reputation and prestige may be particularly important in this process of coming to know who the gurus are.

Accessibility

Accessibility, both in terms of physical propinquity and timely response is also important (Borgatti and Cross 2003; Cross, Rice, and Parker 2001; Hirsch and Dinkelacker 2004). One of the classic observations about communication is that it is more likely to occur when individuals are within a rather limited physical distance (Johnson 1993), with profound implications for information seeking (Allen 1977) as we have seen in Chapter 7. Timely response is an increasingly important issue in the frenetic world of the contemporary organization, as is the quality of the response. Will the person be engaged and problem-solve, or just provide a knowledge dump (Cross, Rice, and Parker 2001)?

Issues of accessibility, approachability, and the quality of the response are often tied up with informal status systems in organizations. As we have seen, admissions of ignorance come at a substantial cost to one's ego. Some individuals just do not have the interpersonal skills to form the informal network relationships necessary for acquiring information (Wilson and Malik 1995).

Transactive memory

> . . . a knowledge community or network would seem to require a human hub or switch, whose function is as much to know who knows what as to know what is known.   (Earl 2001, p. 225)

Knowing who knows what is a fundamental issue for KN; it answers the know-who question (Borgatti and Cross 2003). Using computer search engines and networks as a metaphor can also lead us to interesting insights into this human systems problem. If people can be considered to be computers, then every social group can be viewed as a computer network with analogous problems and solutions (Wegner 1995), developing means of retrieving and allocating information to collective tasks (Palazzolo *et al.* 2006). But we are not focused here on the hardware and software available to search for expertise, the classic knowledge management tools used in many organizations (e.g., SPIFI, directories, "yellow pages"). Perhaps the most serious limit on these technologies is the recurring preference of individuals for interpersonal information sources who can digest and summarize vast quantities of information for individual seekers (Johnson 1996b). Publishing in an organizational data base can serve as a signal to others in the organization that one is knowledgeable in certain areas, thus leading to contacts between two parties (Contractor and Monge 2002) as when relying on a dating service. Some have argued, then, that the fundamental unit of transactive memory is task–expertise–person (TEP) units that answer in fundamental ways the know-who question (Brandon and Hollingshead 2004).

Transactive memory explains how people develop cognitive knowledge networks that help them identify the skills and expertise of others (Monge and Contractor 2003; Palazzolo 2006; Palazzolo *et al.* 2006). It can improve the efficiency and effectiveness of a group by promoting a division of labor in certain information-processing tasks, while also providing mechanisms for integration (Brandon and Hollingshead 2004; Hollingshead 1998). Groups in which members' expertise is made public have been found to share more unique information (Thomas-Hunt, Ogden, and Neale 2003). Several interrelated processes are involved including retrieval coordination, directory updating, and information allocation (Palazzolo 2006; Palazzolo *et al.* 2006; Wegner 1995). Retrieval coordination specifies procedures for finding information. Directory updating involves learning who knows what, while information allocation assigns memory items for group members. So, an *ad hoc* work team might initially meet to determine the expertise of its members, assigning them research tasks and specifying procedures for gathering information related to their tasks in a format that can be shared. For ongoing groups, TEP can be assigned formally, based on individuals' roles, from memory, from various social constructions, from documents, and so on (Brandon and Hollingshead 2004). Once someone's expertise is known, they are more likely to become the objects of information searches (Borgatti and Cross 2003). In a recent empirical test, Palazzolo (2006) found that actual work-team networks depend more on others' perception of one's expertise, than on one's self-reported expertise.

Small-world strategies

Most people lack information skills and have a limited repertoire of search behaviors (Johnson 1996b). Here the formal structure of an organization and professional training can be of considerable assistance, since a large portion of it imparts a formalized set of rules for gathering information in support of decision making (Leckie 2005) (see Table 12.1). However, searches outside these parameters are not governed by the same elaborate set of rules as programmed decision searches. Fortunately, well-established programs of research in two areas can provide us with some clues as to how people go about non-programmed, idiosyncratic searches.

Informal status is often associated with expertise, which can provide one cue for information searches. The twist is that we are not seeking a particular target other, but rather targeted information that another may possess. So one clue may lie in the reputation of radial others, or in assumptions that others might have of their unique attributes (e.g., they have wide-ranging contacts that might lead me to my target). In this sort of "expertise" network, knowledge may substitute for formal authority for identification of targets, but similar problems of access, managing attention, overload, and queuing may result (Krackhardt 1994).

In the classic small-world problem the task is for an individual to contact a distant target other, previously unknown to them, through intermediaries (Barabasi 2003; Buchanan 2002). Most of the research in this area has focused on the overall structural aspects of the linkages through which an individual goes; less attention has been given to how individuals strategically target particular intermediaries. So, recent findings in e-mail networks suggest individuals are more likely to forward a message when the intended recipient appears easier to reach (Newman, Barabasi, and Watts 2006). Watts (2003) has recently examined the latter aspect of the problem. He suggests individuals start with two broad strategies. One is to engage in a broadcast search in which one tells everyone one knows. They in turn tell everyone they know until a target is reached or, in this case, an answer is found. This approach is crude and has some obvious problems: (1) it reveals one's ignorance widely; (2) it implicates a large number of others, distracting them from their other tasks; (3) it may produce large volumes of information that need then to be filtered by some criteria (e.g., credibility, relevance, and so on). Reach and selectivity are often conflicting strategies for information dissemination in organizations. In an ideal world one might want to reach everyone with an inquiry, but the costs of pursuing this strategy are prohibitive (Monge and Contractor 2003), especially for problems one would like to keep secret.

The alternative, a directed search, may start by deciding on some criteria (e.g., one will only ask scientists). Here search targets may be categorized in broadly stereotypic ways as potentially having the information that is needed. Of course, the best of all criteria is some indication of a target's position in the overall social structure (e.g., are they well connected to diverse others; what social groups do they belong to; are they homophilous to me?) (Watts 2003). In general, Watts (2003) has found networks to be more easily searchable when individuals can judge their similarity to target others along multiple dimensions. Interestingly, when individuals are required to do repeated directed searches an overall structure evolves that does not result in bottlenecks at the top of the hierarchy, that is highly searchable (partly because of the recognition of more weak ties), and that is relatively robust in response to environmental changes. Watts goes on to suggest that developing effective social structures may be a better solution to search problems than reliance on centrally designed problem-solving tools and data bases.

Feedback seeking

The area related to individual information seeking in organizations that has probably received the most research attention over the last two decades has been feedback seeking related to individual performance (Ashford, Blatt, and VandeWalle 2003; Ashford and Tsui 1991), especially during organizational entry or job changing (e.g., Brett, Feldman, and Weingart 1990; Comer 1991; Morrison and Bies 1991; Morrison 1993a, b). Of particular interest have been the strategies that individuals use to uncover information about task, cultural, and other expectations an organization might have related to their performance (Miller and Jablin 1991). The information newcomers acquire is critical for determining their adjustment to the organization and their performance within it. Information seeking thus becomes a significant coping mechanism for individuals (Brett, Feldman, and Weingart 1990). Typically feedback seeking about performance is associated with positive adjustment of newcomers and poor adjustment for job changers (Brett, Feldman, and Weingart 1990), who perhaps thought they knew more about a job from their past, tacit experiences than they really did.

A newcomer in the organization is often confronted with a vast array of information of which s/he must make sense in order to determine appropriate behaviors. Formally his/her supervisor may lay out a set of expectations, which are then reinforced by a job description sheet. Informally s/he may be told that job performance is not the critical issue; how well you perform in the company bowling team is. Feedback seeking often complements formal organizational socialization efforts, filling in the gaps and interpreting seeming discrepancies in the information provided to employees. Active information seeking is often necessary because organizations withhold information inadvertently or purposively (Miller and Jablin 1991). Organizations, on the dark side, may not want to share all their secrets until someone has passed an initiation period and can be trusted. They also may want to "protect" employees during the initial "honeymoon" period. At times they also may try to keep employees from coming into contact with dissidents who may impede socialization efforts. They also may want to keep employees "on edge" because they assume withholding positive feedback will heighten employee effort. Whatever information is acquired must be assimilated quickly because typically, especially in American companies, impressions are formed very rapidly about an organizational member's capabilities.

The vast array of information to which newcomers are exposed, and the gaps in the information with which they are provided, often result in high levels of uncertainty. This uncertainty affects people's perceptions of role ambiguity and can impede an employee's job satisfaction and productivity, and ultimately affect his/her tenure. With such uncomfortable feelings, employees are driven to seek information that would reduce the uncertainty they are experiencing (Miller and Jablin 1991). But here they may be doubly vexed because they may be inexperienced information seekers who do not know what strategies are appropriate or useful in their organization. So, often a naive employee will think that question asking is the only available information strategy they have, little realizing that asking direct questions about sensitive areas may be taboo. Counterbalancing the uncertainty newcomers are experiencing are the social costs of seeking information (Miller and Jablin 1991) and a desire to manage the impression they give others (Morrison and Bies 1991). However, impression management is often a subtle process, with the active seeking of negative information being associated with positive impressions of supervisors (Ashford and Tsui 1991), since it appears to be motivated by a desire to improve.

Costs, as we have seen, are real and numerous, and may impede information-seeking behaviors. Individuals may be afraid of going to the well once too often and being cut off from information from a particular source. They may assume that someone will think they are dumb for asking a particular question. They may think that information seeking reflects poorly on their competence and their training to perform a particular job (Ashford 1986). These factors may result in individuals pursuing less overt means of acquiring information (Miller and Jablin 1991), as we have seen in the Blau case study (Box 11.1).

Information seeking for newcomers differs in several ways from that of established organizational members. As we have seen it may involve much more uncertainty and urgency. It also may be more thoughtful, with newcomers consciously weighing the efficacies of various strategies they might employ, since they have not yet established the habits of information seeking particular to their profession and a specific organizational context (Miller and Jablin 1991). Newcomers also focus on three primary types of content: referent (what are my job requirements?), appraisal (how well am I doing?), and relational (do other people like me?) (Miller and Jablin 1991).

Strategies for individual feedback seeking

While we will primarily focus on strategies that have been identified for newcomers in this section, we also will try to develop a comprehensive list of strategies that are more generally used by individuals in organizations. Thus, information seeking can be directly related to self-performance assessment, where individuals determine if they are meeting personal standards and goals (Ashford 1986, 1989; Ashford and Cummings 1985; Ashford and Tsui 1991).

The most obvious strategy, and seemingly the most efficient (Comer 1991), is to ask overt questions on the topic of interest. So, if I am a new administrative assistant, I may ask if I am expected to make coffee every morning. Asking overt questions may be expected and encouraged early in someone's tenure in an organization. This strategy is more likely to be used when an individual feels comfortable with a situation; when they want a direct, immediate, and authoritative reply. Individuals may feel uncomfortable asking direct questions if they perceive others will view them as constantly pestering them for information, or a question reveals more about themselves (e.g., I do not know how to perform my job) than they want others to know (Miller and Jablin 1991). Use of questioning also involves a choice for the target of the question (Ashford 1986), which in itself may be difficult (Morrison 1993b), as we have seen earlier. Similarly, there is also the risk that a question (e.g., how well am I doing?) will result in a negative answer (Brett, Feldman, and Weingart 1990) that both supervisor and employee would like to avoid (Ashford 1986; Larson 1989).

Indirect questions are often employed in cases where someone is uncomfortable (Miller and Jablin 1991). They usually take the form of a simple declarative sentence or observation that is meant to solicit information, often disguised within an apparently casual conversation. Blau (1955) observed workers establishing occasions for information seeking by hanging out with others, i.e., merely being present at informal events.

Yet another strategy is to use a third party as an intermediary to gather information. Thus, rather than asking your supervisor, who serves as a primary source, you might ask his/her assistant as a secondary source of information (Miller and Jablin 1991). This strategy would be used most often when a primary source is unavailable or the seeker feels uncomfortable approaching him/her directly. The downside to this strategy is that the secondary source must be trustworthy and a true surrogate for the primary source. At times the most approachable individuals for a newcomer are those individuals who are most likely to lead them astray, who may have their own motivations for undermining a supervisor or giving an alternative version of an organization's culture.

Another, more dangerous strategy in which individuals might engage is testing limits (Miller and Jablin 1991). So, if an individual really wants to find out how his/her supervisor will react to tardiness, s/he might try getting to work progressively later each day. Obviously this strategy is potentially confrontational and the employee runs the risk of the supervisor generalizing from the specific behavior to more global assessments (e.g., this employee is untrustworthy). Still, individuals might use this as a last resort, especially when the issue is of paramount personal importance to them.

A less direct strategy is that of observing (Miller and Jablin 1991). Employees can watch the actual behaviors of their supervisors and co-workers and weigh them against their words. Managers, too, are likely to give special credence to what they observe (McKinnon and Bruns 1992). Employees can often learn how to handle critical situations from just being with an experienced hand. Thus, an individual can inconspicuously imitate another's behavior. There are limits, however, to what a new employee can directly observe, especially concerning the thought processes that may underlie particular actions.

Beyond the newcomer's information-seeking strategies traditionally identified in the literature, there are other strategies (e.g., skimming, berrypicking [Bates 1989, 2005], chaining, monitoring key sources for developments [Ellis 1989]) that have been identified in the information science literature, which also might pertain to this problem, and, more generally, to other information-seeking situations. Probably, the most interesting of these is browsing, because of its random, non-rational surface appearance.

Browsing essentially involves scanning the contents of a resource base (Chang 2005). It is often used as a strategy early in a search process or when someone is scanning his/her environment (O'Conner 1993). A key element of browsing is preparedness to be surprised and to follow up (Chang and Rice 1993). Thus, in researching this book I would look at book titles surrounding those identified by more formal, rational computerized searches. In doing this I often found works that were more interesting to me than the immediate objects of my search. Inadequate browsing capacity has been traditionally a major shortcoming of most computerized search software (Chang and Rice 1993). Browsing in social contexts often takes the form of informal networking. Casual conversations (e.g., gossip) in a group may take on elements of browsing, with more intensive follow-up on topics that interest an individual. Even the classic principle of management by walking around (e.g., touring a plant) has been identified as a type of browsing. Browsing is facilitated by accessibility, flexibility, and interactivity (Chang and Rice 1993).

In sum, while many strategies have been identified, we know less about what factors will trigger the use of any one strategy. We also do not know answers to such fundamental questions as how many strategies individuals are aware of and actually use in their behavioral repertoire. We also know very little about the sequencing of strategies and how individuals might use them in combination for particular effects (Miller and Jablin 1991). We do know that newcomers use a variety of channels and obtain information on a range of contents (Comer 1991), with particular channels and sources being associated with one another. So, for example, accountants are more likely to use a questioning strategy for technical problems and are more likely to consult co-workers for normative and social information (Morrison 1993b).

Information foraging

More recently, another systematic approach to individual information gathering has developed in evolutionary psychology, based on earlier anthropological and behavioral ecology literatures on how humans gather food. Information foraging theory suggests that people will modify their strategies and the structure of their information fields to maximize the rate of gaining valuable information. It develops three classes of models designed to describe how individuals adapt their information seeking to the flux of information in their environment. First, information patch models deal with the amount of time allocated, filtering, and enrichment activities when information is detected in clusters in an individual's environment. Second, information scent models address the cues individuals use to determine the potential value of information. Third, information diet models focus on decision making related to the selection and pursuit of certain information items. Fundamentally, providing people with access to information is not the problem in today's environment; "the problem is one of maximizing the allocation of human attention to information that will be useful . . ." (Pirolli and Card 1999, p. 643).

This discussion suggests several clear classes of strategy that could be used to enhance information seeking. Interestingly, the authors of this approach were researchers at Xerox's famed Palo Alto Research Center, who were directly confronting information technology needed to enhance organizational information seeking. First, we can increase the proximity of individuals to information patches, thus decreasing "down time" when they cannot forage. Second, we can enhance people's skill in detecting information scents so they have an easier time detecting the correct patches in which to forage. Third, we can enhance their capabilities of foraging once they are in a patch by filtering and enrichment activities that mold the environment to fit available strategies. Specialists focus on high-density patches, while generalists gather information from a wide variety of patches (Jacoby 2005).

Like all metaphors this one has a particularly appealing set of concepts that can be applied to knowledge acquisition, but it also may not perfectly fit prior empirical findings. While all humans have some appetite for food, there is still individual variation in what kinds of nourishment they seek, and as we have seen, the information-seeking literature suggests that not all individuals have a drive to forage for information, in spite of characterizations of the human species as "informavores" (Pirolli and Card 1999).

Summary

Information seeking in KN is often a great challenge to individuals. They have to overcome their tendency to deny the possibility of bad news, and perhaps some of the distasteful problems associated with organizational life. They also have to be willing to believe that their individual actions can make a difference, that by seeking information they gain some control and mastery over their tasks. They also have to overcome the limits of their education and knowledge base. They have to possess skills as information seekers, a knowledge of data bases, familiarity with the Internet, and an ability to weigh conflicting sources of information and to make judgments about their credibility. In short, any one of the factors in this rather long-linked chain could severely impede, if not halt, the acquisition of knowledge.

Many of these traditional barriers to information seeking can be addressed. Training programs and support structures can be designed to overcome individual lack of skills and awareness of information sources. They also can increase the salience of KN development as an important life/career skill. Perhaps, most importantly, new technologies, which were explored in detail in Chapter 6, offer the possibility of overcoming and/or substituting for the traditional problems of accessibility, inertia, and the limitations of humans as information processors. But, as Paisley (1993) details, knowledge dissemination research has gone through similar cycles of excitement over promising new technologies that have fallen by the wayside. Perhaps the most serious limit to these technologies is the recurring preference of individuals for interpersonal information sources who can digest and summarize vast quantities of information for individual seekers. For most of us the problem is not finding nourishment, but rather finding the highest energy input for the effort we expend.

Management's role

The dilemma is clear: on the one hand, managers receive too much information, while on the other hand, they don't get enough of the right information.   (Katzer and Fletcher 1992, p. 227)

... a tentative profile of the superior who is likely to promote increased information flow from lower organizational levels. Such an individual will have power and upward influence, will be employee oriented, will generally not be overloaded, and will value information coming from subordinates. (Glauser 1984, p. 622)

Managers face a daunting task in today's information environment that has been variously described by words ranging from a "mosaic" (McKinnon and Bruns 1992) to a "jungle" (Holsapple and Whinston 1988). They must come to intelligent judgments based on the welter of facts, forecasts, gossip, and intuition which make up their information environment. Perhaps most importantly, however, managers are not only responsible for themselves, but they also must nurture and enhance the information capabilities of their subordinates. They provide a source of information, as well as a link to the larger information environment of the organization (Madzar 2001).

It seems that almost every issue in organizational behavior can be examined on two levels: its impact on individuals and its impact on the organization as an institution. In this section we will first describe traditional search strategies used by managers to get information from often recalcitrant bureaucracies; we will then turn to what managers can do to facilitate the KN of others in their organization. As we saw when we discussed formal structures, the central problem for management is condensing a wealth of information in such a way as to obtain an accurate picture of the organization, an area where new technologies have been of considerable assistance (Porter and Millar 1985). Yet, this imperative often provides the opportunity for subordinates actively to distort and withhold needed information from managers.

Bureaucracies encourage managers to think of a one-way, top-down flow of communication. Historically, managers have relied on the mass media, especially written channels, to efficiently reach large numbers of workers in their campaigns (e.g., to improve safety or quality). These authoritative dicta and the lack of interactivity in the communication mode were meant more to discourage KN than to stimulate them. Many approaches and assumptions of traditional media research were often implicit in this style.

Somewhat akin to the mass media's historical bullet theory, workers were thought to be a relatively passive, defenseless audience. Communication, in effect, could be shot into them (Schramm 1973). This view of communication was embedded in the more general stimulus–response notions popular in psychological research at this time (Rogers and Storey 1987). However, it soon became apparent that, while there were some notable successes, audiences could be remarkably resistant to campaigns, especially when the message of a campaign did not correspond to the views of their immediate social network (Huckfeldt, Johnson, and Sprague 2004; Katz and Lazersfeld 1955; Rogers and Storey 1987).

There developed a tendency among theorists of communication campaigns to cast "the audience as 'bad guys' who are hard to reach, obstinate, and recalcitrant" (Dervin 1989, p. 73). The term "obstinate audience" was coined by Bauer in his classic research article detailing the active role audience members play in the processing of communication messages (Bauer 1972). In natural situations, Bauer contends, the audience selects what it will attend to. These selections often depend on interests, and the interests of audience members are reflected in their level of knowledge and the strength of their convictions. While exposure is the first step to persuasion (McGuire 1989), the audience members most likely to attend to messages related to management's interests are those organizational members already committed to them. Dervin (1989), in this connection, has suggested that the most appropriate strategy might be to change the institutions delivering the message, rather than to expect the audience to change deeply seated behavior patterns. In effect, management campaigns may be reaching the already converted. While this might have a beneficial effect of further reinforcing beliefs, the organizational members who are most in need of being reached are precisely those members who are least likely to attend to management's message.

Management campaigns often fail because their recommended beneficial effects are not apparent to employees and they do not identify market segments within the total audience who require different communication approaches in line with their specific needs (Robertson and Wortzel 1977). The bottom-line issue is that interested people acquire on their own most of the information available on any subject (Hyman and Sheatsley 1947).

One essential pragmatic benefit of the perspective adopted in this book is an increase in the "match" between management communication efforts and their audiences. A focus on individuals is necessary since their perceptions of the information environment will determine their usage irrespective of the "objective" nature of this environment. Individuals are active agents, not just passive recipients; the dynamic nature of their KN patterns has proven to be a more powerful predictor of their information acquisition than a focus on such traditional areas as demographics or past media exposure (Dervin, Jacobson, and Nilan 1982). This suggests that finer-grain discriminations of the social structure of the audience may be necessary to insure effective communication campaigns.

As we have seen, perhaps the best strategy is to achieve a "match" between the information carriers to whom managers choose to disseminate information and the information-seeking profiles of individuals. Thus, the question becomes the much more sophisticated one of placing the most appropriate content, in the most appropriate channel, where it is most likely to be used by a predetermined audience.

Management efforts also suffer from unrealistic expectations. Most advertising campaigns would be happy with a level of change in their audience of 3–5 percent a year (Robertson and Wortzel 1977). McGuire (1989) has also pointed out the very low probabilities of success of communication campaigns given the long string of steps that must be fulfilled (e.g., first get the audience's attention), each of which only has a moderate probability of success.

Modern views of managerial communication are more likely to stress a dialogic view of interaction, with both parties initiating and attending to messages in turn. These views also incorporate a much more specific role for KN, which in traditional views were almost totally ignored. Management's most important role in these perspectives is as a stimulus or cue to action. They must define the most important issues that an organization needs to face, setting the agenda.

Rogers (1995) has identified agenda setting as a central role of management in the diffusion of innovations. In this view, management identifies and prioritizes a need, as well as encouraging information scanning in an organization's environment for potential solutions. Interestingly, in this process, organizations often find solutions for problems which they did not know existed, leading to innovation implementation that was not on anyone's radar screen.

A letter from the president in a company newsletter may identify a top organizational priority (e.g., developing new products to meet increased competition). This is not an answer; it is an implied set of questions for KN: why are our competitors succeeding? What can we do in response? Successfully establishing this agenda will result in numerous proactive information-seeking behaviors by workers. Thus, a critical role of management in the innovation process is that of managing attention (Van de Ven 1986).

Management's KN

Elsewhere we have detailed the powerful barriers that exist to management's search for information in traditional bureaucratic structures: segmentation, contrary individual motives, lack of trust, and so forth. Here we focus on strategies managers can use to acquire knowledge in traditional organizational structures. Unfortunately, many organizations have dual structures. The networked collaborative structure exists side-by-side with the traditional formal one, with the former used for getting the work done and the latter used for preserving and maintaining power and for the accomplishment of narrow productivity goals. The consistent use of some of the strategies discussed in this section may result in a tilt by management to the old ways, which prevents the coming of the new.

Many of the early sections of this book covered structures and communication channels which managers use to support their information needs. Many of the strategies used by newcomers to uncover information that we discussed earlier in this chapter also can be used by managers. For example, browsing, especially because of its random, unstructured nature, can alert managers to potential problems that might exist in their organization. Management by walking around is but one form of browsing, especially useful for the early stages of decision making (Saunders and Jones 1990), that managers might employ (Peters and Waterman 1982: Chang and Rice 1993). So managers might set aside a couple of hours a week for seemingly random tours of facilities; they also might take a random walk through the paperwork done at lower levels, rather than relying on more formal, condensed reports.

Savvy managers listen to and learn from their subordinates. While managers are walking around they might pause to "shoot the breeze" with workers. This conversation will do very little good in a KN sense if a manager spends all the time talking or tries to persuade workers to adopt a new approach to work. A manager must be prepared to ask neutral questions and listen with care to responses. Thus, browsing is also a specific example of a more general strategy of going directly to the source of information rather than letting information be filtered by various intermediaries in the formal structure. Almost 90 percent of managers report learning of significant organizational changes through these sorts of informal information strategies (Katzer and Fletcher 1992).

It helps managers to have key informants for particular domains of information (Mintzberg 1976). Traditionally, these individuals have been described as gatekeepers because of their role in filtering information, often in a condensed understandable fashion (Downs 1967). The modern trend is to eliminate the middleman, keeping the hierarchy flat, reflecting the need of managers to be closer to information sources if messages are not going to be distorted (Downs 1967). Still, no manager can regularly go to the direct source of information; there is not sufficient time. Here a manager can use many of the suggestions of Burt (1992) related to structural holes, developing a wide range of non-redundant sources strategically located so that they give the manager the widest possible view of the organization. In doing this, managers also should develop sources of information external to their organization (e.g., customers, suppliers, and media) who can give them an idea of how their organization is functioning (Downs 1967).

At the same time as managers are developing a breadth of ties, they need to insure that they have sufficient redundant ties to give them alternative sources of information on critical issues (Burt 1992). Creating competitive sources for the same information, with overlapping responsibilities and rewarding a diversity of views (Downs 1967), also overcomes the disturbing tendency of many to distort information. While the carrot may be preferable to the stick, it helps to have a visible, even if unused, stick around. For example, performance appraisal systems should explicitly reward information sharing and punish hoarding. Employees should realize that there is the threat of investigation and that a manager will follow up on problems (Downs 1967) and correct them. Managers who have influence and contacts with those above them in the hierarchy are more likely to be the target of upward communication from their subordinates (Glauser 1984), partly because this entails access to rewards and to punishments. So, when someone passes information on to a manager, it is important that s/he knows what the manager did with it, that it did have some impact.

While managers often have compelling reasons to hoard information and not share it with others, the efficiency and effectiveness of modern organizations depend on information sharing. Managers should realize they have a vested interest in upgrading the information-seeking skills and capabilities of their subordinates if for no other reason than it will enhance the quality of information that they in turn pass on to their supervisors and any decisions they reach (More 1990). However, as Marshall and Stoll (1993) found in their study of network participation and empowerment, managers often resist wide-scale worker involvement, seeing it as detracting from more narrow productivity goals.

Facilitating information seeking

> Efficiency requires members of the audience to be treated amorphously and to
> bend to the institution. Effectiveness requires that individuals be helped on
> their own terms.   (Dervin 1989, p. 85)

While at its core almost every large organization has a bureaucracy, the issues
that are emerging in contemporary organizations arise from a cluster of new
technologies and horizontal coordination processes that many argue are resulting
in a new organizational form: the networked organization (Nohria and Eccles
1992). In this new organization the principle function of management is not to
extract information from ungrateful workers, nor to provide information from the
top down. Management's role in networked organization comes in facilitating
the flow of information and insuring that there is support for the organization's
information infrastructure, which was described in detail in Chapter 6. Many
organizations have realized that there are real strategic advantages, especially
in enhancing quality and developing innovations, in investing in technologies
that enable a networked form of highly collaborative organization that enhances
needed coordination relationships.

As Porter and Millar (1985) point out, competitive advantages come not just
from enhancing performance, but in giving organizations new ways to outperform
competitors and in developing new information businesses. Improving information management, associated analytic skills, and knowledge utilization should
be a top priority of management (McGee and Prusak 1993). However, too often
information systems are ignored by users because they are not accessible or
user-friendly (McKinnon and Bruns 1992), and improving employees' access to
internal knowledge has proven more difficult than it might first appear (Gray and
Meister 2004).

The basic task of management is to change structures, information infrastructure and technology, and culture (e.g., transmission rules) (Downs 1967) to
promote information sharing and seeking in a KN. In effect, management should
serve as a guide to what areas and sources are most likely to have valuable
information. In more modern organizational forms the basic job of management
is not finding information, but rather facilitating the search for information by
all members of the organization. Managers must serve as the chief designers
of more effective information systems and organizational structures (Galbraith
1995), providing the elaborate information infrastructure discussed in Chapter 6.

In part, enhancing KN can be accomplished by improving the climate of the
organization. Satisfied, secure, high-performing, and ambitious employees are
less likely to distort communication messages (Glauser 1984) and thus block
the acquisition of information by others. There may also be a contagion effect
which increases my willingness to share information with others in a growing,
vibrant organization. In this situation a rising tide raises all boats and the success of my peers can contribute to my success as well. Organizations which
are no longer growing become more characterized by zero-sum games, that is,

one member only succeeds at the expense of others, which can have disastrous consequences on the flow of information in informal networks. A focus on information about what the organization should be doing in the future, rather than the more ego-threatening what we have done in the past (Downs 1967), contributes to the development of more positive climates; so does promoting a feeling of problem solving – encouraging feelings of experimentation and inquiry. The best managers in these new organizational environments are practical theorists who solve puzzles, focusing on quantitative, objective information whenever possible (Downs 1967).

A cornerstone of any strategy to facilitate information seeking is the removal of various access barriers. Firms have to support the sharing and use of information (Menon and Varadarajan 1992). Workers must have access to up-to-date, detailed, technical information. They should be able to serve themselves from a common pool of available information through modern telecommunication and data base systems. In creating such systems, management must be willing to let workers' inquiries go where they will. It is self-defeating to listen in on bulletin boards and other electronic forms of communication (Zuboff 1988), since this defeats their primary information-sharing function.

Perhaps most importantly, management must be willing to share its interpretations of information and what types of information it considers to be the most critical to the organization's future. In short, managers must be willing objects/resources for information searches by organizational employees. A precursor to a better dialog would be to increase the organizational members' knowledge base. To provide better information, subordinates need to understand what messages are relevant to their supervisors and what is important to them (Glauser 1984).

In the emerging market-based organizations, rewards are inherent in the search and exchange of information. Markets allow for the possibility of a few central rules governing relationships that can be easily enforced, that permit a delegation of authority to individuals to determine for themselves the ultimate value of any information exchange. Management must think carefully about the incentives for more active information seeking. In many organizational contexts sharing ideas is an "unnatural act," especially where individual performance is the sole focus of reward systems (*Business Week* 1994). As a general rule, managers should encourage employees to develop weak ties to encourage information sharing throughout the organization. Traditionally, information seeking has been punished in various ways. If you uncovered something wrong in the organization, you were placed in the position of the classic messenger to the emperor whose head was chopped off for bringing bad news.

Somewhat relatedly, to coordinate most effectively there must be compatibility among various information systems (Malone, Yates, and Benjamin 1987) and some form of organization-wide standards for information processing (Hoffman 1994). Coordination costs increase with distributed work and more extensive lines of communication (Keen 1990) and the problem of information asymmetries (e.g., quality) may be insurmountable in terms of creating totally open corporate information infrastructures (Connolly and Thorn 1990). For example, in hospital settings CEOs received twice as much decision-making information as their boards and three times as much as their medical staffs (Thomas, Clark, and Gioia 1993). As a result, they have considerably different knowledge bases and interpretive frameworks. The type of information processed by functional specialties also differs, with production-based information more certain and quantifiable than the typical mix of marketing and sales information (McKinnon and Bruns 1992). This fragmentation, which can be augmented and enhanced by information technology, makes it much harder for differing groups to communicate across their boundaries (Hoffman 1994).

Educate organizational members on capabilities of information carriers

Currently workers can easily "avoid" management communications because they often use channels and sources that are unfamiliar to them. Managers need to understand workers' normative expectations of information carriers, and where this is misguided, agencies may want to correct this with their training programs, since avoiding authoritative sources can impede individual performance, often resulting in individuals working at cross-purposes with organizational goals.

Increasing an individual's familiarity with possible authoritative sources of information, such as those formally assigned to particular projects, should be one aspect of any training program. There is a vast literature in information science relating to differences in information seeking and use in different professions (Case 2007). Even highly trained scientists may be unaware of sophisticated bibliographic tools. One objective of training programs should be to sensitize individuals to other sources of communication and to increase their information-seeking capabilities.[2] More knowledgeable individuals have "a better view of the structure ... [and are] more capable of locating the specific resources embedded in structure" (Lin 2001, p. 57). Increasingly, when employees use sources like the Internet, which contain many conflicting voices, they need to be trained in how to weigh the credibility of various sources as well. Exposure to a diverse array of sources increases the validity of any synthesis and allows people to triangulate conflicting information. For enhanced information seeking, training and skill development are essential, but one major concern related to increased use of technology is deskilling, the use of information technology to reduce the level of expertise of human operators of a system. At its simplest level, this can often be seen in counter and clerical people in retail organizations who interface with increasingly sophisticated management information systems that do their work for them (e.g., scan for the price of individual items and automatically calculate the costs of a group of purchases for customers). These machines can

---

[2] Companies that successfully implement information technologies often must spend three dollars in training for every dollar spent on hardware (Hoffman 1994).

monitor the pace of workers, insuring they are performing at high levels. These systems provide for more managerial control; at the same time they demand less from a worker (Palmquist 1992). Offsetting these trends is the possibility of a system "informating" a work task, providing workers with constant feedback on their performance and, in doing so, upgrading skill levels. For example, computer monitoring of athletic performance can provide essential feedback on technique that can result in enhanced performance. In effect, the athlete partners with an automatic trainer that provides him/her with an increasingly sophisticated view of his/her behaviors.

One key outcome of training programs should be enhanced decision making. The point is not just to acquire information, but to acquire information that is goal- or job-related. At one extreme some high information users spend so much time communicating that they have very little time left over to be productive (Brittain 1970; McGee and Prusak 1993). At the other extreme are individuals who try to make the decision search as easy as possible, looking for a cause near its effect and looking for a solution near an old one (MacCrimmon and Taylor 1976).

Creating rich information fields

> By enabling top managers to obtain local information quickly and accurately, management information systems reduce ignorance and help managers make decisions that they, otherwise, may have been unwilling to make …
> (Huber 1990, p. 56)

> Everyone is entitled to their own opinion, but not their own data.
> (Galbraith 1995, p. 94)

> The big payoff of this approach is that by understanding how people search socially, we can hope to design more effective *procedures* by which robust organizations can be constructed without having to specify the precise details of the organizational architecture itself.   (Watts 2003, p. 289, italics in original)

Another possible approach to enhancing KN is to increase the richness of an individual's information fields and the larger corporate information infrastructure (Grover and Davenport 2001). This is an especially appropriate strategy for individuals who are not normally active seekers, but who are interested and concerned about organizational issues. This strategy can potentially broaden awareness of larger corporate issues beyond someone's immediate job, since it removes barriers to the acquisition of information. It can also increase the knowledge base of individuals, making it more likely they can communicate effectively with managers when a problem develops. Conversely, it also has the effect of undermining the power of managers who depend on information hoarding for control (Hoffman 1994).

Increasing the availability of information is particularly appropriate for individuals who are only casually motivated to seek out information. Allen's (1977) work in research and development laboratories suggests that increased familiarity with information carriers increases perceptions of accessibility, but this does little good if the information is not perceived as useful. These strategies are also essential to creating information equity (Siefert, Gerbner, and Fisher 1989) that might serve to reduce critical gaps in the knowledge and awareness of organizational issues. Managers must make it easy for workers to change, since most individuals will resist change, especially change related to information technology (Hoffman 1994).

Because of the unwillingness of individuals to devote much effort to information acquisition noted earlier, it is important that managers arrange to have information easily available for target audiences by increasing the physical access to information in the immediate work environment. As we have seen, physical access provides the opportunity and occasion for interactions (Sykes 1983). Meetings are a particularly rich setting for sharing information and should also be considered to be part of an organization's information infrastructure (Johnson 2005). They are the occasion for storytelling, arguing, explaining, and focusing, all primary forms of information discovery (Solomon 2002). In research and development laboratories considerable effort has been devoted to discovering the ideal physical layout to insure there is a sharing of ideas (e.g., Allen 1977).

All this suggests the increasing importance of information as a strategic asset to organizations that should be systematically incorporated in the planning of upper management (Marchand and Horton 1986). Corporations also need to recognize the potential benefit of marketing unique corporate knowledge and expertise to other information seekers. For example, large-scale agricultural enterprises may have developed unique ancillary knowledge related to weather prediction that could lead to new spinoff industries that others would like to acquire.

Summary

In this chapter we have focused on strategies for finding knowledge. Individual strategies must recognize the basic limits of human beings, who are not the rational information seekers often assumed in the literature or by developers of information systems. Disconcertingly, while studies have demonstrated that people are very unsophisticated users of seemingly ubiquitous online search engines, they are satisfied with their own ability to get the answers they want (Markey 2007). Similarly, people typically have only a limited understanding of where they can go in KN to receive answers to their questions. They tend to rely on easily accessible human agents, such as opinion leaders, and tend not to be very sophisticated in seeking feedback that would enhance their own performance. Management's role in the modern organization becomes one of recognizing these limits and designing systems that ameliorate them. From a resource-based view, organizations that confront these realities will have substantial strategic advantages.

Further reading

Ashford, S. J., Blatt, R., and VandeWalle, D. 2003. Reflections on the looking glass: a review of research on feedback-seeking behavior in organizations. *Journal of Management*, 29: 773–799.

Comprehensive review of this literature by Ashford, perhaps the leading authority in this area.

Case, D. O. 2007. *Looking for Information*, 2nd edn. Academic Press.

The comprehensive contemporary book on the information-seeking literature.

Fisher, K. E., Erdelez, S., and McKechnie, L. (eds.) 2005. *Theories of Information Behavior*. Information Today.

Useful summary of major theories in the information science literature.

Johnson, J. D. 1996. *Information Seeking: An Organizational Dilemma*. Quorum.

Early comprehensive review of information-seeking literature in organizations.

Wegner, D. M. 1995. A computer network model of human transactive memory. *Social Cognition*, 13: 319–339.

Seminal article on transactive memory.

13 Decision making

The only point at which knowledge can affect a social system is through its impacts on decisions.

(Boulding 1966, p. 30)

Decisions require clarity, closure, and confidence. As a result, decisive action comes more easily from the ignorant than from the wise, more easily from the short-sighted than from those who anticipate the long run.

(March 1991, p. 265)

Decision makers look for information, but they see what they expect to see and overlook unexpected things.

(March 1994, p. 11)

We take it as a given that some of the information that is important for the organization to make good decisions is not directly available to those charged with making the decisions. Instead, it is lodged with or producible only by other individuals or groups that are not empowered to make the decisions but may have a direct interest in the resulting outcomes . . . In such situations, the members of the organization may have an incentive to try to manipulate the information they develop and provide in order to influence decisions to their benefits.

(Milgram and Roberts 1988, p. 156)

Every day we see the consequences of poorly made decisions, especially in our political life. The term groupthink has come to symbolize the very human, group processes (e.g., cohesiveness, conformity) that conspire against "good," rational decision making. Janis (1971), in tracing the decision making of the US foreign policy establishment regarding Vietnam, the Cuban missile crises, and the Bay of Pigs, found one recurring theme – how group processes and the limits of human decision making restricted the range of information that was sought and the consideration of a range of alternatives once information was obtained. Box 13.1, on *How Doctors Think*, details the impact of similar decision-making processes on physician–patient interactions, revealing some deep-seated problems in KN.

Traditionally, the primary impetus for information seeking in organizational KN has been in terms of its role in decision making. This has been true of information behavior more generally (Case 2007) and can be seen as the ultimate outcome of these processes. The behavioral decision school of organizational theory, which we turn to first and is represented primarily by Cyert, March, Simon, and Carnegie Mellon University, has cast the central issue in organizational

Box 13.1. *How Doctors Think*

Groopman's *How Doctors Think* is a book about decision making: how doctors gather information, primarily focusing on their relationships with patients, and how they deal (or not) with uncertainty in weighing alternatives to makes diagnoses. Jerome Groopman, MD, holds an endowed chair at Harvard Medical School. He is also chief of experimental medicine at Beth Israel Deaconness Medical Center. He is perhaps best known for his popular writings that appear in leading national magazines and newspapers. His work is an interesting complement to Box 13.2, on clinical decision-making systems, since it is often written in opposition to them, a plea for more humanistic decision making.

The book starts with chapters that lay the groundwork for what follows, emphasizing the uniqueness of each patient and the resulting criticality of physician–patient interaction in jointly creating a successful diagnosis. Through detailed case studies, it focuses on Groopman's initial training and exposure to "flesh-and-blood decision-making", his initial, shaky encounter with a patient with a torn aortic valve, and the difficulties of an intern translating "book knowledge" to actual situations. It then details several cases that highlight classic problems in decision making, such as representativeness, and other errors resting on stereotyping and emotional processes; this is the common managerial problem of juggling many tasks at once. It focuses on the Nobel Prize winning work of Tversky and Kahneman and classic cognitive errors in decision making such as availability heuristics, confirmation biases, and anchoring, with special application to ER settings. It focuses on pediatricians who often operate in a sleep-deprived, limited attention mode owing to the frenetic nature of their practices. Intensive care units have such classic decision-making problems as forming mental prototypes, retreating from zebras (e.g., focusing on novel diagnoses), and diagnosis momentum. It deals with the uncertainty of the expert by focusing on children with malformed hearts and the traditional problems of making decisions when one lacks all of the relevant information. It dwells on Groopman's own problems in finding the appropriate diagnoses, even from some of the leading experts in the country, for a problem he had with tendonitis in his wrists. Again, we see the operation of traditional problems in decision making, such as a commission bias, the tendency to prefer action, often as a result of desperate pleas from the patient to do something – anything rather than inaction – which also can be a form of satisficing. The objective, gold standard of modern medicine, medical tests of various sorts, particularly radiological imagery, are often inaccurate. As a result, for serious problems, you should not only get a second opinion, but a second test. This creates an interesting two by two table with only one cell, correct test/correct diagnosis, likely to lead to optimal outcomes. The book concludes with an epilog that focuses on how patients' questions can shape their treatment, overcoming some of the problems highlighted in the prior chapters, and how patients can act as true partners with the physician in diagnosis and treatment.

The book highlights the following disturbing research findings. First, doctors rush to judgment, often interrupting patients with questions to confirm their initial diagnosis (typically made within twenty seconds of the beginning of interviews with them). Second, an algorithmic approach and a focus on decision trees in medical decision making (detailed in Box 13.2 on clinical decision systems), which may be appropriate in limited situations, encourages poor listening and observing with blinders on, and prevents the patient from telling their own story. Third, doctors quickly form stereotypes that affect their interactions with patients; for example, quite humanly, they many shun sick people because of their own powerlessness in dealing with them. Fourth, doctors' decision making is subject to classic biases found in decision-making research in a number of different settings. Fifth, little attention has been focused on how to correct these known flaws in the medical system, which contribute to the unacceptably high level of medical errors in the American system highlighted in the Institute of Medicine's disturbing 2000 report "To err is human." Increasingly medical decision making is embedded in the work of teams that form their own KN for treating patients, which further complicates these problems.

Dr. Groopman suggests remedies for the problems he describes: avoiding snap judgments; listening carefully and observing keenly; an emphasis on joint decision making with patients; embracing uncertainty; reflecting on things that went wrong; and a return to the tenets of classic practice. He also suggests helpful hints for patients to aid doctors in their decision making, and have the patients correct the systemic problems he identifies. He directly contradicts the current emphasis on clinical decision-making systems using evidence-based medicine. He pleas for a return to more humanistic decision making, although he concedes this was often a very haphazard method for training clinicians in the old craft system.

research as decision making and KN play a central role in these processes (Farace, Monge, and Russell 1977). Next in this chapter we turn to a discussion of the role of cohesive groups and the associated processes of bandwidth and echo in shaping decision making. We then discuss the need to balance various concerns in making decisions, focusing on exploration versus exploitation and the important limits played by managing attention and satisficing processes. Finally, we turn to the limits placed on decision making by cognitive processes and more technical search problems.

Behavioral decision school and uncertainty

> ... returns from exploration are systematically less certain, more remote in
> time, and organizationally more distant from the locus of action and adaption.
> (March 1991, p. 73)

In the behavioral decision school, an organization can be conceived of as a
system for supporting the decision-making process, and the critical issue for organizations is that well-formed decisions be made. Information processing, uncertainty, and decision making have been inextricably interwoven in this school.
The communication network in which an individual is embedded plays a critical
role in the decision-making process (Connolly 1977). It influences the diversity
of an individual's information sources as well as the volume of information to
which an individual will be exposed to. Following these arguments, the primary
purpose of communication networks is "to ensure the presence of certain types
of information" (O'Reilly, Chatham, and Anderson 1987, p. 610) to support
decision-making processes (Daft and Huber 1987; March 1994). This school has
also been responsible for some central concepts critical to KN, such as bounded
rationality, satisficing, and uncertainty reduction. In alignment with this approach,
many communication theorists historically have argued that the primary function
of communication is the reduction of uncertainty.

Much of the current information-seeking literature is also based on the centrality of uncertainty reduction (Kuhlthau 2004), essentially a drive reduction (Case
2005), problem-solving approach, which is accepted as fundamentally rational.
This is the underlying approach of Dervin's popular approach to information gaps
(Dervin 2003) and Belkin's (2005) frequently cited ASK (anomalous states of
knowledge) approach. As Kuhlthau (1991) has suggested, gap-bridging moves
beyond just uncertainty reduction and often encompasses considerable anxiety
evoked in the individual when s/he faces unknowns. In these views, mere ignorance, by itself, is not typically a motivator for information seeking. People are
only motivated to seek information when both they know that they are ignorant
and the missing information becomes salient. So acquiring information is to
be desired not merely for its instrumental value (i.e., "doing something" about
a potential threat) but also for its emotional value (e.g., feeling assured that
the threat is not imminent). Since uncertainty has been seen as equivalent to
lacking the appropriate information (MacCrimmon and Taylor 1976) the structure of KN is critical to uncertainty reduction. Recently Problematic Integration
Theory (Brashers, Goldsmith, and Hsieh 2002) and Uncertainty Management
Theory (Babrow 2001) have questioned the assumption that humans always
desire to reduce uncertainty. Uncertainty Management, in particular, highlights
how people sometimes deliberately increase uncertainty (e.g., for stimulation or
entertainment).

Alternatively, uncertainty has been defined as a function of the number of alternative patterns identified in a set and the probability of each alternative (Farace,

Monge, and Russell 1977). Information can remove uncertainty by helping to define relative probabilities, but it also can increase uncertainty when it leads us to recognize additional alternatives or to change the assessment of probabilities. Uncertainty quite naturally has been associated with cognitive attributes of individuals.

The key element of any definition of decision making is the selection from alternatives. If there are no true alternatives, then the decision is already made. But, if there are many alternatives, all equally beneficial or problematic, then we have no basis for making distinctions and are left with a highly uncertain decision, since we do not have any basis for deciding which of the alternatives is best. So, the number of alternatives, from two to infinity, has much to do with the complexity of decision making and of information seeking in support of it. Not only do we have to gather information on each alternative relating to the various criteria that differentiate them, but we also have to gather information on how they interact and compare. In this way cohesive, dense networks decrease uncertainty, while wide-ranging networks of weak ties may increase it.

An interesting paradox in the literature pertains to the relationship between information load and decision making. Decision makers often seek more information than is needed, even when it induces overload. While this overload of information decreases decision quality, it increases decision makers' confidence (O'Reilly, Chatham, and Anderson 1987) and satisfaction (O'Reilly 1980). In effect, information becomes very addictive for some individuals, with a constant desire for more, even when it has harmful cognitive effects on them. Somewhat paradoxically, scholars in decision making are increasingly turning away from the more rational base of cognition (Dow 1988). This movement is partially a result of the recognition of the non-rational basis of much information acquisition in support of decisions and the ambiguous positions in which many people find themselves.

Cultural norms and expectations also have an impact on the level of information processing in organizations. Organizations often gather more information than they need to make decisions as a result of social norms (Feldman and March 1981). Thus there is a critical distinction between information used to make decisions and information used to support them (O'Reilly, Chatham, and Anderson 1987).

Decision making and its associated formal rules can be taken to be the ultimate expression of general societal norms and specific organizational norms related to the value of rationality (March 1994). The gathering of information often provides ritualistic assurance that the appropriate norms are being followed (Feldman and March 1981) and someone acting as an effective decision maker is fulfilling his/her role in the organization's culture (March 1994). In group contexts, members are more likely to share information they have already discussed than to share unique information in their possession with the group (Stasser, Taylor, and Hanna 1989). It appears that much repetitive information seeking is really aimed at increasing the confidence of decision makers in a choice they have already made (March 1994). People engage in value seeking rather than information seeking, since new knowledge may be threatening (Bates 2005). KN then becomes a ritual which supports the appearance of rational decision making.

Bandwidth, echo, and cohesive groups

> ... the goal of the decision process is to see the world with confidence rather than accuracy ...   (March 1994, p. 40)

The link between decision making and the rational processing of information is often much weaker than we would like to believe (Feldman and March 1981) with insidious interactions with individual cognitive and group processes. To a certain extent, we are all prisoners of our pasts and of our ideologies. Some have argued that the first stage of decision making really rests on the frame, or knowledge base, which an individual has developed because of their preexisting information fields and positioning within communication structures (Carley 1986). The communication structure in which an individual is embedded is a critical part of the decision-making process (Connolly 1977), influencing the volume of information and the diversity of information sources (Johnson 1993). So, in effect, we are doubly vexed: the support structures we rely on for determining alternatives may have already formed the alternatives we are likely to identify. Thus, the essential insight of strength of weak ties arguments also can be applied to decision-making approaches, especially for unique non-programmed decisions; we need to expand the range of communication sources to which we attend if we are to optimize our decision making.

As we have seen repeatedly, membership of cohesive groups results in limiting the range of considered alternatives through both conformity pressures and, somewhat relatedly, the development of trusting relationships. Group members do not share information that does not support: perceived group opinions; the position of a plurality of other group members; their preferences; or the information already in the possession of other group members (Stasser and Titus 1985). These findings were replicated in spite of more structured discussions and instructions to focus on group process so that information would be more likely to be shared (Stasser, Taylor, and Hanna 1989).

Mindguarding acts to severely limit information seeking after a decision is reached; indeed, often organizational decision makers will ignore the information they have available (Feldman and March 1991). In effect, information is only sought from supportive sources, and even experts within one's organization are frozen out of the decision-making process (Janis 1971). Several laboratory studies have also found that individuals require less information to arrive at a decision favorable to them than at one against their interests (O'Reilly and Pondy 1979). Unfortunately, the more uncertain the information, the more subject it is to favorable distortions by those reporting it (Downs 1967) and when information is vitally required there is a tendency to treat it as more reliable than it actually is (Adams 1980). Especially under conditions of threat, organizations may restrict their information seeking and fail to react to changing environmental conditions (Staw, Sandelands, and Dutton 1981). Organizations in these circumstances rely on existing behaviors, narrow their information fields, and reduce the number of information channels consulted.

In terms of echo, discussed in more detail in Chapter 11, the social system of which decision makers are a part acts to reinforce existing approaches, rather than to suggest true alternatives. Decision makers are more likely to use networks to learn how to make legitimate decisions than to improve the information they use to make decisions; this creates imitative pressures that are especially likely to apply to those of lower status (March 1994). Decision makers often ask for more information (it is after all a part of the decision-making ritual) even when they have sufficient information on hand to make a decision (Feldman and March 1981). They know that very seldom will they be criticized for gathering additional information, but they might be blamed for failing to gather a critical piece of information (Feldman and March 1981). Especially later in the decision-making process, sources are sought solely because they may say that the seeker can terminate the decision-making process (Saunders and Jones 1990). Unfortunately the interaction of these processes means that KN reinforce a subjective level of confidence.

So, information is often gathered to justify a decision already made, instead of being used to make an optimal decision (Staw, Sandelands, and Dutton 1981). Over the last three decades observational and research studies have repeatedly demonstrated that decision making is an irrational process. Ironically, because of forces related to bandwidth and echo (Burt 2005), perhaps the ultimate support for the "rightness" of a decision must come from outside an individual's cohesive network of strong ties (Cross, Rice, and Parker 2001). Having a well-defined, explicit problem domain reduces the importance of trust (Cross, Rice, and Parker 2001) and group processes, and makes rational decision making more likely; however, these are often the problems that are the least critical to the organization.

Exploration vs. exploitation

Glorification of exploration obscures the fact that most new ideas are bad ones, most changes are detrimental, and most original inventions are not worth the effort devoted to producing them.   (March 1994, p. 238)

The weak link in the information chain is the increasingly inadequate absorption capacity of individuals and organizations. Computer technology does not help much – unless underlying information is quantitative and structured, and questions are well defined.   (Noam 1993, p. 203)

If I have settled into a routine for making a decision, the premises of the decision and the information used to support it will be well known to me. This ritualistic acquisition of information, characteristic of exploitation, is often troublesome, since organizations often do not recognize the costs of gathering information, especially in terms of opportunity costs or benefits forgone (Feldman and March

1981). These forgone opportunities are reflected in March's classic treatment of exploration discussed in Chapter 10.

Programmed decisions are routine, repetitive ones for which the organization has developed a specific process, often computerized and quantitative (Mac-Crimmon and Taylor 1976; Simon 1960). Programmed decisions are highly formalized, with set rules to follow and penalties associated with the breaking of the rules. So, for example, government procurement is based on some means of finding the lowest bidder. On the surface, this is a rational, cost-effective means of making a purchasing decision. But, as the old joke goes, how comfortable would you feel if you were an astronaut on top of a rocket launcher containing thousands of parts, all selected on the basis that they were the cheapest available.

Decisions are non-programmed to the extent they are novel, unstructured, and important, and to which only very general models of decision making can be applied (Cyert, Simon, and Trow 1956; Simon 1960). In their classic case study of an early business decision, focusing on the adoption of an information processing technology, Cyert, Simon and Trow (1956) point out how tortuous and cumbersome non-programmed decisions can be. In effect, the organization has to decide how to decide. The decision-making process involves at least two major decisions, the first of which can contain many surprises. It may be the case that you discover that a major issue, that you had not specified at first, needs to be included in the decision-making process. So, the whole decision has to be put on hold while you go back to square one on this aspect of the decision. When you gather information on it, you discover it interacts in unexpected ways with things you already thought you knew, which then forces you to rethink some already settled aspects of the decision. For some highly complex, novel, important decisions, organizations can literally go round and round for months, if not years, before they can reach the final stages of making a decision. One basic problem with most technologically driven support structures for decision making is that they are grounded in rational decision-making processes, whereas the actual decision making of upper-level managers, often focuses on non-programmed decisions. As a result, it is often irrational (Mintzberg 1975a, b) and/or intuitive (Simon 1987).

Relatedly, since information seeking operates in support of making a decision, you also can be faced with decisions on how to gather information, how to structure your KN. So, this is also a critical distinction in organizations, with some individuals arguing that organizations make two classes of decisions: one class on the substance of the matter and another on how to search for information (O'Reilly, Chatham, and Anderson 1987).

As we have seen, the role of KN comes primarily in supporting the decision-making process by determining alternatives and gathering information related to them. The primary issue here is that a complete range of alternatives should be selected and that the pertinent information related to each of them should be gathered. One key factor that distinguishes organizational, as opposed to purely individual decision making, is the central role of communication, especially in the selection of information sources and how they inevitably "filter" information (Cyert, Simon, and Trow 1956). Communication processes also play a critical role in how the alternatives are discussed and eventually how decisions are implemented, as we saw in Chapter 9.

While the selection of an exhaustive list of alternatives seems to be a straightforward process, any casual review of case studies of decision making would suggest that often decision makers seize on a limited range of alternatives and then tend to gather information to support these early choices, prematurely limiting exploration. American organizations appear to be so focused on developing solutions to problems that they do not pay enough attention to the earlier aspects of decision making (Jablin and Sussman 1983; Nutt 1984). In fact, it appears that executives "prefer to copy the ideas of others or search for ready-made solutions instead of seeking innovation" (Nutt 1984, p. 445). This occurs partly because being the first to experiment or use new ideas increases the probability of failure, that is often more costly to the individual than would be any rewards from a successful innovation (Nutt 1984).

Once the major alternatives have been identified, then information needs to be gathered on the crucial dimensions of each of them and their consequences (Cyert, Simon, and Trow 1956). In many ways, this area, though it has been understudied when compared to the psychological processes associated with decision making (O'Reilly, Chatham, and Anderson 1987; Saunders and Jones 1990), represents some of the most intriguing findings related to decision-making research. Particularly so, for the oft-repeated finding, across several contexts, that people will knowingly use lower-quality, accessible information sources (Johnson 1996b; Case 2007), which also directly relates to a manager's strong preferences for oral/interpersonal sources of information (Mintzberg 1975a, b; O'Reilly, Chatham, and Anderson 1987).

In reviewing seventy-eight case studies, Nutt (1984) describes two basic search strategies employed by organizations in decision making. A sequestered search, used in 60 percent of the cases, was carried out when a manager felt a need was ill-defined and threatening, precisely the case for most non-programmed decisions. In this situation, passive and defensive strategies were often employed, with only a few others involved in the search and often managers awaiting the serendipitous discovery of information. An open search, seemingly the kind most frequently promoted in the academic literature, was used when needs were seen as trivial and/or vague and only then were subordinates brought into help.

Advanced IT has often been cited as a boon to decision-making processes since it is said to lead to more individuals, representing greater variety, participating as information sources; fewer people composing the actual decision unit; fewer organizational levels involved; greater spread of relevant information across the organization; less time devoted to meetings and other related activities; higher-quality decisions; and more timely decisions (Fulk and Boyd 1991; Huber 1990). IT, as Box 13.2, on clinical decision support, details, can also facilitate individual decision making.

Box 13.2. Decision support systems

A variety of software systems exist to aid decision-making processes. They often focus on access to data bases and other types of information that can facilitate work. These systems have been around essentially as long as computers have been, and several systems have been commercialized, but they have not often fulfilled the hype devoted to them (Power 2007).

In medicine these systems have been used to facilitate the decision making of patients, physicians, and other health professionals. They do this by leading the decision maker step-by-step through often complicated decision trees. More advanced systems can take on a game-like feel and are linked to authoritative evidence. In clinical work these systems are often used to reduce medical errors by decreasing reliance on memory and increasing access to evidence-based medicine. These systems provide alerts and reminders, diagnostic assistance, therapy critiquing and planning, prescribing information, image recognition, and interpretation guidance (Coiera 2003). While often improving practitioner performance, a systematic review has found only inconsistent evidence that they improve patient outcomes (Garg *et al.* 2005).

Algorithms constituting an inference engine to facilitate clinical decision making are often embedded in electronic medical records, where they often rest on evidence-based practice and are used as diagnostic aids (Coiera 2003). However, their use has been criticized by physicians as being as much of a hindrance as a facilitator in clinical judgment (Groopman 2007; Sweeney 2006), as we have detailed in Box 13.1. They also can require more time and effort than traditional methods (Coiera 2003; Garg *et al.* 2005).

Another popular application is group decision support systems (GDSS) that essentially support group decision-making processes by using sophisticated computer software to facilitate making a decision and providing ready access for group members to data bases and data manipulation systems. GDSS software is designed to systematically take members through each stage of the decision process, insuring for example that multiple alternatives are weighed and evaluated. Once alternatives are assessed they also permit various methods for reaching a decision, from simple voting to a proportional weighting of various group members (e.g., upper managers, different divisions).

Recent attempts at GDSS, and the general use of technology to support decision-making processes, often appear to be attempts to reintroduce rationality into decision making, by shifting the focus away from people and toward ideas. GDSS are designed to overcome many problems symptomatic of groupthink by promoting critical thinking and removing status considerations. GDSS encourage consensus approaches to decision making, and equality of participation. The resulting increased cohesiveness and competitiveness of their members also can act to promote information seeking (Smith and Jones 1968).

Their proponents make very strong claims about the improved decision making that would result from these rather expensive systems (Hoffman 1994). Unfortunately these claims have yet to be supported in research studies (Fulk and Boyd 1991), in part because organizations modify these systems in use to reflect their cultures. Clinical decision support systems are often "home-grown" products of local champions. As a result, they have limited exportability and problematic updates to new enterprise systems and other software upgrades (Garg *et al.* 2005). There are literally hundreds of systems that have been developed, which creates problems in sharing data (Raghavan 2005). However, in actual use they may also be limited in the same way that other processes are; by the limits of human decision making and the artificial boundaries imposed upon them by an organization's culture (Poole and DeSanctis 1990).

Increasingly organizations must structure themselves to promote the gathering and sharing of information. There is a constant dilemma for organizations: the imperative, in part stemming from efficiency needs, to limit the availability of information; and the recognition that structural designs are flawed and circumstances change, requiring individuals to seek information normally unavailable to them. Still, the formal structure, and the rewards associated with it (e.g., promotion), often are designed specifically to discourage the sharing of information (Powell 1990). Not only are there structural limits on the amount and kinds of information to which any individual is likely to be exposed, but there are also real limits to the amount of information that individuals can process given their limits (Guetskow 1965) and the constraints of their formal roles. How managers resolve these conflicting imperatives is a critical question for the modern organization.

Managing attention and satisficing

The most basic limit on most organizational members is time, a key factor in medical decision making as Box 13.1, on the book *How Doctors Think*, details. Even the most trivial organizational tasks could theoretically consume a lifetime, if all the information needed to understand them was gathered. The problem then is not in deciding to seek information, but in deciding when to stop. Adept decision makers know intuitively when they have gathered enough information for any particular purpose. They satisfice. They develop their own intuition on when they have spent as much energy as they can in deciding what they should do about any particular problem that confronts them and searching for information related to it (March 1994). They also learn to approximate, or to reach a judgment on when they can make a sufficiently good decision for any particular event (Farace, Monge, and Russell 1977). Thus, decision makers search for an appropriate solution, not the optimal solution (Hickson 1987). They reach these judgments because they have developed an appreciation for what their limits are; they can mentally weigh only so much information at any given time.

The ultimate goals of rationality may be to develop a sense of coherence, and a simple one at that, with satisficing, rather than maximizing, the standard (Bates 2005; Pirolli and Card 1999). Many have argued that most people do not want a wide range of options, in part because our cognitive limits for processing information have been exceeded (Schwartz 2004). In a related way, people may pursue information not for new insights, but for validation, legitimation, and reformulation (Cross, Rice, and Parker 2001). We tend to assume people will expend a lot of energy to attack important problems and will also make sure of the quality of sources and of answers – but they clearly do not (Case 2002, 2007; Johnson 1996b, 1997a; Johnson et al. 2006). The accessibility of sources is often a key determinant of their use (Bates 2005), even for heavily rational engineers (Case 2002, 2007). Most theorists confront the world with a scientific model that implies exhaustive searching and testing to come to the correct conclusion. However, most seekers will stop searching when they discover the first somewhat plausible answer to their query. It may, indeed, be deeply rational to preserve ignorance, and to experience its many benefits (Johnson 1996b).

The pace of managers' activities and the variety of tasks in which they are engaged heighten the problems associated with any one decision, since their optimal level of performance is degraded to the extent that their energies are focused on other problems, as Box 13.1, on *How Doctors Think*, details. So, the more decisions with which they are faced, the less they can really engage in concentrated information seeking on any one of them. When this is coupled with the vast amount of information available on most business-related topics, managers are faced with daunting sets of judgments.

Beyond these factors is the even more depressing fact that some critical information related to a decision may be unavailable. One of the ironies of the age of information, and the constant, clichéd arguments that we all are overloaded with information, is that there never seems to be enough information to answer very specific operational questions that we might have. Most importantly, we never know how the future may hold unexpected events that will alter even the most carefully laid plans.

How do I decide to go ahead and make a decision though I am missing some information? First, I need to decide how useful and available the information really is. If the missing information (e.g., what my competitor is planning) is easily available from trade sources and is critical to what I will do, I may decide to wait until I have spent the extra time and energy needed to gather it. If it is unavailable, in spite of my best efforts, and only of tangential relevance I may decide to press ahead and make a decision, realizing that at least I will have learned that this alternative does not work. (Postponing a decision is always a decision for the *status quo ante*.) The best managers have an intuitive feel for when they have reached the optimal balance of these factors; they have reached a subjective level of confidence that they know enough to make the best decision they can make in their current circumstances.[1]

Cognitive limits

In the field of organizational research there has also been great interest in cognition (Weick 1979), especially in terms of organizational learning (Daft and Huber 1987; Duncan and Weiss 1979) as it relates to information processing. There even has been a tendency to characterize the entire organization as a thinking entity.

As we have seen, there are cognitive limits on the amount of information individuals can process, especially in short-term memory. Miller's classic observation that we can only viably keep seven things in mind at any one time establishes an absolute barrier to information processing. Beyond this absolute limit, the presence of additional information, especially in overload conditions, lowers even this limited capacity (Mintzberg 1975a). While it has become a truism that learning how to search for information should be a major focus of our educational systems, rather than imparting perishable knowledge, the limits on short-term memory suggest having a sound and deep knowledge base is critical to management decision making (Lord and Maher 1990; Mintzberg 1975a).

There is evidence that individual information processing can be substantially enhanced by holding positions that demand higher levels of processing (Zajonc and Wolfe 1966) and by long experience in managerial roles. So, somewhat akin to chess masters who can instantly react to complex patterns based on experience, upper-level managers develop an intuitive feel, tacit knowledge, for how to react to complex information patterns in organizations (Simon 1987).

Beyond the limits of memory, humans have a limited ability to process and interpret information. They tend to exaggerate information they do register (Wales, Rarick, and Davis 1963). They consistently tend to a confirmation bias, ignoring or discounting disconfirming evidence. But, they also often ignore their existing base of information (the base-rate fallacy) and will focus on compelling new information. So, for example, a prodigal employee, who has been a consistent low performer, may still be viewed favorably if there is one recent positive experience. They also engage in the sample-size fallacy, generalizing from very limited experience. So, if one recent product has met with success in a new market, they may assume other products will meet with similar success. At best, humans are limited in their capacity to seek, to process, and to correctly interpret information (Smithson 1989).

---

[1] Managers also can take some comfort in knowing that they often control how things turn out (e.g., they can provide more resources if they are needed to make something work), and they control, to a certain degree, how outcomes are interpreted (Thayer 1988).

Individuals in organizations often need to process information of incredible range and diversity, often outside the range of the requirements of their formal position, which needs to be synthesized in novel ways to form decisions. Cognitive complexity is a concept which directly links individual cognitive abilities to the differing information environments of individuals and may be linked to individual preferences for certain positions in KN.

As explicated by Schroder, Driver, and Streufert (1967), cognitive complexity refers to an individual's ability to differentiate, discriminate, and integrate information. Differentiation refers to the number of dimensions or attributes needed by the individual to distinguish one stimulus from another in a given set of stimuli. Discrimination is defined as the ability of an individual to order stimuli along a given dimension. Integration refers to the ability of an individual to place the stimuli in some coherent fashion in his/her preexisting cognitive structure. In this framework, cognitive complexity is assumed to be a trait of individuals; thus, cognitive complexity is an antecedent condition for the occupancy of particular structural positions.

Communication network roles in KN are naturally linked to notions of cognitive complexity, as we developed in Chapter 3. Differing communication network roles imply different patterning in an individual's information processing. A liaison, because of their linkages to different groups, is naturally exposed to more diverse communication than is an isolate. The role of sales manager reveals a rather typical organizational situation. A person occupying this position must contend with inherently different languages and perspectives and establish a framework for dealing with these often conflicting perspectives which still satisfies most if not all the parties that s/he must deal with. This individual not only has to deal with intraorganizational communication, but interorganizational communication as well. Thus, s/he also has to deal with environmental uncertainty arising outside the organization. An individual in this position, as do boundary spanners generally, in addition to being comfortable with uncertainty, must be able to synthesize information into unique perspectives, developing their own tacit views. Thus the information-processing characteristics of an individual are naturally linked to their role performance. They may also be linked to their desire to occupy certain roles.

These contentions are borne out in many of the empirical findings associated with liaison emergence and structural hole brokerage (Johnson 2004). For example, liaisons tend to be of higher organizational status, have more structurally diverse contacts, be first sources of information, be dyadic opinion leaders, and have longer organizational tenure. Weak ties have also been associated with more cognitively flexible individuals (Granovetter 1982). Because communication networks are not necessarily governed by formal rules, individuals who can process information from diverse sources are sought out by others, and when they are found, because of their unique cognitive abilities, they become liaisons.

Cognitive complexity determines the amount, kind, and diversity of information an individual can process. It structures an individual's cognitive patterns in much the same way that networks structure the patterns of communication relationships in organizations. Thus cognitive complexity should have important impacts on an individual's preference to occupy certain positions in a network of relationships. This is so partially because marked departures from an individual's cognitive capabilities in role incumbency should result in tension and uncertainty in individuals. Individuals eventually assume the network roles which most closely match their cognitive structure. Thus, the liaison role requires individuals who have a preference for uncertainty because this role is characterized by a necessarily high amount of uncertainty absorption. It has also been suggested that individuals who have a tolerance for ambiguity will perceive equivocal information as being less uncertain than will individuals with lower tolerances, and thus they can occupy these positions with less tension (Downey and Slocum 1975).

Several empirical studies have found a relationship between cognitive complexity and positions in communication networks. Schreiman and Johnson (1975) found moderate support for a linkage between cognitive complexity and the amount and variety of communication in social networks. Albrecht (1979) has found that key communicators (individuals occupying linking roles in networks) have more coherent cognitive spaces than do non-key communicators. There also is empirical evidence that entrepreneurs structure their business's information environments according to their integrative complexity (McGaffey and Christy 1975). Sypher and Zorn (1986) found that cognitive differentiation accounted for substantial variation in job level and upward mobility in an insurance firm. Walker (1985), in research conducted on a software firm, found that network position was a stronger and more stable predictor of differences in cognition than the type of function an individual had and the type of product worked on.

Perhaps the most interesting research study in this area was done by Zajonc and Wolfe (1966). Unlike the previous studies, they viewed this problem from a formal perspective. They argued that the hierarchy of organizations resulted in an imbalance in the nature of information flowing into certain positions, particularly in terms of its diversity. Employees of an industrial company who held different administrative positions at different status levels were examined. While somewhat different in labeling, similar dimensions of cognitive complexity to the ones discussed here were examined in this research. The essential argument of this study was that an individual's "cognitive structure is influenced by the individual's access to information" (p. 144). Importantly they found that high vs. low levels of formal communication were more likely to lead to cognitive differentiation, complexity, segmentation, and organization, while no significant relationship was found between the levels of informal communication and these variables. This suggests, in part, that individuals may be compelled to broaden their cognitive structures as a result of certain role requirements. Thus there is empirical evidence that individuals' cognitive structures are related to their positioning in organizational structures.

Cognitive maps

> Organizations exist largely in the mind and their existence takes the form of cognitive maps. Thus, what ties an organization together is what ties thoughts together.   (Weick and Bougon 1986, p. 102)

Cognitive maps represent the patterns of personal knowledge of individuals derived from their experiences in organizations. They also relate to how people identify sources of information, a problem we discussed in the last chapter. One form of such a map is a strip map, which specifies a routinized pathway to get from one point to another. These strip maps may be directly related to the routing of messages through formal and informal structures, such as KN, in organizations.

Another, more complex form of mapping is a cause map which represents concepts tied together by causal relations. These maps remove equivocality by placing concepts in relation to one another and by imposing structure on vague situations. Individuals can interact with each other on the basis of an assemblage of their maps, a composite or an average. The general aims of analysis of cause maps of individuals within an organization is to discover structural regularities. Cause maps have been directly related to two basic components of cognitive complexity: differentiation and integration. The concepts contained in cause maps can also serve as a means of linking individuals together in organizations (Weick and Bougon 1986).

At a somewhat lower level of complexity and abstraction, scripts have also been used to explain the behavior of individuals in organizations. A script is a knowledge structure held in memory which specifies sequences of behavior which are appropriate in familiar situations (Gioia and Poole 1984; Lord and Kernan 1987). Scripts can be applied unconsciously to particular situations, especially conventional, predictable, and frequently encountered ones (Gioia and Poole 1984). This scripting is intimately related to the performance of rituals, such as staff meetings (Gioia and Poole 1984). Scripts are said to serve two roles for organizational members: they aid understanding of organizational events and they provide a guide to appropriate behavior. Scripts often incorporate multiple paths to goals which can be used in hierarchical means–ends structures (Lord and Kernan 1987).

These scripts are important because they also reveal the normative base of information to which individuals will expose themselves, their habitual patterning of sources which they consult in particular situations (Lord and Kernan 1987). Weak scripts are ones which specify particular behavioral events which are expected in a given situation, while strong scripts specify the sort of progressive sequencing of behaviors contained in this example (Gioia and Poole 1984). Scripts and maps provide clear antecedents to people's communication behaviors, and thus structures, within organizations.

Search limitations

> Organizations may be unable, because of organizational or human limitations, to process the information they have.   (Feldman and March 1981, p. 875)

Barriers related to technical search problems primarily relate to awareness of and access to information sources. Since they result from a lack of familiarity with or access to information sources, they appear on the surface to be much more amenable to rational solutions. Regrettably, and somewhat disconcertingly, the threshold where these issues become absolute barriers to information seeking is low (Johnson 1996b; Case 2007). A large part of technical education consists of defining for individuals what are appropriate sources of information and how one can gain access to these sources. An individual's education level probably is the most important factor in their subsequent information seeking (Chen and Hernon 1982).

However, education and experience have potentially insidious side effects, since once someone is familiar with a source they tend to continue to use it (Culnan 1983). This leads to a certain amount of inertia in the use of information sources. Individuals are reluctant to move from the old tried and true sources, partly because they hold off evaluating a source until they have some experience using it (Culnan 1983). Interestingly, almost two-thirds of respondents in a regional survey said they would return to a source even when they had placed it in the "least helpful" category (Chen and Hernon 1982).

The problem of inertia is exacerbated by the number of competing sources of information available on any one subject. Most individuals find, partly because of time pressures, that they cannot engage in a comprehensive search for information. Given that there may be ten sources of information available and they are familiar with two, which they trust on the basis of prior experience, there may be little perceived benefit in consulting any of the remaining eight. Most often, "the search for alternatives terminates when a satisfactory solution has been discovered even though the field of possibilities has not been exhausted" (Cyert, Simon, and Trow 1956, p. 246). This happens, in part, because each additional piece of information makes it more difficult to determine what might be relevant to a particular problem (O'Reilly and Pondy 1979). Individuals also fall into competency traps; they will not learn new, often superior techniques, because they are performing well with the old ones (March 1994).

Of course, each additional source of information adds confidence in a course of action if they corroborate each other. But, if the sources do not provide consistent answers, a not unlikely circumstance, then someone has complicated their decision making. In fact, more communication can result in greater ambiguity and uncertainty, not improved decision making (Rice and Shook 1990). While inconsistent information may often be a spur for additional information seeking to find a "tie-breaking" source, there is no guarantee that this additional source will not present yet another major alternative. So, it becomes easier to understand why there might be real benefits, at least in terms of the amount of effort expended, in consulting only a limited range of familiar sources.

Access

In many ways the findings related to the importance of access are some of the most compelling in the social science literature. What is fascinating, if not downright amazing, is the consistent set of findings suggesting that the threshold point where a source is considered inaccessible is very low. For example, people will not invest much of their time to learn Internet search engines and typically rely on a very limited number of commands (Markey 2007).

Even more disturbing is that access also may be the single most important criterion in evaluation by users of an information system (Rice and Shook 1986). So accessibility outweighs quality in determining usage of information from particular sources. In fact, it is a common finding that individuals will knowingly rely on inferior information sources for answers to their problems because it would take too much effort to get authoritative information (Case 2007; Johnson 1996b). A number of studies document cases where organizational members will seek out information from inferior sources because of the reduced costs involved (Allen 1977; Blau 1954). Allen (1977), in his research stream involving communication in research and development laboratories, has consistently found that professionals will seek the most readily accessible source of information, both in terms of physical distance and comprehensibility, rather than the "best" sources, which offer more professionally authoritative information. Somewhat relatedly, less than 20 percent of the general populace followed up on referrals by information specialists to professionals or institutions for answers to their questions (Chen and Hernon 1982). Beyond accessibility, the relevance of the information also is more important than its quality to managers (Menon and Varadarajan 1992) and respondents are not very concerned with how up-to-date information is (Chen and Hernon 1982).

Even when individuals need information they often do not actively and comprehensively search for it; rather they will wait until they accidentally stumble across the information, often in interpersonal encounters (Scott 1991), which increases the importance of the range of contacts someone has in KN. "Many respondents reported that they made use of an information provider only as an afterthought in relation to another need" (Chen and Hernon 1982, p. 57).

Search problems are often related to the "costs" of information seeking compared to the value or benefit of the information sought, particularly in relation to decision making (March 1994). The costs of information acquisition are many:

psychological, temporal, and material. Most seekers appear to assume it is better to rely on easily obtained information – they have an answer after all, no matter how dubious – than to spend the effort necessary to get complete information. The "costs" in terms of extra time and effort for a complete information search, which may result in delaying opportunities, complicating decision making, and increasing information overload, are real. There are also additional psychological costs, such as loss of self-esteem and frustration, that result from an unsuccessful search (Hudson and Danish 1980).

Summary

Traditionally, the behavioral decision school of organizational theory argued that the primary impetus for KN in organizations was their role in supporting decision making. As we have seen, theorizing in this area has increasingly moved away from a strictly rational approach to decision making to an appreciation of uncertainty and the very human limits in processing an ever-increasing volume of information. People have come to a greater appreciation of the dilemmas posed by decision making and the need to balance various competing forces: while cohesive groups are necessary for tacit knowledge, they also operate to limit consideration of a range of alternatives; relatedly, organizations need to balance exploration of the new with the efficient exploitation of existing knowledge; and, finally, the need to simultaneously attend to many competing problems leads to satisficing processes and an increasing realization of the limits that make "perfect" decision making unlikely.

Further reading

Groopman, J. 2007. *How Doctors Think*. Houghton Mifflin.
> **Application of decision-making principles to the problems confronted by physicians in making clinical judgments. Described in more detail in Box 13.1.**

Janis, I. L. 1971. Groupthink. *Psychology Today*, November: 43–76.
> **Classic examination of case studies of irrational decision making brought on by group processes. Helpful condensation of practices that can be used to overcome the problems identified.**

March, J. G. 1991. Exploration and exploitation in organizational learning. *Organizational Science*, 2: 71–87.
> **Detailed examination of the classic dilemma organizations confront in making decisions, between exploring for new ideas and exploiting existing ones.**

March, J. G. 1994. *A Primer on Decision Making: How Decisions Happen*. New Free Press.
> **A primer for executives, condensing findings of a lifetime of research on decision making.**

14 Summary and commentary

> People underestimate the value of what they do not know, and overestimate the value of what they do know.
>
> (Bates 2005, p. 5)

> Information has always been a source of power, but it is now increasingly a source of confusion. In every sphere of modern life, the chronic condition is a surfeit of information, poorly integrated or lost somewhere in the system.
>
> (Wilensky 1968, p. 331)

> Simply proposing more or better communication is the oldest consulting recommendation in the book – and no one today really needs more meetings.
>
> (Cross *et al.* 2004, p. 67)

In this chapter I bring together my central themes and point to the future. A compelling feature of research on KN is that it stands at the intersection of so many important theoretical and policy issues such as the converging trends surrounding globalization and the "flattening" of our world; the increasing complexity and blurring boundaries represented in new organizational forms; difficult individual challenges selecting career paths and loyalty, or the lack thereof, on everyone's part, cited in Chapter 1. These trends lead to dilemmas, for both individuals and organizations, in the development and sharing of knowledge in KN.

I discussed the fundamental concepts, the building blocks of KN, in Chapters 2 and 3. In Chapter 2 I defined knowledge, distinguishing it from such common terms as information and wisdom. This chapter also discussed the various forms that knowledge can take within organizations, thus making critical distinctions that can be used in defining relationships. I also discussed the contrasting concept of ignorance in this chapter, something to which I will return in concluding this work. Chapter 3 focused on the burgeoning field of network analysis; describing how such basic concepts as entities, linkages, and boundaries can be used to build ever more sophisticated analyses of pathways, cliques, centralization, and density, which are critical to understanding the transfer and diffusion of knowledge within organizations.

The next unit focused on the contexts within which knowledge is embedded. As Chapter 4 details, contexts shape and situate knowledge in various governance structures, determining its distribution. If knowledge is the ultimate expression of our social relationships, then an understanding of the role of context is essential since contextualizing and sense-making are intertwined processes. Chapter 5 focused on the central concern of managers for the basic framework of organizations – formal structure and design issues – that promote or inhibit the flow of knowledge. Much of the current excitement related to KN is associated with new information and telecommunication technologies discussed in Chapter 6. Chapter 7 detailed the spatial distribution of knowledge that constrains its spread, especially revealing new ways of representing knowledge in space. Organizational boundaries are becoming increasingly blurry, so Chapter 8 focused on how firms bring the world outside into the organization through boundary spanning and the development of consortia.

The pragmatics unit focused on using knowledge for various ends. Chapter 9 examined KNs' role in the critical organizational processes of creativity and innovation. Chapter 10 detailed how KN relate to productivity, efficiency, and effectiveness. We then turned, in Chapter 11, to the related topics of the human and the dark side of KN. How people find knowledge and then use it for decision making were the subjects of Chapters 12 and 13.

In this chapter I will focus on some overarching issues raised by KN. I first discuss various ethical (and at times legal) issues that impact the flow of knowledge in organizations. Next I turn to broad policy issues surrounding information haves and have nots in our broader society. Work on KN is just now beginning, so I discuss some high-priority issues for the next round of research, including a deeper view of relationships in network analysis. There are many paradoxes and dilemmas surrounding the management of KN, which emphasizes the importance of managerial judgment. These include the possibility that they simultaneously both empower individuals and subject them to more control. I conclude with perhaps the ultimate paradox – the need for organizations and individuals to promote ignorance at the same time they are facilitating the development of knowledge.

Ethical issues

Not surprisingly there are a number of ethical issues associated with KN. Since knowledge is something that can have great value it is protected by various property rights and sometimes hoarded by individuals. It is also something whose beauty is often in the eye of the beholder, so what is of little value to one person can be of great value to another. As we have seen, these issues are associated with free-riders who often benefit when knowledge is shared, but who do not fully participate in the process, and with the development of public goods, like data bases, in organizations. In part because of these issues, there are numerous concerns over how data might be gathered empirically about the particular relationships and people involved in KN, and this raises more specific concerns about privacy and human subject protections.

Intellectual property

Organizations increasingly see knowledge as one of their key strategic resources, which has resulted in an increased appreciation of the importance of intellectual property exploitation (Earl 2001), with workers often reluctant to share knowledge with outsiders because it may harm their firm's competitive position (Hew and Hara 2007). One essential problem related to knowledge is that it is difficult for it to be "owned" in the same sense that physical objects can be. It also can emerge from interactions with others. Often these interactions are with individuals outside of the organization (e.g., customers, members of one's profession, the scientific community). These communities, and the relationship of constituent organizations and their members to them, present very difficult issues involving protecting one's interest while at the same time benefiting from membership (Lee and Cole 2003).

One of the essential functions of any KM system is protection of intellectual property (Gold, Malhotra, and Segars 2001). However, monitoring, metering, and surveillance of the development of intellectual property are not only expensive and often impractical, but also may be counter-productive (Jarvenpaa and Staples 2001). Panopticon issues associated with formal bureaucratic control and centralization (D'Urso 2006) can easily stifle the flow of knowledge.

Whose knowledge is it anyway, especially if we recognize knowledge as inherently social? There is also an interesting distinction between the expertise that one has developed (that might result in future goods) and the products one has developed while working for an organization (Jarvenpaa and Staples 2001). Organizations are increasingly recognizing that it is not what one knows, but an enhanced capacity to know – to generate new actionable knowledge more quickly than one's peers – that is the critical issue (Dyer and Nobeoka 2000). Beliefs concerning who owns the products of work have important implications for employee motivations, with strong organizational culture norms, resulting from socialization processes, for sharing some of these issues (Constant, Kiesler, and Sproull 1994). Interestingly, a perception of partnership, of knowledge as a joint good, with joint ownership of the products of one's work, may be the most effective approach (Jarvenpaa and Staples 2001).

Privacy issues

It has been estimated that 80 percent of organizations employ some form of employee surveillance, with most forms being associated with electronic monitoring enabled by information technologies (D'Urso 2006). These are features that may be inherent in KM systems which often enhance the potential for, and sophistication of, any surveillance systems. Some of this surveillance is aimed at preventing the spread of proprietary knowledge and/or intellectual property (D'Urso 2006).

This may be mitigated somewhat by tacit knowledge which is based on local experience that is difficult for management to understand. This is somewhat akin to slang developed by subcultures formed in opposition to a dominant culture. Management may have very little understanding of what is critical tacit knowledge.

One theoretical approach to this problem is found in Communication Privacy Management Theory which rests on the following tenets: (1) individuals or collectives believe they own private information; (2) accordingly they have the right to control its flow; (3) privacy rules determine the access of others perceived to be outside of a social boundary; (4) individuals who disclose assume the other will be bound by the same rules they observe, or explicitly negotiate new ones; and (5) management of privacy information at the boundaries is imperfect, resulting in mistrust, anger, and suspicion about the sharing of private information (Petronio 2007).

Human subjects

Network analysis in evaluation research becomes a way of supporting relationships that are critical to KN and of suggesting relationships that should be nurtured (Introcaso 2005). Consultants/researchers often describe how management can use information to help specific individuals in a remedial way (e.g., Cross, Nohria, and Parker 2004), or to connect people to bridge structural holes (Krebs 2008), even in highly charged situations such as labor disputes (e.g., Michael 1997), but neglect to mention the potential problem the sharing of these results may have for the individual. Increasingly, network analysis research must confront issues related to human subject protection.

A fundamental requirement of census-based approaches to network analysis is that they require the identification of specific individuals with whom one communicates. This can lead to problems of "guilt by association," among other things, but it also creates problems for others who may choose not to respond out of concern for privacy issues. The analyst still has a one-sided picture, in the reports of others, of that individual's position in the social structure. There is a fundamental associated question of the differences between an individual's reports on their own attitudes and their reports of another's behavior in which they are involved (e.g., a report of a social tie). The subtlety of these issues has provoked widely different responses among institutional review boards (Borgatti and Molina 2003).

Automated data collection of explicit knowledge, related to enhanced surveillance of employees, is increasingly possible, but for tacit knowledge, the interpretation involved in self-reports is critical. One recurring difficulty with network research, then, is that often the results need further interpretation,[1] often based on discussions with the participants involved. This further complicates human subjects review issues (Durland 2005) both because communigrams often make little sense without identifying the characteristics of the people who occupy certain positions and because the additional information provided for interpretation may be highly personal.

---

[1] Network results are very much like projective tests in psychology, they often reveal much about the mindset of the beholder.

This also raises issues of truly informed consent. While most people are aware of the implications of psychological and intelligence testing, they have little familiarity with how their individual reports might be aggregated (e.g., communigram, constraint, centralization, brokerage) in network analysis research (Borgatti and Molina 2003). As people become more familiar with network analysis, they may become increasingly sophisticated in filling out questionnaires strategically (Zwijze-Koning and de Jong 2005). So, even if they are a social isolate, they may claim ties with others who are perceived to be more central in the network.

In sum, the combination of human subject review problems, the pronounced impact of non-response on network data, and savvy respondents may severely impact the validity of network analysis findings, limiting their application to pragmatic/policy issues and their usefulness in a scientific sense as well (Borgatti and Molina 2003).

Policy issues

The concepts of an "information gap" and the "information poor" have been advanced as important policy issues, generally in terms of their broad societal ramifications, including ethical ones. At a societal level, classically very few people use our existing information infrastructure (Dervin 1980; Dervin and Nilan 1986). It has been argued that there is a growing difference in access to information for different segments of our society and that increasingly this gap also reflects other demographic classifications, such as socioeconomic status. These individuals risk becoming members of a permanent underclass.

New technologies create an increasingly fragmented and privatized information environment, as opposed to the mass public access technologies represented by television and radio (Siefert, Gerbner, and Fisher 1989). Recently there have been countervailing integrative forces with the advent of social networking sites. However, instead of being equalizers, new information technologies may serve to increase the information gaps among organizational members that interact in interesting ways with organizational demography.

The knowledge gap hypothesis (Tichenor, Donohue, and Olien 1970) argues that over time gaps will increase, since highly educated individuals assimilate new information faster than poorly educated ones; they also have more relevant social contacts who are likely to discuss issues with them – an earlier version of power law and preferential attachment arguments. In addition, technology and software access is likely to be greater for privileged groups. Inevitably, differential access to information (and understanding of it in the classic tacit/explicit distinctions) produces differential participation rates in any collectivity (Lievrouw 1994), be it an organization or society. Classically, our mass media infrastructures have produced information fields that are informing. They are geared to providing information they select that is then consumed by their audiences. Information technologies offer the possibility of involving audience members through their interactive capabilities and enhanced possibilities for information seeking (Lievrouw 1994). One underlying reason for creating equity is that the wider the range of ideas available to individuals the more likely it is that a plurality will gravitate toward the correct one, thereby avoiding invidious groupthink processes.

A major impediment to information seeking for some groups is a lack of necessary skills, some as fundamental as a lack of literacy. Information seeking clearly differs with the educational levels of individuals. So, it is important not only to provide access to the information superhighway; people also must receive the training necessary to use it. Rather than stressing simple access to ideas, it may be better to stress access to playful intellectual tools that allow individuals to make sense of an overwhelming information environment (Entman and Wildman 1992).

We have always had among us Luddites who reject new technologies because they are socially and economically disadvantaged by them. We also have many individuals (whom we typically do not like to talk about), who really do not want to know things, who are more interested in "vegging out" and being entertained (Fortner 1995). While over and over again corporations emphasize their need for individuals who will constantly grow and develop into perpetual lifelong learners, it must be acknowledged that some individuals would prefer a comfortable world where they do not need to change nor expend the necessary effort to become full-fledged participants in the information society.[2]

It has been estimated that as few as 10 percent of top executives use the information technologies available to them (Fortner 1995). Some more cynical observers of KN in the professions suggest that perhaps the most powerful motivation for doctors and lawyers to keep up-to-date is the ever present threat of a malpractice suit (Paisley 1993). Most other professions do not have similarly compelling external motivations to keep current; they do not have sanctions for "remediable ignorance," for actions which duplicate or overlook existing knowledge (Paisley 1980). These professions can in effect conspire to say it is pointless to try to keep up. They also have substantial interests in the preservation of personal knowledge unique to their professions by insuring there are heavy information costs to memberships in their priesthood, discouraging intermediation. However, never has secret knowledge been more accessible to those who are interested in it.

Most of the people who write about, think about, and implement information technologies are information "junkies" who have very little understanding of (or tolerance for) these individuals. Some exhibit pathologies at the other extreme and are so concerned with acquiring information that it becomes an end in itself, rather than serving any particular organizational purpose. These individuals, who

---

[2] KN are overwhelmingly thought of as forces for good, but dark networks (e.g., organized crime, monopolistic forces, terrorist) also exist (Raab and Milward 2003). These networks pay more attention to issues of concealment and survivability if links are removed, balancing this against the countervailing pressure to coordinate and control the activities of their members, and thus adopt highly localized structures.

are often information professionals, tend to overburden information systems they design, providing users with too much information and too many options. They fail to distinguish between what people "need to know" and what it would be "nice to know" if you had unlimited time (Paisley 1993).

Even more disturbing than the information gap is the understanding gap that is developing between individuals who have access to a rich array of diverse information sources and the resources necessary to synthesize information. "... bad ideas spread more rapidly among the ignorant than among the informed, and good ideas spread more rapidly among the informed than the ignorant" (March 1994, p. 246). Our elites, both institutions and individuals, are developing a considerably different view of the world than other members of our society, in part because of their differential levels of KN capacities and skills. Even between elites, constant self-selection of information sources is producing different views of the world. The information revolution is contributing to the accelerating fragmentation of our culture (Fortner 1995).

Increasingly there are organizational analog for these societal trends. Many organizations do not have the resources to support elaborate internal information infrastructures, which can be very expensive. A variety of governmental programs have arisen to assist organizations, especially small businesses, in their information needs. Larger enterprises, with sufficient resources, are increasingly finding competitive advantage in the growing gap between themselves and other organizations (e.g., WalMart). In a resource-based view, organizations seek to exploit such disparities for competitive advantage. This has led to considerable concern that individuals and organizations with resources and access will perpetuate (or even widen) gaps in information to preserve or enhance their power and economic advantages.

Until recently most information processing activities in organizations have targeted automating tasks; increasingly computers are being used to augment human capabilities by informating tasks; the wave of the future may lie in restructuring tasks so that they are transformed (Cash *et al.* 1994). For example, the next-wave computers may quickly pass human capacities to simulate complex models, including many more variables than humans are capable of considering, and to visualize them and produce scenarios of various degrees of plausibility for human decision makers. Increasingly, seeking and interpretation will be delegated to intelligent software (Maes 1995). These software systems will not, however, be able to make policy and ethical decisions related to issues facing societies and the role of human beings within them. It has become a truism that computer-based information and decision systems excel at programmed tasks that reflect explicit knowledge. They do not perform well, and may even be dangerous, for tacit tasks that are ambiguous, that need creativity and judgment (Keen and Morton 1978). So, the relentless drive for efficiency, in part brought on by global economic trends, may directly confront human needs for more participation and democratization, that open access to information encourages (Cheney 1995).

Future directions for KN research

The study of knowledge, how it is managed and how it flows in networks, is inherently interdisciplinary, encompassing a number of substantive areas – diffusion of innovations, information technology, cognition, information sciences, management, organizational communication, computer-supported cooperative work, and so on. It also has important implications for organizational learning since it directly relates to three of the four commonly recognized components of it: acquisition, dissemination, shared interpretation, and development of organizational memory[3] (Tippins and Sohi 2003).

However, since research related to KN is proceeding in so many areas it is difficult to accumulate findings and insure that orderly academic progress is being made (Argote, McEvily, and Reagans 2003). There has also been a preponderance of conceptual over empirical papers (Argote, McEvily, and Reagans 2003) in part because of the difficult methodological issues we discussed in Chapter 3. In this section the focus will be on four meta-theoretical issues which concern structure: context, the nature of relationships, the linkages between deep and surface levels of structure, and planned vs. emergent views of structure. These issues have constituted recurring themes throughout this book and point to some major unresolved problems which should guide future inquiry into KN.

Context and individual action

While context is an integral part of the definition of knowledge, and is often fundamental to the development of tacit knowledge, the extent to which it can be systematically related to other issues is limited by the dearth of literature related to it at any meaningful level (Johnson 2003). We explored these issues more fully in Chapter 4; here we will contrast two different ways of conceptualizing context, fields and pathways, that have direct implications for KN (Johnson *et al.* 2006). The notion of fields has been fundamental to sociometric approaches from the outset (Scott 2000), although it is difficult to express in network terms; pathways have more direct linkages to graph theory, as we discussed in Box 10.1. Fields most directly describe the immediate radial networks that characterize someone's strong direct ties. Beyond these ties, however, lie small-world notions of how you can link to someone who may have something you want (e.g., information, knowledge). This brings us to concept of pathways, reachability, zone size, and so on.

An individual's information field provides the more static context for KN. It contains resources, constraints, and carriers of information. The nature of an individual's stable information field can shape his/her more active information

---

[3] Even this component may relate to some views of transactive memory in groups.

seeking, since it provides a starting point for information searches. People are embedded in information fields that determine their level of awareness and knowledge of particular issues. The nature of these fields also determines the likelihood that they will be exposed to information that may trigger a desire to seek more information or to change their behavior in some way. The presence of weak ties may expose them to information that suggests the possibility of change should at least be explored and this may trigger an expansion of the individual's information field. In addition, the mediated channels to which individuals are recurrently exposed through information terminals may incidentally contain information related to a communication campaign which causes them to seek more information.

Individuals can pursue their quest for knowledge by negotiating pathways within an information matrix formed by channels, sources, and messages. This concept of the context of KN is substantially different than that of field. It is more dynamic and active, focusing on individual actions over time in response sequences (Emirbayer and Mische 1998).[4] It also highlights time specificity, or the extent to which information loses its value if it is not used soon after it becomes available (Christiaanse and Venkatraman 2002). Organizations engage in sequential searches, stopping their search when they feel they have sufficient information. This movement over time may result in changing contexts (or surrounds) that are the direct result of individual choice and a response to what an individual has uncovered. In this sense, individual action is more mindful. However, individuals may come, over time, to have habitual pathways and/or plans for negotiating this matrix (Taylor 1968). A pathway, then, is the route someone follows in the pursuit of answers to questions within the information-seeking matrix.

These different approaches imply different relationships between actors and their information environments and thus also encapsulate different views of the relationship between individual actions and contexts. Fields are associated with classic causal approaches to human action, while pathways reflect more modern notions of narrative (Sharf and Vanderford 2003) and a search for typical patterns (Abbott 1990).[5] In many ways, comparisons of fields and pathways are fundamentally about the difference between sequenced, dependent actions and more deterministic clusters of variables. For pathways, more of a process, narrative approach that departs from the standard longitudinal, cross-sectional methodological approach is needed (Poole *et al.* 2000). Small-world, weak ties approaches offer much hope of reclaiming specifics, the pathways by which knowledge is diffused in organizations and the sources to which an individual is exposed.

---

[4] It is also a view that is more difficult to capture sequentially in conventional approaches to communigrams.

[5] Similarly these conceptions in some ways represent the distinction between "objectified" and "interpretive" approaches to context (Talja, Keso, and Pietilainen 1999).

Pathways imply longitudinal research designs and special analytic techniques that are only slowly being developed in the social sciences. The results, especially at the further reaches of one's journey, may be highly idiosyncratic, shaped by unique events. Fields, a more conventional approach with somewhat settled static methods and analytic techniques,[6] are often the starting points for these journeys, providing a set of initial conditions, often determined by accessibility, that shape the likelihood of someone's ultimate success – the starting points for paths individuals might take. In some ways these two approaches are akin to the classic differences between strategies and tactics, with the former determining a general approach to an ultimate goal and the latter the specific actions that result in the goal's accomplishment. Ultimately, mastery of life depends on both approaches operating in concert.

These contemporary approaches also draw our attention to the active role individuals play in contextualizing their environments. Several observers have made trenchant comments concerning the lack of a meaningful focus on context in communication research (e.g., Dervin 1997) and organizational research (Baker and Cullen 1993; Cappelli and Sherer 1991; Porter 1996). When there is so obvious a need, and still little is done, there must be powerful countervailing pressures that preserve the status quo. This need is especially critical for KN since the contexts in which knowledge is embedded often determine its usefulness, the possibility of discovering it, and the likelihood of its transfer (Postrel 2002). Most researchers become embedded in a taken-for-granted reality in which context becomes a set of initial assumptions or limiting conditions on their area of inquiry. We are McLuhan's fish who do not recognize the fundamental enabling presence of water or realize what other possibilities might exist outside this embedding medium. So contexts become conceived of in terms of constraints and limits on individual action (Valsiner and Leung 1994), rather than as enablers.

This problem is reinforced by the habitual, unchanging nature of many environments, at least within short cross-sectional time frames, which leads to a lack of interest in (or awareness of) them (Thorngate 1995). For many researchers, especially ones who focus on limited time frames, it may make sense to ignore the effects of context. It is no accident that the researchers who have been most interested in contexts are those confronted with constantly changing ones (e.g., developmental psychologists), a factor in our often tumultuous world that has renewed interest in studying context in organizations. So, most organizational scholars examining contextual frames focus on processes of organizational change or innovation (e.g., Bartunek and Franzak 1988). In addition, context may also interact with time, with differing levels of context operative in different periods. So, in the long view culture may be determinant, while in the short run structures may be critical to the success of organizations (Ranson, Hinings, and Greenwood 1980).

---

[6] Not so coincidentally, more and more network research is determined by a focus on an individual's immediate radial network of direct ties (Burt 2007).

There is also the problem of levels of analysis (Rousseau 1985). In effect, for lower-level phenomena (e.g., dyadic communication) one must study the contexts of context. This introduces another problem because of the implicit hierarchy of effects in many approaches to levels, which subordinates lower-level phenomena to higher-order ones (Rickert 1994; Rousseau 1985). Many context effects in communication settings are reflections of much more encompassing organizational (Gresov and Stephens 1993) and/or societal trends.[7] Specific lower-level contexts may be determined by larger social, economic, or historical ones (Thorngate 1995), but this view may also short-change emergent properties represented in bottom-up phenomena.

Differing standards for explanation and what is meaningful as an object of study also impede cross-level research. For example, network analysis researchers introduce simplicity at the dyadic level, that is at least disturbing to interpersonal, discourse, and social interaction scholars, to focus on complexity at the social system level (Burt and Schott 1985). Somewhat similarly, cross-level studies proceed at such a high level of abstraction and are so general that they are just not valuable (Schon and Rein 1994), raising echoes of the classic etic–emic distinction in intercultural research (Pike 1966).

In complex social systems everyone's context is somewhat unique, giving the appearance of individual differences attributable to individual locus variables (Richards 1993). The concept of field has a long tradition in the social sciences going back to the seminal work of Lewin (Scott 2000), with interesting recent variants such as the information horizons approach suggested by Sonnenwald, Wildemuth, and Harmon (2001), information grounds (Fisher, Durrance, and Hinton 2004), and small worlds (Huotari and Chatman 2001). These common contexts are important for transferring knowledge in our increasingly virtual organizations. So, individual action and choices may be context-driven, but the diversity of contexts makes this difficult to uncover. Individuals may also choose contexts that best match their characteristics, factors which may play a role in liaison emergence (discussed in Chapter 3), which further clouds the impact of context (Kindermann and Valsiner 1995a, b).

In sum, then, individuals are embedded in an "heuristic field" that encompasses their tacit knowledge (Polanyi 1974) and shapes the context of their KN. The nature of this field determines their exposure to information that triggers a desire to seek more information. For example, weak ties may expose an individual to information that suggests changes should be explored, triggering an expansion of the individual's information field. In addition, the mediated channels in information terminals may incidentally contain information that causes them to seek more information, or to expand their information field by exploring new pathways to obtain information concerning potential threats to them or to their organization.

---

[7] For example, Barley and Kunda's (1992) analysis of the normative social ideologies' impact on managerial discourse over a century and a half

Relationships

In network analysis research, there has been increasing concern over the nature of relationships. This research tends to approach relationships in a binary sense; either they exist or they do not (Johnson 1989). Clearly, however, there are gradations in the strength of relationships and even more interestingly there are various probabilities that a relationship may or may not occur. Network analysis tends to focus on a more narrow sense of relationships involving direct linkages between human entities. However, relationships which do not occur (e.g., no communication between two interrelated work units) may be almost as important as those that do (Knoke and Kuklinski 1982), especially in the context of constraints and their implications for knowledge sharing. Fundamentally, knowledge assets lie in relationships and suffer when those relationships are harmed (Introcaso 2005). Examining missing relationships may be more fruitful in identifying underlying factors which shape structures than examining relationships which do exist.

Gradients and structural equivalence concepts can move us in the direction of broader thinking about relationships, since they suggest a more probabilistic world of forces and fields, which we discussed in the prior section, where locations may be entities as well as individuals. Gradients might be better thought of in terms of relative intensities which are spatially bound. Thus, considering a wide range of approaches also compels us to expand our view of what relationships are; a compelling topic for future theoretical inquiry.

As we noted in the previous chapter, a major trend in the decision-making literature has been toward more and more irrational views of human behavior. Somewhat similarly, a major trend in organizational communication over the last several decades has been to a more subjective, post-modern concept of organizations. A related problem in the development of network analysis within communication has been the richness of its definition of relationships (Susskind et al., 2005).[8] A focus on tacit knowledge only heightens the need for richer concept. As we established in Chapters 2 and 3, the distinction between tacit and explicit knowledge is fundamental to KN. Classically, however, network methods have focused on simplistic operationalizations of surface content and frequencies. But movement to KN, and recognition of the importance of discourse and social construction approaches, make these oscillating movements toward and away from rationality even more important.

In some ways a focus on tacit knowledge is itself a recognition of the subjective, idiosyncratic nature of personal experience. A focus on the technological tools available for modern information searches and technology associated with KM, however, reintroduces the logical and rational, since these systems often demand very logical approaches (e.g., keyword searches) by users (Corman

---

[8] There have been some promising recent attempts to link network and formal structures to more micro, discourse-oriented processes (Gibson 2005).

2005). Information-as-thing, as commodity, may be the only sense of information that makes sense for information systems (Buckland 1991). In fact, information systems are often very mechanistic, a theoretic approach to organizations that clearly has gone out of fashion. As Drucker (1974) has argued, while information may be inherently rational, it is the perception and interpretation of it that is subjective.

A key problem for structural research is the linkage between function and form, between deeper and surface levels. How does one type of knowledge inform another? The nature of these linkages and their consequences for organizations are only poorly understood (see Nonaka 1991). These issues also imply a much richer approach to multiplexity. Assortative mixing of relationships in most networks is a major empirical issue, and may be a new approach to multiplexity (Newman, Barabasi, and Watts 2006), especially as it relates to the complex combinations of tacit and explicit networks detailed in Chapter 3. How we capture this richness is a major methodological issue.

The boundaryless organization

Establishing boundaries around networks has been a continuing problem, with tasks like trying to identify the invisible college of researchers in particular areas nearly boundaryless in conventional organizational terms. Increasingly, KN are also a boundaryless phenomenon, especially with the advent of virtual organizations (DeSanctis and Monge 1999). Professionals seek answers to their questions wherever they may easily be available, whether inside or outside the organization. Sophisticated search agents and brokers only accelerate this trend. Therefore, it will be much harder to define the limited domain of any one organization, or profession, as the context for KN. In fact, linkages between knowledge workers may further encourage alliances between firms (Corman 2005). Organizations form consortia where the dissemination of information and knowledge generation and synthesis are the focus. In doing this, they often partner with think-tanks and key university personnel. Thus a more modern basis for establishing boundaries might be to look at communities of tacit knowledge. Toyota has a way of addressing this by moving learning to the network-of-suppliers level. Thus, organizations learn by collaborating with others who have a shared purpose, not just by observing and importing; this then becomes the most appropriate unit of analysis or level (Dyer and Nobeoka 2000).

Planned vs. emergent views

The fourth meta-theoretical problem lies in whether or not structures, such as KN, should be thought of as planned or emergent. KN can be thought of as islands of highly dense activity surrounded by a sea of (hopefully) planned ignorance. Increasingly, market-oriented views of structure may compel us to recant the underlying determinism of structure conceptualizations.[9] That is, structures may be an expression of individual needs, and while these needs are predictable, and temporally stable, the level of agency is still the individual. It is then the joint activity of organizational actors over time which reveals structures. Greater understanding of emergent KN properties can help in the design of information systems since their designers often ignore human needs (Solomon 2002). Organizational designers could be somewhat akin to landscape architects on campuses in putting sidewalks where footpaths naturally develop.

Managing KN

> Put bluntly, the more management, the less knowledge to "manage." And the more "knowledge" matters, the less space there is for management to make a difference.   (Alvesson and Karreman 2001, p. 996)

In some ways traditional views of management, with an emphasis on the development of explicit knowledge, anticipating problems, documenting them, and ultimately controlling them,[10] are antithetical to the development of KN in organizations, thus fostering a view that managers govern best by letting go. However, a fundamental component of any definition of knowledge is that it provides a basis for action and action is the key preserve of leadership. As we develop in more detail in this section, perhaps the fundamental role of management is mindfully to confront the many paradoxes and dilemmas swirling around KN to insure that a balance is achieved between change and stability, between the known and the unknown.

Paradoxes

> What knowledge the firm can hold on to, it can't use. And what it might use, it can't hold on to.   (Brown and Duguid 2002, p. 150)

As we have seen repeatedly there are a number of paradoxes in KN. For example, Hansen and Hass (2001) found an interesting paradox in knowledge markets – the less information a supplier provided the more it was used, because of a reputation the supplier developed for focus and quality. Such paradoxes reveal contradictory and/or inconsistent qualities, statements that seem absurd but which may be true in fact. They stimulate us to deeper thought and a desire to resolution that may be a stimulus to theory development. They also reveal the need for human, managerial intervention in KN.

---

[9] On the other hand, network studies generally have had an unfortunate tendency to ignore formal hierarchy, seldom reporting a formal organizational chart so we can compare it to networks formed on the basis of other sorts of relationship (Grandori and Kogut 2002).

[10] As do helicopter managers that do not let their workers grow through failure and experimentation.

Poole and Van de Ven (1989) have suggested four ways of working with paradox which are instructive for future development of theory in KN. First, one can accept the paradox and use it constructively, which may be the best approach for the dilemmas we present in the next section. So, savvy organizational experts will hire consultants to tell the organization what they already know, since they realize that external information will be valued more (Menon and Pfeffer 2003). Second, one can clarify differing levels of analysis that can serve to resolve the paradox. So it may be the case that at one and the same time development of tacit knowledge advances a profession and resolves conflict, while it leads to greater conflict and impedes progress at the whole-organization level where many professions may contest for resolution of problems. Third, examining underlying temporal dynamics may also be one way of resolving certain issues. I have made much of differentiation and integration, but it may also be the case that greater differentiation is inherent in organizational growth which then must be redressed eventually by the subsequent development of appropriate integrative mechanisms. Finally, new terms, such as structural hole brokers, may include both underlying dimensions of the paradox, with structural holes often representing underlying differentiation processes, and brokers representing one approach to integration.

Dilemmas

> The weak link in the information chain is the increasingly inadequate absorption capacity of individuals and organizations. Computer technology does not help much – unless underlying information is quantitative and structured, and questions are well defined.   (Noam 1993, p. 203)

While paradoxes reveal seemingly contradictory elements of KN, dilemmas often reveal contrasting forces that may represent opposite, orthogonal ends of an underlying continuum. Being forced to choose between unpleasant, disagreeable, unfavorable alternatives is often very difficult, but the important thing is that managers should be conscious of them so that they are clear as to their costs and benefits, since there are often unintended consequences or tradeoffs in choosing one over the other. So, for example, while managers may design an organization to maximize one key concern (e.g., customers, products, functional specialties), they must through their own actions try to ameliorate the effects of their designs on other key organizational values. Thus, in this view, management's central role becomes one of absorbing uncertainty for the remainder of the organization. Sometimes, as in Eastern religions' concepts of *yin/yang*, it is perhaps better to accept the presence of a two-sided coin and relish the interplay between the two sides (Gupta, Smith, and Shalley 2006), rather than maximize one at the expense of the other. We have highlighted several such dilemmas in the course of this work. Here we will focus on four sometimes intertwining dilemmas: the need to balance cooperation and competition, focusing attention, managing uncertainty, and forgetting.

First, a balance of cooperation and competition must be achieved, most notably in sharing information that is in the interest of the collective, in spite of individual motivations to hoard (Kalman *et al.* 2002). The more and more effort that is devoted to specialization, which implies one benefits from the work of others, the more reluctant someone will be to give up what they know, especially to perceived free-riders.[11] Some have suggested that the best motivator for knowledge sharing is a sense of collectivism and reciprocity (Hew and Hara 2007).[12] But, how much do you give and how much do you receive may be the key problem to be resolved in consortia, with companies like Toyota realizing the essential competitive advantage of resolving this dilemma by creating dynamic learning capabilities so that they learn and assimilate their knowledge into routine practices more quickly than their rivals (Dyer and Nobeoka 2000).

Managers need tacit knowledge and deep understanding for fundamental change, but this knowledge is supported by existing communication structures and various inertial forces. KN can result in coalitions and power struggles (which often are a by-product of tacit knowledge) and, the development of taboos and priesthoods. A key social outcome of the development of KN is tacit knowledge; however, it can lead to problems of concertative control resulting in conformity and influence. While we need the support of others, they also limit our action.

Second, management must focus the attention of organizational members on key issues, which they often do through agenda-setting processes. Many observers have commented that attention rather than information is the scarce resource in organizations (e.g., Hansen and Hass 2001; Pirolli and Card 1999; Simon 1987; Van de Ven 1986); fundamentally, we must accept human limits to information processing. Some people have just reached a saturation point; they cannot spend any more time communicating (Fortner 1995). But there is always a demand to do more, to recognize key threats in the environment, for example, by actively contextualizing or expanding one's noosphere. While more and more information can be produced more efficiently, there is a concomitant increase in the costs of consuming (e.g., interpreting, analyzing) this information (More 1990). Firms increasingly will be organized as knowledge specialists and professionals reacting to a common theme, emulating many characteristics of symphony orchestras (Drucker 1988). In orchestras there must be some common thread that all the members are working from if their individual efforts are not to become too discordant. Some simplifying melody is required so that the players can react to and build on the solo performances, upon which the whole effort depends. Another variant of this approach is to identify a few Critical Success Factors (e.g., orders) that can be quantified and widely shared (McKinnon and Bruns 1992).

---

[11] This may be somewhat akin to the recently developed understanding that paradigms in the sciences do not really change until the dominant cohort ages and leaves the arena.

[12] People are also reluctant to share information with those they think are incapable of understanding it (Hew and Hara 2007).

Third, organizational designers, classically, were concerned with reducing uncertainty, but more modern views have suggested the real issue is managing it in an increasingly turbulent world. The ultimate goals of rationality may be to develop a sense of coherence, and a simple one at that, with satisficing the standard rather than maximizing (Bates 2005; Pirolli and Card 1999). Many have argued that most people do not want a wide range of options, in part because our cognitive limits for processing information have been exceeded (Schwartz 2004). In a related way, people may pursue information not for new insights, but for validation, legitimation, and reformulation (Cross, Rice, and Parker 2001).

Given traditional problems individuals have in developing certainty related to their roles, it is perhaps understandable that they have difficulties reintroducing uncertainty into their lives. This has been referred to as the "curse of knowledge," reflecting the difficulty people have in abandoning prior knowledge (Carlile 2004). Often, when confronted with crisis situations, a failure to adopt appropriate, sometimes creative responses is related to an unwillingness to "drop one's tools" (Weick 1996), to abandon one's competencies (Leonard 2006; Rosenkopf and Nerkar 2001). Knowledge disavowal is indeed an important organizational process; it allows for the dismissal of disconfirming ideas and the recognition of ideas as not fully formed, at least not developed enough to overturn conventional organizational wisdom, and is one way of coping with information overload (Zaltman 1994). These trends also suggest a need to reintroduce organizational simplicity and to think carefully about what information should be excluded from organizational information processing.

Finally, and relatedly, while an organization must maintain the essence of its being (DNA), how an organization goes about forgetting is a critical issue (Argote 1999; Argote and Epple 1990; Govindarajan and Trimble 2005). Managers should think as carefully and deeply about what information they should discard and ignore as about what they should acquire, another aspect of figure/ground issues critical to contextual inquiry. The dark side of the quest for uncertainty reduction is that once an answer is arrived at and a decision made, blockage from future information seeking may occur (Smithson 1989). How long do we hold on to an answer we struggled so hard to attain? These issues are further complicated by the intersection of knowledge with organizational identification, where knowledge becomes the source of identity for organizational members and its discarding comes to mean discarding what people thought the organization was, further supporting strategic inertia (Nag, Corley, and Gioia 2007). As we have seen, disastrous consequences often arise from situations where group ideas become accepted as truth, discouraging even the possibility of seeking discordant information.

There is also an implicit perception of progress in the literature, but knowledge that is found is not always retained as in Box 2.2 on Stradivari. The knowledge of individuals is often lost when they retire or move on, which was one of the key reasons for the interest in expert systems as a means of preservation. Similarly, when organizations die, in the forces of creative destruction that

Table 14.1. *Benefits and costs of differing levels of ignorance*

Level of ignorance	Benefits	Costs
High	(1)	(2)
	Comfort of denial	Don't confront problems
	Easier control	Lack of coordination
	Less redundancy	Fragmented networks
	More efficient	Lower integration
	Structural hole brokers have many rewards	More structural holes anomie
	Easier to manipulate	Opportunities forgone
	Lower information processing costs	Primarily explicit knowledge
	Preservation of inertial states	
Low	(3)	(4)
	More likely to confront problems	Avoidance
	Greater coordination	Increased conflict
	Higher levels of tacit knowledge	Control more difficult
	Higher integration	Higher information processing costs
	Opportunities addressed	Reduced specialization

Schumpeter trumpeted, their collective, social wisdom can also pass, especially if it is private, reflecting high tacitness (Hoetker and Agarwal 2007). Various social processes can also cause people to shun knowledge from failed firms since it is tainted by this very failure. Organizations must constantly struggle with the question of whether to explore new possibilities or exploit old certainties (March 1991), which often relates to forgetting and ignoring, as we discussed in Chapter 9.

A final word

As a way of summarizing, we will organize our discussion around the dimensions presented in Table 14.1. The cells in this table are classified by levels of ignorance (awareness of things known to others in the organization), and the costs and benefits of ignorance for organizational members. Typically research and theory has dwelled on Cells 2 and 3 to the exclusion of Cells 1 and 4. It is by analyzing these latter cells, however, that a greater understanding of the persistence of ignorance, and conversely the role of KN, will result. Ultimately, the final paradox may be that we can only promote the development of deeper levels of knowledge by actively promoting ignorance; there needs to be a recognition that there are enormous amounts of ignorance in organizations, that no one can know what is being maximized overall.

Cell 2 is the straw man to which Cell 3 is often compared, the worst-case scenario of high levels of ignorance and high costs to the organization. In this situation the organization does not confront problems and therefore does not correct them in a timely fashion. It also does not seize opportunities that can result from successful problem solutions. As in the case of the classic segmented organization discussed earlier, there is a general lack of coordination and integrative efforts toward common organizational goals. Thus, you have a highly fragmented network with many structural holes. As a result, at the very least there is a lot of wasted energy; at worst, members of this type of organization often work at cross-purposes to each other.

People underinvest in information seeking (Bates 2005), because uncovering more may entail a need to change, or perhaps more dangerously, they do not have a sense of self-efficacy that they will be able to correctly interpret and react to any new information with which they are presented. Conventionally, given Western attitudes to knowledge and progress, ignorance is viewed as something that needs to be overcome. A critical corollary of this assumption is that acquiring information inevitably helps the inquirer (Case 2007). We also have a taken-for-granted assumption that people correctly interpret and apply the information they acquire; however, Hersh and his colleagues (2000, 2002) have found that a disturbing percentage of health professionals did not correctly interpret medical information they retrieved from medical information systems and, even worse, searching, at times, resulted in changing correct information to incorrect. This research, therefore, extends a generalized concern for information literacy even to our most highly trained professionals.

However, as we have seen, there are also benefits to high levels of ignorance in organizations (Cell 1). This is the set of conditions that serve to maintain ignorance (often overlooked by management theorists) that have been neglected in the research arena. Managers in traditional hierarchical organizations can use these segmented organizations to divide and conquer, just as structural hole brokers can (Johnson 2003). They can always maintain to any employee pressing for change, "If only you knew what I know, then you would act in the same way that I do." So control in this type of organization is easier to achieve. In addition, there are lower levels of information load and therefore lower information processing costs. Individuals also have the comfort of denying the existence of problems that they would have to work to overcome. This can act to preserve powerful inertial forces in organizations. Particularly for individuals then, the benefits of high levels of ignorance may offset the costs, which are largely borne by future organizational members; this builds up pressures that result in powerful episodic changes (Weick and Quinn 1999). We also are reluctant to give up our relationships, and the heavy investments we have in them, even if we see substantial knowledge gains from developing new ones (Kim, Oh, and Swaminathan 2006).

The costs of achieving low levels of ignorance are substantial, especially for effective information processing systems (Hoffman 1994). These costs (Cell 4) are often the impetus for the development of more effective KN. Curiously, more detailed knowledge of how the system really works can sometimes result in higher levels of cynicism (Bellah *et al.* 1991; Greider 1992). Some have suggested that since coordinated action is what is important in an organization, sharing information about values and beliefs may be dysfunctional because of the possibility for increasing conflict (Eisenberg and Riley 1988), especially among professions. Since traditional behaviors and value maintenance often depend in part on ignorance of alternatives (Moore and Tumin 1949), ignorance often serves to reinforce ultimate values and heighten a sense of community (Smithson 1989).

In many ways Cell 3, characterized by low levels of ignorance and many benefits, is the optimal cell, since this is the set of conditions many management theorists and popularizers of management issues, and many advocates of KN, seem to suggest we should be striving toward (Dean and Bowen 1994; Galbraith 1995; Peters and Waterman 1982). In this utopian world we have high levels of coordination and integration. We have knowledgeable organizational members confronting and then solving problems, thus not letting opportunities slip through their grasp.

Conventionally, given Western attitudes to knowledge and progress, ignorance is viewed as something that needs to be overcome, in part by increased attention to information seeking (Smithson 1989). This belief structure is so ingrained that it is difficult for social science to come to grips with ignorance as an area of inquiry (LaFollette 1993; Ravetz 1993; Smithson 1989, 1993), although interestingly uncertainty has been legitimated as an area of study (Smithson 1993). Yet, sometimes in organizations ignorance is planned for and overcoming it may detract from efficiency and specialization goals, thereby presenting organizations with a substantial dilemma. Indeed, ignorance persists because it is useful on several levels, if not a necessity for organizations and their members (Moore and Tumin 1949; Smithson 1989, 1993). In fact, it has been suggested that instead of becoming more complex, organizations that are successful in their environmental niche strive to become more simple as a result of a number of factors – managerial, structural, cultural, and processual (Miller 1993). The question for many organizations is whether the benefits of facilitating KN, and resulting complications, are worth the very real risk to the organization of any strategies that might be used to overcome ignorance. Traditionally, it has been argued that the way to improve organizations is not to produce more information, but to reduce the amount of information any one subsystem must process (March and Simon 1958).

In the end, as we have seen, there are deep-seated barriers to KN – structural, cultural, the limits of individual decision makers, and so forth. Unfortunately, many of these barriers present insurmountable dilemmas, paradoxes, and delicate balancing acts for anyone interested in facilitating knowledge flows and transfers, partly because maximizing knowledge means minimizing an often more important organizational process (e.g., preserving existing power bases, maintaining group norms). As in our larger society – and perhaps to an even greater extent, since there are fewer individual protections (e.g., freedom of speech) – there may be more forces supporting ignorance in organizations than supporting the development and sharing of knowledge in KN.

Further reading

Argote, L. 1999. *Organizational Learning: Creating, Retaining and Transferring Knowledge*. Kluwer.

Summarizes the author's extensive research program on organizational learning, with a focus on underlying factors leading to differential learning curves and the related issue of forgetting.

Borgatti, S. P., and Molina, J. L. 2003. Ethical and strategic issues in organizational social network analysis. *Journal of Applied Behavioral Science*, 39: 337–349.

Systematic treatment of a range of human subject concerns, but clearly tilted toward the interest of researchers.

D'Urso, S. C. 2006. Toward a structural-perceptual model of electronic monitoring and surveillance in organizations. *Communication Theory*, 16: 281–303.

Overview of electronic monitoring and surveillance of social communication in the workplace with application of traditional panopticon issues.

Moore, W. E., and Tumin, M. M. 1949. Some social functions of ignorance. *American Sociological Review*, 14: 787–795.

Classic early discussion of ignorance with a focus on its benefits and functions.

Poole, M. S., and Van de Ven, A. H. 1989. Using paradox to build management and organizational theories. *Academy of Management Review*, 14: 562–578.

Very useful treatment of paradox and its role in theory development.

References

Dictionaries

American Heritage Dictionary of the English Language. 1979. Houghton Mifflin.
Merriam-Webster's Collegiate Dictionary, 4th edn. 1995. Merriam-Webster.

Other works

Abbott, A. 1990. Conceptions of time and events in social science methods: causal and narrative approaches. *Historical Methods*, 23: 140–154.

Abelson, R. P. 1964. Mathematical models of the distribution of attitudes under controversy. In N. Frederiksen and H. Gulliksen (eds.), *Contributions to Mathematical Psychology*: 141–160. Holt, Rinehart, and Winston.

Adams, J. S. 1976. The structure and dynamics of behavior in organizational boundary roles. In M. D. Dunnette (ed.), *Handbook of Industrial and Organizational Psychology*: 1175–1199. Rand McNally.

1980. Interorganizational processes and organizational activities. In S. B. Bacharach (ed.), *Research in Organizational Behavior*, vol. II: 321–355. JAI Press.

Adelman, M. B., Parks, M. R., and Albrecht, T. L. 1987. Beyond close relationships: support in weak ties. In T. L. Albrecht and M. B. Adelman (eds.), *Communicating Social Support*: 126–147. Sage.

Adler, P. S., and Kwon, S.-W. 2002. Social capital: prospects for a new concept. *Academy of Management Review*, 27: 17–40.

Agrell, A., and Gustafson, R. 1996. Innovation and creativity in work groups. In M. West (ed.), *Handbook of Work Group Psychology*: 317–343. Wiley.

Ahuja, G. 2000. Collaboration networks, structural holes, and innovation: a longitudinal study. *Administrative Science Quarterly*, 45: 425–455.

Ahuja, M. K., and Carley, K. M. 1999. Network structure in virtual organizations. *Organization Science*, 10: 741–757.

Aiello, J. R., and Thompson, D. E. 1980. Personal space, crowding, and spatial behavior in a cultural context. In I. Altman, A. Rapoport, and J. F. Wohlwill (eds.), *Human Behavior and Environment: Advances in Theory and Research*: 107–178. Plenum.

Aiken, M., and Hage, J. 1971. The organic model and innovations. *Sociology*, 5: 63–82.

Alba, R. D. 1982. Taking stock of network analysis: a decade's results. In S. B. Bacharach (ed.), *Research in the Sociology of Organizations*: 39–74. JAI Press.

Albert, R., Jeong, H., and Barabasi, A. 2000. Error and attack tolerance of complex networks. *Nature*, 406: 378–381.

Albrecht, T. L. 1979. The role of communication in perceptions of organizational climate. In D. Nimmo (ed.), *Communication Yearbook*, 3: 343–357. Transaction Books.

Albrecht, T. L., and Adelman, M. B. 1987a. Communication networks as structures of social support. In T. L. Albrecht and M. B. Adelman (eds.), *Communicating Social Support*: 40–63. Sage.

1987b. Dilemmas of supportive communication. In T. L. Albrecht and M. B. Adelman (eds.), *Communicating Social Support*: 240–254. Sage.

1987c. Rethinking the relationship between communication and social support: an introduction. In T. L. Albrecht and M. B. Adelman (eds.), *Communicating Social Support*: 13–16. Sage.

Albrecht, T. L., and Hall, B. 1989. Relational and content differences between elites and outsiders in innovation networks, presented to the Annual Convention of the International Communication Association. San Francisco.

Albrecht, T. L., and Ropp, V. A. 1984. Communicating about innovation in networks of three US organizations. *Journal of Communication*, 34: 78–91.

Aldrich, H., and Herker, D. 1977. Boundary spanning roles and organizational structure. *Academy of Management Review*, 2: 217–230.

Alexander, J. W., and Randolph, W. A. 1985. The fit between technology and structure as a predictor of nursing subunits. *Academy of Management Journal*, 28: 844–859.

Allen, B., and Kim, K. 2000. Person and context in information seeking: interactions between cognitive and task variables. *New Review of Information Behaviour Research*, 1: 1–16.

Allen, M. W. 1989. Factors influencing the power of a linking role: an investigation into interorganizational boundary spanning. Louisiana State University.

Allen, T. J. 1966. Performance of information channels in the transfer of technology. *Industrial Management Review*, 8: 87–98.

1977. *Managing the Flow of Technology: Technology Transfer and the Dissemination of Technological Information within the R&D Organization*. MIT Press.

Allen, T. J., and Gerstberger, P. G. 1973. A field experiment to improve communications in a product engineering department: the non-territorial office. *Human Factors*, 15: 487–498.

Almeida, P., and Phene, A. 2004. Subsidiaries and knowledge creation: the influence of the MNC and host country on innovation. *Strategic Management Journal*, 25: 847–864.

Alvesson, M., and Karreman, D. 2001. Odd couple: making sense of the curious concept of knowledge management. *Journal of Management Studies*, 38: 995–1018.

Amabile, T. M., Patterson, C., Mueller, J., Wojcik, T., Odomirok, P. W., Marsh, M. M., and Kramer, S. J. 2001. Acedemic–practitioner collaboration in management research: a case of cross-profession collaboration. *Academy of Management Journal*, 44: 418–431.

Amidon, D. M., and Mahdjoubi, P. 2003. An atlas for knowledge innovation: migration from business planning to innovation strategy. In C. W. Holsapple (ed.), *Handbook for Knowledge Management: Knowledge Directions*: 331–351. Springer Verlag.

Anand, N., Gardner, H. K., and Morris, T. 2007. Knowledge-based innovation: emergence and embedding of new practice areas in management consulting firms. *Academy of Management Journal*, 50: 406–428.

Andersen, T. J., and Segars, A. H. 2001. The impact of IT decision structure on firm performance: evidence from the textile and apparel industry. *Information and Management*, 39: 85–100.

Antonovsky, H. F., and Antonovsky, A. 1974. Commitment in an Israeli kibbutz. *Human Relations*, 27: 95–112.

Applegate, J. L. 2001. Engaged graduate education: skating to where the puck will be. *Spectra*, 37: 1–5.

    2002. Skating to where the puck will be: engaged research as a funding strategy for the communication discipline. *Journal of Applied Communication Research*, 30: 402–410.

Archea, J. 1977. The place of architectural factors in behavioral theories of privacy. *Journal of Social Issues*, 33: 16–37.

Argote, L. 1999. *Organizational Learning: Creating, Retaining and Transferring Knowledge*. Kluwer.

Argote, L., and Epple, D. 1990. Learning curves in manufacturing. *Science*, 247: 920–924.

Argote, L., McEvily, B., and Reagans, R. 2003. Managing knowledge in organizations: an integrative framework and review of emerging themes. *Management Science*, 49: 571–582.

Ashford, S. J. 1986. Feedback seeking in individual adaptation: a resource perspective. *Academy of Management Journal*, 29: 465–487.

    1989. Self assessments in organizations: a literature review and integrative model. In S. B. Bacharach (ed.), *Research in Organizational Behavior*, vol. XI: 133–174. JAI Press.

Ashford, S. J., Blatt, R., and VandeWalle, D. 2003. Reflections on the looking glass: a review of research on feedback-seeking behavior in organizations. *Journal of Management*, 29: 773–799.

Ashford, S. J., and Cummings, L. L. 1985. Proactive feedback seeking: the instrumental use of the information environment. *Journal of Occupational Psychology*, 58: 67–79.

Ashford, S. J., and Tsui, A. S. 1991. Self regulation for managerial effectiveness: the role of active feedback seeking. *Academy of Management Journal* 34: 251–280.

Ashforth, B. E. 1985. Climate formation: issues and extensions. *Academy of Management Review*, 10: 837–847.

Astley, W. G., and Zajac, E. J. 1991. Intraorganizational power and organizational design: reconciling rational and coalitional models of organization. *Organization Science*, 2: 399–411.

Atkin, C. 1979. Research evidence on mass mediated health communication campaigns. In D. Nimmo (ed.), *Communication Yearbook*, 3: 655–668. Transaction Books.

    1981. Mass communication research principles for health education. In M. Meyer (ed.), *Health Education by Television and Radio: Contributions to an International Conference with a Selected Bibliography*: 41–55. Saur.

Axley, S. R. 1984. Managerial and organizational communication in terms of the conduit metaphor. *Academy of Management Review*, 9: 428–437.

Ba, S., Stallaert, J., and Whinston, A. B. 2001. Optimal investment in knowledge within a firm using a market mechanism. *Management Science*, 47: 1203–1219.

Babrow, A. S. 1992. Communication and problematic integration: understanding diverging probability and value, ambiguity, ambivalence and impossibility. *Communication Theory*, 2: 95–130.

2001. Guest editor's introduction to the special issue on uncertainty, evaluation, and communication. *Journal of Communication*, 51: 453–455.

Babrow, A. S., and Mattson, M. 2003. Theorizing about health communication. In T. L. Thompson, A. M. Dorsey, K. I. Miller, and R. Parrott (eds.), *Handbook of Health Communication*: 35–61. Lawrence Erlbaum Associates.

Bach, B. 1989. The effect of multiplex relationships upon innovation adoption: a reconsideration of Rogers' model. *Communication Monographs*, 56: 133–150.

Bach, B. W., and Bullis, C. 1989. An explication and test of relationship multiplexity as a predictor of organizational identification, presented to the Annual Convention of the International Communication Association. San Francisco.

Bacharach, S. B., and Aiken, M. 1977. Communication in administrative bureaucracies. *Academy of Management Journal*, 20: 365–377.

Backer, T. E., Dearing, J., Singhal, A., and Valente, T. 2005. Writing with Ev – Words to transform science into action. *Journal of Health Communication*, 10: 289–302.

Baker, D. D., and Cullen, J. B. 1993. Administrative reorganization and configurational context: the contingent effects of age, size, and change in size. *Academy of Management Journal*, 36: 1251–1277.

Baker, L. M., and Pettigrew, K. E. 1999. Theories for practitioners: two frameworks for studying consumer health information-seeking behavior. *Bulletin of Medical Library Association*, 87: 444–450.

Baker, W. E. 1992. Network organization in theory and practice. In N. Nohria and R. G. Eccles (eds.), *Networks and Organizations: Structure, Form, and Action*: 397–429. Harvard Business School Press.

Bakos, J. Y. 1991. Information links and electronic marketplaces: the role of interorganizational information systems in vertical markets. *Journal of Management Information Systems*, 8: 31–52.

Baldridge, J. V., and Burnham, R. A. 1975. Organizational innovation: individual, organizational, and environmental impacts. *Administrative Science Quarterly*, 20: 165–176.

Bales, R. F. 1950. *Interaction Process Analysis*. Harvard University Press.

Baliga, B. R., and Jaeger, A. M. 1984. Multinational corporations: control systems and delegation issues. *Journal of International Business Studies*, 14: 25–40.

Balkundi, P., and Harrison, D. A. 2006. Ties, leaders, and time in teams: strong inference about network structure's effect on team viability and performance. *Academy of Management Journal*, 49: 49–68.

Balkundi, P., and Kilduff, M. 2005. The ties that lead: a social network approach to leadership. *Leadership Quarterly*, 16: 941–961.

Bandura, A. 2001. Social cognitive theory: an agentic perspective. *Annual Review of Psychology*, 52: 1–26.

2006. On integrating social cognitive and social diffusion theories. In A. Singhal and J. W. Dearing (eds.), *Communication and Innovations: A Journey with Ev Rogers*: 111–135. Sage.

Banker, R. D., and Kauffman, R. J. 2004. The evolution of research on information systems: a fiftieth-year survey of the literature in management Science. *Management Science*, 50: 281–298.

Barabasi, A. L. 2003. *Linked: How Everything is Connected to Everything Else and What It Means for Business, Science, and Everyday Life*. Plume.

Barley, S. R., and Kunda, G. 1992. Design and devotion: surges of rational and normative ideologies of control in managerial discourse. *Administrative Science Quarterly*, 37: 363–399.

Barnes, J. A. 1972. *Social Networks*. Addison-Wesley.

Barnett, G. A., and Rice, R. E. 1985. Longitudinal non-Euclidean networks: applying Galileo. *Social Networks*, 7: 287–322.

Bartunek, J. M., and Franzak, F. J. 1988. The effects of organizational restructuring on frames of reference and cooperation. *Journal of Management*, 14: 579–592.

Bates, D. W., and Gawande, A. A. 2003. Improving safety with information technology. *New England Journal of Medicine*, 348: 2526–2534.

Bates, M. J. 1989. The design of browsing and berrypicking techniques for the online search interface. *Online Review*, 13: 407–424.

   1990. Information as an economic good: a reevaluation of theoretical approaches. In B. D. Ruben and L. A. Lievrouw (eds.), *Information and Behavior*, vol. III: 379–394. Transaction Books.

   2005. An introduction to metatheories, theories, and models. In K. E. Fisher, S. Erdelez, and L. McKechnie (eds.), *Theories of Information Behavior*: 1–24. Information Today.

   2006. Fundamental forms of information. *Journal of the American Society for Information Science and Technology*, 57: 1033–1045.

Bauer, R. A. 1972. The obstinate audience: the influence process from the point of view of social communication. In W. Schramm and D. F. Roberts (eds.), *The Process and Effects of Mass Communication*: 326–346. University of Illinois Press.

Baum, A., and Valens, S. 1977. *Architecture and Social Behavior: Psychological Studies of Social Density*. Lawrence Erlbaum Associates.

Becker, G. S., and Murphy, K. M. 1992. The division of labor, coordination costs, and knowledge. *Quarterly Journal of Economics*, 107: 1137–1160.

Becker, H. 1960. Notes on the concept of commitment. *American Journal of Sociology*, 66: 32–42.

Becker, M. H. 1970. Factors affecting diffusion of innovations among health professionals. *American Journal of Public Health*, 60: 294–304.

Bedian, A. G., Mossholder, K. W., and Armenikas, A. A. 1983. Role perception–outcome relationships: moderating effects of situational variables. *Human Relations*, 36: 43–71.

Belkin, N. J. 2005. Anomalous state of knowledge. In K. E. Fisher, S. Erdelez, and E. F. McKechnie (eds.), *Theories of Information Behavior*: 44–48. Information Today.

Bellah, R. N., Madsen, R., Sullivan, W. M., Swidler, A., and Tipton, S. M. 1991. *The Good Society*. Knopf.

Beninger, J. R. 1986. *The Control Revolution: Technological and Economic Origins of the Information Society*. Harvard University Press.

1990. Conceptualizing information technology as organization, and vice versa. In J. Fulk and C. Steinfield (eds.), *Organizations and Communication Technology*: 29–45. Sage.

Bennett, C. 1977. *Spaces for People: Human Factors in Design*. Prentice Hall.

Bennis, W. G. 1965. Theory and method in applying behavioral science to planned organizational change. *Applied Behavioral Science*, 1: 337–360.

Benson, J. K. 1975. The interorganizational network as a political economy. *Administrative Science Quarterly*, 20: 229–249.

Berelson, B., and Steiner, G. A. 1964. *Human Behavior: An Inventory of Scientific Findings*. Harcourt, Brace & World.

Berger, P. L., and Luckmann, T. 1967. *The Social Construction of Reality*. Anchor Books.

Berlo, D. K. 1960. *The Process of Communication: An Introduction to Theory and Practice*. Holt, Rinehart, and Winston.

1969. Human communication: the basic proposition. Department of Communication, Michigan State University.

Bernard, H. R., and Killworth, P. D. 1977. Informant accuracy in social network data II. *Human Communication Research*, 4: 3–18.

Bernard, H. R., Killworth, P. D., and Sailer, L. 1980. Informant accuracy in social network data, IV: A comparison of clique-level structure in behavioral and cognitive network data. *Social Networks*, 2: 191–218.

1982. Informant accuracy in social network data, V: An experimental attempt to predict actual communication from recall data. *Social Science Research*, 11: 30–66.

Berscheid, E. 1966. Opinion change and communicator–communicatee similarity and dissimilarity. *Journal of Personality and Social Psychology*, 4: 670–680.

Beyer, J. M., and Trice, H. M. 1994. Current and prospective roles for linking organizational researchers and users. In K. W. Thomas, H. Kilmann, D. P. Slevein, R. Nath, and S. L. Jerell (eds.), *Producing Useful Knowledge for Organizations*: 675–702. Jossey-Bass.

Bianconi, G., and Barabasi, A. L. 2001. Competition and multiscaling evolving networks. *Europhysics Letters*, 54: 436–442.

Birkinshaw, J., Nobel, R., and Ridderstrale, J. 2002. Knowledge as a contingency variable: do the characteristics of knowledge predict organization structure? *Organization Science*, 13: 274–289.

Blackler, F. 1995. Knowledge, knowledge work, and organizations: an overview and interpretation. *Organization Studies*, 16: 1021–1046.

Blau, P. M. 1954. Patterns of interaction among a group of officials in a government agency. *Human Relations*, 7: 337–348.

1955. *The Dynamics of Bureaucracy: A Study of Interpersonal Relations in Two Government Agencies*. University of Chicago Press.

1974. Formal theory of differentiation in organizations. In P. M. Blau (ed.), *On the Nature of Organizations*: 297–322. Wiley.

Blau, P. M., and Schoenherr, R. 1971. *The Structure of Organizations*. Basic Books.

Boahene, M., and Ditsa, G. 2003. Conceptual confusions in knowledge management and knowledge management systems: clarifications for better KMS development. In E. Coakes (ed.), *Knowledge Management: Current Issues and Challenges*: 12–24. IRM Press.

Bolman, L. G., and Deal, T. E. 1991. *Reframing Organizations: Artistry, Choice, and Leadership*. Jossey-Bass.

Bolton, P., and Dewatripoint, M. 1994. The firm as a communication network. *Quarterly Journal of Economics*, 109: 809–839.

Boone, M. E. 1991. *Leadership and the Computer*. Prima Publishing.

Borgatti, S. P. 2005. Centrality and network flow. *Social Networks*, 27: 55–71.

Borgatti, S. P., and Cross, R. 2003. A relational view of information seeking and learning in social networks. *Management Science*, 49: 432–445.

Borgatti, S. P., Everett, M. G., and Freeman, L. C. 2002. *UCINET for Windows: Software for Social Network Analysis*. Analytic Technologies.

Borgatti, S. P., and Foster, P. C. 2003. The network paradigm in organizational research: a review and typology. *Journal of Management*, 29: 991–1013.

Borgatti, S. P., and Molina, J. L. 2003. Ethical and strategic issues in organizational social network analysis. *Journal of Applied Behavioral Science*, 39: 337–349.

Borgman, C. L. 2006. Disciplines, documents, and data: convergence and divergence in the scholarly information infrastructure, presented to plenary session of I-School Conference, Ann Arbor, MI.

Boulding, K. E. 1966. The economics of knowledge and the knowledge of economics. *American Economic Review*, 56: 1–13.

Boulos, M. N. K., and Wheeler, S. 2007. The emerging Web 2.0 social software: an enabling suite of sociable technologies in health and health care education. *Health Information and Library Journal*, 24: 2–23.

Boyd, N. R., Sutton, C., Orleans, C. T., McClatchey, M. W., Bingler, R., Fleisher, L., Heller, D., Baum, S., Graves, C., and Ward, J. A. 1998. *Quit Today!*: a targeted communications campaign to increase use of the Cancer Information Service by African-American smokers. *Preventive Medicine*, 27: S50–S61.

Bradach, J. L., and Eccles, R. G. 1989. Price, authority, and trust: from ideal types to plural forms. *Annual Review of Sociology*, 15: 97–118.

Bradley, E. H., Webster, T. R., Baker, D., Schlesinger, M., Inouye, S. K., Barth, M. C., Lapane, K. L., Lipson, D., Stone, R., and Koren, M. J. 2004. Translating research into practice: speeding the adoption of innovative health care programs www.commonwealthfund.org/publications/publications_show.htm?doc_id=233248

Brailer, D. 2005. Presentation to National Governors' Association Conference. www.louhie.org/library.htm

Brandon, D. P., and Hollingshead, A. B. 2004. Transactive memory systems in organizations: matching tasks, expertise, and people. *Organization Science*, 15: 633–644.

Branham, R. J., and Pearce, W. B. 1985. Between text and context: toward a rhetoric of contextual reconstruction. *Quarterly Journal of Speech*, 71: 19–36.

Brashers, D. E., Goldsmith, D. J., and Hsieh, E. 2002. Information seeking and avoiding in health contexts. *Human Communication Research*, 28: 258–272.

Brass, D. J. 1981. Structural relationships, job characteristics, and worker satisfaction and performance. *Administrative Science Quarterly*, 26: 331–348.

    1985. Men's and women's networks: a study of interaction patterns and influence in an organization. *Academy of Management Journal*, 28: 327–343.

Brett, J. M., Feldman, D. C., and Weingart, L. R. 1990. Feedback seeking behavior of new hires and job changers. *Journal of Management*, 16: 737–749.

Brewer, J. 1971. Flow of communications, expert qualifications and organizational authority structures. *American Sociological Review*, 36: 475–484.

Brief, A. P., and Aldag, R. J. 1976. Correlates of role indices. *Journal of Applied Psychology*, 61: 468–472.

Brittain, J. M. 1970. *Information and its Users: A Review with Special Reference to the Social Sciences*. Bath University Press.

Broadbent, M., and Koenig, M. E. D. 1988. Information and information technology management. In M. E. Williams (ed.), *Annual Review of Information Science and Technology*, vol. XXIII. Elsevier Science.

Brody, M. 1986. NASA's challenge: isolation at the top, *Fortune*, May 12: 26–32.

Brower, S. N. 1980. Territory in urban settings. In I. Altman, A. Rapoport, and J. F. Wohlwill (eds.), *Human Behavior and Environment: Advances in Theory and Research*: 179–207. Plenum.

Brown, J. S., and Duguid, P. 1991. Organizational learning and communities-of-practice: toward a unified view of working, learning, and innovation. *Organization Science*, 2: 40–57.

   1998. Organizing knowledge. *California Management Review*, 40: 90–111.

   2002. *The Social Life of Information*. Harvard Business School Press.

Brown, M. H., and McMillan, J. J. 1988. Constructions and counterconstructions: organizational power revisited, presented to the annual Convention of the Speech Communication Association. New Orleans.

Browning, L. D., Beyer, J. M., and Shetler, J. C. 1995. Building cooperation in a competitive industry: SEMATECH and the semiconductor industry. *Academy of Management Journal*, 38: 112–151.

Buchanan, B. I. 1974. Building organizational commitment: the socialization of managers in work organization. *Administrative Science Quarterly*, 19: 533–546.

Buchanan, M. 2002. *Nexus: small worlds and the groundbreaking science of networks*. W.W. Norton.

Buckland, M. 1991. *Information and Information Systems*. Greenwood Press.

Burke, R. J., and Bolf, C. 1986. Learning within organizations: Sources and content. *Psychological Reports*, 59: 1187–1196.

Burt, R. S. 1980. Innovation as a structural interest: rethinking the impact of network position on innovation adoption. *Social Networks*, 2: 327–355.

   1982. *Toward a Structural Theory of Action: Network Models of Social Structure, Perception, and Action*. Academic Press.

   1983. A note on inference concerning network subgroups. In R. S. Burt and M. J. Minor (eds.), *Applied Network Analysis: A Methodological Introduction*: 283–301. Sage.

   1987. Social contagion and innovation: cohesion versus structural equivalence. *Applied Journal of Psychology*, 92: 1287–1335.

   1991. Structure reference manual, version 4.2, Center for the Social Sciences, Columbia University.

   1992. *Structural Holes: The Social Structure of Competition*. Harvard University Press.

   1999. The social capital of opinion leaders. *Annals of the American Academy*, 566: 37–54.

   2000. The network structure of social capital. *Research in Organization Behavior*, 22: 345–423.

2001. Bandwidth and echo: trust, information, and gossip in social networks. In J. E. Rauch and A. Casella (eds.), *Networks and Markets*: 30–74. Russel Sage Foundation.

2002. Bridge decay. *Social Networks*, 24: 333–363.

2003. Social capital and good ideas, presented to the Gatton College of Business and Economics, University of Kentucky.

2004. Structural holes and good ideas. *American Journal of Sociology*, 110: 349–399.

2005. *Brokerage and Closure: An Introduction to Social Capital*. Oxford University Press.

2007. Secondhand brokerage: evidence on the importance of local structure for managers, bankers, and analysts. *Academy of Management Journal*, 50: 119–148.

Burt, R. S., and Bittner, W. M. 1981. A note on inferences regarding network subgroups. *Social Networks*, 3: 71–88.

Burt, R. S., and Doreian, P. 1982. Testing a structural model of perception: conformity and deviance with respect to journal norms in elite sociological methodology. *Quality and Quantity*, 16: 109–150.

Burt, R. S., and Schott, T. 1985. Relation contents in multiple networks. *Social Science Research*, 14: 287–308.

Burt, R. S., and Uchiyama, T. 1989. The conditional significance of communication for interpersonal influence. In M. Kochen (ed.), *The Small World*: 67–87. Ablex.

Burton-Jones, A. 1999. *Knowledge Capitalism: Business, Work, and Learning in the New Economy*. Oxford University Press.

Bush, J. B., Jr., and Frohman, A. L. 1991. Communication in a "network" organization. *Organizational Dynamics*, 20: 23–36.

Business Week. 1994. The information revolution. Special issue, no. 107.

Buster, R. L., Friedland, M. H., Eckert, M. B., and Johnson, J. D. 1988. The impact of communication rituals on role ambiguity and commitment in a high-tech organization, presented to the Annual Convention of the International Communication Association. New Orleans.

Buttimer, A. 1980. Social space and the planning of residential areas. In A. Buttimer and D. Seamon (eds.), *The Human Experience of Space and Place*: 21–54. St. Martin's Press.

Canter, D. 1983. The physical context of work. In D. J. Osborne and M. M. Gruneberg (eds.), *The Physical Environment at Work*: 11–38. Wiley.

Canter, D., and Kenny, C. 1975. The spatial environment. In D. Canter and P. Stringer (eds.), *Environmental Interaction: Psychological Approaches to our Physical Surroundings*: 127–163. International University Press.

Caplow, T. 1947. Rumors in war. *Social Forces*, 25: 298–302.

Cappelli, P., and Sherer, P. D. 1991. The missing role of context in OB: the need for a meso-level approach. *Research in Organization Behavior*, 13: 55–110.

Carley, K. 1986. An approach for relating social structure to cognitive structure. *Journal of Mathematical Sociology*, 12: 137–189.

Carlile, P. R. 2004. Transferring, translating, and transforming: an integrative framework for managing knowledge across boundaries. *Organization Science*, 15: 555–568.

Carroll, G. R., and Teo, A. C. 1996. On the social networks of managers. *Academy of Management Journal*, 39: 421–440.

Carter, N. M. 1984. Computerization as a predominate technology: its influence on the structure of newspaper organizations. *Academy of Management Journal*, 27: 247–271.

Carter, N. M., and Culnan, J. B. 1983. *The Computerization of Newspaper Organizations: The Impact of Technology on Organizational Structuring*. University Press of America.

Case, D., Johnson, J. D., Andrews, J. E., Allard, S., and Kelly, K. M. 2004. From two-step flow to the Internet: the changing array of sources for genetics information seeking. *Journal of the American Society for Information Science and Technology*, 55: 660–669.

Case, D. O. 2002. *Looking for Information*. Academic Press.

2005. Principle of least effort. In K. E. Fisher, S. Erdelez, and L. McKechnie (eds.), *Theories of Information Behavior*: 289–292. Information Today.

2007. *Looking for Information*, 2nd edn. Academic Press.

Case, D. O., Andrews, J. E., Johnson, J. D., and Allard, S. L. 2005. Avoiding versus seeking: the relationship of information seeking to avoidance, blunting, coping, dissonance and related concepts. *Journal of the Medical Libraries Association*, 93: 48–57.

Cash, J. I., Jr., Eccles, R. G., Nohria, N., and Nolan, R. L. 1994. *Building the Information Age Organization: Structure, Control, and Information Technologies*. Irwin.

Chang, S. J., and Rice, R. E. 1993. Browsing: a multidimensional framework. In M. E. Williams (ed.), *Annual Review of Information Science and Technology*, vol. XXVIII: 231–276. Learned Information.

Chang, S. L. 2005. Chang's browsing. In K. E. Fisher, S. Erdelez, and E. F. McKechnie (eds.), *Theories of Information Behavior*: 69–74. Information Today.

Chang, S. L., and Lee, Y. 2001. Conceptualizing context and its relationship to the information behaviour in dissertation research process. *New Review of Information Behaviour Research*, 2: 29–46.

Chen, C., and Hernon, P. 1982. *Information Seeking: Assessing and Anticipating User Needs*. Neal-Schuman.

Cheney, G. 1995. Democracy in the workplace: theory and practice from the perspective of communication. *Journal of Applied Communication Research*, 23: 167–200.

Cheney, G., and Ashcraft, K. L. 2007. Considering "the professional" in communication studies: implications for theory and research within and beyond the boundaries of organizational communication. *Communication Theory*, 17: 146–175.

Cheng, J. L. C. 1983. Interdependence and coordination in organizations: a role system analysis. *Academy of Management Journal*, 26: 156–162.

Child, J., and McGrath, R. G. 2001. Organizations unfettered: organizational form in an information-intensive economy. *Academy of Management Journal*, 44: 1135–1148.

Choi, B. C. K. 2005. Understanding the basic principles of knowledge translation. *Journal of Epidemiology and Community Health*, 59: 93.

Choo, C. W. 2006. *The Knowing Organization: How Organizations Use Information to Construct Meaning, Create Knowledge, and Make Decisions*, 2nd edn. Oxford University Press.

Choo, C. W., and Auster, E. 1993. Environmental scanning: acquisition and use of information by managers. In *Annual Review of Information Science and Technology*, vol. XXVIII: 279–314. Learned Information.

Choudhury, V., Hartzel, K. S., and Konsynski, B. R. 1998. Uses and consequences of electronic markets: an empirical investigation in the aircraft parts industry. *MIS Quarterly*, 22: 471–507.

Christiaanse, E., and Venkatraman, N. 2002. Beyond Sabre: an empirical test of expertise exploitation in electronic channels. *MIS Quarterly*, 26: 15–38.

Cicourel, A. V. 1972. Basic and normative rules in the negotiation of status and role. In D. Sudnow (ed.), *Studies in Social Interaction*: 229–258. Free Press.

Clark, M. S. 1984. Record keeping in two types of relationships. *Journal of Personality and Social Psychology*, 47: 549–557.

Clemons, E. K., and Row, M. C. 1991. Sustaining IT advantage: the role of structural differences. *MIS Quarterly*, 15: 275–292.

Cleveland, H. 1985. The twilight of hierarchy: speculations on the global information society. In S. R. Corman, S. P. Banks, C. R. Bantz, and M. E. Mayer (eds.), *Foundations of Organizational Communication*: 370–374. Longman.

Coase, R. H. 1937. The nature of the firm. *Economica*, 4: 386–405.

Coff, R. W., Coff, D. C., and Eastvold, R. 2006. The knowledge-leveraging paradox: how to achieve scale without making knowledge imitable. *Academy of Management Review*, 31: 452–465.

Cohen, W. M., and Levinthal, D. A. 1989. Innovation and learning: the two faces of R&D. *Economic Journal*, 99: 569–596.

1994. Fortune favors the prepared firm. *Management Science*, 40: 227–251.

Coiera, E. 2003. *Guide to Health Informatics*, 2nd edn. Arnold.

Cole, C. 1994. Operationalizing the notion of information as a subjective construct. *Journal of the American Society for Information Science*, 45: 465–476.

Coleman, J., Katz, E., and Menzel, H. 1957. The diffusion of an innovation among physicians. *Sociometry*, 20: 253–270.

Collins, C. J., and Smith, K. G. 2006. Knowledge exchange and combination: the role of human resource practices in the performance of high-technology firms. *Academy of Management Journal*, 49: 544–560.

Collins, R. 1981. On the microfoundations of macrosociology. *American Journal of Sociology*, 86: 984–1014.

Comer, D. R. 1991. Organizational newcomers' acquisition of information from peers. *Management Communication Quarterly*, 5: 64–89.

Connolly, T. 1977. Information processing and decision making in organizations. In B. M. Staw and G. R. Salancik (eds.), *New Directions in Organizational Behavior*: 205–234. St. Clair Press.

Connolly, T., and Thorn, B. K. 1990. Discretionary databases: theory, data, and implications. In J. Fulk and C. Steinfield (eds.), *Organizations and Communication Technology*: 219–234. Sage.

Conrad, C. 1985. *Strategic Organizational Communication*. CBS College Publishing Co.

Constant, D., Kiesler, S., and Sproull, L. 1994. What's mine is ours, or is it? A study of attitudes about information sharing. *Information Systems Research*, 5: 400–421.

Contractor, N. S., and Eisenberg, E. M. 1990. Communication networks and new media in organizations. In J. Fulk and C. Steinfield (eds.), *Organizations and Communication Technology*: 143–172. Sage.

Contractor, N. S., and Monge, P. R. 2002. Managing knowledge networks. *Management Communication Quarterly*, 16: 249–258.

Contractor, N. S., and Seibold, D. R. 1993. Theoretical frameworks for the study of structuring process in group decision support systems: adaptive structuration theory and self-organizing system theory. *Human Communication Research*, 19: 528–563.

Cook, K. S. 1982. Network structures from an exchange perspective. In P. V. Marsden and N. Lin (eds.), *Social Structure and Network Analysis*: 177–199. Sage.

Cool, C. 2001. The concept of situation in information science. *Annual Review of Information Science and Technology*, vol. XXXV: 5–42. Learned Information.

Corman, S. R. 2005. The reticulation of quasi-agents in systems of organizational communication. In G. A. Barnett (ed.), *Organizational Communication: Emerging Perspectives, vol. VI: Power, Gender, and Technology*: 65–82. Ablex.

Corman, S. R., Kuhn, T., McPhee, R. D., and Dooley, K. J. 2002. Studying complex discursive systems: centering resonance analysis of communication. *Human Communication Research*, 28: 157–206.

Corman, S. R., and Scott, C. R. 1994. Perceived networks, activity foci, and observable communication in social collectives. *Communication Theory*, 4: 171–190.

Crane, L. A., Leakey, T., Ehrsam, G., Rimer, B. K., and Warnecke, R. B. 2000. Effectiveness and cost-effectiveness of multiple outcalls to promote mammography among low-income women. *Cancer Epidemiology, Biomarkers, and Prevention*, 9: 923–931.

Crane, L. A., Leakey, T. A., Woodworth, M. A., Rimer, B. K., Warnecke, R. B., Heller, D., and George, V. S. 1998. Cancer information service-initiated outcalls to promote screening mammography among low-income and minority women: design and feasibility testing. *Preventive Medicine*, 27: S29–S38.

Cross, R., Borgatti, S. P., and Parker, A. 2003. Making invisible work visible: using social network analysis to support strategic collaboration. In R. Cross, A. Parker, and L. Sasson (eds.), *Networks in the Knowledge Economy*: 261–282. Oxford University Press.

Cross, R., and Cummings, J. N. 2004. Tie and network correlates of individual performance in knowledge-intensive work. *Academy of Management Journal*, 47: 928–937.

Cross, R., Nohria, N., and Parker, A. 2004. Six myths about informal networks – and how to overcome them. In E. Lesser and L. Prusak (eds.), *Creating Value with Knowledge: Insights from the IBM Institute for Business Value*: 47–60. Oxford University Press.

Cross, R., Parker, A., Prusak, L., and Borgatti, S. P. 2004. Knowing what we know: supporting knowledge creation and sharing in social networks. In E. Lesser and L. Prusak (eds.), *Creating Value with Knowledge: Insights from the IBM Institute for Business Value*: 61–81. Oxford University Press.

Cross, R., Parker, A., and Sasson, L. E. (eds.) 2003. *Networks in the Knowledge Economy*. Oxford University Press.

Cross, R., and Prusak, L. 2002. The people who make organizations go – or stop. *Harvard Business Review*, 80(6): 104–111.

—— 2003. The people who make organizations go – or stop. In R. Cross, A. Parker, and L. Sasson (eds.), *Networks in the Knowledge Economy*. Oxford University Press.

Cross, R., Rice, R. E., and Parker, A. 2001. Information seeking in social context: structural influences and receipt of information benefits. *IEEE Transactions on Systems, Man, and Cybernetics. Part C: Applications and Reviews*, 31: 438–448.

Cross, R., and Sproull, L. 2004. More than an answer: information relationships for actionable knowledge. *Organization Science*, 15: 446–462.

Crowston, K. 1997. A coordination theory approach to organizational process design. *Organization Science*, 8: 157–175.

Cullen, P., Cottingham, P., Doolan, J., Edgar, B., Ellis, C., Fisher, M., Flett, D., Johnson, D., Sealie, L., Stoklmayer, S., Vanclay, F., and Whittington, J. 2001. Knowledge-seeking strategies of natural resource professionals, Technical Report 2/2001, Cooperative Research Centre for Freshwater Ecology.

Cullen, P. W., Norris, R. H., Resh, V. H., Reynoldson, T. B., Rosenberg, D. M., and Barbour, M. T. 1999. Collaboration in scientific research: a critical need for freshwater ecology. *Freshwater Biology*, 42: 131–142.

Culnan, M. J. 1983. Environmental scanning: the effects of task complexity and source accessibility on information gathering behavior. *Decision Sciences*, 14: 194–206.

Culnan, M. J., and Markus, M. L. 1987. Information technologies. In F. M. Jablin, L. L. Putnam, K. H. Roberts, and L. W. Porter (eds.), *Handbook of Organizational Communication: An Interdisciplinary Perspective*: 420–443. Sage.

Cyert, R. M., Simon, H. A., and Trow, D. B. 1956. Observation of a business decision. *Journal of Business*, 29: 237–248.

Czepiel, J. A. 1975. Patterns of interorganizational communications and the diffusion of a major technological innovation in a competitive industrial community. *Academy of Management Journal*, 18: 6–24.

D'Aprix, R. 1988. Communication as process: the managers' view. In G. M. Goldhaber and G. A. Barnett (eds.), *Handbook of Organizational Communication*: 265–272. Ablex.

D'Urso, S. C. 2006. Toward a structural-perceptual model of electronic monitoring and surveillance in organizations. *Communication Theory*, 16: 281–303.

Daft, R. L. 1978. A dual-core model of organizational innovation. *Academy of Management Journal*, 21: 193–210.

Daft, R. L., and Huber, G. P. 1987. How organizations learn: a communication framework. In N. D. Tomoso and S. B. Bacharach (eds.), *Research in Organizational Behavior*: 1–36. JAI Press.

Daft, R. L., and Lengel, R. H. 1986. Organizational information requirements: media richness and structural design. *Management Science*, 32: 554–571.

Dahlin, K. B., Weingart, L. R., and Hinds, P. J. 2005. Team diversity and information use. *Academy of Management Journal*, 48: 1107–1123.

Dalton, D. R., Todor, W. D., Spendolini, M. J., Fielding, G. J., and Porter, L. W. 1980. Organization structure and performance: a critical review. *Academy of Management Review*, 5: 49–64.

Damanpour, F. 1991. Organizational innovation: a meta-analysis of effects of determinants and moderators. *Academy of Management Journal*, 34: 555–590.

Danes, J. E., Hunter, J. E., and Woelfel, J. 1978. Mass communication and belief change: a test of three mathematical models. *Human Communication Research*, 4: 243–252.

Danowski, J. A. 1980. Group attitude uniformity and connectivity of organizational communication networks for production, innovation, and maintenance content. *Human Communication Research*, 6: 299–308.

  1988. Organizational infographics and automated auditing: using computers to unobtrusively gather as well as analyze communication. In G. M. Goldhaber and G. A. Barnett (eds.), *Handbook of Organizational Communication*: 385–434. Ablex.

  1993. Network analysis of message content. In W. D. Richards Jr., and G. A. Barnett (eds.), *Progress in Communication Sciences*: 197–221. Ablex.

Dansereau, F., and Markham, S. E. 1987. Superior subordinate communication: multiple levels of analysis. In F. M. Jablin, L. L. Putnam, K. H. Roberts, and L. W. Porter (eds.), *Handbook of Organizational Communication: An Interdisciplinary Perspective*: 343–388. Sage.

Darnell, D. K. 1972. Information theory: an approach to human communication. In R. W. Budd and B. D. Ruben (eds.), *Approaches to Human Communication*: 156–169. Spartan Books.

Davenport, T. H., and Prusak, L. 1998. *Working Knowledge: How Organizations Manage What They Know*. Harvard Business School Press.

Davies, E. 2005. Communities of practice. In K. E. Fisher, S. Erdelez, and L. L. McKechnie (eds.), *Theories of information behavior*: 104–107. Information Today.

Davis, K. 1973. The care and cultivation of the corporate grapevine. *Dun's Review*, 108: 44–47.

Davis, T. R. 1984. The influence of the physical environment in offices. *Academy of Management Review*, 9: 271–283.

de Chardin, P. 1961. *The Phenomenon of Man*. Harper.

de Nooy, W., Mrvar, A., and Batagelj, V. 2005. *Exploratory Social Network Analysis with Pajek*. Cambridge University Press.

de Tocqueville, A. 1835/1966. *Democracy in America*. Harper & Row.

Dean, A., and Kretschmer, M. 2007. Can ideas be capital? Factors of production in the postindustrial economy: a review and critique. *Academy of Management Review*, 32: 573–594.

Dean, J. W., Jr., and Bowen, D. E. 1994. Management theory and total quality: improving research and practice through theory development. *Academy of Management Review*, 19: 392–418.

Dearing, J. 2000. Dilemmas of evaluation research, *ICA News*, 5 and 7.

Dearing, J. W. 2006. The emerging science of translational research, presented to Kentucky Conference on Health Communication. Lexington, KY.

Dearing, J. W., Meyer, G., and Kazmierczak, J. 1994. Portraying the new: communication between university innovators and potential users. *Science Communication*, 16: 11–42.

Denison, D. R. 1996. What is the difference between organizational culture and organizational climate? A native's point of view on a decade of paradigm wars. *Academy of Management Review*, 21: 619–654.

Dent, E. B., and Goldberg, S. G. 1999. Challenging "resistance to change." *Journal of Applied Behavioral Science*, 35: 25–41.

Dervin, B. 1980. Communication gaps and inequities: moving toward a reconceptualization. In B. Dervin and M. J. Voight (eds.), *Progress in Communication Sciences*: 74–112. Ablex.

1989. Users as research inventions: how research categories perpetuate inequities. *Journal of Communication*, 39: 216–232.

1997. Given a context by any other name: methodological tools for taming the unruly beast. In P. Vakkari, R. Savolainen, and B. Dervin (eds.), *Information Seeking in Context*: 13–38. Taylor Graham.

1998. Sense-making theory and practice: an overview of user interests in knowledge seeking and use. *Journal of Knowledge Management*, 2: 36–46.

2003. Human studies and user studies: a call for methodological inter-disciplinarity. *Information Research*, 9: 1–27.

Dervin, B., Jacobson, T. L., and Nilan, M. S. 1982. Measuring aspects of information seeking: a test of quantitative/qualitative methodology. In M. Burgoon (ed.), *Communication Yearbook 6*: 419–444. Sage.

Dervin, B., and Nilan, M. S. 1986. Information needs and uses. In M. A. Williams (ed.), *Annual Review of Information Science and Technology*, vol. XXI: 3–33. Knowledge Industry Publications.

DeSanctis, G., and Monge, P. 1999. Introduction to the special issue: communication processes for virtual organizations. *Organization Science*, 10: 693–703.

Dess, G. G., Rasheed, A. M. A., McLaughlin, K. J., and Priem, R. L. 1995. The new corporate architecture. *Academy of Management Executive*, 9: 7–20.

Devaraj, S., and Kohli, R. 2000. Information technology payoff in the health care industry: a longitudinal study. *Journal of Management Information Systems*, 16: 41–67.

Diesner, J., Frantz, T. L., and Carley, K. M. 2005. Communication networks from the Enron Email Corpus "It's always about the people. Enron is no different." *Computational and Mathematical Organization Theory*, 11: 201–228.

Dietz, D., Cook, R., and Hersch, R. 2005. Workplace health promotion and utilization of health services: follow-up data findings. *Journal of Behavioral Health Services and Research*, 32: 306–319.

Doctor, R. D. 1992. Social equity and information technologies: moving toward information democracy. In M. E. Williams (ed.), *Annual Review of Information Science and Technology*, vol. XXVII: 44–96. Learned Information.

Donohew, L., Helm, D. M., Cook, P. L., and Shatzer, M. J. 1987. Sensation seeking, marijuana use, and response to prevention messages: implications for public health campaigns, presented to International Communication Association meeting. Montreal.

Donohew, L., Tipton, L., and Haney, R. 1978. Analysis of information seeking strategies. *Journalism Quarterly*, 55: 25–31.

Dorsey, A. M. 2003. Lessons and challenges from the field. In T. L. Thompson, A. M. Dorsey, K. I. Miller, and R. Parrott (eds.), *Handbook of Health Communication*: 607–608. Lawrence Erlbaum Associates.

Dow, G. K. 1988. Configurational and coactivational views of organizational structure. *Academy of Management Review*, 13: 53–64.

Downey, H. K., and Slocum, J. W. 1975. Uncertainty: measures, research and sources of variation. *Academy of Management Journal*, 18: 562–577.

Downs, A. 1967. *Inside Bureaucracy*. Little, Brown.

Downs, C. W., Clampitt, P. G., and Pfeiffer, A. L. 1988. Communication and organizational outcomes. In G. M.Goldhaber and G. A. Barnett (eds.), *Handbook of Organizational Communication*: 171–212. Ablex.

Downs, C. W., and Hain, T. 1982. Productivity and communication. In M. Burgoon (ed.), *Communication Yearbook 5*: 435–453. Transaction Books.

Drake, L. E., and Donohue, W. A. 1996. Communication framing theory in conflict resolution. *Communication Research*, 23: 297–322.

Drazin, R., Glynn, M. A., and Kazanjian, R. K. 1999. Multilevel theorizing about creativity in organizations: a sensemaking perspective. *Academy of Management Review*, 24: 296–307.

Drazin, R., and Van de Ven, A. 1985. Alternative forms of fit in contingency theory. *Administrative Science Quarterly*, 30: 514–539.

Drucker, P. F. 1974. *Management – Tasks, responsibilities, practices*. Harper & Row.
  1988. The coming of the new organization. *Harvard Business Review*, 66: 45–53.

Duncan, R. 1988. What is the right organization structure? Decision tree analysis provides the answer. Organizational Dynamics Special Report, American Management Association.

Duncan, R., and Weiss, A. 1979. Organizational learning: implications for organizational design. In S. B. Bacharach (ed.), *Research in Organizational Behavior*: 75–123. JAI Press.

Durland, M. E. 2005. A formative evaluation of the integration of two departments. *New Directions for Evaluation*, 107: 81–83.

Dyer, J. H., and Nobeoka, K. 2000. Creating and managing a high-performance knowledge-sharing network: the Toyota case. *Strategic Management Journal*, 21: 345–367.

Earl, M. 2001. Knowledge management strategies: toward a taxonomy. *Journal of Management Information Systems*, 18: 215–233.

Ebadi, Y. M., and Utterback, J. M. 1984. The effects of communication and technical innovation. *Management Science*, 30: 572–585.

Eccles, R., and White, H. 1988. Price and authority in inter-profit center transactions. *American Journal of Sociology* supplement, 94: S17–S51.

Edwards, J. A., and Monge, P. R. 1977. The validation of mathematical indices of communication structure. In B. D. Ruben (ed.), *Communication Yearbook 1*: 183–193. Transaction Books.

Egelhoff, W. G. 1982. Strategy and structure in multinational corporations: an information processing approach. *Administrative Science Quarterly*, 27: 435–458.

Eisenberg, E. M. 1984. Ambiguity as strategy in organizational communication. *Communication Monographs*, 51: 227–242.
  1990. Jamming: transcendence through organizing. *Communication Research*, 17: 139–164.

Eisenberg, E. M., Contractor, N. S., and Monge, P. R. 1988. Semantic networks in organizations, presented to International Communication Association meeting. New Orleans.

Eisenberg, E. M., Farace, R. V., Monge, P. R., Bettinghaus, E. P., Kurchner Hawkins, R., Miller, K. I., and Rothman, L. 1985. Communication linkages in interorganizational systems: review and synthesis. In B. Dervin and M. Voight (eds.), *Progress in Communication Sciences*, vol. VI: 231–261. Ablex.

Eisenberg, E. M., Monge, P. R., and Miller, K. I. 1983. Involvement in communication networks as a predictor of organizational commitment. *Human Communication Research*, 10: 179–202.

Eisenberg, E. M., Murphy, A., and Andrews, L. 1998. Openness and decision making in the search for a university provost. *Communication Monographs*, 65: 1–23.

Eisenberg, E. M., and Riley, P. 1988. Organizational symbols as sense making. In G. M. Goldhaber and G. A. Barnett (eds.), *Handbook of Organizational Communication*: 131–150. Ablex.

Eisenberg, E. M., and Whetten, M. G. 1987. Reconsidering openness in organizational communication. *Academy of Management Review*, 12: 418–426.

Elliott, D. S., and Mihalic, S. 2004. Issues in disseminating and replicating effective prevention programs. *Prevention Science*, 5: 47–53.

Ellis, D. 1989. A behavioral model for information retrieval system design. *Journal of Information Science*, 15: 237–247.

Emery, F., and Trist, E. 1965. The causal texture of organizational environment. *Human Relations*, 18: 21–32.

Emirbayer, M., and Mische, A. 1998. What is agency? *American Journal of Sociology*, 103: 962–997.

Entman, R. M., and Wildman, S. S. 1992. Reconciling economic and non economic perspectives on media policy: transcending the "marketplace of ideas." *Journal of Communication*, 42: 5–19.

Erickson, B. H. 1982. Networks, ideologies, and belief systems. In P. V. Marsden and N. Lin (eds.), *Social Structure and Network Analysis*. Sage.

Eveland, W. P. J., Marton, K., and Seo, M. 2004. Moving beyond "just the facts": the influence of online news and the content and structure of public affairs knowledge. *Communication Research*, 31: 82–108.

Fairhurst, G. T. 1986. Male–female communication on the job: literature review and commentary. In M. L. McLaughlin (ed.), *Communication Yearbook 9*: 83–116. Sage.

Fairhurst, G. T., and Snavely, B. K. 1983. A test of the social isolation of male tokens. *Academy of Management Journal*, 26: 353–361.

Farace, R. V., and Johnson, J. D. 1974. Comparative analysis of human communication networks in selected formal organizations, presented to the Annual Convention of the International Communication Association. New Orleans.

Farace, R. V., and Mabee, T. 1980. Communication network analysis methods. In P. R. Monge and J. N. Cappella (eds.), *Multivariate Techniques in Human Communication Research*: 365–391. Academic Press.

Farace, R. V., Monge, P. R., and Russell, H. 1977. *Communicating and Organizing*. Addison-Wesley.

Farace, R. V., Taylor, J. A., and Stewart, J. P. 1978. Criteria for evaluation of organizational communication effectiveness: review and synthesis. In D. Nimmo (ed.), *Communication Yearbook 2*: 271–292. Transaction Books.

Farrell, A., and Geist-Martin, P. 2005. Communicating social health: perceptions of wellness at work. *Management Communication Quarterly*, 18: 543–592.

Feldman, M. S., and March, J. G. 1981. Information in organizations as signal and symbol. *Administrative Science Quarterly*, 26: 171–186.

Ferlie, E., Fitzgerald, L., Wood, M., and Hawkins, C. 2005. The nonspread of innovations: the mediating role of professionals. *Academy of Management Journal*, 48: 117–134.

Ferratt, T. W., Agarwal, R., Brown, C. V., and Moore, J. E. 2005. IT human resource management configurations and IT turnover: theoretical synthesis and empirical analysis. *Information Systems Research*, 16: 237–255.

Festinger, L., Schacter, S., and Back, K. 1950. *Social Pressures in Informal Groups: A Study of a Housing Project*. Harper.

Fidler, L. A., and Johnson, J. D. 1984. Communication and innovation implementation. *Academy of Management Review*, 9: 704–711.

Fink, G., and Holden, N. 2005. The global transfer of management knowledge. *Academy of Management Executive*, 19: 5–8.

Fiol, C. M. 1994. Consensus, diversity, and learning in organizations. *Organization Science*, 5: 403–420.

Fisher, C. D., and Gitelson, R. 1983. A meta-analysis of the correlates of role conflict and ambiguity. *Journal of Applied Psychology*, 68: 320–333.

Fisher, K. E., Durrance, J. C., and Hinton, M. B. 2004. Information grounds and the use of need-based services by immigrants in Queens, New York: a context-based, outcome evaluation approach. *Journal of the American Society for Information Science and Technology*, 55: 754–766.

Fisher, K. E., Erdelez, S., and McKechnie, L. (eds.). 2005. *Theories of Information Behavior*. Information Today.

Fleisher, L., Woodworth, M., Morra, M., Baum, S., Darrow, S., Davis, S., Slevin-Perocchia, R., Stengle, W., and Ward, J. A. 1998. Balancing research and service: the experience of the Cancer Information Service. *Preventive Medicine*, 27: S84–S92.

Florida, R., and Cohen, W. H. 1999. Engine or infrastructure? The university role in economic development. In L. M. Branscomb, F. Kodoma, and R. Florida (eds.), *Industrializing Knowledge: University–Industry linkages in Japan and the United States*: 589–610. MIT Press.

Fontaine, M. A. 2004. Keeping communities of practice afloat: understanding and fostering roles in communities. In E. Lesser and L. Prusak (eds.), *Creating Value with Knowledge: Insights from the IBM Institute for Business Value*: 124–133. Oxford University Press.

Foray, D. 2001. Continuities and ruptures in knowledge management practices. In J. de la Mothe and D. Foray (eds.), *Knowledge Management in the Innovation Process*: 43–52. Kluwer.

Ford, C. M. 1996. A theory of individual creative action in multiple social domains. *Academy of Management Review*, 21: 1112–1142.

Ford, D. P. 2003. Trust and knowledge management: the seeds of success. In C. W. Holsapple (ed.), *Handbook on Knowledge Management*, vol. I: *Knowledge Matters*: 553–575. Springer-Verlag.

Ford, E. W., Duncan, J. W., Bedeian, A. G., Ginter, P. M., Rousculp, M. D., and Adams, A. M. 2003. Mitigating risks, visible hands, inevitable disasters, and soft variables. *Academy of Management Executive*, 17: 46–60.

Ford, J. D., and Slocum, J. W., Jr. 1977. Size, technology, environment and the structure of organizations. *Academy of Management Review*, 2: 561–575.

Form, W. H. 1972. Technology and social behavior of workers in four countries: a sociotechnical perspective. *American Sociological Review*, 37: 727–738.

Fortner, R. S. 1995. Excommunication in the information society. *Critical Studies in Mass Communication*, 12: 133–154.

Fouche, B. 1999. Knowledge networks: emerging knowledge work infrastructures to support innovation and knowledge management. *ICSTI Forum*, 32.

Frances, J., Levacic, R., Mitchell, J., and Thompson, G. 1991. Introduction. In G.Thompson, J. Frances, R. Levacic, and J. Mitchell (eds.), *Markets, Hierarchies, and Networks: The Coordination of Social Life*: 1–19. Sage.

Freeman, A. C., and Sweeney, K. 2001. Why general practictioners do not implement evidence: qualitative study. *British Medical Journal*, 323: 1100–1110.

Freeman, L. C. 1977. A set of measures of centrality based on betweenness. *Sociometry*, 40: 35–41.

   1992. Filling in blanks: a theory of cognitive categories and the structure of social affiliation. *Social Psychology Quarterly*, 55: 118–127.

Freeman, L. C., Romney, A. K., and Freeman, S. C. 1987. Cognitive structure and informant accuracy. *American Anthropologist*, 89: 310–324.

Freimuth, V. S. 1987. The diffusion of supportive information. In T. L. Albrecht and M. B. Adelman (eds.), *Communicating Social Support*: 212–237. Sage.

French, J. R. P. 1956. A formal theory of social power. *Psychological Review*, 63: 181–194.

French, J. R. P., Jr., and Raven, B. 1959. The bases of social power. In D. Cartwright (ed.), *Studies in Social Power*: 150–167. Institute for Social Research.

Friedkin, N. E. 1980. A test of structural features of Granovetter's strength of weak ties theory. *Social Networks*, 2: 411–422.

   1982. Information flow through strong and weak ties in intraorganizational social networks. *Social Networks*, 3: 273–285.

   1984. Structural cohesion and equivalence: explanation of social homogeneity. *Sociological Method and Research*, 12: 235–261.

   2001. *Snap: Social Network Analysis Procedures*. Aptech Systems, Inc.

Friedman, R. A., and Podolny, J. 1992. Differentiation of boundary spanning roles: labor negotiations and implications for role conflict. *Administrative Science Quarterly*, 37: 28–47.

Friedman, T. 2005. *The World is Flat: A Brief History of the Twenty-first Century*. Farrar, Strauss, and Giroux.

Frisee, M. E. 2005. State and community-based efforts to foster interoperability. *Health Affairs*, 24: 1190–1196.

Froehlich, T. J. 1994. Relevance reconsidered: towards an agenda for the 21st century (introduction to special topic issue on relevance research). *Journal of the American Society for Information Science*, 45: 124–134.

Fry, L. W., and Smith, D. A. 1987. Congruence, contingency, and theory building. *Academy of Management Review*, 12: 117–132.

Fulk, J., and Boyd, B. 1991. Emerging theories of communication in organizations. *Journal of Management*, 17: 407–446.

Fulk, J., Heino, R., Flanigan, A. J., Monge, P. R., and Bar, F. 2004. A test of the individual action model for organizational information commons. *Organization Science*, 15: 569–585.

Fund for the Improvement of Post-Secondary Education. 2003. Innovation and impact: the comprehensive program FY 2004. Fund for the improvement of Post-Secondary Education, Washington, DC.

Galbraith, J. R. 1973. *Designing Complex Organizations*. Addison-Wesley.

　1974. Organizational design: an information processing view. *Interfaces*, 4: 28–36.

　1982. Designing the innovating organization. *Organizational Dynamics*, 10: 5–25.

　1995. *Designing Organizations: An Executive Briefing on Strategy, Structure, and Process*. Jossey-Bass.

Gales, L., Porter, P., and Mansour-Cole, D. 1992. Innovation project technology, information processing and performance: a test of the Daft and Lengel conceptualization. *Journal of Engineering and Technology Management*, 9: 303–338.

Gans, D., Kralewski, J., Hammons, T., and Dowd, B. 2005. Medical groups' adoption of electronic health records and information systems. *Health Affairs*, 24: 1323–1333.

Garg, A. X., Adhikari, N. K. J., McDonald, H., Rosas-Arellano, M. P., Devereaux, P. J., Beyene, J., Sam, J., and Haynes, R. B. 2005. Effects of computerized clinical decision support systems on practitioner performance and patient outcomes. *Journal of American Medical Association*, 293: 1223–1238.

Gargiulo, M., and Benassi, M. 2000. Trapped in your own net? Network cohesion, structural holes, and the adaption of social capital. *Organization Science*, 11: 183–196.

Geertz, C. 1973. *The Interpretation of Cultures*. New York: Basic Books.

　1978. The bazaar economy: information and search in peasant marketing. *American Economic Review*, 68: 28–37.

Geist-Martin, P., Horsley, K., and Farrell, A. 2003. Working well: communicating individual and collective wellness initiatives. In T. L. Thompson, A. M. Dorsey, K. I. Miller, and R. Parrott (eds.), *Handbook of Health Communication*: 423–443. Lawrence Earlbaum Associates.

Georgoudi, M., and Rosnow, R. L. 1985. The emergence of contextualism. *Journal of Communication*, 35: 76–88.

Ghoshal, S., and Bartlett, C. A. 1990. The multinational corporation as an interorganizational network. *Academy of Management Review*, 15: 603–625.

Gibson, D. R. 2005. Taking turns and talking ties: networks and conversational interaction. *American Journal of Sociology*, 110: 1561–1597.

Gibson, D. V., and Rogers, E. M. 1994. *R&D Collaboration on Trial*. Harvard Business School Press.

Giddens, A. 1985. Time, space and regionalization. In D. Gregory and J. Urry (eds.), *Social Relations and Spatial Structures*: 265–295. Macmillan.

　1991. Structuration theory: past, present and future. In C. G. A. Bryant and D. Jary (eds.), *Giddens' Theory of Structuration: A Critical Appreciation*: 201–221. Routledge.

Gioia, D. A., and Poole, P. P. 1984. Scripts in organizational behavior. *Academy of Management Review*, 9: 449–459.

Gittell, J. H., and Weiss, L. 2004. Coordination networks within and across organizations: a multi-level framework. *Journal of Management Studies*, 41: 127–153.

Glasgow, R. E., Klesges, L. M., Dzewaltowski, D. A., Bull, S. S., and Estabrooks, P. 2004. The future of health behavior change research: what is needed to improve translation of research into health promotion practice? *Annals of Behavioral Medicine*, 27: 3–12.

Glasgow, R. E., Lichtenstein, E., and Marcus, A. C. 2003. Why don't we see more translation of health promotion research to practice? Rethinking the efficacy-to-effectiveness transition. *American Journal of Public Health*, 93: 1261–1267.

Glasgow, R. E., Marcus, A. G., Bull, S. S., and Wilson, K. M. 2004. Disseminating effective cancer screening interventions. *Cancer Supplement*, 101: 1239–1250.

Glasgow, R. E., Vogt, T. M., and Boles, S. M. 1999. Evaluating the public health impact of health promotion interventions: The RE-AIM framework. *American Journal of Public Health*, 89: 1322–1327.

Glauser, M. J. 1984. Upward information flow in organizations: review and conceptual analysis. *Human Relations*, 37: 613–643.

Goerzen, A. 2005. Managing alliance networks: emerging practices of multinational corporations. *Academy of Management Executive*, 19: 94–106.

Goffman, E. 1974. *Frame Analysis: An Essay on the Organization of Experience*. Harvard University Press.

Gold, A. H., Malhotra, A., and Segars, A. H. 2001. Knowledge management: an organizational capabilities perspective. *Journal of Management Information Systems*, 18: 185–214.

Goldberg, S. C. 1954. Three situational determinants of conformity to social norms. *Journal of Abnormal and Social Psychology*, 9: 449–459.

Goldenson, R. M. 1984. *Longman Dictionary of Psychology and Psychiatry*. Longman.

Goldhaber, G. M., Yates, M. P., Porter, T. D., and Lesniak, R. 1978. Organizational communication: 1978. *Human Communication Research*, 5: 76–96.

Goldhar, J. D., Bragaw, L. W., and Schwartz, J. J. 1976. Information flows, management styles, and technological innovation. *IEEE Transactions on Engineering Management*, 23: 51–62.

Goodall, H. L. 1989. On becoming an organizational detective: the role of context, sensitivity, and intuitive logics in communication consulting. *Southern Communication Journal*, 55: 42–54.

Gottlieb, L. K., Stone, E. M., Stone, D., Dunbrack, L. A., and Calladine, J. 2005. Regulatory and policy barriers to effective clinical data exchange: lessons learned from MedsInfo-Ed. *Health Affairs*, 24: 1197–1204.

Gough, C. 2000. Science and the Stradivarius. http://physicsworld.com/cws/article/print/696.

Govindarajan, V., and Trimble, C. 2005. Organizational DNA for strategic innovation. *California Management Review*, 47: 47–76.

Grandori, A., and Kogut, B. 2002. Dialogue on organization and knowledge. *Organization Science*, 13: 224–231.

Granovetter, M. S. 1973. The strength of weak ties. *American Journal of Sociology*, 78: 1360–1380.

1982. The strength of weak ties: a network theory revisited. In P. V. Marsden and N. Lin (eds.), *Social Structure in Network Analysis*: 105–130. Sage.

1985. Economic action and social structure: the problem of embeddedness. *American Journal of Sociology*, 91: 481–510.

Gray, B. 1996. Review of "Frame reflection." *Academy of Management Review*, 21: 576–579.

Gray, P. H., and Meister, D. B. 2004. Knowledge sourcing effectiveness. *Management Science*, 50: 821–834.

Green, L. A., and Seifert, C. M. 2005. Translation of research into practice: why we can't "just do it." *Journal of American Board of Family Medicine*, 18: 541–545.

Green, L. W., and Glasgow, R. E. 2006. Evaluating the relevance, generalization, and applicability of research: issues in external validation and translation methodology. *Evaluation and the Health Professions*, 29: 126–153.

Greene, C. N. 1978. Identification modes of professionals: relationships with formalization, role strain, and alienation. *Academy of Management Journal*, 21: 486–492.

Gregory, D. 1985. Suspended animation: the stasis of diffusion theory. In D. Gregory and J. Urry (eds.), *Social Relations and Spatial Structures*: 296–336. Macmillan.

Gregory, D., and Urry, J. 1985. Introduction. In D. Gregory and J. Urry (eds.), *Social Relations and Spatial Structures*: 1–8. Macmillan.

Gregory, K. L. 1983. Native-view paradigms: multiple cultures and culture conflicts in organizations. *Administrative Science Quarterly*, 28: 359–376.

Greider, W. 1992. *Who will tell the people?: the betrayal of American democracy*. Simon & Schuster.

Gresov, C., and Drazin, R. 1997. Equifinality: functional equivalence in organization design. *Academy of Management Review*, 22: 403–428.

Gresov, C., and Stephens, C. 1993. The context of interunit influence attempts. *Administrative Science Quarterly*, 38: 252–276.

Grimshaw, J. M., Thomas, R. E., MacLennan, G., Fraser, C., Ramsay, C. R., Vale, L., Whitty, P., Eccles, M. P., Matowe, L., Shirran, L., Wensing, M., Dijkstra, R., and Donaldson, C. 2004. Effectiveness and efficiency of guideline dissemination and implementation strategies. *Health Technology Assessment*, 8: viii–73.

Groopman, J. 2007. *How Doctors Think*. Houghton Mifflin.

Grover, V., and Davenport, T. H. 2001. General perspectives on knowledge management: fostering a research agenda. *Journal of Management Information Systems*, 18: 5–21.

Guetskow, H. 1965. Communication in organizations. In J. G. March (ed.), *Handbook of Organizations*: 534–573. Rand-McNally.

Guetskow, H., and Simon, H. A. 1955. The impact of certain communication nets upon organization and performance in task oriented groups. *Management Science*, 1: 233–250.

Gulati, R. 2007. *Managing Network Resources: Alliances, Affiliations, and other Relational Assets*. Oxford University Press.

Gulati, R., and Kletter, D. 2005. Shrinking core, expanding periphery: the relational architecture of high-performing organizations. *California Management Review*, 47: 77–104.

Gullahorn, J. T. 1952. Distance and friendship as factors in the gross interaction matrix. *Sociometry*, 15: 123–134.

Gupta, A. K., and Govindarajan, V. 1991. Knowledge flows and the structure of control within multinational organizations. *Academy of Management Review*, 16: 768–792.

Gupta, A. K., Smith, K. G., and Shalley, C. E. 2006. The interplay between exploration and exploitation. *Academy of Management Journal*, 49: 693–706.

Gurbaxani, V., and Whang, S. 1991. Knowledge flows and the structure of control within multinational organizations. *Communications of the ACM*, 24: 59–73.

Hackbarth, G., and Milgate, K. 2005. Using quality incentives to drive physician adoption of health information technology. *Health Affairs*, 24: 1147–1149.

Hackman, J. 1983. Group influences on individuals. In M. Dunette (ed.), *Handbook of Industrial and Organizational Psychology*: 1455–1525. Wiley.

Hägerstrand, T. 1953. *Innovation Diffusion as a Spatial Process*. University of Chicago Press.

　1982. Diorama, path and project. *Tijdschrift voor Economische en Sociale Geografie*, 73: 323–339.

Hage, J. 1999. Organizational innovation and organizational change. *Annual Review of Sociology*, 25: 597–622.

Hage, J., and Aiken, M. 1970. *Social Change in Complex Organizations*. Random House.

Hage, J., Aiken, M., and Marrett, C. B. 1971. Organization structure and communications. *American Sociological Review*, 36: 860–871.

Halamka, J., Overhage, J. M., Ricciardi, L., Rishel, W., Shirky, C., and Diamond, C. 2005. Exchanging health information: local distribution, national coordination. *Health Affairs*, 24: 1170–1179.

Hall, H. 2003. Borrowed theory: applying exchange theories in information science research. *Library and Information Science Research*, 25: 287–306.

Hammond, W. E. 2005. The making and adoption of health data standards. *Health Affairs*, 24: 1205–1213.

Hansen, M. T. 1999. The search-transfer problem: the role of weak ties in sharing knowledge across organization subunits. *Administrative Science Quarterly*, 44: 82–111.

　2002. Knowledge networks: explaining effective knowledge sharing in multiunit companies. *Organization Science*, 13: 232–248.

Hansen, M. T., and Hass, M. R. 2001. Competing for attention in knowledge markets: electronic document dissemination in a management consulting company. *Administrative Science Quarterly*, 46: 1–28.

Hansen, M. T., Mors, M. L., and Lovas, B. 2005. Knowledge sharing in organizations: multiple networks, multiple phases. *Academy of Management Journal*, 48: 776–793.

Hanser, L. M., and Muchinsky, P. M. 1978. Work as an information environment. *Organizational Behavior and Human Performance*, 21: 47–60.

Hanson, R., Porterfield, R. I., and Ames, K. 1995. Employee empowerment at risk: effects of recent NLRB rulings. *Academy of Management Executive*, 9: 45–54.

Hargadon, A., and Fanelli, A. 2002. Action and possibility: reconciling dual perspectives of knowledge in organizations. *Organization Science*, 13: 290–302.

Hargadon, A., and Sutton, R. I. 1997. Technology brokering and innovation in a product development firm. *Administrative Science Quarterly*, 42: 716–749.

2000. Building an innovation factory, *Harvard Business Review*, 78: 156–166.

Harris, L., and Associates. 2005. *At a Tipping Point: Transforming Medicine with Health Information Technology – A Guide for Consumers*. L. Harris and Associates.

Harter, L. M., and Krone, K. J. 2001. The boundary-spanning role of a cooperative support organization: managing the paradox of stability and change in non-traditional organizations. *Journal of Applied Communication Research*, 29: 248–277.

Hartman, R. L., and Johnson, J. D. 1989. Social contagion and multiplexity: communication networks as predictors of commitment and role ambiguity. *Human Communication Research*, 15: 523–548.

1990. Formal and informal group communication structures: an examination of their relationship to role ambiguity. *Social Networks*, 12: 127–151.

Hatch, M. J. 1987. Physical barriers, task characteristics, and interaction activity in research and development firms. *Administrative Science Quarterly*, 32: 387–399.

Hellweg, S. A. 1987. Organizational grapevines. In B. Dervin and M. J. Voight (eds.), *Progress in Communication Sciences*, vol. VIII: 213–230. Ablex.

Hersh, W. R., Crabtree, M. K., Hickman, D. H., Sacherek, L., Friedman, C. P., Tidmarsh, P., Mosbaek, C., and Kraemer, D. 2002. Factors associated with success in searching MEDLINE and applying evidence to answer clinical questions. *Journal of the American Medical Informatics Association*, 9: 283–293.

Hersh, W. R., Crabtree, M. K., Hickman, D. H., Sacherek, L., Rose, L., and Friedman, C. P. 2000. Factors associated with successful answering of clinical questions using an information retrieval system. *Bulletin of Medical Library Association*, 88: 323–331.

Hew, K. F., and Hara, N. 2007. Knowledge sharing in online environments: a qualitative case study. *Journal of the American Society for Information Science and Technology*, 58: 2310–2324.

Hickson, D. J. 1987. Decision making at the top of organizations. *Annual Review of Sociology*, 13: 165–192.

Hillestad, R., Bigelow, J., Bower, A., Girosi, F., Meili, R., Scoville, R., and Taylor, R. 2005. Can electronic medical record systems transform health care? Potential health benefits, savings, and costs. *Health Affairs*, 24: 1103–1117.

Hinds, P. J., and Pfeffer, J. 2003. Why organizations don't "know what they know": cognitive and motivational factors affecting the transfer of expertise. In M. S. Ackerman, V. Pipek, and V. Wulf (eds.), *Sharing Expertise: Beyond Knowledge Management*: 3–26. MIT Press.

Hirsch, S., and Dinkelacker, J. 2004. Seeking information in order to produce information: an empirical study at Hewlett Packard Labs. *Journal of the American Society for Information Science and Technology*, 55: 807–817.

Hjorland, B. 2007. Information: objective or subjective/situational? *Journal of the American Society for Information Science and Technology*, 58: 1448–1456.

Hoetker, G., and Agarwal, R. 2007. Death hurts, but it isn't fatal: the post exit diffusion of knowledge created by innovative companies. *Academy of Management Journal*, 50: 446–467.

Hoffman, G. M. 1994. *The Technology Payoff: How to Profit with Empowered Workers in the Information Age*. Irwin.

Hollingshead, A. B. 1998. Communication, learning, and retrieval in transactive memory systems. *Journal of Experimental Social Psychology*, 34: 423–442.

Holsapple, C. W. 2003. Knowledge and its attributes. In C. W. Holsapple (ed.), *Handbook of Knowledge Management*, vol. I: *Knowledge Matters*: 165–188. Springer-Verlag.

Holsapple, C. W., and Whinston, A. B. 1988. *The Information Jungle: A Quasi Novel Approach to Managing Corporate Knowledge*. Dow Jones–Irwin.

Howell, J. M. 2005. The right stuff: identifying and developing effective champions of innovation. *Academy of Management Executive*, 19: 108–119.

Huber, G. P. 1990. A theory of the effects of advanced information technologies on organizational design, intelligence, and decision making. *Academy of Management Review*, 15: 47–71.

Huber, G. P., and Daft, R. L. 1987. The information environment in organizations. In F. M. Jablin, L. L. Putnam, K. H. Roberts, and L. W. Porter (eds.), *Handbook of Organizational Communication: An Interdisciplinary Perspective*: 130–164. Sage.

Huber, G. P., and McDaniel, R. R., Jr. 1988. Exploiting information technologies to design more effective organizations. In M. Jarke (ed.), *Managers, Micros and Mainframes*: 221–236. Wiley.

Huckfeldt, R., Johnson, P. E., and Sprague, J. 2004. *Political Disagreement: The Survival of Diverse Opinions within Communication Networks*. Cambridge University Press.

Hudson, J., and Danish, S. J. 1980. The acquisition of information: an important life skill. *Personnel and Guidance Journal*, 59: 164–167.

Huff, C., Sproull, L., and Kiesler, S. 1989. Computer communication and organizational commitment: tracing the relationship in a city government. *Journal of Applied Social Psychology*, 19: 1371–1391.

Huotari, M., and Chatman, E. 2001. Using everyday life information seeking to explain organizational behavior. *Library and Information Science Research*, 23: 351–366.

Huysman, M., and van Baalen, P. 2002. Editorial. *Trends in Communication*, 8: 3–5.

Hyman, H. H., and Sheatsley, P. B. 1947. Some reasons why information campaigns fail. *Public Opinion Quarterly*, 11: 412–423.

Ibarra, H. 1993. Personal networks of women and minorities in management: a conceptual framework. *Academy of Management Review*, 18: 56–87.

Inkpen, A. C., and Tsang, E. W. K. 2005. Social capital, networks, and knowledge transfer. *Academy of Management Review*, 30: 146–165.

Inman, T. H., Olivas, L., and Golden, S. P. 1986. Desirable communication behaviors of managers. *Business Education Forum*, 40: 27–28.

Introcaso, D. M. 2005. The value of social network analysis in health care delivery. *New Directions for Evaluation*, 107: 95–98.

Iverson, J. O., and McPhee, R. D. 2002. Knowledge management in communities of practice: being true to the communicative character of knowledge. *Management Communication Quarterly*, 16: 259–266.

Jablin, F. M. 1978. Message response and "openness" in superior–subordinate communication. In B. D. Ruben (ed.), *Communication Yearbook 2*: 293–309. Transaction Books.

　　1980. Organizational communication theory and research: an overview of communication climate and network research. In D. Nimmo (ed.), *Communication Yearbook 4*: 327–347. Transaction Books.

　　1981. An exploratory study of subordinates' perceptions of supervisory politics. *Communication Quarterly*, 28: 269–275.

　　1987. Formal organization structure. In F. M. Jablin, L. L. Putnam, K. H. Roberts, and L. W. Porter (eds.), *Handbook of Organizational Communication: An Interdisciplinary Perspective*: 389–419. Sage.

Jablin, F. M., Putnam, L. L., Roberts, K. H., and Porter, L. W. (eds.) 1987. *Handbook of Organizational Communication: An Interdisciplinary Perspective*. Sage.

Jablin, F. M., and Sussman, L. 1983. Organizational group communication: a review of the literature and model of the process. In H. H. Greenbaum, R. L. Falcione, and S. A. Hellweg (eds.), *Organizational Communication: Abstracts, Analysis, and Overview*: 11–50. Sage.

Jackson, S. E., and Schuler, R. S. 1985. A meta-analysis and conceptual critique of research on role ambiguity and role conflict in work settings. *Organizational Behavior and Human Decision Processes*, 36: 16–78.

Jacoby, J. 2005. Optimal foraging. In K. E. Fisher, S. Erdelez, and L. McKechnie (eds.), *Theories of Information Behavior*: 259–264. Information Today.

James, L. R., and Jones, A. P. 1974. Organizational climate: a review of theory and research. *Psychological Bulletin*, 16: 74–113.

Janis, I. L. 1971. Groupthink. *Psychology Today*, November: 43–76.

Jansen, J. J. P., van den Bosch, F. A. J., and Volberda, H. W. 2005. Managing potential and realized absorptive capacity: how do organizational antecedents matter? *Academy of Management Journal*, 48: 999–1016.

Jarvenpaa, S. L., and Staples, D. S. 2001. Exploring perceptions of organizational ownership of information and expertise. *Journal of Management Information Systems*, 18: 151–183.

Jensen, M. C., and Meckling, W. H. 1995. Specific and general knowledge, and organizational structure. *Journal of Applied Corporate Finance*, 8: 4–18.

Johnson, B. M., and Rice, R. E. 1987. *Managing Organizational Innovation: The Evolution of Word Processing to Office Information Systems*. Columbia University Press.

Johnson, J. D. 1983. A test of a model of magazine exposure and appraisal in India. *Communication Monographs*, 50: 148–157.

　　1984a. International communication media appraisal: tests in Germany. In R. N. Bostrom (ed.), *Communication Yearbook 8*: 645 658. Sage.

　　1984b. Media exposure and appraisal: Phase II, tests of a model in Nigeria. *Journal of Applied Communication Research*, 12: 63–74.

　　1987. Multivariate communication networks. *Central States Speech Journal*, 38: 210–222.

　　1988a. On the use of communication gradients. In G. M. Goldhaber and G. Barnett (ed.), *Handbook of Organizational Communication*: 361–383. Ablex.

　　1988b. Structure: a software review. *Communication Education*, 37: 172–174.

1989. Technological and spatial factors related to communication structure, presented to the Annual Convention of the International Communication Association. San Francisco.

1990. Effects of communicative factors on participation in innovations. *Journal of Business Communication*, 27: 7–24.

1992. Approaches to organizational communication structure. *Journal of Business Research*, 25: 99–113.

1993. *Organizational Communication Structure*. Ablex.

1996a. Approaches to communication structure: applications to the problem of information seeking. In M. West (ed.), *Handbook of Work Group Psychology*: 451–474. Wiley.

1996b. *Information Seeking: An Organizational Dilemma*. Quorum Books.

1997a. *Cancer-related Information Seeking*. Hampton Press.

1997b. A framework for interaction (FINT) scale: extensions and refinement in an industrial setting. *Communication Studies*, 48: 127–141.

1998. Frameworks for interaction and disbandments: a case study. *Journal of Educational Thought*, 32: 5–21.

2002. Researcher–practitioner relationships in consortia: the Cancer Information Services Research Consortium. *AIC Journal of Business*, 14: 34–56.

2003. On contexts of information seeking. *Information Processing and Management*, 39: 735–760.

2004. The emergence, maintenance, and dissolution of structural hole brokerage within consortia. *Communication Theory*, 14: 212–236.

2005. *Innovation and Knowledge Management: The Cancer Information Services Research Consortium*. Edward Elgar.

2006. A sociometric analysis of influence relationships within a community of practice. *Studies in Communication Sciences*, 6: 63–92.

2008. Dosage: a bridging metaphor for theory and practice. *International Journal of Strategic Communication*, 2: 137–153.

Johnson, J. D., Andrews, J. E., Case, D. O., Allard, S. L., and Johnson, N. E. 2006. Fields and/or pathways: contrasting and/or complementary views of information seeking. *Information Processing and Management*, 42: 569–582.

Johnson, J. D., Case, D. O., Andrews, J. E., and Allard, S. L. 2005. Genomics-: the perfect information seeking research problem. *Journal of Health Communication*, 10: 323–329.

Johnson, J. D., and Chang, H. J. 2000. Internal and external communication, boundary spanning, innovation adoption: an over-time comparison of three explanations of internal and external innovation communication in new organization form. *Journal of Business Communication*, 37: 238–263.

Johnson, J. D., Donohue, W. A., Atkin, C. K., and Johnson, S. 1994. Differences between formal and informal communication channels. *Journal of Business Communication*, 31: 111–122.

1995a. A comprehensive model of information seeking: tests focusing on a technical organization. *Science Communication*, 16: 274–303.

1995b. Differences between organizational and communication factors related to contrasting innovations. *Journal of Business Communication*, 32: 65–80.

Johnson, J. D., LaFrance, B. H., Meyer, M., Speyer, J. B., and Cox, D. 1998. The impact of formalization, role conflict, role ambiguity, and communication quality on perceived organizational innovativeness in the Cancer Information Service. *Evaluation and the Health Professions*, 21: 27–51.

Johnson, J. D., and Meischke, H. 1993. A comprehensive model of cancer related information seeking applied to magazines. *Human Communication Research*, 19: 343–367.

Johnson, J. D., Meyer, M., Berkowitz, J., Ethington, C., and Miller, V. 1997. Testing two contrasting models of innovativeness in a contractual network. *Human Communication Research*, 24: 320–348.

Johnson, J. D., and Oliveira, O. S. 1988. A model of international communication media appraisal and exposure: a comprehensive test in Belize. *World Communication*, 17: 253–277.

1992. Communication factors related to closer international ties: an extension of a model in Brazil. *International Journal of Conflict Management*, 3: 267–284.

Johnson, J. D., Oliveira, O. S., and Barnett, G. A. 1989. Communication factors related to closer international ties: an extension of a model in Belize. *International Journal of Intercultural Relations*, 13: 1–18.

Johnson, J. D., and Smith, D. A. 1985. Effects of work dependency, response satisfaction and proximity on communication frequency. *Western Journal of Speech Communication*, 49: 217–231.

Johnson, J. D., and Tims, A. R. 1985. Communication factors related to closer international ties. *Human Communication Research*, 12: 259–273.

Joshi, A. 2006. The influence of organizational demography on the external networking behavior of teams. *Academy of Management Journal*, 31: 583–595.

Kahn, R. L., Wolfe, D. M., Quinn, R. P., Snoek, J. D., and Rosenthal, R. 1964. *Organizational Stress: Studies in Role Conflict and Ambiguity*. Wiley.

Kahn, W. A. 1990. Psychological conditions of personal engagement and disengagement at work. *Academy of Management Journal*, 33: 692–724.

Kalman, M. E., Monge, P. R., Fulk, J., and Heino, R. 2002. Motivations to resolve communication dilemmas in database-mediated collaboration. *Communication Research*, 29: 125–154.

Kane, G. C., and Alavi, M. 2008. Casting the net: a multimodal network perspective on user–system interactions. *Information Systems Research*, 19: 253–272.

Kanter, R. M. 1977. *Men and Women of the Corporation*. Basic Books.

1983. *The Change Masters: Innovation and Entrepreneurship in the American Corporation*. Simon & Schuster.

1988. When a thousand flowers bloom: structural, collective, and social conditions for innovation in organizations. *Research in Organizational Behavior*, 10: 169–211.

Kashy, D. A., and Kenny, D. A. 1990. Do you know whom you were with a week ago Friday? A re-analysis of the Bernard, Killworth, and Sailer studies. *Social Psychology Quarterly*, 53: 55–61.

Kasperson, C. J. 1978. An analysis of the relationship between information sources and creativity in scientists and engineers. *Human Communication Research*, 4: 113–119.

Katila, R., and Ahuja, G. 2002. Something old, something new: a longitudinal study of search behavior and new product introduction. *Academy of Management Journal*, 45: 1183–1194.

Katz, D., and Kahn, R. L. 1966. *The Social Psychology of Organizations*. Wiley.

1978. *The Social Psychology of Organizations*, 2nd edn. Wiley.

Katz, E. 1957. The two step flow of communication: an up to date report on an hypothesis. *Public Opinion Quarterly*, 21: 61–78.

1968. On reopening the question of selectivity in exposure to mass communications. In R. P. Abelson (ed.), *Theories of Cognitive Consistency*: 788–796. Rand-McNally.

Katz, E., and Lazersfeld, P. F. 1955. *Personal Influence: The Part Played by People in the Flow of Mass Communications*. Free Press.

Katz, N., Lazer, D., Arrow, H., and Contractor, N. 2004. Network theory and small groups. *Small Group Research*, 35: 307–332.

Katz, R., and Allen, T. J. 1982. Investigating the not invented here (NIH) syndrome: a look at the performance, tenure, and communication patterns of 50 R&D project groups. *R&D Management*, 12: 7–19.

Katz, R., and Tushman, M. L. 1981. An investigation into the managerial roles and career paths of gatekeepers and project supervisors in a major R&D facility. *R&D Management*, 11: 103–110.

Katzer, J., and Fletcher, P. T. 1992. The information environment of managers. In *Annual Review of Information Science and Technology*: 227–263. Learned Information.

Kayworth, T., and Leidner, D. 2003. Organizational culture as a knowledge resource. In C. W. Holsapple (ed.), *Handbook of Knowledge Management*, vol. I: *Knowledge Matters*: 235–252. Springer-Verlag.

Kearns, G. S., and Lederer, A. L. 2003. A resource-based view of strategic IT alignment: how knowledge sharing creates competitive advantage. *Decision Sciences*, 34: 1–29.

Keen, M., and Stocklmayer, S. 1999. Science communication: the evolving role of rural industry research and development corporations. *Australian Journal of Environmental Management*, 6: 196–206.

Keen, P. G. W. 1990. Telecommunications and organizational choice. In J. Fulk and C. Steinfield (eds.), *Organizations and Communication Technology*: 295–312. Sage.

Keen, P. G. W., and Morton, M. S. S. 1978. *Decision Support Systems: An Organizational Perspective*. Addison-Wesley.

Keidel, R. W. 1984. Baseball, football, and basketball: models for business. *Organizational Dynamics*, 12: 4–18.

Keller, R. T. 1989. A cross-national study of communication networks and technological innovation in research and development organizations, presented to the National Meetings of the Academy of Management. Washington, DC.

2001. Cross-functional product groups in research and new product development: diversity, communications, job stress, and outcomes. *Academy of Management Journal*, 44: 547–555.

Kenney, D. A., Kashy, D. A., and Cook, W. L. 2006. *Dyadic Data Analysis*. Guilford Press.

Kerwin, A. 1993. None too solid: medical ignorance. *Knowledge: Creation, Diffusion, Utilization*, 15: 166–185.

Ketchen, D. J., Jr., Thomas, J. B., and Snow, C. C. 1993. Organizational configurations and performance: a comparison of theoretical approaches. *Academy of Management Journal*, 36: 1278–1313.

Kilduff, M., and Krackhardt, D. 1994. Bringing the individual back in: a structural analysis of the internal market for reputation in organizations. *Academy of Management Journal*, 37: 87–108.

Kilduff, M., and Tsai, W. 2003. *Social Networks and Organizations*. Sage.

Killworth, P. D., and Bernard, H. R. 1976. Informant accuracy in social network data. *Human Organizations*, 35: 269–286.

1979. Informant accuracy in social network data, III: A comparison of triadic structure in behavioral and cognitive data. *Social Networks*, 2: 10–46.

Killworth, P. D., Bernard, H. R., and McCarty, C. 1984. Measuring patterns of acquaintanceship. *Current Anthropology*, 25: 381–392.

Kilmann, R. H., Slevin, D. P., and Thomas, K. W. 1983. The problem of producing useful knowledge. In R. H. Kilmann, K. W. Thomas, D. P. Slevin, R. Nath, and S. L. Jerrell (eds.), *Producing Useful Knowledge for Organizations*: 1–21. Jossey-Bass.

Kim, L. 1980. Organizational innovation and structure. *Journal of Business Research*, 2: 225–245.

Kim, T., Oh, H., and Swaminathan, A. 2006. Framing interorganizational network change: a network inertia perspective. *Academy of Management Review*, 31: 704–720.

Kimberly, J. R., and Evanisko, M. J. 1981. Organizational innovation: the influence of individual, organizational, and contextual factors on hospital adoption of technological and administrative innovations. *Academy of Management Journal*, 24: 689–713.

Kindermann, T. A., and Valsiner, J. 1995a. Directions for the study of developing person–context relations. In T. A. Kindermann and J. Valsiner (eds.), *Development of Person–Context Relationships*: 227–240. Lawrence Erlbaum Associates.

1995b. Individual development, changing contexts and the co-construction of person–context relations in human development. In T. A. Kindermann and J. Valsiner (eds.), *Development of Person–Context Relationships*: 1–9. Lawrence Erlbaum Associates.

Kirman, A. 2001. Market organization and individual behavior: evidence from fish markets. In J. E. Rauch and A. Casella (eds.), *Networks and Markets*: 155–195. Russel Sage.

Klein, K. J., Palmer, S. L., and Conn, A. B. 2000. Interorganizational relationships: a multilevel perspective. In K. J. Klein and S. W. J. Kozlowski (eds.), *Multilevel Theory, Research, and Methods in Organizations*: 267–307. Jossey-Bass.

Klesges, L. M., Estabrook, P. A., Dzewaltowski, D. A., Bull, S. S., and Glasgow, R. E. 2005. Beginning with application in mind: designing and planning health behavior change interventions to enhance dissemination. *Annals of Behavioral Medicine*, 29: 66–75.

Klovdahl, A. S. 1981. A note on images of networks. *Social Networks*, 3: 197–214.

Knoke, D., and Kuklinski, J. H. 1982. *Network Analysis*. Sage.

Kogut, B. 2000. The network as knowledge: generative rules and the emergence of structure. *Strategic Management Journal*, 21: 405–425.

Kogut, B., and Zander, U. 1996. What firms do? Coordination, identity, and learning. *Organization Science*, 7: 502–518.

Koka, B. R., Madhavan, R., and Prescott, J. E. 2006. The evolution of interfirm networks: environmental effects on patterns of network change. *Academy of Management Review*, 31: 721–737.

Komsky, S. H. 1989. Electronic mail and democratization of organizational communication, presented to the Annual Convention of the International Communication Association. San Francisco.

Korzenney, F. 1978. A theory of electronic propinquity: mediated communication in organizations. *Communication Research*, 5: 3–24.

Krackhardt, D. 1989. Graph theoretical dimensions of informal organizations, presented to the National Meeting of the Academy of Management, Washington, DC.

  1992. The strength of strong ties: the importance of philos in organizations. In N. Nohria (ed.), *Networks and Organizations: Structure, Form, and Action*: 216–239. Harvard Business Review.

  1994. Constraints on the interactive organization as an ideal type. In C. Heckscher and A. Donnelon (eds.), *The Post-bureaucratic Organization: New Perspectives on Organizational Change*: 211–222. Sage.

  2007. Closing remarks, presented to the Intra Organizational Network Conference, Lexington, KY.

Krackhardt, D., and Porter, L. W. 1985. When friends leave: a structural analysis of the relationship between turnover and stayers' attitudes. *Administrative Science Quarterly*, 30: 242–261.

Kratzer, J., Leenders, R. T. A. J., and van Engelen, J. M. L. 2004. Stimulating the potential: creative performance and communication in innovation teams. *Creativity and Innovation Management*, 13: 63–71.

Krebs, V. 2008. Mapping community networks, presented to INSNA Annual Conference. St. Petersburg Beach, FL.

Krippendorf, K. 1986. *Information Theory: Structural Models for Qualitative Data*. Sage.

Krizner, I. M. 1973. *Competition and Entrepreneurship*. University of Chicago Press.

Kuhlthau, C. 1991. Inside the search process: information seeking from the user's perspective. *Journal of the American Society for Information Science*, 12: 361–371.

  2004. *Seeking Meaning: A Process Approach to Library and Information Services*, 2nd edn. Libraries Unlimited.

Kuhn, T. 2002. Negotiating boundaries between scholars and practitioners: knowledge, networks, and communities of practice. *Management Communication Quarterly*, 16: 106–112.

Kuhn, T., and Corman, S. R. 2003. The emergence of homogeneity and heterogeneity in knowledge structures during a planned organizational change. *Communication Monographs*, 70: 198–229.

Kuhn, T. S. 1970. *The Structure of Scientific Revolutions*, 2nd edn. Chicago: University of Chicago Press.

Kumbasar, E., Romney, A. K., and Batchelder, W. H. 1994. Systematic biases in social perception. *American Journal of Sociology*, 100: 477–505.

Kurke, L. B., Weick, K. E., and Ravlin, E. C. 1989. Can information loss be reversed? Evidence for serial construction. *Communication Research*, 16: 3–24.

LaFollette, M. C. 1993. Editorial. *Knowledge: Creation, Diffusion, Utilization*, 15: 131–132.

Lane, P. J., Koka, B. R., and Pathak, S. 2006. The reification of absorptive capacity: a critical review and rejuvenation of the construct. *Academy of Management Review*, 31: 833–863.

Larson, J. R., Jr. 1989. The dynamic interplay between employees' feedback seeking strategies and supervisor's delivery of performance feedback. *Academy of Management Review*, 14: 408–422.

Laumann, E. O., Marsden, P. V., and Prensky, D. 1983. The boundary specification problem in network analysis. In R. S. Burt and M. J. Minor (eds.), *Applied Network Analysis*: 18–34. Sage.

Laumann, E. O., and Schumm, L. P. 1992. Measuring social networks using samples: Is network analysis relevant to survey research?, presented to a symposium at the National Opinion Research Center, Chicago.

Lawrence, P. R., and Lorsch, J. W. 1967. *Organization and Environment: Managing Differentiation and Integration*. Harvard Business School Press.

Leavitt, H. J. 1951. Some effects of certain communication patterns on group performance. *Journal of Abnormal and Social Psychology*, 46: 38–50.

Leckie, G. J. 2005. General model of the information seeking of professionals. In K. E. Fisher, S. Erdelez, and E. F. McKechnie (eds.), *Theories of Information Behavior*: 158–163. Information Today.

Lee, A. M. 1970. *Systems Analysis Frameworks*. Macmillan.

Lee, G. K., and Cole, R. E. 2003. From a firm-based to a community-based model of knowledge creation: the case of Linux kernel development. *Organization Science*, 14: 633–649.

Lee, J., Miranda, S. M., and Kim, Y. 2004. IT outsourcing strategies: universalistic, contingency, and configurational explanations of success. *Information Systems Research*, 15: 110–131.

Leifer, R., and Delbecq, A. 1978. Organizational/environmental interchange: a model of boundary spanning activity. *Academy of Management Review*, 20: 40–50.

Lenz, E. R. 1984. Information seeking: a component of client decisions and health behavior. *Advances in Nursing Science*, 6: 59–72.

Leonard, D. 1995. *Wellsprings of Knowledge: Building and Sustaining the Source of Innovation*. Harvard Business School Press.

Leonard, D., and Sensiper, S. 1998. The role of tacit knowledge in group innovation. *California Management Review*, 40: 112–132.

Leonard, D. A. 2006. Innovation as a knowledge generation and transfer process. In A. Singhal and J. W. Dearing (eds.), *Communication of Innovations: A Journey with Ev Rogers*: 83–111. Sage.

Leonard-Barton, D., and Deschamps, I. 1988. Managerial influence in the implementation of new technology. *Management Science*, 34: 1252–1265.

Lesser, E., and Prusak, L. (eds.) 2004. *Creating Value with Knowledge: Insights from the IBM Institute for Business Value*. Oxford University Press.

Lesser, E. L., and Cothrel, J. 2004. Fast friends – virtuality and social capital. In E. Lesser and L. Prusak (eds.), *Creating Value with Knowledge: Insights from the IBM Institute for Business Value*: 24–35. Oxford University Press.

Lesser, E. L., and Storck, J. 2004. Communities of practice and organizational performance. In E. Lesser and L. Prusak (eds.), *Creating Value with Knowledge: Insights from the IBM Institute for Business Value*: 107–123. Oxford University Press.

Levacic, R. 1991. Markets: introduction. In G.Thompson, J. Frances, R. Levacic, and J. Mitchell (eds.), *Markets, Hierarchies and Networks: The Coordination of Social Life*: 21–23. Sage.

Levin, D. Z., Cross, R., Abrams, L. C., and Lesser, E. L. 2004. Trust in knowledge sharing: a critical combination. In E. Lesser and L. Prusak (eds.), *Creating Value with Knowledge: Insights from the IBM Institute for Business Value*: 36–46. Oxford University Press.

Levine, J. M., and Moreland, R. L. 2004. Collaboration: the social context of theory development. *Personality and Social Psychology Review*, 8: 164–172.

Lewin Group. 2005. Health information technology leadership panel: final report (March).

Lewis, L. K., and Seibold, D. R. 1993. Innovation modification during interorganizational adoption. *Academy of Management Review*, 18: 322–354.

1996. Communication during intraorganizational innovation adoption: predicting users' behavioral coping responses to innovations in organizations. *Communication Monographs*, 63: 131–157.

Lewis, M. L., Cummings, W. W., and Long, L. W. 1982. Communication activity as a predictor of the fit between worker motivation and worker productivity. In M. Burgoon (ed.), *Communication Yearbook 5*: 473–501. Sage.

Lewis, R. S. 1988. *Challenger: The Final Voyage*. Columbia University Press.

Li, L. 2002. Information sharing in a supply chain with horizontal competition. *Management Science*, 48: 1196–1212.

Liberman, S., and Wolf, K. B. 1997. The flow of knowledge: scientific contacts in formal meetings. *Social Networks*, 19: 271–283.

Lievrouw, L. A. 1994. Information resources and democracy: understanding the paradox. *Journal of the American Society for Information Science*, 45: 350–357.

Liker, J. K., Haddad, C. J., and Karlin, J. 1999. Perspectives on technology and work organization. *Annual Review of Sociology*, 25: 575–596.

Likert, R. 1967. *The Human Organization: Its Management and Value*. McGraw-Hill.

Lin, N. 2001. *Social Capital: A Theory of Social Structure and Action*. Cambridge University Press.

Lincoln, J. R., and McBride, K. 1985. Resources, homophily, and dependence: organizational attributes and asymmetric ties in human service networks. *Social Science Research*, 14: 1–30.

Lodahl, T. M. 1964. Patterns of job attitudes in two assembly technologies. *Administrative Science Quarterly*, 8: 482–519.

Lord, R. G., and Kernan, M. C. 1987. Scripts as determinants of purposeful behavior in organizations. *Academy of Management Review*, 12: 144–156.

Lord, R. G., and Maher, K. J. 1990. Alternative information processing models and their implications for theory, research, and practice. *Academy of Management Review*, 15: 9–28.

Lorenz, E. H. 1991. Neither friends nor strangers: informal networks of subcontracting in French industry. In G.Thompson, J. Frances, R. Levacic, and J. Mitchell (eds.), *Markets, Hierarchies and Networks: The Coordination of Social Life*: 183–192. Sage.

Lorenzoni, G., and Lipparini, A. 1999. The leveraging of interfirm relationships as distinctive organizational capability: a longitudinal study. *Strategic Management Journal*, 20: 317–338.

Lukasiewicz, J. 1994. *The Ignorance Explosion: Understanding Industrial Civilization.* Carlton University Press.

MacCrimmon, K. R., and Taylor, R. N. 1976. Decision making and problem solving. In M. D. Dunnette (ed.), *Handbook of Industrial and Organizational Psychology*. Rand-McNally.

Mackenzie, K. D. 1984. Organizational structures as the primal information system: an interpretation. In S. Chang (ed.), *Management and Office Information Systems*: 27–46. Plenum.

1986. Virtual positions and power. *Management Science*, 32: 622–642.

MacMorrow, N. 2001. Knowledge management: an introduction. *Annual Review of Information Science and Technology*, 35: 381–422.

Madzar, S. 2001. Subordinates' information inquiry: exploring the effects of perceived leadership style and individual differences. *Journal of Occupational and Organizational Psychology*, 74: 221–232.

Maes, P. 1995. Intelligent software. *Scientific American*, 273(3): 84–86.

Mahmood, M. A., and Mann, G. J. 2000. Special issue: impacts of information technology investment on organizational performance. *Journal of Management Information Systems*, 17: 3–10.

Malone, T. W., and Crowston, K. 1994. The interdisciplinary study of coordination. *Computing Surveys*, 26: 87–119.

Malone, T. W., Yates, J., and Benjamin, R. I. 1987. Electronic markets and electronic hierarchies. *Communications of the ACM*, 30: 484–497.

March, J. G. 1991. Exploration and exploitation in organizational learning. *Organizational Science*, 2: 71–87.

1994. *A Primer on Decision Making: How Decisions Happen*. Free Press.

2000. Citigroup's John Reed and Stanford's James March on management research and practice. *Academy of Management Executive*, 14: 52–64.

March, J. G., and Simon, H. A. 1958. *Organizations*. John Wiley.

Marchand, D. A., and Horton, F. W., Jr. 1986. *Infotrends: Profiting from your Information Resources*. Wiley.

Marchionini, G. 1992. Interfaces for end user information seeking. *Journal of the American Society for Information Science*, 43: 156–163.

Marcus, A. C. 1998a. The Cancer Information Service Research Consortium: a brief retrospective and preview of the future. *Preventive Medicine*, 27: S93–S100.

1998b. Introduction: The Cancer Information Service Research Consortium. *Preventive Medicine*, 27: S1–S2.

Marcus, A. C., Heimendinger, J., Wolfe, P., Rimer, B. K., Morra, M. E., Cox, D., Lang, P. J., Stengle, W., Van Herle, M. P., Wagner, D., Fairclough, D., and Hamilton, L. 1998. Increasing fruit and vegetable consumption among callers to the CIS: results from a randomized trial. *Preventive Medicine*, 27: S16–S28.

Marcus, A. C., Morra, M. E., Bettinghaus, E., Crane, L. A., Cutter, G., Davis, S., Rimer, B. K., Thomsen, C., and Warnecke, R. B. 1998. The Cancer Information Service Research Consortium: an emerging laboratory for cancer control research. *Preventive Medicine*, 27: S3–S15.

Marcus, A. C., Woodworth, M. A., and Strickland, C. J. 1993. The Cancer Information Service as a laboratory for research: the first 15 years. *Journal of the National Cancer Institute*, Monograph 14: 67–79.

Markey, K. 2007. Twenty-five years of end-user searching, part 2: Future research directions. *Journal of the American Society for Information Science and Technology*, 58: 1123–1130.

Markus, M. L. 1994. Electronic mail as the medium of managerial choice. *Organization Science*, 5: 502–527.

Marrone, J. A., Tesluk, P. E., and Carson, J. B. 2007. A multilevel investigation of antecedents and consequences of team member boundary-spanning behavior. *Academy of Management Journal*, 50: 1423–1439.

Marsden, P. V. 1987. Core discussion networks of Americans. *American Sociological Review*, 52: 122–131.

1990. Network data and measurement. *Annual Review of Sociology*, 16: 435–463.

Marshall, A. A., and Stohl, C. 1993. Participating as participation: a network approach. *Communication Monographs*, 60: 137–157.

Matei, S. A., and Ball-Rokeach, S. 2005. Watts, the 1965 Los Angeles riots, and the communicative construction of the fear epicenter of Los Angeles. *Communication Monographs*, 72: 301–323.

Matson, E., Patiath, P., and Shavers, T. 2003. Stimulating knowledge sharing: organization's internal knowledge market. *Organizational Dynamics*, 32: 275–285.

Matthews, R., and Shoebridge, A. 1993. The strategic importance of executive information systems. In R. Ennals, and P. Molyneaux (eds.), *Managing with Information Technology*: 22–36. Springer-Verlag.

McCain, B. E., O'Reilly, C., and Pfeffer, J. 1983. The effects of departmental demography on turnover: the case of a university. *Academy of Management Journal*, 26: 626–641.

McCarrey, M. W., Peterson, L., Edwards, S., and von Kulmiz, P. 1974. Landscape office attitudes: reflections of perceived degree of control over transactions with the environment. *Journal of Applied Psychology*, 59: 401–403.

McCarthy, D., and Saegert, S. 1978. Residential density, social overload, and social withdrawal. *Human Ecology*, 6: 253–271.

McCrosky, J. C., Richmond, V. P., and Daly, J. A. 1975. The development of a measure of perceived homophily in interpersonal communication. *Human Communication Research*, 1: 323–332.

McDermott, R. 1999. Why information technology inspired but cannot deliver knowledge management. *California Management Review*, 41: 103–117.

McDonald, C. J., Overhage, J. M., Barnes, M., Schadow, G., Blevins, L., Dexter, P. R., Mamlin, B., and the INPC Management Committee 2005. The Indiana network for patient care: a working local health information infastructure. *Health Affairs*, 24: 1214–1220.

McGaffey, T. N., and Christy, R. 1975. Information processing capability as a predictor of entrepreneurial effectiveness. *Academy of Management Journal*, 18: 857–863.

McGee, J. V., and Prusak, L. 1993. *Managing Information Strategically*. Wiley.

McGrath, C., and Krackhardt, D. 2003. Network conditions for organizational change. *Journal of Applied Behavioral Science*, 39: 324–336.

McGuinness, T. 1991. Markets and managerial hierarchies. In G. Thompson, J. F. R. Levacic, and J. Mitchell (eds.), *Markets, Hierarchies, and Networks: The Coordination of Social Life*: 66–81. Sage.

McGuire, W. J. 1983. A contextualist theory of knowledge: its implications for innovation and reform in psychological research. In L. Berkowitz (ed.), *Advances in Experimental Social Psychology*, vol. XVI: 1–47. Academic Press.

    1989. Theoretical foundations of campaigns. In R. E. Rice and C. K. Atkin (eds.), *Public Communication Campaigns*: 43–66. Sage.

McIntosh, J. 1974. Processes of communication, information seeking and control associated with cancer: a selective review of the literature. *Social Science and Medicine*, 8: 167–187.

McKinney, M. M., Barnsley, J. M., and Kaluzny, A. D. 1992. Organizing for cancer control: the diffusion of a dynamic innovation in a community cancer network. *International Journal of Technology Assessment in Health Care*, 8: 268–288.

McKinnon, S. M., and Bruns W. J., Jr. 1992. *The Information Mosaic*. Harvard Business School Press.

McLaughlin, M. L., and Cheatam, T. R. 1977. Effects of communication isolation on job satisfaction of Bank tellers: a research note. *Human Communication Research*, 3: 171–175.

McNeil, K., and Thompson, J. D. 1971. The regeneration of social organizations. *American Sociological Review*, 36: 624–637.

McPhee, R. D. 1988. Vertical communication chains: toward an integrated approach. *Management Communication Quarterly*, 1: 455–493.

McPherson, M., Smith-Lovin, L., and Cook, J. M. 2001. Birds of a feather: homophily in social networks. *Annual Review of Sociology*, 27: 415–444.

Mead, S. P. 2001. Using social network analysis to visualize project teams. *Project Management Journal*, 32: 32–38.

Melville, N., Kraemer, K., and Gurbaxani, V. 2004. Information technology and organizational performance: an integrative model of IT business value. *MIS Quarterly*, 28: 283–322.

Menon, A., and Varadarajan, P. R. 1992. A model of marketing knowledge use within firms. *Journal of Marketing*, 56: 53–71.

Menon, T., and Pfeffer, J. 2003. Valuing internal vs. external knowledge: explaining the preference for outsiders. *Management Science*, 49: 497–513.

Meyer, M. 1996a. *The Effects of Weak Ties on Perceived Organizational Innovativeness and Innovation Characteristics*. Michigan State University.

    1996b. Reconceptualizing innovation characteristics: a confirmatory factor analysis of the pros and cons of three contrasting preventive health innovations, presented to the convention of the Central States Speech Association, St. Paul, MN.

Meyer, M., and Johnson, J. D. 1997. The effects of weak ties on perceived organizational innovativeness and innovation characteristics, presented to the Annual Convention of the National Communication Association. Chicago.

Michael, J. H. 1997. Labor disputed reconciliation in a forest products manufacturing facility. *Forest Products Journal*, 47: 41–45.

Miles, R. E., and Snow, C. C. 1994. The network firm: a spherical structure built on a human investment policy. *Organizational Dynamics*, 23: 5–18.

Miles, R. E., Snow, C. C., Mathews, J. A., Miles, G., and Coleman, H. J. J. 1997. Organizing in the knowledge age: anticipating the cellular form. *Academy of Management Executive*, 11: 7–20.

Milgram, P., and Roberts, J. 1988. An economic approach to influence activities in organizations. *American Journal of Sociology*, 94: S154–S179.

Miller, D. 1993. The architecture of simplicity. *Academy of Management Review*, 18: 116–138.

Miller, D. J., Fern, M. J., and Cardinal, L. B. 2007. The use of knowledge for technological innovation with diversified firms. *Academy of Management Journal*, 50: 308–326.

Miller, G. R. 1969. Human information processing: some research guidelines. In R. J. Kibler and L. L. Barker (eds.), *Conceptual Frontiers in Speech Communication*: 51–68. Speech Communication Association.

Miller, K. D., Zhao, M., and Calantone, R. J. 2006. Adding interpersonal learning and tacit knowledge to March's exploration–exploitation model. *Academy of Management Journal*, 49: 709–722.

Miller, K. I. 1995. *Organizational Communication: Approaches and Processes*. Wadsworth.

Miller, P., and O'Leary, T. 1989. Hierarchies and American ideals. *Academy of Management Review*, 14: 250–265.

Miller, R. H., West, C., Brown, T. M., Sim, I., and Ganchoff, C. 2005. The value of electronic health records in solo or small group practices. *Health Affairs*, 24: 1127–1137.

Miller, V. D., and Jablin, F. M. 1991. Information seeking during organizational entry: influences, tactics, and a model of the process. *Academy of Management Review*, 16: 92–120.

Miller, V. D., Johnson, J. R., and Grau, J. 1994. Antecedents to willingness to participate in a planned organizational change. *Journal of Applied Communication Research*, 22: 59–80.

Milo, R., Shen-Orr, S., Itzkovitz, S., Kashten, N., Chklovskii, D., and Alon, U. 2002. Network motifs: simple building blocks of complex networks. *Science*, 298: 824–827.

Minor, M. J. 1983. New directions in multiplexity analysis. In R. S. Burt and M. J. Minor (eds.), *Applied Network Analysis: A Methodological Introduction*: 223–244. Sage.

Mintzberg, H. 1975a. *Impediments to the Use of Management Information*. National Association of Accountants.

1975b. The manager's job. *Harvard Business Review*, 53: 49–61.

1976. Planning on the left side and managing on the right. *Harvard Business Review*, 54: 49–58.

Mitchell, J. C. 1969. The concept and use of social networks. In J. C. Mitchell (ed.), *Social Networks in Urban Situations: Analyses of Personal Relationships in Central African Towns*: 1–50. Manchester University Press.

Mitchell, O. S. 1988. Worker knowledge of pensions provisions. *Journal of Labor Economics*, 6: 21–39.

Mizruchi, M. S., and Galaskiewicz, J. 1993. Networks of interorganizational relations. *Sociological Methods and Research*, 22: 46–70.

Moch, M. K. 1980. Job involvement, internal motivation, and employees' integration into networks of work relationships. *Organizational Behavior and Human Performance*, 25: 15–31.

Moch, M. K., and Morse, E. V. 1977. Size, centralization and organizational adoption of innovations. *American Sociological Review*, 42: 716–725.

Mohr, L. B. 1971. Organizational technology and organizational structure. *Administrative Science Quarterly*, 16: 444–459.

Mohrman, S. A., Gibson, C., and Mohrman, A. M., Jr. 2001. Doing research that is useful to practice: a model and empirical exploration. *Academy of Management Journal*, 44: 357–375.

Mohrman, S. A., Tenkasi, R. V., and Mohrman, A. M., Jr. 2003. The role of networks in fundamental organizational change: a grounded analysis. *Journal of Applied Behavioral Science*, 39: 301–323.

Monge, P. R., and Contractor, N. S. 1987. Communication networks: measurement techniques. In C. H. Tardy (ed.), *A Handbook for the Study of Human Communication*: 107–138. Ablex.

2001. Emergence of communication networks. In F. M. Jablin and L. L. Putnam (eds.), *The New Handbook of Organizational Communication: Advances in Theory, Research, and Methods*: 440–502. Sage.

2003. *Theories of Communication Networks*. Oxford University Press.

Monge, P. R., Edwards, J. A., and Kirste, K. K. 1978. The determinants of communication and communication structure in large organizations: a review of research. In B. D. Rubin (ed.), *Communication Yearbook 2*: 311–331. Transaction Books.

Monge, P. R., and Eisenberg, E. M. 1987. Emergent communication networks. In F. M. Jablin, L. L. Putnam, K. H. Roberts, and L. W. Porter (eds.), *Handbook of Organizational Communication: An Interdisciplinary Perspective*: 304–342. Sage.

Monge, P. R., and Miller, K. I. 1988. Participative processes in organizations. In G. M. Goldhaber and G. A. Barnett (eds.), *Handbook of Organizational Communication*: 213–230. Ablex.

Monkhouse, F. J., and Wilkinson, H. R. 1971. *Maps and Diagrams: Their Compilation and Construction*. Methuen.

Moore, W. E., and Tumin, M. M. 1949. Some social functions of ignorance. *American Sociological Review*, 14: 787–795.

More, E. 1990. Information systems: people issues. *Journal of Information Science*, 16: 311–320.

Moreno, J. L. 1934. *Who Shall Survive?* Nervous and Mental Disease Publishing.

Morgan, G. 1986. *Images of Organization*. Sage.

Morra, M. E., Van Nevel, J. P., O'D.Nealon, E., Mazan, K. D., and Thomsen, C. 1993. History of the Cancer Information Service. *Journal of the National Cancer Institute*, Monograph 14: 7–34.

Morris, J. H., Steers, R. M., and Koch, J. L. 1979. Impacts of role perceptions on organizational commitment, job involvement, and psychosomatic illness among three vocational groupings. *Journal of Vocational Behavior*, 14: 88–101.

Morrison, E. W. 1993a. Longitudinal study of the effects of information seeking on newcomer socialization. *Journal of Applied Psychology*, 78: 173–183.

1993b. Newcomer information seeking: Exploring types, modes, sources, and outcomes. *Academy of Management Journal*, 36: 557–589.

Morrison, E. W., and Bies, R. J. 1991. Impression management in the feedback seeking process: a literature review and research agenda. *Academy of Management Review*, 16: 522–541.

Morton, J. A. 1971. *Organizing for innovation*. New York: McGraw-Hill.

Mowday, R. T., Steers, R. M., and Porter, L. M. 1979. The measurement of organizational commitment. *Journal of Vocational Behavior*, 14: 224–247.

Mumby, D. K., and Putnam, L. L. 1992. The politics of emotion: a feminist reading of bounded rationality. *Academy of Management Review*, 17: 465–486.

Nadler, D. A., and Tushman, M. L. 1997. *Competing by Design: The Power of Organizational Architecture*. Oxford University Press.

Nag, R., Corley, K. G., and Gioia, D. A. 2007. The intersection of organizational identity, knowledge, and practice: attempting strategic change via knowledge grafting. *Academy of Management Journal*, 50: 821–847.

Nahapiet, J., and Ghoshal, S. 1998. Social capital, intellectual capital, and the organizational advantage. *Academy of Management Review*, 23: 242–266.

Nass, C., and Mason, L. 1990. On the study of technology and task: a variable based approach. In J. Fulk and C. W. Steinfield (eds.), *Organizations and Communication Technology*: 46–68. Sage.

Nathan, M. L., and Mitroff, I. I. 1991. The use of negotiated order theory as a tool for the analysis and development of an interorganizational field. *Journal of Applied Behavioral Science*, 27: 163–180.

National Cancer Institute. 2003. The nation's investment in cancer research. National Cancer Institute, Rockville, MD.

National Institutes of Health. 2006. NIH launches national consortium to transform clinical research (October 3).

Naumer, C. 2005. Flow theory. In K. E. Fisher, S. Erdelez, and L. McKechnie (eds.), *Theories of Information Behavior*: 153–157. Information Today.

Nebus, J. 2006. Building collegial information networks: a theory of advice network generation. *Academy of Management Review*, 31: 615–637.

Newman, M., Barabasi, A., and Watts, D. J. (eds.). 2006. *The Structure and Dynamics of Networks*. Princeton University Press.

Newman, M. E. J. 2005. A measure of betweenness centrality based on random walks. *Social Networks*, 27: 39–54.

Nicholson, J., P. J., and Goh, S. C. 1983. The relationship of organization structure and interpersonal attitudes to role conflict and ambiguity in different work environments. *Academy of Management Journal*, 26: 148–155.

Noam, E. 1993. Reconnecting communications study with communications policy. *Journal of Communication*, 43: 199–206.

Noelle-Neumann, E. 1974. The spiral of silence. *Journal of Communication*, 24: 43–51.

Nohria, N. 1992. Is a network perspective a useful way of studying organizations? In N. Nohria and R. G. Eccles (eds.), *Networks and Organizations: Structure, Form, and Action*. Harvard Business School Press.

Nohria, N., and Eccles, R. G. (eds.). 1992. *Networks and Organizations: Structure, Form, and Action*. Harvard Business School Press.

Nonaka, I. 1991. The knowledge-creating company. *Harvard Business Review*, 69: 21–45.

Nonaka, I., and Takeuchi, H. 1995. *The Knowledge-creating Company: How Japanese Companies Create the Dynamics of Innovation*. Oxford University Press.

Nord, W. R., and Tucker, S. 1987. *Implementing Routine and Radical Innovations*. Lexington Books.

Nutt, P. C. 1984. Types of organizational decision processes. *Administrative Science Quarterly*, 29: 414–450.

O'Conner, B. C. 1993. Browsing: a framework for seeking functional information. *Knowledge: Creation, Diffusion, Utilization*, 15: 211–232.

O'Dell, C., and Grayson, C. J. 1998. If only we knew what we know: identification of internal best practices. *California Management Review*, 40: 154–174.

Oh, H., Labianca, G., and Chung, M. 2006. A multilevel model of group social capital. *Academy of Management Review*, 31: 569–582.

Oldenburg, B. F., Sallis, J. F., French, M. L., and Owen, N. 1999. Health promotion research and the diffusion and institutionalization of interventions. *Health Education Research*, 14: 121–130.

Oldham, G. R., and Cummings, A. 1996. Employee creativity: personal and contextual factors at work. *Academy of Management Journal*, 39: 607–634.

O'Mahony, S., and Ferraro, F. 2007. The emergence of governance in an open source community. *Academy of Management Journal*, 50: 1079–1106.

O'Neill, B. 1984. Structures for nonhierarchical organizations. *Behavioral Science*, 29: 61–77.

Ordanini, A. 2005. The effects of participation in B2B exchanges: a resource-based view. *California Management Review*, 47: 97–113.

O'Reilly, C. A., III. 1980. Individuals and information overload in organizations: is more necessarily better? *Academy of Management Journal*, 23: 684–696.

O'Reilly, C. A., III, Chatham, J. A., and Anderson, J. C. 1987. Message flow and decision making. In F. M. Jablin, L. L. Putnam, K. H. Roberts, and L. W. Porter (eds.), *Handbook of Organizational Communication: An Interdisciplinary Perspective*: 600–623. Sage.

O'Reilly, C. A., III, and Pondy, L. R. 1979. Organizational communication. In S. Kerr (ed.), *Organizational Behavior*: 119–150. Grid.

Organ, D., and Greene, C. 1981. The effects of formalization on professional involvement: a compensatory process approach. *Administrative Science Quarterly*, 26: 237–252.

Organ, D. W., and Bateman, T. 1986. *Organizational Behavior: An Applied Psychology Approach*, 3rd edn. Business Publications.

Orleans, C. T. 2005. The behavior change consortium: expanding the boundaries and impact of health behavior change research. *Annals of Behavioral Medicine*, 29: 76–79.

Orlikowski, W. J. 2002. Knowing in practice: enacting a collective capability in distributed organizing. *Organization Science*, 13: 249–273.

Ouchi, W. G. 1981. *Theory Z*. Avon.

Pacanowsky, M. E., and O'Donnell Trujillo, N. 1982. Communication and organizational cultures. *Western Journal of Speech Communication*, 46: 115–130.

Paisley, W. 1980. Information and work. In B. Dervin and M. J. Voight (eds.), *Progress in Communication Sciences*, vol. II: 114–165. Ablex.

1993. Knowledge utilization: the role of new communication technologies. *Journal of the American Society for Information Science*, 44: 222–234.

Palazzolo, E. T. 2006. Organizing for information retrieval in transactive memory systems. *Communication Research*, 16: 726–761.

Palazzolo, E. T., Serb, D. A., She, Y., Su, C., and Contractor, N. S. 2006. Coevolution of communication and knowledge networks in transactive memory systems: using computational models for theoretical development. *Communication Theory*, 16: 223–250.

Palmgreen, P. 1984. Uses and gratifications: a theoretical perspective. In R. N. Bostrom (ed.), *Communication Yearbook 8*: 20–55. Sage.

Palmquist, R. A. 1992. The impact of information technology on the individual. In M. E. Williams (ed.), *Annual Review of Information Science and Technology*, vol. XXVII: 3–42. Learned Information.

Pan, S., Pan, G., and Hsieh, M. H. 2006. A dual-level analysis of the capability development process: a case study of TT&T. *Journal of the American Society for Information Science and Technology*, 57: 1814–1829.

Parise, S., and Henderson, J. C. 2004. Knowledge resource exchange in strategic alliances. In E. Lesser and L. Prusak (eds.), *Creating Value with Knowledge: Insights from the IBM Institute for Business Value*: 145–167. Oxford University Press.

Park, S. H., and Ungson, G. R. 1997. The effect of national culture, organizational complementarity, and economic motivation on joint venture dissolution. *Academy of Management Journal*, 40: 279–307.

Parks, M. R., and Adelman, M. B. 1983. Communication networks and the development of romantic relationships: an expansion of uncertainty reduction theory. *Human Communication Research*, 10: 55–79.

Patchen, T. 1970. *Participation, Achievement, and Involvement on the Job*. Prentice Hall.

Pearce, W. B., and Conklin, R. 1979. A model of hierarchical meanings in coherent conversation and a study of "indirect responses." *Communication Monographs*, 46: 75–87.

Peng, M. W., and Shenkar, O. 2002. Joint venture dissolution as corporate divorce. *Academy of Management Executive*, 16: 92–105.

Perrow, C. 1972. *Complex Organizations: A Critical Essay*. Scott, Foresman.

Perry, D. K. 1988. Implications of a contextualist approach to media-effects research. *Communication Research*, 15: 246–264.

Perry-Smith, J. E. 2006. Social yet creative: the role of social relationships in facilitating individual creativity. *Academy of Management Journal*, 49: 85–101.

Perry-Smith, J. E., and Shalley, C. E. 2003. The social side of creativity: a static and dynamic social network perspective. *Academy of Management Review*, 28: 89–106.

Perse, E. M., and Courtright, J. A. 1993. Normative images of communication media: mass and interpersonal channels in the new media environment. *Human Communication Research*, 19: 485–503.

Peters, T. J., and Waterman, R. H., Jr. 1982. *In Search of Excellence: Lessons from America's Best Run Companies.* Harper & Row.

Petronio, S. 2007. Translational research endeavors and the practice of communication privacy management. *Journal of Applied Communication Research*, 35: 218–222.

Pettigrew, A. 1971. Managing under stress, *Management Today, April*: 99–102.

Pettigrew, K. E., Fidel, R., and Bruce, H. 2001. Conceptual frameworks in information behavior. *Annual Review of Information Science and Technology*, 35: 43–78.

Pfeffer, J. 1978. *Organizational Design.* AHM Publishing.

    1982. *Organizations and Organization Theory.* Pitman.

    1983. Organizational demography. *Research in Organizational Behavior*, 5: 299–357.

Pfeffer, J., and Leblebici, H. 1977. Information technology and organizational structure. *Pacific Sociological Review*, 20: 241–259.

Picherit-Duthler, G., and Freitag, A. 2004. Researching employees' perceptions of benefits communication: a communication inquiry on channel preferences, understanding, decision-making, and benefits satisfaction. *Communication Research Reports*, 21: 391–403.

Pickrell, J. 2004. Did "Little Ice Age" create Stradivarius violins' famous tone? *National Geographic News* (January 7).

Pike, K. L. 1966. *Language in Relation to a Unified Theory of the Structure of Human Behavior.* N. V. Uitgeverij Mouton en Co.

Pile, J. 1978. *Open Office Planning.* Whitney Library of Design.

Pirolli, P., and Card, S. 1999. Information foraging. *Psychological Review*, 106: 643–675.

Podolny, J. M. 2001. Networks as the pipes and prisms of the market. *American Journal of Sociology*, 107: 33–60.

Polanyi, M. 1974. *Personal Knowledge: Towards a Post-critical Philosophy.* University of Chicago Press.

Polanyi, M., and Prosch, H. 1975. *Meaning.* University of Chicago Press.

Pollock, T. G., Porac, J. F., and Wade, J. B. 2004. Constructing deal networks: brokers as network "architects" in the US IPO market and other examples. *Academy of Management Review*, 29: 50–72.

Poole, M. S., and DeSanctis, G. 1990. Understanding the use of group decision support systems: the theory of adaptive structuration. In J. Fulk and C. Steinfield (eds.), *Organizations and Communication Technology*: 175–295. Sage.

Poole, M. S., and McPhee, R. D. 1983. A structurational analysis of organizational climate. In L. L. Putnam and M. E. Pacanowsky (eds.), *Communication and Organizations: An Interpretive Approach*: 195–220. Sage.

Poole, M. S., Van de Ven, A., Dooley, K., and Holmes, M. E. 2000. *Organizational Change and Innovation Processes: Theory and Methods for Research.* Oxford University Press.

Poole, M. S., and Van de Ven, A. H. 1989. Using paradox to build management and organizational theories. *Academy of Management Review*, 14: 562–578.

Porter, L., and Lawler, E. E. 1965. Properties of organizational structure in relation to job attitudes and job behavior. *Psychological Bulletin*, 64: 23–51.

Porter, L. W. 1996. Forty years of organization studies: reflections from a micro perspective. *Administrative Science Quarterly*, 41: 262–269.

Porter, L. W., Allen, R. W., and Angle, H. L. 1981. The politics of upward influence in organizations. In S. M. Bacharach (ed.), *Research in Organizational Behavior*. JAI Press.

Porter, L. W., Lawler, E. E., III, and Hackman, J. R. 1975. *Behavior in Organizations*. McGraw-Hill.

Porter, M. E., and Millar, V. E. 1985. How information gives you competitive advantage. *Harvard Business Review*, 63: 149–160.

Postrel, S. 2002. Islands of shared knowledge: specialization and mutual understanding in problem-solving teams. *Organization Science*, 13: 302–320.

Poverny, L. M., and Dodd, S. J. 2000. Differential patterns of EAP service utilization: a nine year follow-up study of faculty and staff. *Employee Assistance Quarterly*, 16: 29–42.

Powell, W. W. 1990. Neither market nor hierarchy: network forms of organization. In S. B. Bacharach (ed.), *Research in Organizational Behavior*: 295–336. JAI Press.

   1998. Learning from collaboration: knowledge and networks in the biotechnology and pharmaceutical industries. *California Management Review*, 40: 228–240.

Powell, W. W., and Smith-Doerr, L. 1994. Networks and economic life. In N. J. Smelser and R. Swedberg (eds.), *The Handbook of Economic Sociology*: 368–402. Princeton University Press.

Power, D. J. 2007. A brief history of decision support systems. www.dssresources.com.

Presthus, R. 1962. *The organizational society*. New York: Random House.

Provan, K. G. 1983. The federation as an interorganizational linkage network. *Academy of Management Review*, 8: 79–89.

Provan, K. G., and Milward, H. B. 2001. Do networks really work? A framework for evaluating public-sector organizations. *Public Administration Review*, 61: 414–423.

Puranam, P., Singh, H., and Zollo, M. 2006. Organizing for innovation: managing the coordination-autonomy dilemma in technology acquisitions. *Academy of Management Journal*, 49: 263–280.

Putnam, L. L., and Holmer, M. 1992. Framing, reframing, and issue development. In L. L. Putnam and M. E. Roloff (eds.), *Communication and Negotiation*: 128–155. Sage.

Qian, Y., Roland, G., and Xu, C. 2003. Coordinating tasks in M-Form and U-Form organizations. University of California at Berkeley.

Raab, J., and Milward, H. B. 2003. Dark networks as problems. *Journal of Public Administration Research and Theory*, 13: 413–439.

Raghavan, S. 2005. Medical decision support systems and knowledge sharing standards. In R. K. Bali (ed.), *Clinical Knowledge Management: Opportunities and Challenges*: 196–217. Idea Group Publishing.

Randolph, W. A., and Finch, F. E. 1977. The relationship between organization technology and the direction and frequency dimensions of task communications. *Human Relations*, 30: 1131–1145.

Ranson, S., Hinings, B., and Greenwood, R. 1980. The structuring of organizational structures. *Administrative Science Quarterly*, 25: 1–17.

Rapoport, A. 1982. *The Meaning of the Built Environment: A Nonverbal Communication Approach*. Sage.

Ravetz, J. R. 1993. The sin of silence: ignorance of ignorance. *Knowledge: Creation, Diffusion, Utilization*, 15: 157–165.

Ray, E. B. 1987. Supportive relationships and occupational stress in the workplace. In T. L. Albrecht and M. B. Adelman (eds.), *Communicating Social Support*: 172–191. Sage.

Reagans, R., and McEvily, B. 2003. Network structure and knowledge transfer: the effect of cohesion and range. *Administrative Science Quarterly*, 48: 240–267.

Real, J. C., Leal, A., and Roldan, J. L. 2006. Information technology as a determinant of organizational learning and technological distinctive competencies. *Industrial Marketing Management*, 35: 505–521.

Redding, W. C. 1972. *Communication within the Organization*. Industrial Communication Council.

Reif, W. E. 1968. *Computer Technology and Management Organization*. University of Iowa.

Renn, O. 1991. Risk communication and the social amplification of risk. In R. E. Kasperson and P. J. Stallen (eds.), *Communicating Risks to the Public*: 287–324. Kluwer.

Reynolds, E. V., and Johnson, J. D. 1982. Liaison emergence: relating theoretical perspectives. *Academy of Management Review*, 7: 551–559.

Rice, R. E. 1989. Issues and concepts in research on computer mediated communication systems. In J. A. Anderson (ed.), *Communication Yearbook 12*: 436–476. Sage.

Rice, R. E., Grant, A., Schmitz, J., and Torobin, J. 1988. Organizational information processing, critical mass and social influence: a network approach to predicting the adoption and outcomes of electronic messaging, presented to the Annual Meeting of the International Communication Association. New Orleans.

Rice, R. E., McCreadie, M., and Chang, S. L. 2001. *Accessing and Browsing Information and Communication*. MIT Press.

Rice, R. E., and Richards, W. D. 1985. An overview of network analysis methods and programs. In B. Dervin and M. J. Voight (eds.), *Progress in Communication Sciences*: 105–165. Ablex.

Rice, R. E., and Shook, D. 1986. Access to and usage of integrated office systems: implications for organizational communication, presented to Annual Convention of the International Communication Association, Montreal, Canada.

1990. Relationships of job categories and organizational levels to use of communication channels, including electronic model: a meta analysis and extension. *Journal of Management Studies*, 27: 196–229.

Richards, W. D. 1985. Data, models, and assumptions in network analysis. In R. D. McPhee and P. K. Tompkins (eds.), *Organizational Communication: Traditional Themes and New Directions*: 109–128. Sage.

Richards, W. D., Jr. 1993. Communication/information networks, strange complexity, and parallel topological dynamics. In W. D. Richards, Jr. and G. A. Barnett (eds.), *Progress in Communication Sciences*, vol. XII 165–195. Ablex.

Richards, W. D., and Seary, A. J. 2000. Eigen analysis of networks, *Journal of Social Structure*. www.heinz.cmv.edu/project/NSNA/joss/ean.html.

Rickert, E. J. 1994. Contextual association. In R. J. Corsini (ed.), *Encyclopedia of Psychology*, 2nd edn., vol. I: 316. Wiley.

Riley, M. W., and Riley, J. W. 1951. A sociological approach to communications research. *Public Opinion Quarterly*, 15: 445–460.

Rivkin, J. W., and Siggelkow, N. 2003. Balancing search and stability: interdependencies among elements of organizational design. *Management Science*, 49: 290–311.

Rizzo, J. R., House, R. J., and Lirtzman, S. I. 1970. Role conflict and ambiguity in complex organizations. *Administrative Science Quarterly*, 15: 150–163.

Roberts, J. 2004. *The Modern Firm: Organizational Design for Performance and Growth*. Oxford University Press.

Roberts, K. H., and O'Reilly, C. A., III. 1979. Some correlations of communication roles in organizations. *Academy of Management Journal*, 4: 283–293.

Robertson, T. S., and Wortzel, L. H. 1977. Consumer behavior and health care change: the role of mass media. *Consumer Research*, 4: 525–527.

Rogers, E. M. 1983. *Diffusion of Innovations*, 3rd edn. Free Press.
  1995. *Diffusion of Innovations*, 4th edn. Free Press.
  2003. *Diffusion of Innovations*, 5th edn. Free Press.

Rogers, E. M., and Adhikayra, R. 1979. Diffusion of innovations: an up-to-date review and commentary. In D. Nimmo (ed.), *Communication Yearbook 3*: 67–81. Transaction Books.

Rogers, E. M., and Agarwala Rogers, R. 1976. *Communication in Organizations*. Free Press.

Rogers, E. M., and Kincaid, D. L. 1981. *Communication Networks: Toward a New Paradigm for Research*. Free Press.

Rogers, E. M., and Shoemaker, F. F. 1971. *Communication of Innovations*, 2nd edn. Free Press.

Rogers, E. M., and Storey, J. D. 1987. Communication campaigns. In C. R. Berger and S. H. Chaffee (eds.), *Handbook of Communication Science*: 817–846. Sage.

Romney, A. K., and Faust, K. 1982. Predicting the structure of a communication network from recalled data. *Social Networks*, 4: 283–304.

Rosenkopf, L., and Nerkar, A. 2001. Beyond local search: boundary-spanning, exploration, and impact in the optical disk industry. *Strategic Management Journal*, 22: 287–306.

Rosenstock, I. M. 1974. Historical origins of the Health Belief Model. In M. H. Becker (ed.), *The Health Belief Model and Personal Health Behavior*: 1–8. Charles B. Slack.

Rouse, W. B., and Rouse, S. H. 1984. Human information seeking and design of information systems. *Information Processing and Management*, 20: 129–138.

Rousseau, D. M. 1985. Issues of level in organizational research: multi level and cross level perspectives. In S. M. Bacharach (ed.), *Research in Organizational Behavior*, vol. VII: 1–37. JAI Press.

Rowley, J. E., and Turner, C. M. D. 1978. *The Dissemination of Information*. Westview Press.

Rowley, T., Behrens, D., and Krackhardt, D. 2000. Redundant governance structures: an analysis of structural and relational embeddedness in the steel and semiconductor industries. *Strategic Management Journal*, 21: 369–386.

Ruef, M., Aldrich, H. E., and Carter, N. M. 2003. The structure of founding teams: homophily, strong ties, and isolation among U.S. entrepreneurs. *American Sociological Review*, 68: 195–222.

Russo, T. C., and Koesten, J. 2005. Prestige, centrality, and learning: a social network analysis of an online class. *Communication Education*, 54: 254–261.

Rynes, S. L., Bartunek, J. M., and Daft, R. L. 2001. Across the great divide: knowl-edge creation and transfer between practitioners and academics. *Academy of Management Journal*, 44: 340–355.

Sabherwal, R., and Robey, D. 1993. An empirical taxonomy of implementation processes based on sequences of events in information system development. *Organization Science*, 4: 548–576.

Sack, R. 1980. Conceptions of geographic space. *Progress in Human Geography*, 4: 313–345.

Saeed, K. A., Malhotra, M. K., and Grover, V. 2005. Examining the impact of interorgani-zational systems on process efficiency and sourcing leverage in buyer–supplier dyads. *Decision Sciences*, 36: 365–396.

Salancik, G. R. 1977. Commitment and control of organizational behavior and belief. In B. M. Staw and G. R. Salancik (eds.), *New Directions in Organizational Behavior*: 1–54. St. Clair Press.

Salancik, G. R., and Pfeffer, J. 1977. An examination of need satisfaction models of job attitudes. *Administrative Science Quarterly*, 22: 427–453.

Salazar, A. 2007. Information technology-enabled innovation: a critical overview and research agenda. In A. Salazar and S. Sawyer (eds.), *Handbook of Information Technology and Electronic Markets*: 415–444. World Scientific.

Saracevic, T. 1975. Relevance: a review of and a framework for the thinking on the notion in information science. *Journal of the American Society for Information Science*, 26: 321–343.

Sarbaugh, L. E. 1979. A systematic framework for analyzing intercultural communication. In N. C. Jain (ed.), *International and Intercultural Communication*, vol. V: 11–22. Speech Communication Association.

Satyadas, A., Harigopal, U., and Cassaigne, N. P. 2001. Knowledge management tutorial: an editorial overview. *IEEE Transactions on Systems, Man, and Cybernetics, Part C: Applications and Reviews*, 31: 429–437.

Saunders, C., and Jones, J. W. 1990. Temporal sequences in information acquisition for decision making: a focus on source and medium. *Academy of Management Review*, 15: 29–46.

Sawyer, S., Crowston, K., Wigand, R. T., and Allbritton, M. 2003. The social embed-dedness of transactions: evidence from the residential real-estate industry. *The Information Society*, 19: 135–154.

Scarbrough, H., and Swan, J. 2002. Knowledge communities and innovation. *Trends in Communication*, 8: 7–18.

Schein, E. H. 1965. *Organizational Psychology*. Prentice Hall.

Schmidt, D. E., and Keating, J. P. 1979. Human crowding and personal control: an integration of the research. *Psychological Bulletin*, 86: 680–700.

Schon, D. A., and Rein, M. 1994. *Frame Reflection: Toward the Resolution of Intractable Policy Controversies*. Basic Books.

Schramm, W. S. 1973. *Men, Messages, and Media*. Harper & Row.

Schreiman, D. B., and Johnson, J. D. 1975. A model of cognitive complexity and network role, presented to the International Communication Association. Chicago.

Schroder, J. M., Driver, J. J., and Streufert, S. 1967. *Human Information Processing*. Holt, Rinehart and Winston.

Schulz, M. 2001. The uncertain relevance of newness: organizational learning and knowledge flows. *Academy of Management Journal*, 44: 661–681.

Schumpeter, J. A. 1943. *Capitalism, Socialism and Democracy*. Routledge.

Schwartz, B. 2004. *Paradox of Choice: Why More is Less*. Harper Collins.

Scott, J. 1991. *Social Network Analysis: A Handbook*. Sage.

   2000. *Social Network Analysis: A Handbook*, 2nd edn. Sage.

Senge, P. M. 1990. *The Fifth Discipline: The Art and Practice of the Learning Organization*. Doubleday Currency.

Sept, R. 1989. Bureaucracy, communication, and information system design, presented to the Annual Meeting of the International Communication Association. San Francisco.

Shah, P. P. 1998. Who are employees' social referents? Using a network perspective to determine referent others. *Academy of Management Journal*, 41: 249–268.

Shannon, C. E., and Weaver, W. 1949. *A Mathematical Theory of Communication*. University of Illinois Press.

Sharf, B. F., and Vanderford, M. L. 2003. Illness narratives and social construction of health. In T. L. Thompson, A. M. Dorsey, K. I. Miller, and R. Parrott (eds.), *Handbook of Health Communication*. Lawrence Erlbaum Associates.

Shaw, M. E. 1971. *Group Dynamics: The Psychology of Small Group Behavior*. McGraw-Hill.

Sherif, M., and Sherif, C. W. 1964. *Reference Groups: Exploration into Conformity and Deviation of Adolescents*. Henry Regnery.

Shortliffe, E. H. 2005. Strategic action in health information technology: why the obvious has taken so long. *Health Affairs*, 24: 1222–1233.

Siefert, M., Gerbner, G., and Fisher, J. 1989. *The Information Gap: How Computers and Other New Communication Technologies Affect the Social Distribution of Power*. Oxford University Press.

Simmel, G. 1955. *Conflict and the Web of Group Affiliations*. Free Press.

Simon, H. A. 1960. "The executive as decision maker" and "Organizational design: man machine systems for decision making." In H. A. Simon (ed.), *The New Science of Management Decision Making*: 1–8. Harper & Row.

   1987. Making management decisions: the role of intuition and emotion. *Academy of Management Executive*, 1: 57–64.

   1991. *Models of My Life*. Basic Books.

Simpson, R. L. 1952. Vertical and horizontal communication in formal organizations. *Administrative Science Quarterly*, 2: 188–196.

Sircar, S., Turnbow, J. L., and Bordoloi, B. 2000. A framework for assessing the relationship between information technology investments and firm performance. *Journal of Management Information Systems*, 16: 69–97.

Smith, A. 1776/1952. *An Inquiry into the Nature and Causes of the Wealth of Nations*. Encyclopaedia Britannica.

Smith, C. G., and Jones, G. 1968. The role of the interaction influence system in planned organizational change. In A. S. Tannebaum (ed.), *Control in Organizations*: 165–184. McGraw-Hill.

Smith, H. A., and McKeen, J. D. 2003. Creating and facilitating communities of practice. In C. W. Holsapple (ed.), *Handbook of Knowledge Management*, vol. I: *Knowledge Matters*: 393–407. Springer-Verlag.

Smith, K. G., Carroll, S. J., and Ashford, S. J. 1995. Intra- and interorganizational cooperation: toward a research agenda. *Academy of Management Journal*, 38: 7–23.

Smith, K. G., Collins, C. J., and Clark, K. D. 2005. Existing knowledge, knowledge creation capability, and the rate of new product introduction in high-technology firms. *Academy of Management Journal*, 48: 346–357.

Smith, R. L., Richetto, G. M., and Zima, J. P. 1972. Organizational behavior: an approach to human communication. In R. Budd and B. Ruben (eds.), *Approaches to Human Communication*. Spartan Books.

Smithson, M. 1989. *Ignorance and Uncertainty: Emerging Paradigms*. Springer-Verlag.

1993. Ignorance and uncertainty: emerging paradigms. *Knowledge: Creation, Diffusion, Utilization*, 15: 133–156.

Solomon, P. 2002. Discovering information in context. *Annual Review of Information Science and Technology*, 36: 229–264.

2005. Rounding and dissonant grounds. In K. E. Fisher, S. Erdelez, and L. McKechnie (eds.), *Theories of Information Behavior*: 308–312. Information Today.

Sonnenwald, D. H., Wildemuth, B. M., and Harmon, G. L. 2001. A research method to investigate information seeking using the concept of information horizons: an example from a study of lower socio-economic students' information seeking behavior. *New Review of Information Behavior Research*, 2: 65–85.

Sparrowe, R. T., Liden, R. C., Wayne, S. J., and Kraimer, M. L. 2001. Social networks and the performance of individuals and groups. *Academy of Management Journal*, 44: 316–325.

Spekman, R. E. 1979. Influence and information: an exploratory investigation of the boundary role person's basis of power. *Academy of Management Journal*, 22: 104–117.

Stasser, G., Taylor, L. A., and Hanna, C. 1989. Information sampling in structured and unstructured discussions of three and six person groups. *Journal of Personality and Social Psychology*, 57: 67–78.

Stasser, G., and Titus, W. 1985. Pooling of unshared information in group decision making: biased information sampling during discussion. *Journal of Personality and Social Psychology*, 48: 1467–1478.

Staw, B. M., Sandelands, L. E., and Dutton, J. E. 1981. Threat rigidity effects in organizational behavior: a multilevel analysis. *Administrative Science Quarterly*, 26: 501–524.

Steele, F. 1973. *Physical Setting and Organizational Development*. Addison-Wesley.

Steers, R. M. 1977. Antecedents and outcomes of organizational commitment. *Administrative Science Quarterly*, 22: 46–56.

Steinfield, C. W. 1985. Dimensions of electronic mail use in an organizational setting. *Proceedings of the Academy of Management*.

Steinfield, C. W., and Fulk, J. 1986. Information processing in organizations and media choice, presented at the Annual Convention of the International Comunication Association. Chicago.

Stewart, T. A. 2001. *The Wealth of Knowledge: Intellectual Capital and the Twenty-first Century Organization*. Currency.

Stigler, G. J. 1961. The economics of information. *Journal of Political Economy*, 69: 213–225.

Stocking, S. H., and Holstein, L. W. 1993. Constructing and reconstructing scientific ignorance: ignorance claims in science and journalism. *Knowledge: Creation, Diffusion, Utilization*, 15: 186–210.

Strassman, W. P. 1959. *Risk and Technological Innovation*. Cornell University Press.

Strauss, A. 1978. *Negotiations: Varieties, Contexts, Processes, and Social Order*. Jossey-Bass.

Strobel, L. P. 1980. *Reckless Homicide? Ford's Pinto Trial*. And Books.

Sundstrom, E., Burt, R. E., and Kamp, D. 1980. Privacy at work: architectural correlates of job satisfaction and job performance. *Academy of Management Journal*, 23: 101–117.

Susskind, A. M., Schwartz, D. F., Richards, W. D., and Johnson, J. D. 2005. Evolution and diffusion of the Michigan State University tradition of organizational communication network research. *Communication Studies*, 56: 397–418.

Sutton, H., and Porter, L. W. 1968. A study of the grapevine in a government organization. *Personnel Psychology*, 21: 223–230.

Swan, J. 2003. Knowledge management in action? In C. W. Holsapple (ed.), *Handbook of Knowledge Management*, vol. I: *Knowledge Matters*: 271–296. Springer-Verlag.

Swap, W., Leonard, D., Shields, M., and Abrams, L. C. 2004. Using mentoring and storytelling to transfer knowledge in the workplace. In E. Lesser and L. Prusak (eds.), *Creating Value with Knowledge: Insights from the IBM Institute for Business Value*: 181–200. Oxford University Press.

Swedberg, R. 1994. Markets as social structures. In N. J. Smelser and R. Swedberg (eds.), *The Handbook of Economic Sociology*: 255–282. Princeton University Press.

Sweeney, K. 2006. Personal knowledge: doctors are much more than simple conduits for clinical evidence. *British Medical Journal*, 332: 129–130.

Swinehart, J. W. 1968. Voluntary exposure to health communications. *American Journal of Public Health*, 58: 1265–1275.

Sykes, R. E. 1983. Initial interaction between strangers and acquaintances: a multivariate analysis of factors affecting choice of communication partners. *Human Communication Research*, 10: 27–53.

Sypher, B. D., and Zorn, T. E., Jr. 1986. Communication-related abilities and upward mobility: a longitudinal investigation. *Human Communication Research*, 12: 420–431.

Szilagyi, A. D., and Holland, W. E. 1980. Changes in social density: relationships with functional interaction and perceptions of job characteristics, role stress, and work satisfaction. *Journal of Applied Psychology*, 65: 28–33.

Szulanski, G. 1996. Exploring internal stickiness: impediments to the transfer of best practice within the firm. *Strategic Management Journal*, 17: 27–43.

  2003. *Sticky Knowledge: Barriers to Knowing in the Firm*. Sage.

Talja, S., Keso, H., and Pietilainen, T. 1999. The production of "context" information seeking research: a metatheoretical view. *Information Processing and Management*, 35: 751–763.

Taylor, A., and Greve, H. R. 2006. Superman or the Fantastic Four? Knowledge combination and experience in innovative teams. *Academy of Management Journal*, 49: 723–740.

Taylor, R., Bower, A., Girosi, F., Bigelow, J., Fonkych, K., and Hillestad, R. 2005. Promoting health information technology: is there a case for more-aggressive government action? *Health Affairs*, 24: 1234–1245.

Taylor, R. S. 1968. Question negotiation and information seeking in libraries. *College and Research Libraries*, 29: 178–194.

1986. Information use environments. In B. Dervin and M. J. Voight (eds.), *Progress in Communication Sciences*, vol. X: 217–255. Ablex.

Tenkasi, R. V., and Chesmore, M. C. 2003. Social networks and planned organizational change: the impact of strong network ties on effective change implementation and use. *Journal of Applied Behavioral Science*, 39: 281–300.

Thayer, L. 1988. How does information "inform"? In B. D. Ruben (ed.), *Information and Behavior*, vol. II: 13–26. Transaction Books.

Thomas, J. B., Clark, S. M., and Gioia, D. A. 1993. Strategic sensemaking and organizational performance: linkages among scanning, interpretation, action, and outcomes. *Academy of Management Journal*, 36: 239–270.

Thomas-Hunt, M. C., Ogden, T. Y., and Neale, M. A. 2003. Who's really sharing? Effects of social and expert status on knowledge exchange within groups. *Management Science*, 49: 464–477.

Thompson, G. 1991. Introduction. In G. Thompson, J. Frances, R. Levacic, and J. Mitchell (eds.), *Markets, Hierarchies, and Networks: The Coordination of Social Life*: 243–245. Sage.

Thompson, J. D. 1967. *Organizations in Action*. New York: McGraw-Hill.

Thompson, T. G., and Brailer, D. J. 2004. The decade of health information technology: delivering consumer-centric and information-rich health care: framework for strategic action. National Coordinator for Health Information Technology, Washington, DC.

Thompson, T. L. 2003. Introduction. In T. L. Thompson, A. M. Dorsey, K. I. Miller, and R. Parrott (eds.), *Handbook of Health Communication*: 1–5. Lawrence Erlbaum Associates.

Thomsen, C. A., and Maat, J. T. 1998. Evaluating the Cancer Information Service: a model for health communications. Part 1. *Journal of Health Communication*, 3: 1–14.

Thorngate, W. 1995. Accounting for person–context relations and their development. In T. A. Kindermann and J. Valsiner (eds.), *Development of Person–Context Relations*: 39–54. Lawrence Erlbaum Associates.

Tichenor, P. J., Donohue, G. A., and Olien, C. N. 1970. Mass media and differential growth in knowledge. *Public Opinion Quarterly*, 34: 158–170.

Tidd, J. 2000. The competence cycle: translating knowledge into new processes, products, and services. In J. Tidd (ed.), *From Knowledge Management to Strategic Competence: Measuring Technological, Market, and Organizational Innovation*: 5–25. Imperial College Press.

Timmerman, C. E., and Scott, C. R. 2006. Virtual working: communicative and structural predictors of media use and key outcomes in virtual work teams. *Communication Monographs*, 73: 108–136.

Tippins, M. J., and Sohi, R. S. 2003. IT competency and firm performance: is organizational learning a missing link? *Strategic Management Journal*, 24: 747–761.

Trevino, L. K., and Webster, J. 1992. Flow in computer mediated communication: electronic mail and voice mail evaluation and impacts. *Communication Research*, 19: 539–573.

Tsai, W. 2001. Knowledge transfer in intraorganizational networks: effects of network position and absorptive capacity on business unit innovation and performance. *Academy of Management Journal*, 44: 996–1004.

Tsoukas, H. 1996. The firm as distributed knowledge system: a constructionist approach. *Strategic Management Journal*, 17: 11–25.

Tsoukas, H., and Vladimirou, E. 2001. What is organizational knowledge? *Journal of Management Studies*, 38: 973–993.

Tsui, A. S., and O'Reilly, C. A., III 1989. Beyond simple demographic effects: the importance of relational demography in superior–subordinate dyads. *Academy of Management Journal*, 32: 402–423.

Turner, K. L., and Makhija, M. V. 2006. The role of organizational controls in managing knowledge. *Academy of Management Review*, 31: 197–217.

Tushman, M. L. 1978. Technical communication in R & D laboratories: the impact of project work characteristics. *Academy of Management Journal*, 21: 624–645.

1979. Work characteristics and subunit communication structure: a contingency analysis. *Administrative Science Quarterly*, 24: 82–98.

Tushman, M. L., and Scanlan, T. J. 1981a. Boundary spanning individuals: their role in information transfer and their antecedents. *Academy of Management Journal*, 24: 289–305.

1981b. Characteristics and external orientations of boundary spanning individuals. *Academy of Management Journal*, 24: 83–98.

Tutzauer, F. 1989. A statistic for comparing behavioral and cognitive networks, presented to the Annual Convention of the International Communication Association. San Francisco.

Urry, J. 1985. Social relations, space and time. In D. Gregory and J. Urry (eds.), *Social Relations and Spatial Structures*: 20–48. Macmillan.

Uzzi, B., and Spiro, J. 2005. Collaboration and creativity: the small world problem. *American Journal of Sociology*, 111: 447–504.

Valente, T. 2006. Communication network analysis and the diffusion of innovations. In A. Singhal and J. W. Dearing (eds.), *A Journey with Ev Rogers*: 61–82. Sage.

Valente, T. W. 1995. *Network Models of the Diffusion of Innovations*. Hampton Press.

Valsiner, J., and Leung, M. C. 1994. From intelligence to knowledge construction: a sociogenetic process approach. In R. J. Sternberg and R. K. Wagner (eds.), *Mind in Context: Interactionist Perspectives on Human Intelligence*: 202–217. Cambridge University Press.

Van de Ven, A. 2000. The President's Message: The practice of management knowledge. *Academy of Management News*, 31: 4–5.

2002. Strategic directions for the Academy of Management: this academy is for you! *Academy of Management Review*, 27: 171–184.

Van de Ven, A. H. 1976. On the nature, formation, and maintenance of relations among organizations. *Academy of Management Review*, 1: 24–36.

1986. Central problems in the management of innovation. *Management Science*, 32: 590–607.

Van de Ven, A. H., Delbecq, A. L., and Koenig, R. 1976. Determinants of coordination modes within organizations. *Administrative Science Quarterly*, 41: 322–338.

Van Den Bulte, C., and Lillien, G. L. 2001. Medical innovation revisited: social contagion versus marketing effort. *American Journal of Sociology*, 106: 1409–1435.

Van Der Vegt, G. S., Bunderson, J. S., and Oosterhof, A. 2006. Expertness, diversity and interpersonal helping teams: why those who need the most help end up getting the least. *Academy of Management Journal*, 49: 877–893.

Van Sell, M., Brief, A. D., and Schuler, R. S. 1981. Role conflict and role ambiguity: an integration of the literature and directions for future research. *Human Relations*, 34: 43–72.

Varlejs, J. 1986. Information seeking: changing perspectives. In J. Varlejs (ed.), *Information Seeking: Basing Services on Users' Behaviors*: 67–82. McFarland & Co.

Vaughan, D. 1999. The dark side of organizations: mistake, misconduct, and disaster. *Annual Review of Sociology*, 25: 271–305.

Voelpel, S. C., Dous, M., and Davenport, T. H. 2005. Five steps to creating a global knowledge-sharing system: Siemens ShareNet. *Academy of Management Executive*, 19: 9–23.

von Hayek, F. 1991. Spontaneous ("grown") order and organized ("made") order. In G. Thompson, J. Frances, R. Levacic and J. Mitchell (eds.), *Markets, Hierarchies, and Networks: The Coordination of Social Life*: 293–301. Sage.

von Hayek, F. A. 1945. The uses of knowledge in society. *American Economic Review*, 35: 519–520.

Wade, M., and Hulland, J. 2004. The resource-based view and information systems research: review, extension, and suggestions for future research. *MIS Quarterly*, 28: 107–142.

Wales, M., Rarick, G., and Davis, H. 1963. Message exaggeration by the receiver. *Journalism Quarterly*, 40: 339–342.

Walker, A. H., and Lorsch, J. W. 1968. Organizational choice: product vs. function. *Harvard Business Review*, 46: 129–138.

Walker, G. 1985. Network position and cognition in a computer software firm. *Administrative Science Quarterly*, 30: 103–130.

Walker, J. M. 2005. Electronic medical records and health care transformation. *Health Affairs*, 24: 1118–1120.

Walton, E. 1975. Self interest, credibility, and message selection in organizational communication: a research note. *Human Communication Research*, 1: 180–181.

Walton, R. E. 1985. Strategies with dual relevance. In E. E. Lawler, III, A. M. Mohrman, Jr., S. A. Mohrman, G. E. Ledford, Jr., and T. G. Cummings (eds.), *Doing Research that is Useful for Theory and Practice*: 176–204. Jossey-Bass.

Wandersman, A., Goodman, R. M., and Butterfoss, F. D. 1997. Understanding coalitions and how they operate: An "open systems" organizational framework. In M. Minkler (ed.), *Community Organizing and Community Building for Health*: 261–277. Rutgers University Press.

Wasserman, S., and Faust, K. 1994. *Social Network Analysis: Methods and Applications*. Cambridge University Press.

Waters, R. 2004. The enigma within the knowledge economy, *Financial Times* (February 2).

Wathen, C. N., and Burkell, J. 2002. Believe it or not: factors influencing credibility on the web. *Journal of the American Society for Information Science and Technology*, 53: 134–144.

Watts, D. J. 2002. A simple model of global cascades on random networks. *Proceedings of the National Academy of Sciences*, 99: 5766–5771.

2003. *Six Degrees: The Science of the Connected Age*. W. W. Norton.

Watts, D. J., and Strogatz, S. H. 1998. Collective dynamics of "small world" networks. *Nature*, 393: 440–442.

Weber, M. 1947. *The Theory of Social and Economic Organization*. Free Press.

Weedman, J. 1992. Informal and formal channels in boundary-spanning communication. *Journal of American Society for Information Science*, 43: 257–267.

Weenig, M., and Midden, C. 1991. Communication network influences on diffusion and persuasion. *Journal of Personality and Social Psychology*, 61: 734–742.

Wegner, D. M. 1995. A computer network model of human transactive memory. *Social Cognition*, 13: 319–339.

Weick, K. E. 1969. *The Social Psychology of Organizing*. Addison-Wesley.

1979. Cognitive processes in organizations. In S. B. Bacharach (ed.), *Research in Organizational Behavior*: 41–74. JAI Press.

1983. Organizational communication: toward a research agenda. In L. L. Putnam and M. E. Pacanowsky (eds.), *Communication and Organizations: An Interpretive Approach*: 13–29. Sage.

1996. Drop your tools: An allegory for organizational studies. *Administrative Science Quarterly*, 41: 301–313.

Weick, K. E., and Bougon, M. G. 1986. Organizations as cognitive maps. In H. P. Sims and D. A. Gioia (eds.), *The Thinking Organization*: 102–135. Jossey-Bass.

Weick, K. E., and Quinn, R. E. 1999. Organizational change and development. *Annual Review of Psychology*, 50: 361–386.

Weimann, G. 1983. The strength of weak conversational ties in the flow of information and influence. *Social Networks*, 5: 245–267.

Wejnert, B. 2002. Integrating models of diffusion of innovations: a conceptual framework. *Annual Review of Sociology*, 28: 297–326.

Wenger, E., McDermott, R., and Snyder, W. M. 2002. *Cultivating Communities of Practice: A Guide to Managing Knowledge*. Harvard Business School Press.

West, E., Barron, D. N., Dowsett, J., and Newton, J. N. 1999. Hierarchies and cliques in social networks of health care professionals: implications for the design of dissemination strategies. *Social Science and Medicine*, 48: 633–646.

Whisler, T. L. 1970. *Information Technology and Organizational Change*. Wadsworth.

Wigand, R. T. 1977. Some recent developments in organizational communication: network analysis – a systematic representation of communication relationships. *Communications*, 3: 181–200.

1988. Communication network analysis: history and overview. In G. M. Goldhaber and G. A. Barnett (eds.), *Handbook of Organizational Communication*: 319–360. Ablex.

Wigand, R. T., Picot, A., and Reichwald, R. 1997. *Information, Organization and Management: Expanding Markets and Corporate Boundaries*. Wiley.

Wilensky, H. L. 1968. Organizational intelligence. In D. L. Sills (ed.), *The International Encyclopedia of the Social Sciences*: 319–334. Free Press.

Williamson, O. E. 1994. Transaction cost economics and organization theory. In N. J. Smelser and R. Swedberg (eds.), *Handbook of Economic Sociology*: 77–107. Russell Sage.

Wilson, D. O., and Malik, S. D. 1995. Looking for a few good sources: exploring the intraorganizational communication linkages of first line managers. *Journal of Business Communication*, 32: 31–48.

Wilson, P. 1983. *Second-hand Knowledge: An Inquiry into Cognitive Authority*. Greenwood Press.

Withey, M., Daft, R. L., and Cooper, W. H. 1983. Measures of Perrow's work unit technology: an empirical assessment and new scale. *Academy of Management Journal*, 26: 45–63.

Woelful, J., Cody, M. J., Gillham, J., and Holmes, R. A. 1980. Basic premises of multidimensional attitude change theory: an experimental analysis. *Academy of Management Journal*, 6: 153–167.

Woodward, J. 1965. *Industrial Organization*. Oxford University Press.

Wright, G., and Taylor, A. 2003. Strategic knowledge sharing for improved public service delivery: managing an innovative culture for effective partnerships. In E. Coakes (ed.), *Knowledge Management: Current Issues and Challenges*: 187–211. IRM Press.

Xu, Y., Tan, C. Y., and Yang, L. 2006. Who will you ask? An empirical study of interpersonal task information seeking. *Journal of the American Society for Information Science and Technology*, 57: 1666–1677.

Yates, J. 2005. *Structuring the Information Age: Life Insurance and Technology in the Twentieth Century*. Johns Hopkins University Press.

Yuan, Y., Fulk, J., Shumate, M., Monge, P. R., Byrant, J. A., and Matsaganis, M. 2005. Individual participation in organizational information commons: the impact of team level social influence and technology-specific competence. *Human Communication Research*, 31: 212–240.

Zahra, S. A., and George, G. 2002. Absorptive capacity: a review, reconceptualization, and extension. *Academy of Management Review*, 27: 185–203.

Zajonc, R. B., and Wolfe, D. M. 1966. Cognitive consequences of a person's position in a formal organization. *Human Relations*, 19: 139–150.

Zaltman, G. 1994. Knowledge disavowal in organizations. In R. H. Kilmann, K. W. Thomas, D. P. Slevin, R. Nath, and S. L. Jerrell (eds.), *Producing Useful Knowledge in Organizations*: 173–187. Jossey-Bass.

Zaltman, G., and Duncan, R. 1977. *Strategies for Planned Change*. Wiley.

Zaltman, G., Duncan, R., and Holbek, J. 1973. *Innovations and Organizations*. Wiley.

Zeng, M. L., and Chan, L. M. 2004. Trends and issues in establishing interoperability among knowledge organization systems. *Journal of American Society for Information Science and Technology*, 55: 377–395.

Zenger, T. R., and Lawrence, B. S. 1989. Organizational demography: the differential effects of age and tenure distributions on technical communication. *Academy of Management Journal*, 32: 353–376.

Zhu, K., and Kraemer, K. L. 2005. Post-adoption variations in usage and value of e-business by organizations: cross-country evidence from the retail industry. *Information Systems Research*, 16: 61–84.

Zimbardo, P. G. 1960. Involvement and communication discrepancy as determinants of opinion conformity. *Journal of Abnormal and Social Psychology*, 60: 86–94.

Zimmerman, S., Sypher, B. D., and Haas, J. W. 1996. A communication metamyth in the workplace: the assumption that more is better. *Journal of Business Communication*, 33: 185–204.

Zipf, G. 1949. *Human Behavior and the Principle of Least Effort: An Introduction to Human Ecology*. Addison-Wesley.

Zuboff, S. 1988. *In the Age of the Smart Machine: The Future of Work and Power*. Basic Books.

Zwijze-Koning, K. H., and de Jong, M. D. T. 2005. Auditing information structures in organizations: a review of data collection techniques and network analysis. *Organizational Research Methods*, 8: 429–453.

Index